Contents

The Byzantine Liturgy
Symbolic Structure and Faith Expression

Hans-Joachim Schulz

THE
BYZANTINE LITURGY

Symbolic Structure and
Faith Expression

Translated by Matthew J. O'Connell

English edition
introduced and reviewed by Robert Taft, S.J.

PUEBLO PUBLISHING COMPANY

NEW YORK

Design: Frank Kacmarcik

Originally published in German as *Die byzantinische Liturgie* ©
1980 Paulinus-Verlag, Trier.

Scriptural pericopes quoted from the Revised Standard Version.

IBSN: 0-916134-72-5

Printed in the United States of America.

Foreword

As a teacher of eastern liturgy I welcome with great satisfaction this English translation of *Die byzantinische Liturgie*, the work of my friend and colleague Hans-Joachim Schulz. Few books on Byzantine liturgy have aroused in me pangs of jealousy. This is one of them. No better explanation exists of the symbolic structure of Byzantine Divine Liturgy and its meaning to those who created it.

Since the appearance of the first edition in 1964, the isolation in which Schulz's book then found itself has been ended definitively by a series of major scholarly studies on the Byzantine eucharistic liturgy: its manuscripts, setting, history, and commentaries. The work of G. Wagner on the Chrysostom anaphora, of J. Mateos and myself on the historical development, of R. Bornert on the commentaries, of A. Jacob on the manuscript tradition, and of F. van de Paverd on the Chrysostom documents, comprises the new material for Part Two of the present English edition.

Apart from new liturgical studies, much has happened in the world of pastoral liturgy and ecumenism since the Second Vatican Council closed shortly after the appearance of the first edition. The Byzantine liturgical tradition still mirrors the dogmatic heritage of the first millenium, and it is in such a mirror that many later developments will have to be reexamined. For the East, "Orthodoxy" also means "right-worshiping," a concept akin to the Latin adage *"ut legem credendi lex statuat supplicandi."* Father Schulz is one of the major Catholic contributors to an ecumenical dialogue that takes liturgy as its point of departure, a starting point congenial to both Orthodox and Catholic communions, as is evidenced by the decision to begin the new Orthodox-Catholic dialogue with a discussion of the sacramental life of the two churches.

Of course there is more than one way to start with liturgy. Some approach eastern liturgy with scholarly background and method, yet fail to comprehend or appreciate the spirit of that worship, the elusive ethos of the Christian East. For others, the opposite is true.

Although they may have imbibed the tradition with their mother's milk, inadequacies in historical knowledge and the inability to be scientifically critical or even objective vitiate much of their work. H.-J. Schulz is an exception on both counts. Not only are his scholarly credentials impeccable; he has also penetrated to the heart of the mystery.

Perhaps more than in any other tradition, Byzantine liturgy equals more than the sum of it component parts, says much more than what its texts affirm. It has a *Symbolgestalt*, an *Erscheinungsbild*, to use Schulz's felicitous terms. This symbolic form goes beyond the verbal or the notional to create a transcendent vision characteristic of the Byzantine spiritual world. There is no better guide to this vision than Schulz. He is easily the best interpreter of Byzantine liturgical theology writing today.

Schulz explains not only this symbolic form. The evolution of both the structure and its interpretation in response to the cultural and spiritual forces of each age is also traced with historical vision and spiritual insight, through a profoundly knowledgeable and sympathetic—that is, truly ecumenical—unfolding of the teaching of the major Byzantine liturgical commentators: Maximus Confessor, Germanus, the *Protheoria*, Nicholas Cabasilas, Symeon of Thessalonica. We have become accustomed to treating medieval liturgical commentaries with a certain disdain, as mere fanciful allegory. Schulz does us the great service of rehabilitating this literary genre, a revisionist view later confirmed by René Bornert's superb study of the Byzantine commentaries. As Schulz shows, one must not be put off by the seeming similarity of method between the Byzantine liturgical commentaries and medieval Latin mass-allegories. In the Byzantine liturgy the very evolution of the rite is linked inseparably to a symbolic method of interpretation that, although perhaps not always felicitous, is in no way *extrinsic* to the structure and meaning of the rites, as are the Latin allegories from Amalar on. Furthermore, these Byzantine commentaries are still a living part of eastern liturgical theology and cannot be ignored, although they must of course be complemented by a genetic understanding of the rites based on contemporary historical scholarship.

Also noteworthy is the role Schulz assigns to the church building, and especially to the developing iconographic program of the Middle Byzantine church as a source of Byzantine liturgical theology. In no tradition is liturgical space so integral to the liturgical experience as in the Byzantine, and in no tradition has liturgical iconography had such influence. The struggle with iconoclasm

(726–843) was a watershed for the development of Byzantine thought in the period after the golden age of Justinian. Schulz's mastery of all this material and its precise place within the broader context of Byzantine liturgical history and theology is apparent in this synthesis of the interplay between liturgical development and the unfolding of dogma, and between liturgical development and liturgical understanding.

Important for contemporary eucharistic understanding are the subtle shifts Schulz indicates as liturgical sign moves from symbolism to representation. The importance of the Seventh Ecumenical Council (Nicea II), the "Council of Orthodoxy" against the iconoclasts in 787, is rightly highlighted, along with the influence of a representational understanding of the liturgy on iconodule theology during the second phase of iconoclasm (815–843). All this is necessary to grasp the relation between Byzantine icon theology and liturgical understanding.

Schulz is also aware of the defects in the Byzantine viewpoint. An excessively realistic representational view of the liturgy spilled over into the crude historicism of medieval eucharistic piety in East as well as West, contrary to what is sometimes thought. While the West was having its bleeding hosts and other eucharistic wonders, the East had its visions of the infant Jesus bleeding on the discos as sacrificial lamb. Schulz's serene ecumenical objectivity permits him to put the finger on this and other less laudable aspects of the Byzantine liturgical outlook without laying himself open to the charge of bias.

This is an excellent book, one I recommend warmly to all who seek a thorough, profound, and nuanced discussion of the growth and meaning of the Byzantine Divine Liturgy within the total context of Byzantine cultural history. It is indeed a *Liturgie in der byzantinischen Geistesgeschichte,* to paraphase the title of A. Mayer's fascinating series of essays that attempted to do something analogous for the West.

Robert Taft, S.J.
Ordinary Professor of Eastern Liturgy
Pontifical Oriental Institute, Rome

First Preface

The encounter with the churches of the East has entered a new phase since the pontificate of John XXIII. A correspondingly greater theological effort will have to be made in the future to render accessible the tradition of the eastern churches. In the process, the study of the Christian East, which has at times been regarded as the preserve of a few specialists, will have to be brought into fruitful communication with the other theological disciplines. This is especially true of relations between liturgical science and the systematic study of the eastern churches. As a matter of fact, in its very beginnings the liturgical renewal went hand in hand with a growing openness to the Christian East. Recall Dom Lambert Beauduin, who not only started the liturgical movement but also became the first prior of the newly founded ecumenical monastery at Amay-sur-Meuse (later at Chevetogne), or of Dom Odo Casel, whose mystery-presence theory, which so closely resembles the Byzantine understanding of the liturgy, was the source of important stimuli for sacramental theology and liturgical science. J. A. Jungmann devoted his inaugural dissertation on the place of Christ in liturgical prayer to a study of the special theological character of the earlier eastern liturgical texts,[1] and in so doing pointed the way for the investigation of the eastern liturgies.

The work presented here is an attempt to advance a step further along this path. Until now there has been no comprehensive description of the Byzantine eucharistic celebration from the early days of the Byzantine patriarchate down to the standardization of this liturgy in the fourteenth century. The ground-breaking works of P. de Meester[2] and J. M. Hanssens[3] have indeed shed light on the origins of most of the liturgical texts and manuscripts, but they have not considered the historico-theological background in which these developments took place. Above all, little attention has been paid until now to the evidence that iconography and the explanations of the liturgy provide for the history of the Byzantine liturgy.

The primary purpose of the present book is to show therefore for each period in the history of Byzantine thought the reciprocal relations between the development of liturgical forms, the statements made in ecclesiastical art, and the interpretative approach taken in commentaries on the liturgy.

For the liturgy of their times the liturgical commentaries are usually as informative in their differing symbolical interpretations as they are in their mention of liturgical details. The similarity between the motifs in these interpretations and those found in the Latin allegories of the mass (which are now, fortunately, a thing of the past) should not lead us to put the two phenomena on the same level. In the eastern liturgies the liturgical development as such is inseparable from the method of symbolical interpretation. Thus, such characteristic parts of the Byzantine liturgy as the prothesis, the two entrances, the addition of hot water (Zeon) to the Precious Blood after the commingling of the species, and many other practices as well, can be understood in their historically developed form only in the light of their symbolic interpretation, in which the very essence of the eucharistic celebration finds expression. The expressive power of these rites, moreover, must be evaluated in terms of the theology of icons. The doctrine of images itself was legitimized by the Seventh Ecumenical Council, although the characteristic Byzantine form of this doctrine was not defined formally.

The liturgy as it developed down to the fourteenth century is still the focal point of the piety of the eastern church. Even in the construction of churches the effort is still made to be faithful to the ancient prototypes. And in writings on the liturgy and in catechisms, the interpretation of the liturgy that is represented by Nicolas Cabasilas (d. after 1363) and Symeon of Thessalonica (d. 1429) is followed even today.[4] Consequently the inclusion of church architecture, iconography, and the interpretation of the liturgy in my study is not a matter of purely historical interest. These areas, too, help us to encounter the churches of the East as living realities. At the same time, however, the course of liturgical development also emerges more clearly, and the necessity of a genetic explanation of the liturgy becomes the more evident. Such an explanation will doubtless win out even in the East; it is a presupposition for a future liturgical renewal such as no church can avoid.

The present work was accepted as an inaugural dissertation by the Catholic Theological Faculty of the University of Münster in December, 1963. I thank the Reverend Professors of the Faculty for this acceptance, and in particular Professor E. J. Lengeling, who played a decisive part in the dissertation from the outset and also wrote the verdict of the experts. My studies were made possible by a doctoral stipend from the Deutsche Forschungsgemeinschaft. I wish to express my gratitude for this grant.

Since the book was expected to be of interest outside scholarly circles, the editors and publishers encouraged its publication in the *Sophia* series—an invitation that was indeed welcome to me.

Hans-Joachim Schulz
Münster
March 1964

The Byzantine Liturgy
as a Witness to Faith Today

The first edition of this book appeared a few weeks after the end of the promising second session of Vatican II. The close of this session was marked by two equally memorable events: the adoption of the Constitution on the Sacred Liturgy, which was meant to ensure a liturgical renewal throughout the entire Catholic church of the Roman rite, and the announcement of the papal pilgrimage to the Holy Land. As a result of this journey, Pope Paul VI and Patriarch Athenagoras initiated that new relationship between eastern and western churches that Paul VI described as a relationship of "sister Churches."[1]

As a result of these developments a new importance attaches to the study of the eucharistic celebration of the Eastern Church. Orthodoxy shares a dogmatic heritage with the Catholic Church of the first millennium. In addition, it has given comprehensive expression to this heritage in its liturgy and has integrated it into an original dogmatico-liturgical[2] expression of faith. For these reasons, an encounter with the faith as conceived in the ancient undivided church and reflected in this liturgy has power to reduce later doctrinal divergences to the secondary rank that is properly theirs in the history of the traditions, and to eliminate them as real differences in faith and as factors justifying a division between the churches.

On the Catholic side the development represented by the Council has led to a reassessment of the dogmatic tradition. In addition, it has created a new awareness that dogmatic "orthodoxy" is inconceivable without "orthopraxy" (in the life of the church in question and in its relation to the other churches) and that the liturgy of the local church reflects and embodies the content and intensity of faith in a unique way.[3]

In the light of those more profound principles that define the church above all as a mystery and as God's people of the new covenant, the Liturgy Constitution of Vatican II laid a heavier emphasis on the importance of the episcopal office and of the local church in reaction against a unilateral view of the primacy. As a result of this new emphasis, those sources in which the church's teaching authority has found nondefinitional expression have once again become important for the doctrinal side of faith, and the liturgical tradition, insofar as this is made visible in a continuity that embraces churches and epochs, has acquired the status of a decisive witness to faith.

The clearest proof of these new orientations may be seen in certain questions that are discussed passionately today: the relation between ministerial office and eucharist,[4] the relation between the pastoral, teaching, and priestly offices of bishop and presbyter,[5] and similar structural questions in ecclesiology and sacramental theology in which, not by chance, the utterances of the extraordinary teaching office play an entirely secondary role in comparison with the clear and unbroken liturgical tradition. The liturgy articulated its historical response to many of these questions long before the beginning of the conciliar era (in the fourth century) and, to some extent, even in the early postapostolic period. The history of the liturgy may fill in many a lacuna in the tradition linking New Testament to later dogmatic tradition.

Like the ecclesiological thinking that has gone on since the Council, the official liturgical reform has also directed theological attention to the pristine liturgical tradition. According to Article 23 of the Constitution on the Sacred Liturgy, "sound tradition" bears witness to the "structure and meaning" of the liturgy and therefore provides a criterion to which careful theological and historical study must be devoted. And among the major concrete reforms affecting the heart of the eucharistic celebration and of sacramental theology, particularly significant are those that attempt to set the eucharistic prayer, the consecration of bishops, and the confession of faith at baptism in visible continuity with early Christian liturgy, as given normative expression in the *Apostolic Tradition* of Hippolytus.[6]

It is true, of course, that borrowing outward forms from early Christianity will not by itself ensure the recovery or strengthening of a genuine continuity of tradition. It is far more important to derive from very early and authentic tradition those normative principles that will enable us to cut away the secondary traditions that have become hardened parts of later theology and church structure. Then the presently separated major confessions will be able to travel a common path to understanding on the basis of the most ancient ecumenical tradition.

In the execution of this task the Orthodox understanding of the tradition is an important witness whose power is manifested in its unique combination of dogmatic tradition (heavily influenced by the liturgy) and directly liturgical tradition. This history of the first seven ecumenical councils (which alone are ecumenical for the Orthodox and which are ecumenical in a privileged way for Catholics) makes vividly clear how the dogmatico-conciliar development of doctrine insofar as its purpose is to defend the faith against heresies, presupposes the liturgical tradition that has its origin in the immanent laws governing the life of the church.

When the Fathers of Nicea (325) defined the teaching of the church they did not so much appeal to their own doctrinal authority as invoke against the Arians the tradition that had long since found its liturgically oriented expression in the Symbol of Caesarea that was used in baptismal catechesis: "God from God, Light from Light."[7] And while the Second Council of Nicea (787), which closed the series of seven ecumenical councils, apparently dealt principally with the liceity of icons and the legitimacy of venerating them, it was concerned in the final analysis to maintain a consistent view of the normative character of liturgical and liturgically shaped tradition, since icons had become an inseparable part of this tradition.

Moreover, in order to safeguard the results of the entire development of christological doctrine (for the Council regarded this as its task), it had to set forth with as much clarity as possible a consequence of that doctrine, namely, the full representation of the mystery of the incarnate Christ in the liturgical life of the Church. This representation is for its part most complete when the sacramental mystery of Christ and its liturgical manifestation can be experienced in their proclamation through icons and in the encounter with Christ that takes place in the veneration of icons.

The reason why Orthodoxy has been able to dispense with further ecumenical councils ever since the eighth century is that the continuity of its liturgically shaped proclamation of the faith and of its liturgical expression of this same faith has itself been an authentic and completely authoritative witness to the tradition.

The most recent contribution of Orthodox theology has been its persuasive development of a "eucharistic ecclesiology" that has long since found a broad ecumenical response.[8] Such an ecclesiology makes strikingly clear how the central action of the liturgical life, the celebration of the eucharist (which in the usage of the Eastern Church is called "the liturgy" without qualification), provides the clearest possible theological manifestation of the basic structures of the church as a community of faith and as a community governed by its shepherds, and at the same time repeatedly brings these structures to their fulfillment in the most intense way possible.

A similar statement can be made about the structure of the content of the faith. The Second Vatican Council spoke of a "hierarchy of truths"[9] and by so doing stirred profound ecumenical hopes. But the hierarchy of truths will not in fact be a source for the renewal of faith and of the church unless it is applied at a level deeper than that of the mere interpretation of dogmas. Rather it will prove to be a principle of realization and evaluation for the life of faith when it is viewed in its inherent connection with the mystery of Christ in the sacramental and liturgical life of the Church. We may venture this formula: the more relevant a dogma proves to be to those decisive moments of life that occur in baptism and the eucharist and that give us an experience of God's saving action in Christ through the working of the Holy Spirit, the more central a role must it be judged to have in the structure of the church's faith.[10]

Such a synthesis of a eucharistic ecclesiology and a pneumatological vision of the church[11] provides the context in which I wish the reader to view this new edition of a book on the symbolic structure of the Byzantine liturgy and on this liturgy as a witness to the faith.

Our journey through the concrete history of liturgical development and interpretation will bring us in contact with various manifestations that today strike us as odd. Nonetheless the overall development bears living witness to the continuity of a properly liturgico-sacramental tradition. That tradition and its continuity manifest themselves above all in the anaphora, or eucharistic prayer, and it is as a reflection of the anaphora that the abundance of forms and language that make up the liturgy as a whole ultimately must be viewed. As will be shown in a special chapter of Part Two, "New Contributions," the anaphora draws upon the sources of a liturgical-dogmatic tradition that the Orthodox Church continued to drawn upon even after its conciliar period had ended in order to express the content of its faith as fully as possible and in a way that even today represents it to the ecumenical movement.

For this reason, over and above the direct influence exercised by representatives of Orthodoxy in the World Council of Churches, the testimony rendered by the eucharistic prayer in the Liturgy of Chrysostom was able to shape decisively the recent Declaration on the Eucharist of the Commission for Faith and Order, and to do so in a way that is full of promise for the future of the ecumenical movement.[12]

As far as the even more recently announced dialogue between the Catholic and Orthodox churches is concerned, the agreement in principle between the liturgical traditions of East and West and the high value set upon this agreement by the Orthodox will lead to an emphasis on the basic presuppositions shared by these churches. It can lead eventually to that full communion in faith and eucharist that has been described strikingly on the Orthodox side as the "source of equal ecclesial status" (in terms of sacramental and hierarchic structure) and the source of a common tradition of faith "based on the first seven ecumenical councils."[13]

As I offer the public a new edition of a book that first appeared in 1964 on the symbolic form of the Byzantine liturgy, I find that the renewed interest in the Byzantine liturgy and its history deserve to be taken into account. Above all, however, one must come to grips with the advances that have been made since in liturgical science, a field that fifteen years ago was but inadequately cultivated.

Probably the most important results achieved since 1964 have been published, usually after many years of work, by R. Bornert (text-critical studies of the Byzantine liturgical commentaries), A. Jacob (examination of all the manuscript material for the Liturgy of Chrysostom with a view to establishing the evolution of the text), J. Mateos and R. F. Taft (editions of texts and studies relating to the major structural units of the liturgical celebration), F. van de Paverd (further examination of the passages in Chrysostom that are relevant to the liturgy), and G. Wagner (proof of the authenticity of the anaphora of Chrysostom).[14]

While publishing a new edition that would include all these findings, I also wanted to preserve that which gave the original book its special character: the comprehensive view of the overall form of the liturgy, and the way in which historical developments in liturgy, dogma, and iconography were each made to shed light on the others. It did not seem advisable to attempt a new and expanded presentation of all these aspects and so I chose an alternative: to add a supplementary section of "New Contributions" (which can be read independently) that would bring to bear the results of research and the theological viewpoints that must now be taken into consideration. These contributions are ordered in relation to the successive parts of the original book.[15] I have altered the original text in only a few places, especially where a view formerly expressed had meanwhile become untenable. It should be noted, however, that although these passages in the original text did not have behind them the results of contemporary science reflected in the "New Contributions," they were formulated in an open-ended way that did not give a false picture of the state of scholarship at that time.

The primary purpose, however, of the "New Contributions" is to help the reader grasp the basic structures of the Byzantine liturgy, as well as the character of this liturgy as witness to faith (above and beyond the technical aspects both of the history of the Byzantine liturgy and of studies in Byzantine theology—aspects necessary in a postdoctoral qualifying dissertation such as the original book was). The reader will also be helped by the addition of a new index that makes it easier to get at the information in the book regarding the sequence of rites in the liturgy and the various liturgical and historical details provided.[16] The bibliography has been expanded and at the same time weeded out. Works published after 1963 are given consideration only in the supplementary essays.

In the context of our renewed consciousness of the church and of the liturgy, may the republication of this book help also to a more profound encounter with the liturgical celebration that is so dear to the churches of the East.

Sources

I. TEXTS OF THE LITURGIES OF BASIL AND CHRYSOSTOM
1. List of manuscripts, editions, and translations in P. de Meester, DACL VI, 1647–1654; list of manuscripts now especially in Jacob (*Recherches; Formulaire*) and Taft, and in selection in Beck 245ff.

2. Edition of the *Codex Barberinus graecus 336*, from the end of the eighth century, in: F. E. Brightman, *Liturgies Eastern and Western* I. *Eastern Liturgies* (Oxford, 1896; repr. 1965), 309–344 (Liturgies of Basil and Chrysostom in parallel columns). Textual criticism and bibliography for the Barberini Codex: A. Strittmatter, "The *Barberinum S. Marci* of J. Goar," ELit 47 (1953) 329–367.

3. Reconstruction of the older text traditions: (a) for the anaphora of Basil: H. Engberding, *Das eucharistische Hochgebet* and "Das anaphorische Furbittgebet" (see Bibliography); (b) for the anaphora of Chrysostom: Jacob, *Recherches*; (c) for the anaphora of James: B. Chr. Mercier, in PO 26/2 (1946) 115–256.

4. Editions of the texts now in use: Br (353–399, 400–411) as well as the many editions for use in the liturgy.

II. LITURGICAL AND PATRISTIC SOURCES
For sources—patristic and ancient liturgical—not available in GCS, PG, PO, SC, and PE, see the texts edited by Borgia, Botte, Funk, and Tonneau-Devreesse (see Abbreviations).

For Nestorian and Jacobite interpretation of the liturgy, see Connolly and Connolly-Codrington (see Bibliography).

For the history of the form of the Byzantine liturgy (in addition to the sources listed above under I), see, in the Abbreviations or Bibliography, Mateos, *Typikon*; Jacob, "Léon Toscan" and "Nicolas d'Otrante"; and Arranz, "Typicon"; also the materials collected by Dmitrievskij, Krasnosel'cev, Moraitis, and Trempelas.

Part One

The Byzantine Liturgy:
The Development of Its Symbolic Form

Chapter One

The Contribution of the Fathers
to the Development of the Byzantine Liturgy

The first phase in the development of the Byzantine liturgy covers the period between the Ecumenical Councils of Constantinople (381) and Ephesus (431). At the first of these councils the capital on the Bosphorus, which originally belonged to the metropolitanate of Heraclea, managed, in its capacity as the "New Rome," to win for its bishops a "primacy of honor"[1] immediately after the Roman pope. The simultaneous express confirmation of all the existing rights of those metropolitanates that would later belong to the Byzantine patriarchate makes it clear that this primacy did not initially mean a patriarchate of jurisdiction.[2] Nonetheless the primacy of honor soon turned into a jurisdictional supremacy over the surrounding dioceses of Thrace, Asia, and Pontus[3] and an effective primacy of rank among the eastern patriarchates. This development would be sealed by the twenty-eighth canon of Chalcedon,[4] which reflected already existing relationships.

While the capital at this time already exercised a major influence in ecclesiastical politics, in matters theological and liturgical it still received its decisive impulses from the older ecclesiastical centers and in particular from Antioch. In fact, the following bishops of the capital came from these other centers: Gregory of Nazianus (379–381), Nectarius of Tarsus (381–397), John Chrysostom (398–404), and Nestorius (428–431).[5]

Similarly, the two Byzantine anaphora texts that bear the names of St. Basil and St. John Chrysostom probably originated in Caesarea and Antioch. In favor of Basil's authorship there is also external evidence and the theological style of the text. The tradition of Chrysostom's authorship, on the other hand, becomes a firm one only in the eighth century; but internal criteria point to an Antiochene origin in the late fourth century and allow the possibility that its use in Constantinople may have been due to Chrysostom's episcopacy there. It was primarily through their theology, however, that these two Fathers contributed to liturgical development: Basil through his teaching on the Holy Spirit, which prepared the way for the Council of Constantinople; Chrysostom (and the same holds for his Antiochene fellow student and friend, Theodore of Mopsuestia) through his teaching on the mysteries, which promoted the development of liturgical symbolism and drama.

Thus the Fathers of this period had a fruitful influence on the liturgy of Constantinople as well as on that of their native places, and the later Byzantine liturgy, in the strict sense of this term, is unintelligible apart from their theology.

A. ORIGIN AND AUTHENTICITY
OF THE BYZANTINE ANAPHORA TEXTS

The Byzantine church ascribes its two liturgical formularies, which differ in their anaphoras and some other presidential prayers,[1] to St. Basil the Great and St. John Chrysostom.[2] The Liturgy of St. Basil appears under this name in all the manuscripts that have survived, the oldest[3] of these being from the end of the eighth century. In the oldest codices, however, the name of St. John Chrysostom does not clearly and unambiguously extend to the entire liturgy or, in some instances, to all the prayers peculiar to this liturgy.[4] On the other hand, even the most consistent ascription of authorship in the text tradition is no guarantee of authorship in the historical sense. The nonhistoricity of such ascriptions is evident, for example, in the case of liturgical formularies that bear the name of an apostle or of an apostle's disciple. This kind of ascription frequently amounts only to a profession of fidelity to the tradition of the local church in question and to its founders. Nonetheless, when the ascription is to a church Father of the fourth century, there is some possibility that the latter had at least a part in the formulation of the liturgy, that is, in the formulation of the nucleus of the anaphora. The likelihood increases when the same anaphora is used under the same name in churches of different liturgical traditions and when the attestation of the text and its authorship reaches back close to the lifetime of the Father in question. This is in fact the case with the anaphora of Basil.

1. St. Basil and the Anaphora of Basil

The unanimous testimony of the liturgical manuscripts that the Liturgy of Basil was used under this name as far back as the eighth century is carried even further back by various older sources. Attestation for the seventh century is given by the thirty-second canon of the Trullan Synod (692), which enjoins anew the custom of mixing some water with the wine in the celebration of the liturgy because such was the tradition received from James, the brother of the Lord and from Basil the Great.[5] Very informative, too, is a passage of Leontius of Byzantium's book against the Nestorians and Eutychians (543[6]): "He [Theodore of Mopsuestia] dared still another blasphemous deed. . . . He composed another anaphora in opposition to the one which the Fathers had passed on to the Churches; he did not respect the anaphora of the Apostles or show reverence to the anaphora which Basil the Great wrote down under the influence of the Holy Spirit. As a result he put together a collection of blasphemies rather than of prayers."[7]

Faustus of Byzantium takes us back even further, to the years shortly after the death of St. Basil. A lengthy passage in his history of the Armenians is composed evidently in imitation of the anaphora of Basil,[8] although the latter is not directly named. There can thus be no doubt that our anaphora goes back at least to the time of St. Basil. The only questions remaining are whether it in fact originated in Cappadocia and was from the beginning diffused under the name of St. Basil, and, if so, what share the archbishop of Caesarea had in its composition.

The historian of the liturgy would be spared a great deal of trouble if he could trust the testimony that claims to be that of Patriarch Proclus of Constantinople (434–446). According to the treatise in question, many pastors and teachers of the holy churches have handed on liturgical formularies; the earliest and most famous of these pastors and teachers were Clement and James. "Then St. Basil, mindful of the laxity and weakness of human beings who find the liturgy burdensome because of its length, gave permission to read a shorter form of the liturgy. Not long afterwards, our Father, John of the golden tongue, wanted . . . to eliminate this same satanic objection completely; therefore he removed a good deal from the liturgy and prescribed that it be celebrated in an even briefer form."[9]

This passage offers a graphic explanation of the origin of the two Byzantine anaphora texts and of their varying length. The explanation is that these texts are an abbreviation of the Clementine Liturgy (in the eighth book of the *Apostolic Constitutions*). Unfortunately, this testimony is not really from Proclus. It has been known for some time that it could not have preceded the seventh century,[10] and it has recently been recognized as a sixteenth-century forgery.[11] But even in what it says the account is full of impossibilities. The Clementine Liturgy is accepted as an authentic work of Clement, the disciple of the apostles, and its length then leads to the conclusion that a longer liturgy is always an older liturgy. In fact, however, the liturgy recorded in the *Apostolic Constitutions* is an ideal formulary from the second half of the fourth century and was probably never used in an actual liturgical celebration.[12] Moreover, even if one were to regard this liturgy as in fact older than those of Basil and Chrysostom, the latter could not have come into existence simply through abbreviation of the older liturgy.[13] As everyone knows, third-century episcopal celebrants of the liturgy exercised a great deal of freedom in formulating the eucharistic prayer,[14] so that when standardized forms did become customary, there were initially a number of independent formularies in use. The idea of one formulary deriving from another through shortening or lengthening is one that can be accepted in retrospect only when the correspondences between different anaphora texts are so extraordinary that the general pattern followed in anaphoras (a pattern affecting the overall structure and certain formulations) is evidently not enough to explain the similarities.

That kind of close similarity does in fact exist between the Greek-Byzantine and the Greek-Egyptian anaphoras of Basil. A. Baumstark has given this explanation: the Egyptian anaphora of Basil is "evidently a shortened version of the Byzantine anaphora of Basil that has been adapted for Egyptian use."[15] The dependence of the one formulary on the other was thus exposed. But could not the dependence run in the opposite direction? In order to reach an unambiguous answer to this question, H. Engberding broadened the comparison of texts to include the Greek anaphoras of James and Mark.[16] It became clear that the comparable sections of the eucharistic prayers in the anaphoras of Mark and James and the Egyptian anaphora of Basil followed a single scheme in both extent and content, and that the Byzantine anaphora of Basil departs from this pattern to a considerable degree by reason of the addition of material peculiar to it. The only possible conclusion is that "it is not the brevity of the Egyptian form but the unparalleled length of the Byzantine form that needs explanation"; it is not shortening but expansion that accounts for the difference in length, and therefore the Byzantine form must be regarded as an expansion of an older formulary.[17] But since the expanded form is attested by Faustus of Byzantium only a few years after the death of St. Basil and since we know from other sources of the great Cappadocian's activity in liturgical reform,[18] it is reasonable to ascribe the expanded parts of

6

the anaphora to the editorial activity of the saint, especially since these passages are consistent with his theological views. This last point is beyond dispute. "Let us go straight to the most convincing passage. . . . How clearly the personality of Christ is presented! The theological knowledge of the incarnate Son of God which the scriptures convey with conceptual clarity is here summarized in truly classical form."[19] "Compare the Apostolic Symbol with the creeds produced by the councils at Nicea and Constantinople, and you will find the same shift in spirit. The Apostolic Symbol is a spare kerygmatic composition; the creeds show speculative theological expansions."[20] These expansions betray the consistent intervention of a theologian, such as Basil was; it is thus very highly probable that he authored the expanded form of the liturgy.

Final certainty came with the work of B. Capelle, who showed the many correspondences between the material peculiar to the Byzantine anaphora of Basil and the writings of the saint, along with the works that Basil used as proofs from tradition for his own teaching.[21] A theologian such as Basil must have felt it indispensable to provide a new version of the christological passages that would be in keeping with the teaching of the Council of Nicea. But no one could be a better authority for this teaching than Athanasius. Thus the first expanded christological passage in the liturgy (Br 322, 28–323,2) shows a striking similarity to Athanasius (PG 25:217BC), especially in its acceptance of the typically Athanasian expression "express image" (sphragis isotupos).[22]

The first mention of the Holy Spirit in the eucharistic prayer must in particular have spurred Basil to expand the text, inasmuch as his theological labors were directed primarily to the right doctrine of the Holy Spirit. And in fact this passage with its many citations of scripture (Br 323,3–11) contain many echoes of other places in Basil. Typically Basilian is the description of the Holy Spirit as "fountain of sanctification" (hê pêgê tou hagiasmou).[23]

In the salvation-historical part of the eucharistic prayer a somewhat lengthy passage (Br 324,14–325,19) after the Thrice Holy is strikingly similar to a corresponding section in the longer monastic Rule. Most revealing are the last four segments of this passage (Br 325,9–19), three of which appear in the longer Rule (PG 31:913C), in the treatise On the Holy Spirit (PG 32:140B), and in Letter 261 (PG 32:969A), while two of them appear in Homily 5 on the Hexaemeron (PG 29:108C).[24] These segments prove to be so characteristic of Basil not only theologically but even stylistically that he is the only possible redactor of the anaphora.

2. St. John Chrysostom and the Chrysostom Anaphora

With respect to the Liturgy of Chrysostom it is far more difficult than it was for the Liturgy of Basil to establish a historical link between the anaphora and the saint whose name it bears. To begin with, prior to the eleventh century the anaphora of Chrysostom played a much less important role at Byzantium than did the anaphora of St. Basil.[25] Moreover, the liturgical text tradition is not clear and consistent in its attribution from the beginning. In the Vatican *Codex Barberini 336* (end of the eighth century) the name of Chrysostom is found only before the Prayer over the Catechumens,[26] before the "Proscomide Prayer"[27] after the Great Entrance, and before the Prayer behind the Ambo.[28] An attribution of the entire formulary to Chrysostom would be implicit if these prayers are also representative of the others that follow them and thus of the entire formulary,[29] and could then be regarded as historically valid for the parts that developed down to the end of the fourth century.[30]

Before the eighth century the external witnesses make no mention of any Liturgy of St. John Chrysostom. However, the silence of the already mentioned canon 32 of the Trullan Synod may be due to the anaphora of Chrysostom having nothing to say about the custom of mingling water and wine, which is the issue in this canon. Only Leontius attests that in addition to the anaphora of Basil there was another of the apostles, which Theodore disfigured as he did that of Basil. Could it be that this other anaphora had come into use in Constantinople in the time of Chrysostom and that his name was subsequently associated with it? As a matter of fact, among the Syrian-Jacobite liturgical formularies there is an anaphora of the Twelve Apostles, very similar to the anaphora of Chrysostom, as was pointed out by I. E. Rahmani.[31] The kinship of the two texts was confirmed brilliantly by H. Engberding after a detailed investigation.[32] Both texts originate in a Greek anaphora of the fourth century that probably saw the light in the region of Antioch.[33]

An adoption of the anaphora of the Apostles at Constantinople in the time of Chrysostom or Nestorius is not improbable. When Leontius of Byzantium asserts that Theodore of Mopsuestia had altered the anaphora of the Apostles, he evidently supposes it to have been in use at least at Mopsuestia in Cilicia. But the tradition of the Nestorian Church ascribes creative liturgical activity to both of its two saints, Theodore and Nestorius. The Liturgy of Nestorius, which is still one of the three regular formularies of the Nestorian Church, is thought to have been regarded as an authentic work of Nestorius himself by Catholicos Mar Abba (d. 552) and to have been translated by the latter from Greek into Syriac at the time when he "was living in the Roman Empire prior to his elevation in 536 to the highest office in the Persian-Nestorian Church."[34] It if could be shown that Nestorius likewise remodeled the anaphora of the Apostles, then we would have to assume that the latter was already the liturgy of his episcopal see, Constantinople, and that therefore the anaphora of Chrysostom, under the name of the anaphora of the Apostles, was in use soon after Chrysostom not only in Cilicia but in Constantinople as well.

A. Baumstark published a comparison of the anaphora of Nestorius (Ne) with those of Basil (Ba) and Chrysostom (C)[35] and concluded that a relation of dependence between Ne and C was undeniable. At the qualitative level the agreement between Ne and C:

"takes on a special significance inasmuch as it extends to all the positive traits which, in the section compared, are characteristic of C in contrast to all the other Greek liturgies[36]: the Trinitarian ending of the introduction to the eucharistic prayer of thanksgiving[37]; the formula of thanksgiving for everything, which concludes the first part of the anaphora (before the Trisagion)[38]; the thanksgiving for this *leitourgia* itself[39]; the concessive "though" which connects the introduction to the Trisagion with what precedes[40]; the *staurou* (cross) without any descriptive adjective,[41] the use of *taphou* instead of *taphês* (= burial, tomb),[42] and the phrase *tês ek dexiôn kathedras* ("the sitting at the right hand"—without saying whose right hand!),[43] all in the anamnesis. Finally, it is to be observed that those elements of wording which the two texts have in common appear in exactly the same order in both. If we consider all these points together, it is impossible to speak of the findings as more or less coincidental; rather a direct relation of dependence between C and Ne must be assumed in one or the other direction."[44]

Baumstark himself initially interpreted the dependence as meaning that C had been derived from Ne through abbreviation. But after Engberding's studies he considered the originality of C to have been demonstrated.[45] According to Baumstark, then, the picture is as follows: it is certain that Ne was derived from C through expansion; it is highly probable that Nestorius himself was the redactor of Ne; it is also probable that C was in use as the liturgy of the capital. All this heightens the independently existing probability

9

that the anaphora of the Apostles made its way from Antioch to Constantinople during the period of brisk liturgical relations before 431.[46]

The texts cited to exemplify the Basilian redaction of the Byzantine anaphora of Basil will already have given a clear indication of the historico-dogmatic situation. It was the efforts in behalf of a further development of christology and the doctrine of the Holy Spirit that provided the stimulus for liturgical reform. In his earlier mentioned study, *The Place of Christ in Liturgical Prayer*, J. A. Jungmann, using primarily the invocations and conclusions of liturgical prayers, demonstrated changes in the eastern liturgies that had their origins in the history of dogma. In the present context I must also investigate the development of the anamnesis and epiclesis formulas that are characteristic of the eastern liturgies.

1. Christology and the Anamnesis

In the fourth century East, resistance to Arianism was an urgent priority. In the process, the conviction of faith regarding the eternally efficacious intercession of the exalted Lord with the Father in our behalf,[1] along with the corresponding liturgical prayer to the Father *"through* our Lord Jesus Christ," had to be deemphasized because of the danger of Arian misinterpretation.[2] In its place came a greater emphasis on the divinity of Christ, and this emphasis found liturgical expression in praise of the Father *"with* the Son." At the heart of this development were the cities of Antioch and Caesarea.

"In Antioch, where, after the banishment of the Catholic Bishop Eustathius in the year 330, the Arians had the upper hand, the two laymen, Diodorus of Tarsus and Flavian, were the focus for the minority of convinced Catholics in this city. The latter felt themselves challenged by the doxology *Doxa patri di'huiou en hagiô pneumati*—most probably recited by the Arians with the necessary emphasis—and about this time they began to use, instead, in their own liturgical assemblies, in the psalm-chant at the sanctuaries of the martyrs and then also in the common Church, the form: *Doxa patri kai huiô kai hagiô pneumati*. The two doxologies thus became passwords of the two parties."[3]

"A similarly critical situation resulted in Caesarea, where likewise there was a strongly Arian-minded party; only here, St. Basil the

Great was on guard as bishop. He began one day, when praying with the people, to use in protest against the Arian interpretation of the old doxology, the formula, "to the God and Father *with* the Son *together* with the Holy Spirit" . . . alongside the other, "*through* the Son *in* the Holy Spirit."[4]

The orthodox theologians of this period energetically defended the divinity of Christ, in the sense of a consubstantiality with the Father, against the Arians. At the same time, when the discussion turned to the mediatorship of Christ, they focused their attention on the historical work of redemption. Statements of scripture and tradition about a subordination of the Son to the Father could thus be understood in terms of the Lord's earthly life and related solely to his humanity.

"After the reform of liturgical prayer at Caesarea and Antioch, the priestly action of Jesus as the here and now active mediator of our prayers and sacrifices—an action that had formerly been the object of keen Christian awareness—was increasingly obscured; the priestly activity of Jesus was increasingly located in his past work of redemption. In consequence, there was also an increasing emphasis on the Mass as a re-presentation, or making present, of the past saving act of Jesus."[5]

"The anamnetic character of the Lord's Supper was seen as the means of making the past saving act present to us and giving us a share in redemption."[6]

The greater stress on the general anamnetic character of the eucharistic celebration led inevitably to a richer development of the anamnesis as a particular prayer. This development cannot be missed in the liturgies of the fourth century. The anaphora of Hippolytus had said simply: "Mindful of his death and resurrection we offer you the bread and cup."[7] Now in the two Byzantine anaphora texts the object of remembrance becomes: the passion, cross, burial, resurrection after three days, ascent into heaven, session at the right hand of the Father, and second coming in glory.[8]

Even more enlightening than the lengthened list of saving acts in the anamnesis proper is the repercussion of the anamnesis on the form of the command to "do in memory" and of the account of institution. In the liturgy of Basil the anamnesis command is so formulated that not only Paul's words: "For as often as you eat this bread and drink this cup, you proclaim the Lord's death until he comes" (1 Cor 11:26), but also its liturgical expansion: "And confess

11

my resurrection," are put into the mouth of the Lord himself as a continuation of his own words: "Do this in remembrance of me."[9]

At this period the idea of the eucharistic celebration as a re-presentation and even an identical image of the Last Supper was interpreted in such concrete terms that the biblical account of institution underwent a further assimilation to current liturgical practice. In the Byzantine anaphora of Basil the words over the bread were: "He gave thanks and blessed it, *sanctified it*,[10] broke it and gave it to his holy disciples." The words over the chalice were: "He *mixed the wine and water*, gave thanks and blessed it, *sanctified it*,[11] and gave it to his holy disciples."

Also indicative of the greater emphasis on the anamnetic character of the eucharist is another alteration in the Basilian redaction of the anaphora. The older expression: "He left us this great mystery of his love,"[12] which occurred in the transition to the account of institution, is now made more concrete, in keeping with the liturgical anamnesis: "He left us as a memorial (*hypomnêmata*) of his saving passion that which we have offered in accordance with his commission."[13]

2. Pneumatology and the Epiclesis

The Basilian redaction of the anaphora already offered an example of how, in the age of the Second Ecumenical Council, the passages of the anaphora that dealt with the Holy Spirit called for greater emphasis and expansion. This was true in particular of the epiclesis. Even an older type of epiclesis that mentioned the Spirit but that in its content would have to be regarded as a Logos epiclesis,[14] could at this period be understood only as an epiclesis of the Holy Spirit. The interpretation of the consecration as the work of the Holy Spirit[15] became prevalent all the sooner because in the struggle with the Peumatomachians that had been going on since Athanasius, special emphasis was laid on the incarnation as a work of the Holy Spirit.[16] Athanasius says: "When the Logos descended into the holy Virgin, the Holy Spirit entered into her with him, and in the Holy Spirit the Logos shaped and formed a body for himself, in order to recapitulate creation through himself and offer it to the Father and once again reconcile all things in himself."[17]

The development of this epiclesis, or invocation, of the Spirit, which corresponds exactly to the dogmatic advance in the doctrine of the Holy Spirit, can be followed easily in the anaphoras of the eastern churches. A very early stage in this development is reflected in the East-Syrian Liturgy of the Apostles Addai and Mari:

12

"And may there come, o my Lord, thine Holy Spirit and rest upon this offering of thy servants and bless it and hallow it that it be to us, o my Lord, for the pardon of offences and the remission of sins and for the great hope of resurrection from the dead and for new life in the kingdom of heaven with all those who have been well pleasing in thy sight. And for all this great and marvellous dispensation towards us we will give thee thanks and praise thee without ceasing in thy Church. . . ."[18]

This form of the epiclesis is reminiscent of the epiclesis in Hippolytus. Common to both are: the invocation of the Holy Spirit upon the gifts, with nothing expressly said of the transformation of these into the body and blood of Christ; the descent of the Holy Spirit in order to sanctify the participants; and the direct transition from epiclesis to praise of God.

The next stage of development is represented by the epiclesis in the Egyptian Liturgy of St. Basil in its original wording. This epiclesis describes the action of the Holy Spirit on the gifts as a *hagiazein* and an *anadeiknumi hagia tôn hagiôn*.[19] Here we already have two consecratory terms (*hagiazein* and *anadeiknumi*[20]), and the effect of the act of consecration is explicitly emphasized as *hagia tôn hagiôn*.[21] But the starting point and end result of the act of consecration (bread into the body of Christ, and wine into the blood of Christ) are not yet contrasted with all the clarity that will be achieved later on.

In order to keep pace with the dogmatico-liturgical development, this epiclesis formula was expanded subsequently in a rather inorganic way by the addition of a section of text[22] that evidently comes from the Liturgy of James. In the latter it emerges organically out of what has preceded, whereas in the Egyptian Liturgy of Basil it gives the impression of being a belated repetition intended to specify further what has already been said.

The progressive form of epiclesis in the Jerusalem Liturgy of James is also attested explicitly for the second half of the fourth century in the *Mystagogical Catecheses* of Cyril[23] and represents a tradition that in all likelihood antecedes the Second Ecumenical Council.

The most clearly defined version of the epiclesis is peculiar to the Liturgy of Chrysostom. Not only are the starting point and end result of the act of consecration stated, but this act is also expressly described in the final words of the epiclesis as the work of the Holy Spirit: "transforming [them] through your Holy Spirit."[24] These

13

words are not in the original anaphora of the Apostles,[25] but they probably did exist in the formulary that the author of the Liturgy of Nestorius used for his redaction.[26] This very specific and pointed form of a Spirit epiclesis, which goes much further than the formulation in the anaphora of Basil, is hardly explicable before the Council of 381.[27] On the other hand, it is quite understandable as a direct result of this Council, especially since the Liturgy of the Apostles, as celebrated in Constantinople, would be almost immediately affected by the action of the Council.

C. THE SACRAMENTAL REALITY OF THE ANAPHORA
WITHIN THE OVERALL SYMBOLIC FORM OF THE LITURGY

The development of the anaphora in the fourth century is characterized chiefly by the trinitarian structuring of the introduction to the Thrice Holy and by the expansion of the special anamnesis and epiclesis. The first result is a clarification of the ancient Christian eucharistic prayer, which now emerges clearly as the textual form of the sacramental reality of the Supper. For the special anamnesis underscores the fact that the church's Supper is a memorial of Christ and, in particular, that it is a reality-filled proclamation of the Lord's death and resurrection. The angelic Thrice Holy, now given prominence by the expanded introduction to it, underscores the significance of the Supper as an anticipation of heavenly reality. Due to the emphasis on ideas from the letter to the Hebrews and the Apocalypse, the eschatological aspect of the Supper, which is attested in the synoptic gospels,[1] is accentuated inasmuch as the eschaton appears no longer as simply an object of expectation but as something shared in the present. The development of the special epiclesis, for its part, turns the idea of an acceptance among the angels at the singing of the Thrice Holy[2] into that of an epiphany of God himself, and at the same time, by reason of the greater emphasis on the act of consecration, calls attention to the eucharist as a sacramental incarnation[3] and a proclamation of death and resurrection, as indicated in the anamnesis.

The anamnesis is now seen as so filled with salvation-historical and heavenly reality that the entire liturgical celebration is drawn into the ambit of that reality. Even those actions of the eucharistic celebration that are not sacramental in the strict sense appear, in the radiance of the mystery event proper, as demanding respect and as "terrifying," although intially no independent salvation-historical or heavenly symbolism is attached to them, as it is to the sacramental event proper of the eucharistic celebration. But in a later stage of development these actions too become actual symbols that give new graphic expression to what the eucharistic celebration effects at the sacramental level, while at the same time they introduce differentiation into the content of the sacramental eucharistic symbolism.

It is easy to follow this development in the Fathers, and especially in the Antiochene Fathers, of the fourth and fifth centuries. Among these, John Chrysostom and Theodore Mopsuestia in particular create the preconditions for the development and interpretation of the later Byzantine liturgy.

1. The Mystery Character of the Liturgy according to John Chrysostom
For John Chrysostom the liturgy is a "mystery." In his view, the entire celebration is so much an anamnesis of the saving work of Christ and a revelation of heavenly reality that its earthly form is wholly irradiated by these aspects. He urges his hearers:

"Believe that even now this is the meal [the farewell meal of Jesus] of which he himself partook. For this meal is in no way different from that one. It is not at all the case that a simple human being prepares this meal while Jesus alone prepared that one; rather, he alone prepares this one as he did that. Therefore, when you see the priest giving you communion, do not think that it is the priest who is doing it. Think instead that it is Christ's hand[4] that is being extended to you."[5]

The preacher is deeply interested even in the external setting past and present. "This table of ours is the same as that one, and what rests upon it is not of any lesser value. . . . Here [in our church] is the upper room where they gathered that evening; it is from here that they departed for the Mount of Olives."[6] The next words, "Let us too, then, go forth to the multitudes of the poor, for they are our Mount of Olives," make it clear that the comparison between past and present applies differently depending on the aspects under consideration and that, for example, the same kind of identity is not being predicated of the supper table as is predicated of the eucharist itself. It remains true, nonetheless, that Chrysostom is concerned to relate even the externals of the liturgy to the mystery character of the eucharistic celebration.

The eucharist is also a rendering present of the incarnation. Here again the preacher sees the entire liturgical celebration as clothed in Christmas splendor: "If we approach with believing hearts, we will undoubtedly see the Lord lying in the manger, for the Supper table takes the place of the manger. Here too the body of the Lord will lie, not wrapped in swaddling clothes as it was then, but surrounded on every side by the Holy Spirit."[7]

As a re-presentation of the death of Christ the liturgy imitates and gives experience of the death of Christ to such an extent that this alone is enough to refute the heretics who call the sacrificial death of Christ into question: "When heretics ask: 'How can we know that Christ was offered in sacrifice?' we reduce them to silence by referring them, among other things, to the mysteries. For if Jesus did not die, what do the liturgical actions[8] symbolize?"[9]

Chrysostom sees the presence of the angels as proof that the liturgy is the sacramental form of heavenly reality: "The priest is surrounded by angels. The sanctuary and the entire temple are filled with heavenly Powers who pay homage to him who is present on the altar."[10]

The extension of eucharistic symbolism to the entire liturgy is especially clear in Chrysostom's broad application of the concept of mystery to it. Chrysostom's concept of mystery, as G. Fittkau has shown, is not derived from the mystery cults,[11] but rather takes as its starting point the basic meaning of the word itself: "a hidden, secret reality,"[12] and then understands this in the specifically Christian sense as referring to God's decree of salvation and its revelation in Jesus Christ.[13] Such a concept of mystery allows this Church Father not only to apply the term to the sacraments, especially the eucharist, and other ecclesial realities as well, but also to make clear the place of all these within the overall order of salvation. As a result it is all the easier to see the importance that Chrysostom assigns to the sphere of worship and sacrament and to the liturgy. For out of the approximately 275 passages in which the word mystery appears in Chrysostom's works, the plural, *mystêria*, occurs in 200; of these the reference in 160 is to worship and the sacraments, while of these in turn 125 are to the eucharistic mysteries.[14]

Insofar as the mysteries are a revelation of divine reality, they are called "divine," "holy," "Spirit-filled." In relation to human unworthiness they are "terrifying" and "awe-inspiring."[15] Expressions of both types are often found together as descriptive of the "mysteries."[16]

It is characteristic of Chrysostom that he indicates the mystery character of various aspects and elements of the eucharistic celebration by referring to them as "terrifying." The altar and the place where the sacred scriptures are kept are terrifying.[17] " 'Holy and terrifying' are, above all, the sanctuary where the Eucharist is celebrated,[18] as well as the time during which it is celebrated,[19] the liturgical prayers,[20] the deacon's call: 'Holy things to the holy,'[21] the Our Father and the creed in the liturgy of dedication,[22] and finally the holy kiss of peace and mutual embrace[23] during the eucharistic meal."[24] Chrysostom sees all of these objects, actions, and prayers as participating in the sacramental mystery, but he does not as it were divide the mystery content of the entire celebration among them, as soon became customary beginning with Theodore of Mopsuestia.

2. The Image Character of the Liturgy according to Theodore of Mopsuestia
Theodore of Mopsuestia devotes more attention than John Chrysostom does to the specific meaning of the outward form of the liturgy. The difference in the approaches of the two great Antiochene writers can already be seen in the way each relates the priest of the earthly liturgy to Christ. The following statement is typical of Chrysostom:

"Christ is present now as well. He who waited on that table of old also waits on this one now. For it is not a human being who causes the sacrificial gifts to become the body and blood of Christ, but Christ himself who was crucified for us. Supplying Christ with a visible form, a priest stands at the altar and speaks the words spoken of old; but the power and the grace are from God."[25]

According to Theodore too, Christ truly acts in the eucharist, but he acts through the mediation of the visible priest. The latter's action mediates and renders present the action of Christ. With this in mind, Theodore can say: "Those whom divine grace chooses as priests of the new covenant do through the sacraments what Christ our Lord did and will continue to do."[26]

Theodore, the most consistent of the Antiochene theologians, is also the most typically Antiochene representative of the new, anti-Arian emphasis on the high priesthood of Christ. He sees Christ as the heavenly high priest, less however by reason of his constant intercession for us than as the one "who is seated at the right hand of the throne of the Majesty in heaven" (Heb 8:1). This means that "he carried out his priestly function when he died, rose and ascended into heaven, in order that all of us too might rise and ascend into heaven."[27] Therefore this priestly activity must also be imaged forth in the liturgy. Just as the priest is an image *(eikon)* of Christ,[28] so too must the liturgical actions become images of the historical work of redemption and in particular of the resurrection.

Theodore thus lays a greater stress than Chrysostom on the idea that the liturgy is an anamnesis of the historical work of salvation, including the resurrection, and that this anamnesis is effected by the liturgical actions as such, which are described and explained more specifically as images, types, and symbols that transmit reality.

We understand, then, why for the first time in the history of liturgical explanation Theodore assigns to individual rites the role of representing the various phases of the work of redemption. In the process the main parts of the liturgy (transfer of gifts; anaphora with the words of institution; epiclesis; fraction and commingling; communion) are as it were synchronized with the stages in the life of Christ frrom his going forth to a sacrificial death to his resurrection. Regarding the transfer of gifts Theodore writes:

"By means of the symbols we must see Christ who is now being led out and going forth to his passion and who, at another moment, is once again laid out for us on the altar in order to be sacrificed. For when the sacrificial gifts to be offered come forth in the sacred vessels, the patens and the chalices, you must think that Christ our Lord is coming forth and being led to his passion. But he is not being led out by the Jews, for it is neither allowed nor fitting that in the symbols of our life and salvation any reference be made to what is evil. Rather these things are images that tell us of the service provided by those invisible powers who long ago were likewise present and serving when the saving passion was taking place."[29]

"You must therefore think of the deacons, when they carry out the gifts for the offering, as images of the invisible serving spirits."[30] To the salvation-historical symbolism of the liturgy Theodore is here adding its heavenly symbolism. Once again, he is the first of the Fathers to link this with the outward forms of the liturgy in such a concrete way. Chrysostom and other Fathers do indeed claim that the angels minister at the eucharistic liturgy; Theodore, however, sees the angelic presence as being symbolized by the deacon, and this not only through his liturgical function but even through his outward garb.[31] The symbolism that Theodore develops for the transfer of the gifts will exercise a particularly lasting influence on the Byzantine liturgy and give this rite a greater importance than it has in the other liturgies.

The deposition of the gifts on the altar is another action of great symbolic importance. When the deacons have brought in the gifts, they place them on the altar "for the complete fulfillment of the passion. Thus we believe that Christ lies on the altar as though in the tomb and has already completed his suffering. For that reason the deacons who spread the linens on the altar provide an image of the burial cloths."[32] The other deacons who take their stand at both sides of the altar as soon as Christ has been laid on it and who fan the sacred body lest anything come near it, represent the angels who stayed by Christ as long as his repose in the tomb lasted, until they saw him rise from the dead.[33]

Like the explanation of the transfer of the gifts, this one of the deposition of the gifts on the altar was to have an important future. Shortly after Theodore, Isidore of Pelusium offers a similar explanation:

"The pure linen that is spread for the sake of the sacrificial gifts represents the liturgical service of Joseph of Arimathea. For just as he wrapped the body of the Lord in a linen cloth and consigned it to the tomb through which our entire race reached its resurrection, so, according to us, the sacrificial bread that we consecrate upon the linen is undoubtedly the body of Christ that is for us the source of immortality imparted by Christ the Savior, who was buried by Joseph but rose from the dead."[34]

Strikingly similar to this passage are the following troparia of the Byzantine liturgy that are recited at the deposition and covering of the gifts after the Great Entrance: "Noble Joseph took your immaculate body from the wood of the cross, anointed it with fragrant ointments, wrapped it in pure linen, and placed it in a new tomb.—O Christ, your tomb, the source of our resurrection, proved itself a giver of life, more fruitful than paradise, more radiant than that royal bridal chamber."[35]

Finally, the symbolism of death and resurrection in the eucharistic liturgy is also to be found in the consecration. Theodore takes account of this in his explanation of the words of institution and the epiclesis:

"As he gave his apostles the two species our Lord said: 'This is my body that is broken for you for the forgiveness of sins' and 'This is my blood that is shed for you for the forgiveness of sins.' In the first statement he reveals his passion, in the second the violence and intensity of his suffering in which a great deal of blood was shed. Therefore in accordance with this tradition we place the two species on the altar in order to show what happened."[36]

The epiclesis and subsequent liturgical actions correspond especially to the resurrection. "From this point on our Christ must rise from the dead in virtue of these actions and must pour out his grace on us; this is not possible except through the coming of the grace of the Holy Spirit. For it was the Spirit who raised him up of old."[37] It is in the light of the epiclesis that Theodore also explains the fraction, the signing, and, above all, the commingling of the species and the communion. Of the commingling he says: "Therefore it is prescribed that we put the lifegiving bread in pieces into the chalice, in order to show that the body and blood are inseparable and one in their power and that they impart one and the same grace to those who receive them."[38]

This dividing of the bread for the commingling proclaims the Easter events in which Christ appeared to the disciples one after another[39] and as it were divided his presence among them. Once again, the communion rite shows "that he rose from the dead in accordance with the type that was fulfilled."[40]

While the Theodoran symbolism of the fraction and signing lives on especially in the Syrian rites,[41] the synoptic vision of the epiclesis and commingling is also to be seen in the Byzantine rite when the priest places a piece of consecrated bread in the chalice with the words: "The fullness of the Holy Spirit."[42] In the Byzantine Church the rite of commingling receives a special further interpretation from the addition of hot water (the Zeon) at the commingling of the species.

After 553, of course, there was no longer any question of Theodore being a direct authority for the Byzantine Church. But by then his approach to the liturgy had become so much a part of ecclesiastical tradition that his interpretative motifs are interwoven inextricably with the later Byzantine explanation of the liturgy.

Chapter Two

The Liturgy of Constantinople
in the Age of the Monophysite Controversy

In the time of Chrysostom and Theodore of Mopsuestia, Constantinople was in close communication, both theological and liturgical, with Antioch. The connection became a burden to Constantinople when Nestorius ascended the patriarchal throne of the capital and his heretical teaching elicited the anathemas of Patriarch Cyril of Alexandria and the Council of Ephesus. The "pope" of Alexandria enjoyed a predominance[1] that showed itself at the Council of Ephesus and was even misused by a heretic at the Robber Synod of 449. The Byzantine patriarchate countered this assertiveness by pushing through the twenty-ninth canon of Chalcedon. While not detracting from the prestige of Old Rome, this canon was intended as a means of outstripping Alexandria in the competition for first place among the eastern patriarchates. But Constantinople's success produced only a hollow victory, since the greater part of the patriarchate of Alexandria succumbed to monophysitism.[2]

The ancient rivalry between the patriarchates and the new dogmatic struggle against monophysitism and its heretically rigid attachment to the terminology of Cyril (largely outmoded by Chalcedon) did not entice orthodox Byzantines into denying the orthodoxy of Cyril, however, as they would that of Theodoret of Cyr and Theodore of Mopsuestia in 553, or into adopting an accentuated Antiochene interpretation of Chalcedon and taking a position directly opposed to monophysitism with its exaggerated Alexandrianism. In fact, when they later adopted the neo-Chalcedonianism of the sixth century, the majority of the Orthodox would be thinking along Alexandrian lines and would as far as possible make use of Cyril's terminology within the Chalcedonian framework. In pursuing this line they would even sacrifice Theodoret and Theodore, Antiochenes hitherto regarded as orthodox.

These changes and debates are reflected even in the Byzantine liturgy. First, the emergence and use of the Trisagion in the Byzantine liturgy is indicative of the polemical position adopted against monophysitism. Second, at the end of the sixth century the work of Dionysius the Areopagite, so important for the Byzantine conception of the liturgy, is the manifestation of an intellectual outlook linking both fronts. Finally, the new liturgical texts of the sixth century, especially the hymn *Ho monogenês* and the Cherubikon, will show Byzantine theology swinging in an orthodox but Alexandrian direction.

A. THE TRISAGION AND THE SOLEMNIZATION
OF THE BISHOP'S ENTRANCE

The first sure information we have on the Trisagion comes from the Council of Chalcedon where the bishops of the diocese of Orient called for the condemnation of Dioscurus with the acclamation "Holy God, Holy Strong One, Holy Immortal One, have mercy on us! Long life to the rulers! May the godless one vanish for ever! Christ has deposed Dioscurus!"[1]

This account shows that the Trisagion hymn was probably regarded from the outset as a kind of polemical chant against the monophysites and as a criterion of orthodoxy, somewhat as the doxology "Glory be to the Father *and* the Son" had been the watchword of the Orthodox in the time of Dioscurus and Flavian. The theological point of the new formula in the struggle against monophysitism was its emphasis on the impossibility of fusing the divine nature with anything else. Even in the hypostatic union and in the passion and death of Christ the divine nature retained its innate "strength" (= impassibility?) and "immortality." Therefore the "Holy God" (it is evidently the Logos that is meant) was also invoked as "Holy Strong One" and "Holy Immortal One."[2]

A formula such as this hit at the disciples of Eutyches rather than at the defenders of the *mia physis* terminology of Cyril, who were much more numerous but equally hostile to Chalcedon. This second group could hardly raise serious objection to the Trisagion formula. They could make a small addition to it, however, that would blunt its edge and make it useful in their own discussions.

At Ephesus (431) the description of Mary as "Theotokos" had already been the watchword of the Orthodox and had served to remove all doubt as to the legitimacy of the "communication of idioms" idea, which the Alexandrians often used to emphasize the unity of Christ. Now the Trisagion could also be turned into a comprehensible example of the communication of idioms, provided it were formulated in this way: "Holy God, Holy Strong One, Holy

Immortal One, who was crucified for us, have mercy on us." It was in this form that Peter Knapheus (Peter the Fuller) introduced the Trisagion among the Monophysites when he became patriarch of Antioch for the first time in 468.[3]

The Orthodox were, of course, not disposed to give a benign interpretation of the expanded formula. They explained that the hymn was addressed to the entire Holy Trinity and that the addition introduced the worst possible heresies. This claim was made even though a very similar theopaschite formula (*Unus ex trinitate passus*) had long since become presentable in Byzantium and had even entered the liturgy in the hymn *Ho monogenês*.[4] Yet John Damascene still regards the addition to the Trisagion as

"blasphemous, because it introduces a fourth person and separates the Son of God, who is the personal "Strength" of the Father, from the crucified one, as though as the "Strong One" he were a different person—or else it has the Holy Trinity suffering and crucifies the Father and the Holy Spirit as well as the Son. . . . We for our part understand "Holy God" to refer to the Father (not attributing the name of God to him alone, but knowing perfectly well that the Son and the Holy Spirit are also God), and we refer "Holy Strong One" to the Son (without denying the same strength to the Father and the Holy Spirit) and "Holy Immortal One" to the Holy Spirit (without depriving the Father and the Son of immortality, but understanding all the names of God as applying without qualification to each of the hypostases)."[5]

Damascene's tortuous explanation shows how implausible was the trinitarian interpretation of the Trisagion, although it had nonetheless been asserted inflexibly ever since the introduction of the "monophysite" addition.

The same arguments against this addition already appear in a series of fictive letters of protest by eminent bishops to Peter Knapheus. These letters had been circulating since about 512.[6] In defense of the correct form of the Trisagion they appeal to a divine revelation in the time of Patriarch Proclus of Constantinople (434–446). John Damascene gives this account of the legend:

"Church historians report that while the people of Constantinople were praying against a divinely threatened calamity in the time of Patriarch Proclus, a boy in the crowd fell into an ecstasy and while in this state was taught the Thrice Holy by angels. . . . When the child regained his senses, the whole assembly sang the song and the threat ceased."[7]

The liturgical use of the Trisagion was probably as old as the formula itself, since only as a liturgical formula could it serve as a watchword of Orthodoxy. The most appropriate place for the singing of this hymn during the celebration of the eucharist was the entrance of the bishop, since the heightened ritual and symbolic importance of this entrance called for a suitable musical accompaniment. Furthermore, since this entrance was the bishop's first appearance in the divine presence, a hymn praising the holiness of God seemed particularly appropriate.

The development of the episcopal entrance into a solemn introductory liturgical rite that included an incensing of the church is attested for the last quarter of the fifth century by Dionysius the Areopagite, who also mentions[8] the confession of faith that was first introduced into the liturgy by Peter Knapheus[9] after 476. According to Dionysius the introductory rite took this form:

"After the hierarch has finished the holy prayer before the divine altar, he begins there the incensing and makes a complete circle of the holy place. Having returned to the altar, he intones the holy psalmody, and the entire congregation with its ordered ranks join him in singing the words of the holy psalms. After this comes the reading of the sacred scriptures."[10]

Dionysius' description is of the Antiochene rite, but the Byzantine entrance must have been similar.

In the light of what Dionysius says, two Byzantine notices regarding the singing of the Trisagion and the incensing of the church yield their meaning. In 512 Emperor Anastasius attempted to introduce the expanded Trisagion into Constantinople and gave instructions to this effect to the cantors of Hagia Sophia. When the people were assembled in the church on Sunday and suddenly heard the theopaschite Trisagion, they broke into a tumult during which the cantors were shouted down by the orthodox formula and were even attacked physically. The uproar then spread throughout the entire city.[11] This occurred evidently during the Sunday morning eucharist at which people were accustomed to hearing the correct formula.

In a life of his teacher, Patriarch Eutychius (552–565, 577–582), Eustratius mentions in passing an incensation of the church by the bishop, although this took place at the beginning of the Easter Vigil solemnities.[12] According to Brightman such an incensation is also to be assumed as part of the regular liturgy in the fifth and sixth centuries.[13]

24

The entrance of the celebrant as an introductory rite before the liturgy of the word continues today in the form of the Little Entrance, although since the eighth century this entrance is itself preceded by the prothesis and enarxis. The solemn beginning described by Dionysius, in which the bishop incenses the church, lives on in the Little Entrance of an episcopal celebrant. During the enarxis the bishop remains on his throne in the nave. At the Little Entrance all the ministers go to him and lead him in solemn procession to the sanctuary. There the bishop takes the censer and incenses the altar, the iconostasis, his fellow celebrants in the sanctuary and the faithful in the nave. Having returned to the altar, he recites the prayer for the Trisagion, and the singing of this hymn follows immediately.

In a nonepiscopal liturgy the Trisagion and the incensation of the altar are separated from one another by the enarxis and various more recent entrance songs. While the Trisagion follows the Little Entrance or, if you prefer, precedes the readings, the incensation takes place after the prothesis and before the beginning of the enarxis, and is done not by the priest but by a deacon.

B. THE SPIRITUAL MEANING OF LITURGICAL FORMS ACCORDING TO DIONYSIUS THE AREOPAGITE

Dionysius the Areopagite is important in the history of the liturgy not only as a witness to the liturgy as celebrated during the patriarchate of Peter Knapheus,[1] but also and above all as an interpreter of liturgical symbols. His explanation of the liturgy in the third chapter of his *Ecclesiastical Hierarchy*[2] became *the* model for later Byzantine explicators of the liturgy. In particular, Maximus the Confessor (d. 662) and Symeon of Thessalonica (d. 1429) appeal to his authority,[3] which they take to be that of the disciple whom Paul the Apostle won on the Areopagus.

The arrangement of Dionysius' explanation of the liturgy is determined by its place within his book on the ecclesiastical hierarchy, which in turn follows upon his meditation on the heavenly hierarchy. According to Dionysius, the function of both the heavenly and the earthly hierarchies is to mediate the divine illumination that radiates from the Most Holy Trinity, the source of all hierarchies, and descends through the ranks of the angelic world and the ordained priesthood to the believing people, and by means of this communication to lead the people to the knowledge of God. The communication of this illumination, "which takes place in a purely spiritual manner in the sphere of the angelic world, is then repeated in the Church in symbols, sacraments and images, that is, in half-spiritual, half-visible forms which at once copy and conceal the spiritual process occurring in the higher sphere."[4]

This description sums up the importance of liturgical forms in the process of mediating salvation and at the same time shows the necessity of understanding the spiritual meaning these forms have as participations in a higher reality and of tracing this meaning back to its ultimate source. This meaning, too, is communicated by the earthly hierarchy, the activity of which is manifested in its highest form in the rites of the synaxis, as the opening action of the synaxis, the incensation of the church by the bishop, shows:

"We must now unveil the meaning of the first ceremony, raise our eyes steadfastly to its godlike beauty, and observe how the hierarch, filled with God, walks from the altar to the farthest reaches of the church with the fragrance rising from the censer and, having completed his round, returns again to the altar.

"Inspired by his own goodness, the blessed God who is supreme above all beings, comes forth from himself to enter into communion with those who share in his holy gifts; and yet he does not abandon his essential and immutable repose and immobility. . . .

"This is also true of the divine sacrament of the Eucharist. . . . Out of love for human beings it *unfolds its being in a varied fulness of symbolic ceremonies* and condescends to become an entire figurative representation of the divinity. But it *returns again to its own unity* and brings with it into unity all those who approach it with a holy mind.

"In the same godlike manner the godlike hierarch in his goodness transmits to his inferiors his simple knowledge of the hierarchical office by making use of a varied multitude of symbols. But then, free and unfettered by lower things and without having suffered any loss, he returns again to his source and accomplishes his spiritual entrance into his own unity. There he contemplates in pure light and in their unity the ideas of the sacramental rite. Thus he derives from his love-inspired descent into the lower world an even more godlike return to the highest realities."[5]

According to Dionysius, then, the opening ceremony of the liturgy already reflects the basic structure of God's saving activity, of the eucharistic celebration, and of the conduct of the hierarchic office. Although Dionysius ascends to dizzying spiritual heights in this explanation of the incensation, he nonetheless does not lose sight of the natural function of the rite,[6] for at that time the solemn beginning of the liturgy served as a kind of overture that sounded the theme of the entire celebration, while the filling of the church with the fragrance of the incense was a symbol of the divine action that fills all of reality. Dionysius' explanation of the incensation is echoed in the Byzantine troparion recited at the first incensing of the church, although the refrain is enriched by the addition of salvation-historical aspects that are either lacking in Dionysius or, if present, are not developed: "In the body, O Christ, you remained in the tomb; as God united with the soul you descended into the lower world; you entered into paradise with the thief, and you sit enthroned with the Father and the Holy Spirit; *you fill all things with your immensity.*"[7]

Dionysius' procedure in explaining the ceremonies is therefore by no means an arbitrary one. On the contrary, for in his system every "*allegoresis*" (relating of one thing to "another") is kept within bounds because in every case the meaning of the rite emerges from a "higher" and never from "another" irrelevant reality. Dionysius sees everything in the perspective of the supratemporal saving divine action and of the service rendered by the angels in this divine action. This orientation admittedly brings with it the danger of paying too little heed to the historical work of redemption. As a matter of fact, the danger can be seen in his explanation of the liturgy, although the incarnation forms as it were the backbone of his entire system. Thus the anaphora is explained as a prayer of praise and thanksgiving for "the great deeds God has done for us,"[8] but the only redemptive actions expressly mentioned are the incarnation itself and the Supper. At most an allusion to the redemptive death of the Lord may be seen in the statement that "the incarnated love of God for the human race" broke the power of the demons over us, "not by way of violence . . . but, according to a mysteriously transmitted saying, through judgment and righteousness."[9] This turn of phrase reminds us of the idea found in Gregory of Nyssa and other Fathers that by redeeming the human race with his blood Christ satisfied the just demands of Satan himself.

The lack of attention to the historical saving actions is a disadvantageous result of Dionysius' neoplatonic intellectual approach,[10] which only accentuates the one-sidedness of an Alexandrian conception of redemption and the liturgy, although on the credit side the Chalcedonian *asynchytos* ("without confusion") is a basic concept in Dionysius.[11] It is characteristic of the Alexandrian Fathers that in interpreting the liturgy their attention is focused primarily on the supratemporally present saving action of God in the eucharist.[12] From this point of view Dionysius must be regarded as an extreme Alexandrian; this is not surprising in view of the monophysite environment in which his writings were composed.[13]

Dionysius' explanation of the liturgy is thus opposed diametrically to that of Theodore of Mopsuestia. The later Byzantine explanation of the liturgy will strike a balance between these two basic possibilities. The star of Dionysius will be in the ascendant in the now beginning age of Justinian, whose most brilliant creation, Hagia Sophia, bears witness to the same view of the world. The christology of the Fifth Ecumenical Council, which was influenced by Alexandria, and the liturgical production of the Justinianic age likewise bear witness to this world-view.

Chapter Three

The Liturgy of the Justinian Age
and Its Interpretation by Maximus the Confessor

The Justinian age, so immensely important in the development of
Byzantine culture, was the period in which the Byzantine liturgy
first displayed its unmistakable character. This claim applies especially to Hagia Sophia—a novel place of worship that was at the
same time a symbol of the entire age—and to the most expressive
rite of the new liturgy—the Great Entrance, with its solemn transfer of gifts and accompanying mystic songs. It was in this period
too that Byzantine church poetry reached its earliest and highest
achievements in the person of Romanos Melodos,[1] while new
feasts[2] such as the solemnities of the Annunciation and Dormition
(Assumption) of Mary typified the rapid development of the liturgical year.

In this period liturgical and dogmatic history was again related
closely. No less a person than Justinian himself composed liturgical
hymns, which are as important as his administrative provisions for
understanding his program in theology and church politics. Justinian was concerned above all with winning back the Severian monophysites; his hope was to achieve this goal by means of a popular
revival, even in Orthodox circles, of the old Cyrillian christology in
the framework of the Chalcedonian system.[3] In 532 a religious dialogue was held with the Severian bishops, who introduced writings
of the Areopagite for the first time. Initially this met with mistrust
from the Orthodox side.[4] Bishop Hypatius of Ephesus, spokesman
for the imperial party, advocated a strict Chalcedonian course. But
toward the end of the proceedings the emperor himself intervened
and recommended the theopaschite formula (*Unus ex trinitate passus*), which had already been propagated by the Scythian monks
and was also acceptable to the Severians. The entire group asked
the pope to approve the formula.[5] Severus, who had been banished by Justin I, was allowed to take up residence in the capital
once again, where he won the favor of the empress.[6]

The hymn *Ho monogenês*[7] originated in the period of these efforts at reunion and found acceptance in the liturgy of both the Orthodox and the Monophysites.[8] Later Byzantine sources name Justinian as its author, while the monophysite tradition ascribes it to Patriarch Severus. As a matter of fact the hymn corresponds very closely to the theological view that the emperor expressed in various writings; even more importantly it matches word for word a passage[9] in Justinian's *Confession of the True Faith Against the Three Chapters*. As a composition of the emperor the hymn could have been adopted by the Monophysites after 532, but not after 536,[10] the year in which Severus was banished for good and the Byzantine Patriarch Anthimus, who had ties with Severus, was deposed. Consequently, Theophanes' statement in his Chronicle for the year 6028 (535)[11] deserves credence: in that year the emperor ordered that the hymn be sung in the churches. The evidence from the period itself does not enable us to determine what part it played in the liturgy. But its role as a song at the Little Entrance in the Melkite liturgies of Mark and James[12] confirms what we know from other sources: that this was also the original place of the hymn in the Byzantine liturgy before it became part of the enarxis during the secondary development of the latter; and it was shifted to the end of the second antiphon.

Despite the setback to the emperor's policy of reconciliation in 536, the Cyrillian interpretation of Chalcedon, or neo-Chalcedonianism, as it is called, won acceptance in Byzantium.[13] In 553 the church of Hagia Sophia witnessed the spectacle of the Fifth Ecumenical Council (Constantinople II) at which the condemnation of the Three Chapters excluded the venerable Antiochene tradition from playing a part in the further development of christology. Toward the end of his life Justinian seems to have been sympathetic to the views of the Aphthartodocetes,[14] but no theological writings along these lines have come down from him. An attempt has been made to prove that this phase of Justinian's theology was the most likely context for the emergence of the rite of the Zeon.[15] According to L. H. Grondijs in a study of eleventh-century sources, the practice of warming the Precious Blood before communion by adding some hot water to it, which is characteristic of the Byzantine liturgy and is first attested in the sixth century, presupposes the conviction that after the death of Christ the blood and water flowing from his side were warm.[16] But this conviction could only have sprung from an Aphthartodocetic outlook, although this could no longer be acknowledged after the sixth century. The rite continued in use, however, and only in the eleventh century did Nicetas Stethatos provide it with a new doctrinal basis by claiming that the vital warmth of the blood shed on the cross after death was due to the Holy Spirit, who remained in the body; in this way Nicetas explained the vital warmth in a phthartolatric way.[17] According to Grondijs, Nicetas' interpretation was generally accepted and was still being proposed in the fourteenth century.[18]

In fact, however, Nicetas did not make use of any new christological arguments, nor did the symbolism of the Zeon require any. The novelty was to be found rather in the fact that people were no longer content with the general eucharistic symbolism of the Zeon[19] and instead altered the meaning to fit in with the eleventh-century view according to which the liturgy copies in detail the incidents of Christ's life, especially those of his death, burial, and resurrection. In keeping with this approach, we find that as early as the eighth century a liturgical lance was used to represent the opening of Christ's side; it was thought that the immediate consequences of this opening were experienced liturgically in the use of the Zeon. As we shall see, the original meaning of the Zeon, which is to be explained in the context of the liturgical symbolism of the sixth century, shows that the origin of this rite has nothing to do with the episode of Aphthartodocetism under Justinian or with any other theories about the condition of Christ's body on the cross.

The second great spiritual force that made its appearance alongside the neo-Chalcedonian christology, and that was in fact linked closely to this in the sixth-century development of the liturgy, was the Dionysian vision of the hierarchic order in the world. When the writings of the Areopagite first surfaced during the religious dialogue of 532 they were viewed with skepticism, but only a few years later John of Scythopolis, the most important of the neo-Chalcedonians, was writing the first scholia on the Corpus Areopagiticum.[20] Of course, the prominence of the world-picture drawn by Dionysius was due only in part to the direct influence of his writings, since they were only the most conceptually rigorous expression of ideas that were the intellectual and spiritual movers of the age. In the political sphere the representational character of Justinian's imperial and ecclesiastical order seems to reflect this vision of the world; many aspects of that vision were brought together as in a burning glass in the liturgy of Hagia Sophia, which was bound up so inseparably with the ceremonial of the imperial court.

The Great Church of Divine Wisdom at Constantinople[1] is the first place of worship in the history of the church and the liturgy that so completely expresses the spiritual power of its age and by its architecture so graphically displays the heavenly dimension of the liturgy performed in it.

The unique role played by Hagia Sophia in Byzantium can be compared only with that of the Temple in Jerusalem, which is precisely how Justinian thought of this structure.[2] It is in this light that we are to understand the words he is reported to have spoken at the dedication on December 27, 537:[3] When the emperor entered the church, he suddenly hurried on ahead of his retinue, threw up his arms, and cried: "Glory and praise to the Most High, who has considered me worthy to complete such a work! Solomon, I have outdone you!"[4] The continued existence of this church was regarded in later times as a symbol of God's guarantee of protection to the empire and to the Christian church; and any damage that the building occasionally suffered from earthquakes was regarded as a misfortune affecting the entire empire. "Ornament and symbol of the sovereign sway of the Rhomaioi"[5] is the decription of Justinian's church of Hagia Sophia by John Cantacuzenus, fourteenth-century emperor and historian.

But while no imitations of the Jerusalem Temple were permitted elsewhere in Israel, the Great Church in Byzantium was looked upon as a model for all new churches in the empire, and its example encouraged builders of other churches to imitate what was imitable in Hagia Sophia: not its function as "heart of the Rhomaic empire" and as display case for the ceremonial of a theocratic court,[6] nor its bold construction, grandeur, and wealth, but rather its layout as a dome-crowned place of worship that is an image of heaven. The shallow-arched dome—an image of heaven that seems to float above the circle of windows—turns the entire place of worship into a hierarchically ordered cosmos whose character is determined by heaven, and shows the church's liturgy to be an imitative or even a direct participation[7] in the heavenly liturgy of the angels. This expressiveness is what makes the Great Church the ideal place of worship and the consummate model[8] for all later Byzantine church architecture.

The sanctuary of Syrian churches in the time of Chrysostom was already identified as a "heaven,"[9] not simply in the context of a comprehensive symbolic conception but through imitative elements: orientation, the closure of the vault, the dome-supporting canopy (ciborium) over the altar,[10] and the chancel curtains, which when drawn aside after the epiclesis "allow the heavens to open and the hosts of angels to come forth."[11]

This symbolism of heaven and light finds stunning expression in the novel architecture of Hagia Sophia. Procopius describes it as follows in his book on the buildings erected by Justinian:

"Rising above this circle is an enormous spherical dome which makes the building exceptionally beautiful. It seems not to be founded on solid masonry, but to be suspended from heaven by that golden chain and so cover the space."[12] "It abounds exceedingly in gleaming sunlight. You might say that the [interior] space is not illuminated by the sun from the outside, but that the radiance is generated from within, so great an abundance of light bathes this shrine all round."[13] "The visitor's mind is lifted up to God and floats aloft, thinking that He cannot be far away, but must love to dwell in this place, which He himself has chosen."[14]

We must not read too much into these passages, which come in fact from different sections of the description, but they doubtless do communicate three impressions that give a visitor an experience of cosmic sacrality. The dome does not seem made of heavy earthly material but to be directly linked to the heavens, of which it is an image. Like the cosmic heavens, the dome is a source and dwelling place of light, which flows down from it into the nave and then, as it were, returns to the dome, lifting the spirit of the praying visitor aloft with it to the heavenly heights.

This experience of light is an experience of the same reality that, in philosophical form, is at work in the two hierarchies of Dionysius the Areopagite. The light that descends from sphere to sphere within the church building is an image of the enlightenment of grace,[15] which according to Dionysius is communicated, via the angelic hierarchies, to the various ranks and states in the church, in order then to bring these up with it to higher regions as it returns to its source. In this sense C. Schneider is justified in saying that the dome of Byzantine churches "was not chosen for practical reasons but as an expression of Neoplatonic Christianity; Byzantine domed churches are Dionysius the Areopagite translated into stone and brick, marble and gold, mosaic and gem."[16]

The hierarchical order characteristic of the Dionysian vision of the world finds expression above all in the vertical dimension, but it is reflected in the horizontal as well. In the church of Hagia Sophia the descent of meaning from bema (sanctuary) to naos (nave) is emphasized by the richly adorned walls enclosing the bema. These are mentioned in the hymn of praise[17] that Paul the Silentiary composed when Hagia Sophia was restored after the dome had collapsed in 558[18] and which he read in the presence of the emperor and the patriarch at the dedication on December 24, 562.[19] In this poem he says: "Not only upon the walls which separate the priest from the choir of singers has he set plates of naked silver, but the columns, too, . . . he has completely covered with the silver metal."[20] "And the screen gives access to the priests through three doors. For on each side the workman's hand has made a small door."[21]

In his day K. Holl made these passages the point of departure for his well-known study of the origin of the iconostasis in Greek churches.[22] He understood the passages as describing a wall completely separating sanctuary and nave, such as became customary later on in Byzantine churches, and he interpreted this arrangement as connected with the proscenium of the Greek theater. According to Holl, the designation of the transfer of gifts as "entrance," a term already used in the seventh century, presupposed an enclosed space as the goal of the transfer.

The details of this view of Holl, which was long regarded as unassailable, have today been abandoned,[23] but some of the suggestions made in it continue to be of value. Thus the walls of the bema in Hagia Sophia give an impression of novelty as compared with the customary arrangement, even though they are still far from forming an unbroken barrier. In any case, the sanctuary is unmistakably an enclosed area as far as its meaning is concerned.[24] As a result of passing through this barrier, the procession with the gifts acquires a dramatic character that is heightened by the slightly later introduction of the Cherubikon. To that extent a comparison with the dramatic effects achieved in the Greek theater is not unjustified, although in its form the bema enclosure can hardly have any connection with the ancient proscenium. In this context we should think rather of the integration into the liturgy of various forms of court ceremonial[25] and of the literary genre of the dramatic sermon, which at this period was to some extent being transmuted into liturgical poetry.[26]

Of course, the emphasis on the separation of bema and naos, clergy and people, not only heightened the dramatic quality and solemnity of the liturgy, but was unfortunately at the same time symbolic of a diminished liturgical participation by the people and, more generally, of a curtailment in prayer and proclamation of the word as compared with ceremonial; this shift was, once again, consonant with Dionysian symbolic thinking.[27] Even the prayer of the priest, although abundant, drew less attention, and Justinian vainly added legislation to prevent the anaphora from now being spoken for the most part in a low voice.[28]

The Byzantine place of worship, which received its ideal form in the sixth-century Hagia Sophia as a cosmos controlled by heaven and filled with heavenly reality, was to manifest its characteristic traits even more clearly in the future through a consistent expansion of decoration.[29] This expansion took place especially in the period after iconoclasm.

B. THE LITURGY IN THE AGE OF JUSTINIAN

As Justinian's church of Hagia Sophia became the model for all later Byzantine church architecture, so also did the symbolic expressiveness of the new liturgy, especially as seen in the creation of the Great Entrance, determine the further development of the liturgy. A line runs from the symbolism of the transfer of gifts to the symbolism of the preparation of gifts, which underwent development especially in the period of iconoclasm. The Great Entrance itself became a high point of the liturgy and attracted the veneration of the faithful to an extraordinary degree. Another expression of the symbolism of the gifts, in this case the consecrated gifts, is the custom of the Zeon, a rite that is just as unmistakably characteristic of the Byzantine liturgy as the Great Entrance in its developed form.

1. The Great Entrance and the Interpretative Chants Accompanying It

The "entrance of the holy mysteries" is what Maximus the Confessor calls the transfer of the bread and wine to the altar at the beginning of the sacrificial liturgy.[1] The description shows a new and higher esteem for what was originally a purely practical procedure, and as such reflects the increasingly solemn form given to this rite in the Byzantine liturgy from the middle of the sixth century on. The rite receives its authentic interpretation in the Cherubikon, or Cherubic Hymn, that Emperor Justin II introduced in the ninth year of his reign (573–574) as an accompaniment to the transfer of gifts.[2] The hymn reads: "We who mystically represent the cherubim and sing the thrice-holy hymn to the life-giving Trinity, let us lay aside all worldly care to receive the King of all escorted unseen by the angelic corps."[3]

The symbolic interpretation that the Cherubikon gives of the transfer of gifts had its precedents. We find Theodore of Mopsuestia already writing: "When the deacons now bring out the gifts for presentation, you must look upon them as images of the spirits who serve invisibly."[4] In the gifts themselves Theodore saw Christ "who is now being led out and going forth to his passion."[5] Theodore thus related the rite primarily to the historical sacrifice of Christ, whereas the Cherubikon emphasizes the supratemporal dimension.

This difference in interpretation shows that it was possible for the ideas of Theodore to enter the Byzantine liturgy of the sixth century only through the transposing medium, as it were, of the Dionysian vision of the world.[6] True enough, in Dionysius himself the mention of the transfer of gifts seems at first sight to have very little of the "Dionysian" about it. At the beginning of chapter 3 of the *Ecclesiastical Hierarchy* Dionysius says quite simply: "Privileged members of the group of celebrants, in conjunction with the priests, place the holy bread and the cup of blessing on the altar of God."[7] Even briefer is the remark in the otherwise prolix interpretative main part of the chapter. After a very detailed appreciation of the confession of faith come the laconic words: "The divine bread and the chalice of blessing are placed on the altar with a veil over them."[8]

The reason for this sober treatment of the transfer of gifts is probably the fact that the action is performed only by "privileged members of the group of celebrants," which is Dionysius' way of referring to the deacons; the priests simply help them, probably by actually placing the gifts on the altar. The bishop has no part in this action, which for this reason is not acknowledged as having any reference to heavenly events; only through the mediation of the bishop do the lower degrees in the hierarchy share in the sanctifying and illuminative power of the higher. Only when the bishop is involved actively with the gifts or is active in their presence do they manifest their symbolic meaning. Thus at the reading of the diptychs Dionysius bids us consider "that after the placing on the altar of the *venerable symbolic* sacrificial gifts through which *Christ is signified and received*, the role of the saints . . . signifies the unbreakable bond that marks their supraterrestrial holy union with Christ."[9] Subsequently, in the interpretation of the washing of the bishop's hands, he twice says that this rite takes place "in the presence of the sacred symbols." When he makes this remark the second time, he adds: ". . . *as in the presence of Christ*, insofar as he sees our most secret thoughts, and the purification is carried out to its ultimate degree *under his all-seeing and penetrating gaze* and his just and incorruptible judgment."[10]

Consequently we must regard the interpretation of the gifts in the Cherubikon as a clarification of Dionysian ideas. And yet there is clearly an essential difference: the angels in the Cherubikon perform a service that is not specifically angelic, that is, incorporeal, as their service would have to be for Dionysius. Accordingly, their service is not really of a higher nature than that of the bishop himself as far as its spiritual meaning goes. Rather the angels simply perform at a higher level a service that is described in the sensible categories provided by ecclesial and liturgical forms, on the one hand, and by court ceremonial, on the other. In view of the sensible character of this service the angels of the Cherubikon are close to those of Theodore of Mopsuestia, who sets such a high value on the temporal and spatial role of the angels in the historical redemptive work of Christ. The popularization of Dionysian interpretative principles in the Cherubikon shows, in a way that is exemplary for later periods, how the unsurpassed influence of Dionysius on the Byzantine interpretation of the liturgy does not at all exclude a simultaneous acceptance of interpretative motifs from the Antiochene school, and in particular from Theodore of Mopsuestia.

So too the hymn that is used nowadays at the Great Entrance in the Liturgy of Basil for the Great—that is, Holy—Saturday (more accurately, the former Easter Vigil), and that originally had its place in the order of the Liturgy of James,[11] sounds like a paraphrase of Theodore's ideas:

"Let all mortal flesh be silent, and stand in fear and trembling and harbor no earthly thoughts; for the King of kings and Lord of lords is entering in to be slain and given as food to the faithful. The choirs of archangels go before him, with all the Principalities and Powers the many-eyed Cherubim and the six-winged Seraphim, who hide their faces and cry out the hymn: Alleluia, alleluia, alleluia."[12]

Some years before the definitive introduction of the Cherubikon under Justin II, the interpretation of the Great Entrance was still much disputed in Byzantium. This is clear from the criticism that Patriarch Eutychius (552–565)[13] directed at the symbolic interpretation of the rite and at the accompanying songs:

"They act stupidly, who have taught the people to sing a certain psalmic chant when the ministers are about to bring up to the altar the bread of oblation and the recently mixed chalice. In this hymn, which they consider suitable to the action being performed, the people say that they bear in the king of glory and refer in this way to the things being brought up, even though they have not yet been consecrated by the high-priestly invocation—unless perhaps what is sung means something else to them. For as Athanasius the Great says in his sermon to the baptized: 'You will see the Levites [i.e. deacons] bearing in breads and a chalice of wine and putting them on the table. And as long as the supplications and prayer have not been completed, it is nothing but plain bread.' "[14]

Is Eutychius' criticism aimed directly at the Cherubikon? Many historians of the liturgy are inclined to assume that it is.[15] If so, then the Cherubikon was already in use in some churches before its introduction was made obligatory under Justin II; Eutychius' phrase "King of glory" would then refer to the words "King of all" in the Cherubikon.[16] But why should Eutychius have cited the words inaccurately?

The phrase cited by Eutychius does, however, occur in the hymn sung in the Liturgy of the Presanctified at the transfer of the already consecrated gifts. But this hymn was not introduced until the year 615 and in all likelihood was composed specifically for the Liturgy of the Presanctified,[17] for which alone it seems appropriate. The Easter Chronicle says with regard to the year 615[18]:

"In this year in the reign of Patriarch Sergius of Constantinople they began to sing [the following]: after the 'Let rise' (*kateuthynthêtô*, Ps 140)[19] at the moment when, after the bishop's cry, 'Through the grace of your Christ,'[20] the presanctified gifts are carried from the skeuophylakion to the sanctuary, the people begin immediately: 'Now the heavenly Powers invisibly worship with us. For, behold, *the King of glory enters in*. Behold, the completed mystical sacrifice is escorted in. With faith and reverence let us approach to become sharers in eternal life. Alleluia!' "[21]

This hymn, which in its present form could hardly have been the one attacked by Eutychius, makes use of Psalm 27 (vs. 7 or 9, depending on the numeration) and suggests that this psalm had already been applied to the Great Entrance. The simplest explanation of Eutychius' reference to a *psalmikos hymnos* and of his criticism of the words "King of glory" is that he was speaking of Psalm 23. At the same time, we can understand how despite this criticism the Cherubikon could become established so quickly. For apart from all their symbolism, the newly introduced poetic hymns were far more appropriate than Psalm 23 to the different situations represented by the Great Entrance in both the ordinary liturgy and in the Liturgy of the Presanctified.

Thus the Cherubikon too allows for the fact that the symbolism attached to the unconsecrated gifts can be fully realized only when these gifts have been consecrated. Therefore at the moment of the Great Entrance the faithful are described as those who are about to "receive" (*hypodexamenoi*) into their midst the King of all. For although this "reception" begins at the Great Entrance, it acquires its full form and realization only at the consecration and communion. Thus the *Protheoria* of Nicholas and Theodore of Andida (eleventh century), for example, unhesitatingly relates the word to the reception of the Lord in communion.[22] Nicolas Cabasilas (d. after 1365) likewise interprets the Great Entrance and the many accompanying manifestations of reverence[23] by the people that were already customary in his day as referring to the sacramental offering of the sacrifice, but he must also admit that not all the faithful correctly distinguish between the consecrated and the unconsecrated gifts:

"The faithful chant during this procession, kneeling down reverently and devoutly, and praying that they may be remembered *when the offering is made*. The priest goes on, surrounded by candles and incense, until he comes to the altar. . . . During this ceremony we must prostrate ourselves before the priest and entreat him to remember us in the prayers which he is about to say. For there is no other means of supplication so powerful . . . as that which takes place through this most holy sacrifice. . . . If any of those who prostrate themselves thus before the priest who is carrying the offerings adores them as if they were the Body and Blood of Christ, and prays to them as such, he is led into error; he is confusing this ceremony with that of "the entry of the presanctified," not recognizing the differences between them. In this entry of the offerings, the gifts are not yet consecrated for the sacrifice; in the liturgy of the Presanctified they are consecrated and sanctified, the true Body and Blood of Christ."[24]

2. The Zeon
The songs accompanying the Great Entrance show that in sixth-century Byzantium the gifts for the offering were regarded as being able, even during their transfer, to symbolize the true sacrificial gift that alone effects a universal reconciliation, namely, Christ who died and rose from the dead for us. In this respect the Cherubikon directs attention more to the "King of all" who has passed through

a sacrificial death, while the hymn "Let all flesh be silent" meditates rather on the sacrifice itself, even if from the standpoint of heaven. Even before the consecration, then, the bread and wine have a representational character of a symbolico-figurative kind, the peculiar nature of which is not lost after the consecration but rather reaches its full form once the species signify the real presence of Christ.

Because the bread and wine had this function, there was a concern to express the essence of the eucharist as far as possible even in the composition of the material for the sacrifice. Thus preference was expressed for either leavened or unleavened bread[25] and for wine that was or was not mixed with water.[26] Especially informative for the sixth-century conception of the liturgy is the symbolic meaning that was assigned to the custom of using wine mixed with water and from which the meaning of the Zeon among the Byzantines becomes clear.

The most important witnesses to the symbolism that was attached to the condition of the wine in the eucharistic celebration come from the controversies on this subject from the sixth century on between the Byzantines and the Jacobites on the one side and the Armenians on the other. For in contrast to all the rest of ecclesial tradition the Monophysite Armenians use wine unmixed with water. They appeal in their own defense to a prescription of their apostle, George the Illuminator,[27] but they frequently offer symbolic considerations as well.

Historians are of the opinion that the custom was introduced in the sixth century[28] after the Armenians had split off from Orthodoxy. In 632 Emperor Heraclitus induced them to follow the custom of mixing water with the wine,[29] but as early as 648 they had returned to their own peculiar practice.[30] Jacob of Edessa (633–708), although himself a Monophysite, reproached the Armenians: "Therefore they agree with the Jews in offering . . . unleavened bread and unmixed wine."[31] The Trullan Synod expressly condemned the custom of using unmixed wine in the eucharist.[32]

The early stages of this controversy provide a first testimony to the mixing of the Zeon with the sacred blood.[33] When Moses II, the Armenian Catholicos, was summoned to Constantinople by Emperor Maurice (582–602), he is reported to have answered: "I will not cross the river Azat nor eat leavened bread nor drink warm water."[34] The words obviously allude to leavened bread and wine mixed with Zeon. Since the Armenians rejected any addition of water, they evidently did not practice the custom of the Zeon.

But what were their reasons for rejecting the mixing of water with the wine? The twelfth canon of the Trullan Synod contains a somewhat strange bit of information.[35] The canon reads: "It has come to our attention that when the unbloody sacrifice is offered in Armenia, pure wine unmixed with water is brought to the altar. In their defense the Armenians appeal to what Chrysostom, holy doctor of the Church, says in his explanation of the gospel of Matthew: 'Why did the risen Lord drink no water?' "[36] It seems that the Armenians tried to prove from this passage that the drinking of wine alone was appropriate for the risen Jesus in his immortal state, and not the drinking of water, which is itself corruptible and corrupts the purity of wine.

The same point is evidently being made in a canon that is ascribed wrongly to Bishop Macarius of Jerusalem (d. 331) but certainly reflects the views of the Armenians at the time of the Trullan Synod: "In keeping with apostolic tradition fresh bread and a chalice of pure wine without any admixture are to be brought to the altar, for we have not been redeemed by corruptible things but by the incorruptible blood and the body of the great and spotless Lamb of sacrifice."[37]

The Jacobite patriarch Johannan bar Susan (d. 1071), who himself defends the necessity of using mixed wine and water with an appeal to the blood and water that flowed from the side of Christ, draws the following inference from the Armenian custom. Since "the blood was his life and the water his death," it follows that "those who use only the wine of life and offer it alone at the altar, deny that he suffered and died for us, since they recognize only his life. . . . Mar Ephraem too says: 'The water proclaims the death, and the blood that he is by his very nature alive.' "[38]

These testimonies in their totality justify the assumption that the Armenians used unmixed wine in order to remove from the eucharistic food of immortality any hint of corruption and death. The objection that the death of the Lord must be proclaimed in the eucharistic celebration could not persuade them to change, since his resurrection too must be proclaimed, and the living, not the dead, body of the Lord be received there.

The Byzantines did not need to get involved in such arguments in their controversy with the Armenians. It was simpler for them to appeal, in behalf of the use of mixed wine, to the tradition of all the patriarchates and the example of the Lord himself.[39] This did not mean, however, that the symbolic aspect of the question was less important to them. They regarded the celebration of the eucharist with unmixed wine as an "imperfect proclamation of the mysteries,"[40] for the reason, evidently, that the proclamation of the death was not carried out in an appropriate way. And if the rite of the Zeon is mentioned for the first time in the context of the dispute with the Armenians, there can hardly be any doubt that the Byzantines regarded this rite precisely as an argument for the completeness of their own proclamation of the mysteries. But since the proclamation of the death was already accomplished through the use of mixed wine, the further addition of the Zeon before communion could only signify the opposite of death and therefore proclaim the resurrection. In fact, the sacred blood could not be better shown to be living and life-giving than by making it warm. Above all, however, the Zeon, being water that has felt the effect of fire, is a symbol of the life-giving power of the Holy Spirit, whose action on the sacred gifts has already been petitioned in the epiclesis and symbolized in the commingling.

According to Theodore of Mopsuestia, the entire course of the liturgy from the epiclesis to the communion is a proclamation of the resurrection.[41] This is true in particular of the epiclesis and the signing and commingling of the species. There is no mistaking Theodore's meaning when he says in connection with the commingling: "It is prescribed that we put the life-giving bread piecemeal into the chalice, in order to show that body and blood are inseparably united with each other."[42] In the sixth century this vital union of body and blood was further indicated by the addition of the Zeon immediately after the commingling and by the resultant warming of the blood.

The significance of the Zeon thus emerges directly from its association with the commingling. For this reason the rite required no separate formula of its own during the first century it was in use.[43] The formula of the commingling sufficed. Thus the oldest liturgical formulary that we have, dating from the end of the eighth century,[44] has in addition to the rubric for the commingling only the short accompanying formula, Eis plerôma Pneumatos Hagiou ("For the fullness of the Holy Spirit").[45] A rubric for the addition of the Zeon is supplied by Brightman from the Canons of Nicephorus.[46] The mention of the Holy Spirit at the commingling should not surprise us, since the effect of the epiclesis is made manifest in the commingling, and since epiclesis, commingling, and Zeon proclaim the Lord's resurrection—which is the work of the Holy Spirit[47]—as well as the presence of the risen body under the species, which results from the invocation of the Holy Spirit.

42

The rite of the Zeon, thus understood, fits without difficulty into the same phase of the Byzantine liturgical development in which the King of glory was seen entering in at the Great Entrance and was praised in hymns. On the other hand, a Zeon rite with the function of symbolizing that the blood shed in an extraordinary moment after death is nonetheless warm would be unthinkable in the framework of sixth-century liturgical symbolism. Only in the eleventh century did Niketas Stethatos hit upon such an explanation of the Zeon, and only in regard to this belated interpretation of the rite can there be any question of a connection with the conceptions of the hypostatic union that L. J. Grondijs regards as responsible for the very origin of the rite.

C. THE MYSTAGOGY OF MAXIMUS THE CONFESSOR

In his *Mystagogy* Maximus the Confessor gives a comprehensive interpretation of both the place of worship and the liturgy itself in the age of Justinian.[1] The complete title of the work is: "An introduction to the mystery, showing what the realities are that are imaged forth in the mysteries accomplished in holy Church at the time of the synaxis." In his preface the author tells us the model he feels obliged to follow:

"Since in his work on the ecclesiastical hierarchy holy Dionysius the Areopagite, a true interpreter of God, has also discussed, in a manner befitting his lofty spirit, the symbols accomplished in the sublime and mysterious consecration of the sacred synaxis, let me say that my discourse will not go back over the same topics nor travel the same paths he travelled. It would be excessively daring and almost senseless for one who is barely capable of grasping or understanding him to attempt to treat anew what he has already dealt with and, as it were, to present as my own invention what the Holy Spirit made known to him regarding the mysteries."[2]

In Maximus' explanation of the liturgy his intention "not to go back over the same topics" can be seen at work especially in the fact that he passes directly from the Thrice Holy (Sanctus) to the Our Father without discussing the anaphora, although, of course, his explanation of the liturgy as a whole does shed some light on the anaphora. The same intention is obviously at work also in the explanation of new rites introduced after Dionysius. Meanwhile Maximus travels "his own path" inasmuch as his work departs significantly from that of Dionysius in its structure and in the kind of symbolic interpretation given.

43

The *Mystagogy* begins with a meditation on the church to which the first five chapters, or about one third of the entire work, are devoted. In Maximus' interpretation of church architecture the "heaven-reflecting" dome plays no part as a vehicle of liturgical meaning; instead the bema symbolizes both the vault of heaven and the supersensible heaven. Nonetheless it may be assumed that in Maximus, to a greater degree than in Dionysius, the sacral expressivity of the entire architecture of the church suggested the church building as a point of departure for interpretation.

Maximus' symbolic interpretation of the church building is independent, however, of the concrete architectural form of basilical or domed church, and even the properly liturgical use of the building seems at first sight to play a secondary role. The chapter titles of the first part of the *Mystagogy* are clear evidence of this. The relation of the church space to the realities represented—the cosmos,[3] humanity,[4] and sacred scripture[5]—and the description of this relation by the words "image," "likeness," and "similarity," show that unlike Dionysius, Maximus makes no effort to develop a *graduated* symbolism of a sacramental or quasi-sacramental kind that *unmistakably ascends* from the reality of the church to the reality of heaven. We discern his intention rather in the constant emphasis on a "heavenly-earthly" bipolarity within the church, cosmos, humanity, and so on, which symbolize each other (only) because of this polarity, and this in a *reciprocal* way.

Thus we read, for example, in the interpretation of the church as symbolic of the cosmos, that in spiritual contemplation

"the holy church of God presents itself as an image and likeness of the entire cosmos, which encompasses visible and invisible beings, inasmuch as the church displays the same unity and variety as the universe. For though as a structure it is a single building, the differentiation within its form gives it variety, inasmuch as it is divided into a section reserved to the priest and officiating ministers (this we call the sacred choir) and another to which the entire believing people has access (this we call the nave). Yet it is one by its nature, not being divided by having parts which are diverse from each other; rather, by subsuming these parts into its own unity, it rescues them from the separateness proper to [ecclesiastical] states and callings and shows that each is one with the other because each signifies to the other that which it is in itself: namely, that the nave is potentially a sacred choir because it has been dedicated to the goal of the consecration of the mystery, and conversely that the sacred choir is also a nave because the nave is the starting point in the exercise of its own consecration of the mystery. It is because of both that the church is the one reality which it is."[6]

The passage is clearly nothing but an expansion of the christological formula of Chalcedon. But Maximus places his greatest emphasis on one part of the formula, taken from the Dogmatic Letter of Pope Leo I: "For each of the two natures performs the functions proper to it in communion with the other."[7] In so doing he also does justice to the concern embodied in neo-Chalcedonianism and already anticipates the content of the definition issued by the Sixth Ecumenical Council.[8]

Maximus finds the church to have a christological structure. But since the hypostatic union is the center of the world's meaning and since the entire universe likewise has a christological structure, he is able to look upon the church as also a symbol of the universe. As the church, so the universe is divided into,

"on the one hand, a spiritual world which is filled with spiritual and incorporeal beings and, on the other, this sensible and corporeal world which is so marvelously composed of various forms and natures and resembles that other church not built with hands that is mystically signified by this physical church erected by men. The world above is, as it were, the universe's sacred choir that is assigned to the higher powers, while its nave is the church here below that is assigned to those who live a life of the senses. But again, this universe is one and is not split up because it has parts."[9]

In adopting the christological formula of Chalcedon, here expanded into a formula for the universe, Maximus chose for his *Mystagogy* a starting point that made his work highly relevant for the christology of his day but that at the same time lessens its value for a theology of the sacraments and the liturgy. The reason for this is that the effort to ensure as broad as possible a range of applications of the christological formula leads only too easily to a relativization of the irreplaceable saving power of the *special* actions and signs ordained by Christ (and the church). This result is especially noticeable in the first part of the *Mystagogy*, but it also shows in the liturgical explanation proper to the second part, for here an undeniable spiritualizing tendency can be seen in the treatment of the natural meaning of liturgical actions.

In Maximus' explanation of the church building the nave was a symbol of the lower regions of the world, while the sacred choir was correlated with the higher powers. Correspondingly, in the explanation of the liturgy the actions of the synaxis that are performed in the naos are a symbol of the salvific operations that take place on earth; the rites performed in the sanctuary, on the other hand, represent events in heaven. The two parts together form the one synaxis, and the "communication of forms" between them becomes visible in the solemn entrance that are, as it were, the hinges on which the entire explanation of the liturgy in the *Mystagogy* pivots. Thus the entrance of the bishop into the nave of the church, which represents the earthly region of the cosmos, must be a symbol of the incarnation, and the ascent to the heavenly sphere of the sanctuary must be a symbol of the ascension.[10]

The fact that the entrance into the sanctuary signifies an entrance into heavenly regions and the beginning of a participation in the liturgy of the angels is expressly brought out in the silent prayer at the Little Entrance.[11] This prayer has been part of the fixed order of the liturgy since the eighth century at the latest, but may have been part of it from the time of Justinian or Maximus.

The people enter with the high priest into the nave and thus into an upright life.[12] They may not, however, follow the high priest directly into the heavenly regions of the sanctuary, for in principle they are still engaged in the battle of earthly life. On the other hand, they do receive important aid from the heavenly activity of the celebrant, while the sacred readings and songs enable them to make continual progress in virtue and gnosis.[13]

A completely new situation arises after the gospel when the celebrant descends from his throne. This descent symbolizes the return of Christ at the end of time, when the good news will be preached to the entire world. The return follows upon the judgment, which divides humanity and is symbolized by the dividing of the faithful from the catechumens.[14] Finally, the "entrance of the holy and venerable mysteries" marks the beginning, at the symbolic level, of the revelation of the glory of the new eon.[15]

It might seem that from this point no further climax is possible in the order of symbols and symbolized. But then what is left of the special character of the anaphora? Oddly enough, as I mentioned earlier, Maximus offers no interpretation of his own of the anaphora. By referring the reader to the *Ecclesiastical Hierarchy* of Dionysius and by stating his intention of not repeating what an expert has already said, he has doubtless excused himself from having to interpret the anaphora. But in this case again the liturgical appropriateness of his explanation of the liturgy depends on whether his interpretations at least leave room for the special place of the anaphora and its possible explanation along the lines of (for example) Dionysius. We may ask, then, what indications in this direction are given by Maximus' explanation of those parts of the liturgy that lie closest to the anaphora.

The explanation of the Great Entrance and the succeeding chapters on the kiss of peace, the confession of faith, the Thrice Holy (Sanctus) and the hymn of praise, "One is holy," lead into the splendors of the new eon. The kiss of peace is said to be "a prefiguration and foreshadowing" of the universal unanimity that will one day become a reality.[16] The confession of faith "signifies in advance" the spiritual thanksgiving that will one day be offered to God.[17] The Thrice Holy hints at the equality with the incorporeal powers that will one day be manifested.[18] The Our Father is the "likeness" of the acceptance as God's children that will one day be granted to us.[19] The relatively weak kind of symbolization that is expressed by such terms as "foreshadowing" and "likeness" leaves open the possibility of an intensified symbolism for the anaphora.

On the other hand, a positive reference to the significance of the anaphora is probably already to be seen in the explanation of the Great Entrance. The "entrance of the holy and venerable mysteries" is said to be

"the beginning and prologue of the new instruction to be given in heaven about God's salvific dealings with us, and of the revelation of the mystery of our redemption that resides in the hidden abysses of the divinity. For thus did the Word, who is God, speak to his disciples: 'I shall not drink again of the fruit of the vine until the day when I drink it new with you in the kingdom of my Father.' "[20]

In this passage statements are made about the kind of symbolization and about the reality symbolized that are intelligible only by reference to the anaphora. For example, there is question here no longer of a "foreshadowing" but of a "beginning and prologue"; the heavenly reality that is designated is called a "revelation of the mystery of our redemption"; finally, the words of the Lord that are cited refer to the Supper and the fulfillment of the remembrance command in the anaphora. The transfer of the gifts is thus here related to the anaphora in a manner similar to that found in Theodore of Mopsuestia or even in the text of the Cherubikon itself. Only thus does the description of the Great Entrance, or "entrance of the holy and venerable mysteries," become intelligible.

The communion likewise has no special chapter devoted to it. But the chapter entitled "What is signified by the ending of the hymns of praise sung during the sacred mysteries, 'One is holy, one is Lord,' and following?" is indirectly related to the communion. In this chapter Maximus writes:

"The hymn of praise that is sung at the end of the holy mysteries by the entire congregation, namely, "One is holy, etc.," signifies the gathering that will one day take place in an unfathomable manner transcending all the concepts of reason, and the unification, in the oneness of the divine simplicity, of those who are to be initiated into the incorruptible eon of spiritual things, wherein they will gaze upon the light of the invisible and utterly ineffable Glory and will become participants, with the higher powers, in that blessed purity . . . so that by decree and grace they will be and will be called gods, because God in his entirety will wholly fill them and allow no part of them not to be filled with his presence."[21]

This is the conclusion of Maximus' explanation of the liturgy insofar as it has to do with the redemption of the whole human race from the incarnation to the revelation of future glory. The saving work accomplished from the incarnation to the ascension is here looked upon as a single act of restoration of earthly reality and is symbolized in an extremely compact way by the Little Entrance. The Great Entrance, for its part, simply alludes to the historical course of redemption from, as it were, a heavenly perspective.

In the next three chapters of the *Mystagogy* Maximus shows "how and in what way the divine and perfect state of the individual soul as such may also be contemplated in what has thus far been said."[22] He once again interprets all the parts of the liturgy that have been discussed previously, but now from two new angles: first, inasmuch as these parts are "a likeness of the virtues of the soul,"[23] and, second, in terms of the mysteries that "the grace of the Holy Spirit" effects and brings to completion "in the faithful through the ordinances carried out in the sacred synaxis."[24]

In the earlier type of explanation, the representation of the concrete historical work of redemption in the liturgy was indicated as being the basis for the liturgy's effectiveness in the order of grace. In this new explanation, however, this aspect fades entirely from view, and the liturgy is seen as a direct image of the soul's ascent to God by grace. Nonetheless, in keeping with his basically christological outlook, Maximus emphasizes throughout that the grace communicated by the liturgy is the grace of Christ with its incarnational structure. This emphasis may be seen above all in the "reception of the spotless and life-giving mysteries,"[25] "by the power of which the human person is enabled to become a god." The hypostatic union in Christ is seen here in a wholly concrete way as the prototype of the union of other human beings with God.

If, then, the course of the liturgy depicts the ever swifter ascent of the soul to God, to the point at which "the human person is enabled to become a god," it is not surprising to find Maximus several times insisting that in this ascent the soul also attains to "insight like that of the angels"[26] and to a "unity and equality of dignity with the holy angels."[27] We are told in another work of the Confessor that Christ "definitively united spirit and matter, because he brought a sensible body and a soul among the choirs of angels and in this way recapitulated the entire creation."[28] Such statements show how different the viewpoint of Maximus is from that of Dionysius, despite all the former's veneration for the earlier writer. In place of all of Dionysius' graduated orders, especially those of the angelic hierarchy, Maximus puts a synthesis in Christ. Thus Origen's idea that "the redeemer unites all levels in himself"[29] is given a new Chalcedonian meaning and made fruitful for seventh-century theology. However, as far as the explanation of liturgical symbolism is concerned, Maximus' dyadic pattern often leads to a neglect of those intermediate symbolic meanings that would be described as *res et sacramentum* in the triadic conceptual scheme of scholastic theology.

Chapter Four

Liturgy and Image in the Age of Iconoclasm

The second main period in which Byzantium fully manifested its uniqueness was the age of iconoclasm. The dispute over the sacred icons called forth great theological efforts on the part of the iconophiles, and their thinking found binding dogmatic expression at the Seventh Ecumenical Council, Nicea II, in 787.

The full cultural fruitfulness of image theology and image veneration became clear, of course, only after the final victory of 843, which the churches of the Byzantine rite still celebrate each year under the characteristic title of the "feast of Orthodoxy." The first representative church built when peace had finally come—the "New Church," consecrated by Photius and known in the history of art as the Nea—will be included in this chapter, for the representational decoration of this church is regarded as a direct expression of the doctrine of images. It is also seen as a first example of the Middle Byzantine system of church decoration that, in its more developed form, is typical of the churches of the eleventh and twelfth centuries, although in large measure it also exercised a decisive influence on the whole of later Byzantine iconography.

The forces that shaped this period exercised no less lasting an influence on the development of the liturgy by building on the foundations already laid in the age of Justinian. Thus the symbolic character of the liturgy became more pronounced due to the introduction of new and highly expressive actions relating to the gifts. While the Justinian age had devoted its creative attention especially to the transfer of the gifts, attention was now focused chiefly on their preparation. The result was the prothesis, which is so characteristic of the Byzantine liturgy.

This period too had its representative commentary on the liturgy. The connection of this commentary with the doctrine of images has inspired its traditional attribution to Patriarch Germanus who, in 730 when iconoclasm was beginning, was ousted from his office because of his advocacy of images. Germanus' authorship has often been challenged, but his century is the only possible period for the origin of the commentary, and as yet no other author has been suggested.

A. THE MIDDLE BYZANTINE SYSTEM OF CHURCH DECORATION AND ITS LITURGICAL FUNCTION

The most brilliant creation that the spirit behind the doctrine on images produced was the Middle Byzantine system of church decoration.[1] Once the veneration of images had been restored definitively, this system became a fixed element in the embellishment of the now usual cruciform, domed church. And while the system underwent modification in later times, it was never abandoned in principle.[2] An early example of this use of images was the mosaics of the Nea (or New Church of the imperial palace), which Photius describes in a festal discourse,[3] while the eleventh-century mosaics in the Greek monasteries of Hosios Lukas, Nea Moni, and Daphni[4] are probably to be regarded as the most mature implementation of the Middle Byzantine program of images.

In this decorative use of images the Byzantine church structure shows itself to be what it had to be according to Dionysius' vision of the world and what Maximus actually saw it as being: a copy of the cosmos that comprises heaven and earth, a cosmos ordered to Christ and filled with a cosmic liturgy. By reason of the images that adorn it the church itself henceforth becomes a liturgy, as it were, because it depicts the liturgico-sacramental presence of Christ, the angels, and the saints, and by depicting it shares in bringing it about. The iconography of the church also shows it to be the place in which the mysteries of the life of Christ are made present. This was already true at the level of program during the period of struggle; the program was then given embodiment in the art of the Nea and achieved its complete form in the liturgical cycle of the fully developed Middle Byzantine system of decoration in the eleventh century.

1. Church Decoration as Proclamation
according to the Discourse against Constantine "Caballinus"

While giving expression to the general presuppositions of ecclesial iconography that are derived from the theology of images, the writings in defense of images during the period of struggle already give a glimpse as well of those principles for the choice of images that will be characteristic of the Middle Byzantine system of decoration.

51

For although all transmitted images were regarded as venerable witnesses to ecclesial tradition, the application of nuanced principles from the theology of images to the various pictorial themes led inevitably to a preference for certain especially representative graphic types that had a clearly proclamatory character.

Especially informative in this respect is the description of the iconographic themes of pictorial decoration that is given in the discourse against the iconoclastic Emperor Constantine V, known as "Caballinus" (741–755).[5] Although the author intends only to tell us "how the church has come down to us, adorned with its images, from the Fathers," emphases pointing to the future are nonetheless unmistakable.

The discourse was long regarded as a work of John Damascene (d. 749)[6] because it was transmitted under the name of a "John" and gives the impression of being a compendium of Damascene's doctrine on images. But the real author was a more recent man, John of Jerusalem, who was synkellos (associate) of Patriarch Theodore of Antioch.[7] In the textual form in which we now have it, the discourse goes back to the period after the deposition of Patriarch Constantine II (766).[8]

In the third chapter of the discourse[9] the author responds to the objection of idolatry by listing the subjects of the images usually venerated in the church. Is it perhaps the images of Apollo or Artemis that the iconophiles venerate? "Or is it not rather the image of our Lord Jesus Christ, which teaches me the economy of his incarnation," together with the images of the Mother of God, John the Baptist, the apostles, the martyrs, and the other saints of God?

"Who will dare apply the word 'idolatry' in connection with such a beautiful exposition of the order of salvation, and by so doing blaspheme against the suffering of Christ and his saints and of those whom holy Church has handed on to us? For the Church we have received from the holy Fathers is a Church adorned [and representing] what the sacred scriptures also teach us: The economy of the incarnation of Christ, his descent among us for our salvation, the annunciation of Gabriel to the Virgin, and the following as well: the birth, the cave, the manger, the midwife and the swaddling clothes, the star and the wise men. In addition: the baptism, the Jordan, John who touches the head of Christ, and the Holy Spirit descending in the form of a dove.

"Let us move further on to his passion and see the children with the palm branches, the basin [for the washing of the feet] and the

towel, the kiss of Judas and the capture by the Jews, the actions of
Pilate. Furthermore: the crucifixion, the nails and the scourging, the
sponge and the lance, and up above, the sign with the inscription:
'Behold, the king of the Jews.' Furthermore: the resurrection, which
is the joy of the world; how Christ descends into hell and raises
Adam from the dead, and likewise the ascension.

"Let us move further on to his miracles [and see]: the giving of
sight to the man born blind, the healing of the paralytic, the touching of the Lord's garments by the woman with the flow of blood,
the same woman who was the first to form an image of Christ from
bronze. Also the figures of the saints as they are condemned and
suffer torments for the sake of Christ our God. How can you use
the word 'idolatry' in connection with these beautiful and salutary
depictions?

"Saint Basil, our great Father, says in his encomium of the Forty
Martyrs: 'The writers of history and the painters often describe the
same things, the former presenting them in words, the latter depicting them on panels.' Thus the holy writer wrote the gospel. . . .
And the painter did the same. In pictures he portrayed the beauty
of the Church from the first Adam down to the birth of Christ and
the entire economy of Christ in the flesh, along with the suffering
of the saints, and he passed this on to the Church. Both, therefore,
put together a *single* account by means of which they instruct us.
. . . Why, then, do you venerate the book but spurn the image?
. . . . What difference is there between the two since both *proclaim
the same message of salvation?*"

In chapter 10 the author writes:

"If a pagan should come to you and ask: 'Show me your faith, so
that I too may believe,' what would you show him? Would you not
lead him from visible to invisible things so that he might willingly
accept the latter? . . . . Listen, then! You lead him into the church
and show him its decoration. You open his eyes to the figures in
the icons. The unbeliever looks for himself and says: 'Who is this
that is crucified? Who is this that arises from the dead and tramples
on the head of this ancient?' Do you not then instruct him with the
help of the icons by telling him: 'This crucified man is God's Son,
who was nailed to the cross for the sins of the world. The man rising from the dead is the same man who is the first of many, and
with him he raises up the first ancestor, Adam.' . . . And in this
way you bring the man to a knowledge of God.

"You lead him then to the sacred bath of baptism. He sees only water in the font, but you, a believer, see water, fire, and the Spirit. . . .

"When led to the mystagogy of the body and blood of the redeemer, he sees only bread and wine, whereas you see the body and the blood that flowed from his spotless side. And when he has become worthy, he too will share therein and gradually rise to the level of your faith and your knowledge. Do you see how you have in this way led him from visible to invisible things? Well, then, please understand the icons as well!"[10]

The passages I have cited reveal the spirit at work in the doctrine of images and also list the themes that according to this doctrine were to be the preferred subjects of images. When icons are contemplated in faith they lead one from bodily gaze to spiritual vision and mystical encounter with the persons and saving deeds that are represented. For one who is still on the way to faith, icons can serve as a prelude to sacramental initiation by giving a first introduction to the mystery; they can thus be compared with baptism and the eucharist and be set directly beside prebaptismal instruction and the proclamation that takes place during the liturgy of the word.

In their systematic writings on images, the theologians, especially Theodore of Studites, press the analogy with the eucharistic action to the point of saying that that which is represented is actually present in its image.[11] Therefore veneration is due the icons, although not in the same measure as is given to the original, since the latter is present not directly but precisely in its image or copy. Thus adoration (*latreia*) is due to Christ himself, but only veneration (*proskynesis*) to his image.[12] More specifically, the Seventh Ecumenical Council prescribes for sacred images the kind of veneration that is also paid to the lifegiving cross and the holy gospels.[13]

The comparison with the gospels is developed from various points of view in the doctrine on images. Like the gospels, images too have been transmitted by ecclesial tradition,[14] and their divine origin is guaranteed.[15] Both gospels and images proclaim the same saving reality in a quasi-sacramental manner: images through vision, gospels through hearing.[16] Just as the gospels are not simply a retelling of what is past but proclaim past events with their perduring effectiveness, so too do images. As we encounter Christ the Lord himself in the words he spoke, so do we encounter him in his image.[17] We see Christ in his every icon as the apostles saw him during his earthly life[18] and as they recognized him anew after his resurrection, in the form in which he withdrew from their sight at his ascension[19] and in which he will come again to bestow upon us the everlasting face-to-face vision.[20] In the icon of Christ, then, we are really able to see "the economy of our Lord in the flesh."

The saints too encounter us in their likeness to Christ. Their icons reproduce their true appearance[21] and at the same time show them to us as men and women who, being filled with grace, entered into eternal life and yet remain close to us in order to aid us with their intercession.

The saving work of Christ reached its consummation in his death and resurrection. Just as the message of the death and resurrection is the focal point of the proclamation of the word, especially in the liturgical year, so too the images of the death on the cross and the resurrection are especially important and are given a place of honor in churches. The comparison of images with baptism and eucharist will no longer surprise us, since every celebration of baptism and eucharist is a proclamation of the death and resurrection of the Lord.

Representations of the other great deeds of salvation must likewise not be absent from the churches, since they play a primary role both in the proclamation of the word and in the celebration of the liturgical year. Some of them are even made a special object of remembrance in the anamnesis of the eucharistic celebration. The author of the discourse we are studying makes special mention therefore of the images of the annunciation, birth, baptism, passion (entry into Jerusalem, washing of the feet, capture), and ascension.

A lesser importance is assigned to representations of the miracles. The author does mention three miracles, but these are probably chosen because they are seen as symbols of the saving action of Christ in the sacraments. They are mentioned only at the end, however, and are not inserted into the series of other scenes from the life of Christ.

If we imagine such a cycle of images in a church, we will realize immediately how it differs from the cycle of images used in the early Byzantine period. It is no longer the historical course of Christ's life but the salvific importance and continuing efficacy of what is represented that primarily determines the rank of images. The images of this period seem comparable in function, therefore, to the liturgical *proclamation* of the gospels according to the liturgical cycle rather than to the *account* as found continuously in the gospels themselves.

We do not know whether at this period the principle governing the new ranking and choice of images was already embodied, at least in a rudimentary way, in an existing cycle of images or whether it existed only in the mind of the author of the discourse. In any case, as an immediate conclusion from the doctrine on images, it certainly provides the key to an understanding of the posticonoclastic system of decoration. The mosaics of the Nea provide the first example of the new system that has come down to us, even if it has reached us only in the form of Patriarch Photius' description.

2. The Decoration of the New Church
as a Rendering Present of Christ, the Angels, and the Saints

The re-presentational character of Middle Byzantine church painting, which already emerges in the discourse against Caballinus, becomes almost exaggeratedly clear in the Nea or New Church in honor of the Mother of God, which Emperor Basil I, founder of the Macedonian dynasty, built next to the imperial palace.[22] Its appointments and decoration are known to us chiefly from the festal discourse that Patriarch Photius pronounced at the dedication on May 1, 881, and in which he praises the mosaics:

"On the very ceiling [of the dome] is painted in colored mosaic cubes a man-like figure bearing the traits of Christ. Thou mightest say He is overseeing the earth, and devising its orderly arrangement and government, so accurately has the painter been inspired to represent, though only in forms and in colors, the Creator's (demiourgou) care for us. In the concave segments next to the summit of the hemisphere a throng of angels is pictured escorting our common Lord. The apse which rises over the sanctuary glistens with the image of the Virgin, stretching out her stainless arms on our behalf and winning for the emperor safety and exploits against the foes. A choir of apostles and martyrs, yea, of prophets, too, and patriarchs fill and beautify the whole church with their images."[23]

According to this description, which certainly does not pass over anything important, the Nea possessed a set of mosaics that was extremely limited in its themes and completely abstained from any depiction of scenes. Since according to the Seventh Council "the execution is the painter's task and his alone"[24] and direction of the enterprise is in the hands of the hierarchy, we must look for some theological intention behind this striking limitation to individual images. Such an intention in turn can only be based on the doctrine of images.

The list of subjects for images in the discourse against Caballinus already showed a certain restriction in regard to the representation of scenes, although the restriction at that point applied only to the representation of the miracles. The builders of the Nea drew more radical conclusions from the doctrine of images: if in an image we really encounter as present what is represented therein, then the only subject suitable for a true icon is one that is by its nature capable of such an encounter. Consequently, it is above all Christ,[25] the angels,[26] and the saints who must be represented, and this in images of a portrait type, since their constant intercession for us is a present reality. Historical facts as such have no place in this kind of iconography.

What is the situation, then, with regard to the representations of Christ's redemptive work, which is historical, although not past, and which becomes present in a unique way precisely during the celebration of the eucharist? The proclamation of the work of redemption certainly cannot be passed over in the pictorial decoration of a church that claims to be consistent with the classical theology of icons. The task can be carried out in the Nea only in the image of the Pantocrator in the dome. For it is the icon of Christ (precisely as an individual image) "that teaches me the economy of his incarnation."[27] That the icon of Christ does in fact act as a comprehensive commemoration of the work of salvation is already taught in canon 82 of the Trullan Synod (692): "We prescribe that from now on, in place of the lamb of old, Christ our God, the Lamb who takes away the sins of the world, is to be portrayed in human form in the icons, so that in his state of abasement the majesty of God the Word may be seen and we may be reminded of his life in the body, his suffering, his saving death and the redemption of the world which his death accomplished."[28]

Of the entire work of the salvation, the incarnation seems to be the part most directly connected with the icons of Christ in general,[29] while the memory of the ascension[30] and the second coming[31] also seems directly linked to the image of the Pantocrator in particular. The program of images in the Nea is thus thought of as a comprehensive proclamation of the Christian order of salvation, but in a concentrated mode of expression that makes the essence of icons extremely clear: the believer encounters the sacral persons in individual pictures marked by frontality and compactness; the impact is not lessened by secondary figures or scenic details; and the image is a rounded expression of the original's constant presence.[32]

Yet such purity of expression could not be maintained, for the usual comparison of images with the gospel called for a direct representation of the saving deeds, as described by the author of the discourse against Caballinus. The demand would be met in the cycles of the eleventh century, although then (more clearly than in the discourse) the major events of salvation, which are also central in the liturgical re-presentation, would determine the choice of images.

The principle that images were to be chosen strictly according to their ability to render present their originals also conditioned an equally strict hierarchic arrangement of images in the church building. Specifically, the more transparent the images were in relation to their originals, the more exactly must their arrangement reflect the hierarchy of the originals. In this descending hierarchy Christ came first, then Mary and the angels, and finally the saints. Among the last-named the apostles were in first place, then the martyrs, and only then the prophets. The sequence that Photius follows in his list corresponds to the primacy assigned to the stage of salvation that is reflected in the New Testament.

The purpose of this hierarchic arrangement was simply to bring the hierarchy of images into harmony with the rank assigned to the separate parts of the building and with their symbolic importance. A double gradient of meaning within the church building had to be taken into account: from sanctuary to nave, and from dome to nave.

To begin with, Hagia Sophia's broad dome, which as it were floated above a circle of windows, succeeded fully in imitating architecturally the weightless, light-filled heavens. But the sanctuary too was interpreted as a heavenly place. Maximus had set aside the decending order of Dionysius, with its many steps, in favor of his own christological formula for the world, and had retained only the unconfused and undivided duality of sanctuary and nave within the one church. After Maximus the interpretation of the dome as an image of heaven, because of its greater vividness, becomes definitive, and as a result the categories of above and below and of the hierarchic descending order again become significant.

By reason of its pictorial decoration the thus structured cosmos that is the church shows itself as taking its character from Christ. In Hagia Sophia, restored in 562 after an earthquake, a gem-encrusted cross shone down from the star-bespangled dome.[33] But due to the

58

influence of image theology, the symbol of redemption was replaced by the image of the redeemer himself in his human form. This doubtless explains why the Pantocrator mosaic of Hagia Sophia, known to us from descriptions of a later age,[34] replaced the old representation of the cross in the ninth or tenth century.[35] From that time on, the dome of every Byzantine church was reserved for the image of the Pantocrator.

From the dome of the Nea, as if from heaven, Christ, the "Creator," looks down upon the earth. This description of Photius, as well as the usual name "Pantocrator" that is given to this type of image (although in the liturgy it is God the Father who is addressed as Pantocrator[36]), reminds us of the words of Christ: "He who has seen me has seen the Father" (Jn 14:9).

The next place of honor in the church is the apse. As terminus of the sanctuary, but closer than the dome is to the nave, it calls for an image that stands in a special relation to the concrete accomplishment of our redemption here on earth. Since only images of individual persons are to be considered and since the image of Christ already has its privileged place in the dome, there is hardly any other image that can be chosen except that of the Theotokos. The incarnation in Mary's maternal womb is represented in the apse, and it is here that the event of redemption, which is rendered liturgically present on the nearby altar, has its start. The most expressive representation of this connection is the Late Byzantine pictorial type known as the Platytera,[37] which shows the Theotokos in the attitude of an orant, while the incarnate Logos floats in an aureole before her breast. In the Nea, Mary is depicted according to the older version of an orant, that is, with arms outstretched, and Photius describes her as the great intercessor and, as in the Akathistos Hymn,[38] the protectress of the empire and the giver of victory.

As heavenly beings, the angels have their place in the dome beneath the Pantocrator, to whom they seem to be related as servants. Since according to the doctrine of images only that which belongs to the visible sphere of revelation can be represented,[39] there is at first sight a difficulty with regard to the angels, but it is one that is resolved easily:

"You object that no one has ever seen an angel. On the contrary: many have seen angels. The Most Blessed Mother of God often saw the angel Gabriel; the myrrh-bearing women saw angels when they came to the tomb; the apostles, too, saw them: again at the tomb, and then, when they were in prison, an angel came to bring them out. The prophets—Isaiah, Ezekiel, and Daniel—and many saints likewise saw angels, each according to his capacity. It is on this basis that Dionysius the Areopagite describes the orders of angels and represents them pictorially; he does not prohibit such representations but even explains why the angels are depicted in a fourfold form as eagles and other animals."[40]

If then angels can be represented on the basis of certain apparitions,[41] we can tell on what concrete vision of the angels the post-iconoclastic images of angels depend for their mode of representation. In fact this is determined easily in the case of angels in representations of scenes; it is more difficult, however, in the case of the angels who surround the Pantocrator in the dome, where they fill out the image of the heavenly hierarchy. But the author of the discourse against Caballinus expressly mentions Isaiah, Ezekiel, and Daniel as among those who saw angels, and he appeals to the Areopagite for the use of the visions of these men in pictorial representations.[42] Then what was the appearance of the angels whom the prophets saw as heavenly beings around the throne of God and who are therefore susceptible of iconographic representation?

We read in Isaiah: "In the year that King Uzziah died I saw the Lord. . . . Above him stood the seraphim; each had six wings: with two he covered his face, and with two he covered his feet, and with two he flew" (Is 6:1f.).

The angels in Ezekiel have the following distinguishing marks. In general their appearance is like that of human beings (1:5), but each has four faces (1:6): in addition to a human face there are the faces of a lion, an ox, and an eagle (1:10). They have four wings and, under these, human hands (1:8); two wings are extended upward, touching the wings of another angel, and two cover their bodies (1:11, 1:23). In addition to feet, there is a wheel beside each (1:15). Body and wings are covered with eyes (10:12). Ezekiel recognizes these beings as Cherubim. Over their heads is something resembling a firmament, and above the firmament there is something resembling a throne, and on the throne something like a human form (1:22f., 1:26f.).

Daniel sees an Ancient of Days on the throne, and "a thousand thousands served him, and ten thousand times ten thousand stood before him" (7:9f.).

Does one of these visions serve as basis for the representation of the angels in the Nea? Photius stresses the point that "a throng of angels is pictured escorting our common Lord," in order to serve him. This trait actually occurs in the vision of the angels in Daniel. We may more readily assume this connection, since the Pantocrator of the Nea, whom Photius describes as "Creator," seems to be inspired by the picture of the "Ancient of Days" in Daniel 7:9.

The angels whom Daniel saw more readily invited iconographic representation than did the Seraphim and Cherubim described by Isaiah and Ezekiel. By reason of their human form, Daniel's angels seemed more in harmony with the incarnational order of salvation in the New Testament, on which the doctrine of images was based, and with the argument used in the Seventh Council for the possibility of representing the angels.[43] On the other hand, the development and esteem for the iconographic representation of the angels was also influenced in the long run by the teaching of the Areopagite. According to Dionysius, the Archangels and Angels, who are active directly in human salvation and who appear in human form, have in fact the lowest place, while the Seraphim and Cherubim occupy the highest rank.[44] Thus in the restorations of Hagia Sophia in the ninth or tenth century, after the mosaics had been for the most part destroyed by the iconoclasts, four mighty Cherubim were represented in the spandrels of the dome[45]; these were understood more specifically as an image of the divine chariot described by Ezekiel.[46]

The decoration of the Nea was completed by the images of a large number of saints. Photius lists four categories of saints, but these are not to be taken as exclusive. The apostles are mentioned first, and their pre-eminence is certainly also reflected in the placement of their images. In the fully developed Middle Byzantine system of decoration their place is in the dome. This is the less surprising since in the early posticonoclastic period the representation of the ascension was a special favorite for the dome, and in this picture the apostles are joined with Mary and the two angels beneath an aureole containing the Lord, who is carried by other angels and depicted as already enthroned and ruling.[47] Dionysius regards the apostles and other hierarchic figures as so closely linked with the angelic orders by reason of their office that he would like to give them too the name of "angels."[48]

The prophets, too, often have a place in the dome, since they had been regarded as worthy of a vision of heaven and converse with the angels even during their lifetime.[49] The four evangelists, whose divinely inspired writings join heaven to earth,[50] appear in the four pendentives that link the dome with the rest of the church building.

The position of the images of the saints in the nave of the Nea is already determined in principle by the organization that is unmistakably operative in the eleventh century:

"While the dome is . . . the place of the heavenly Church, the lowest . . . area of decoration becomes an image of the earthly Church. A choir of saints, made up of simple individual figures, is spread about the nave in accordance with the principles of rank and function that have already been applied in the heavenly area; their sequence in the calendar is also taken into account. Patriarchs, doctors of the Church, and priests have their place near the main apse, in the sanctuary and its adjoining rooms, or in niches of the nave that are directly beneath the dome. The holy martyrs, arranged in groups, cover the main arches of the dome, and the walls, pillars and vaults of the nave. Finally, ascetics, simple monks, and local saints are exhibited in the western part of the church, close to the entrance."[51]

B. THE LITURGY AS REPRESENTATIONAL

Like the pictorial decoration of the church, so too the development and interpretation of the liturgy at this period is to be understood in light of the doctrine on images, for liturgical symbols were now conceived after the manner of sacred images and, where possible, were even assimilated externally to these. Thus the defenders of image veneration appealed to the liturgy, and the explicators of the liturgy described it as a cycle of images. Theodore of Studites mentions some of these "images" in liturgical use, the meaning of which he regards as undisputed, in order to ensure that their acceptance will be accompanied by the veneration of images as well.

"Do you not think that the divine myron [chrism] is to be regarded as a type of Christ, the divine table as his lifegiving tomb, the linen as that in which he was buried, the lance [for the Eucharist] of the priest as that which pierced his side, and the sponge as that in which he received the drink of vinegar? Set all these aside, and what will be left to render present the divine mysteries?"[1]

Those, then, who reject images—be these icons, symbolic objects, or rites—must in the final analysis reject the entire order of salvation and even the incarnation, since they refuse to acknowledge that divine reality can link itself to an earthly form.[2] On the other

62

hand, those who believe in the images and symbolic rites of the liturgy find in them a new confirmation of the reality of the incarnation and of Christ's presence in the eucharist.[3]

Correspondingly, as many new symbolic elements as possible were introduced into the liturgy. Given the traditional and sacrosanct organization of the liturgy, that kind of development was, of course, possible only to a limited degree.[4] As a result, it manifested itself primarily in the prothesis, which was able to expand freely since it came at the beginning of the liturgy and outside the directly preanaphoric rites.

1. Iconographic and Ritual Proclamation of Christ

The pictorial decoration of the New Church of Emperor Basil I turned the Middle Byzantine cruciform, domed church into an image of the cosmos that has been transfigured by Christ's incarnation. This impression was due above all to the great image of the Pantocrator in the dome, for, in accordance with canon 82 of the Trullan Synod, this showed the Lord in his earthly form and thereby rendered superfluous for the pictorial decoration of a church all of the Old Testamental foreshadowings and symbols. This is how the Synod argued:

"Some venerable icons display a lamb, with the Precursor pointing to it as a symbol of grace, just as the lamb of the Law represents the true Lamb, Christ our Lord. Although we lovingly accept the ancient shadows and images that have been handed down to the Church as symbols and hints of the truth, we nonetheless give preference to grace and truth themselves, which we acknowledge to be the fulfillment of the Law. In order, then, that at least in images this fulfillment may be proposed to all eyes, we prescribe that from now on, in place of the lamb of old, Christ our God, the Lamb who takes away the sins of the world, is to be portrayed in human form in the icons. . . ."[5]

The demand to turn away from shadows and symbols and to the perspicuous reality of the life of Christ was also applied to the shaping of the liturgy. For the celebration of the eucharist involves the very reality of Christ himself, and it was necessary that this be presented in its full New Testament clarity.

But the eucharist also involves the reality-filled commemoration of his saving work. In accordance with what is said further on in the same canon, it seemed that a single image of Christ was an adequate iconographic expression of this commemoration in the case of the Nea. The discourse against Caballinus, for its part, had high-lighted the importance of the images of Christ's death and resurrection, and these also played a large role in the fully developed Middle Byzantine system of decoration. In any case, the command that the commemoration of redemption be proclaimed in a perspicuously visible way was applied not only in iconography but also and especially in the development of the liturgy.

The commandment of remembrance in the account of institution was understood along these lines. Moreover, since the Liturgy of Basil was still the one more frequently celebrated, the command was usually cited in its expanded form: "Do this in remembrance of me. For as often as you eat this bread and drink the cup, you proclaim the Lord's death until he comes." In this form the command seemed to require not only a properly sacramental fulfillment but in addition a symbolico-ritual proclamation that, as a fuller accomplishment of the command, would be most appropriate if it (like the confection of the sacrament proper) were connected with the gifts. Above all, it was those gift-connected actions, which originally had a purely practical significance or at best a meaning heightened by simple symbolism, that now like so many "images and shadows" called for symbolic expansion or at least symbolic interpretation. I refer to the preparation of the gifts, the placing of them on the altar, and the fraction and commingling before communion. It was the preparation of the gifts that underwent the most startling development.

2. The Prothesis[6]

Liturgical development had been moving toward a symbol-oriented reformulation of the preparation of the gifts ever since the transfer of the gifts came to be regarded as the entrance of the heavenly king for his sacrifice, in keeping with the words of the accompanying hymn. As long as people agreed with Patriarch Eutychius that before the consecration the gifts were "nothing but bread and wine,"[7] the preparation and transfer were primarily practical procedures, and there could hardly be any question of heightened solemnity or symbolic actions. Moreover, the final preparation of the gifts could come immediately before the transfer.[8] Thus Eutychius could speak of the "chalice just now mixed" being brought to the altar. But once the Great Entrance gave solemn expression to the gifts offered in sacrifice as the body and blood of Christ, the preparation of the gifts inevitably came to be viewed in light of the same symbolism.

64

The commentary of Patriarch Germanus on the liturgy describes the symbolism of the preparation of the gifts in the first half of the eighth century[9]: "The preparation of the gifts (*hê proskomidê*), which takes place in the sanctuary (*thysiastêrion*) or in the skeuophylakion, symbolizes the Place of Skulls where Christ was crucified. . . . Like a lamb he was slain, his side pierced through with a lance."[10] Here the preparation of gifts for the sacrifice has turned into a preparation of the sacrificial victim, in the sense of a symbolic introduction to the sacramental rendering present of the sacrifice of the cross.

The passage cited comes before the description of the Great Entrance; this position may indicate that the preparation of the gifts still took place just before the Entrance.[11] However, it seems that the gifts on the table of preparation already had this sacrificial symbolism at the very beginning of the liturgy. The commentary of Germanus mentions bread, wine, and lance for the first time in connection with the description of the church, its appointments, and the vestments. The sacrificial bread that lies on the table of preparation reminds the author of the words: "I am the bread which came down from heaven" (Jn 6:51) and insinuates that the Son of God became man and surrendered himself in a redemptive and expiatory sacrifice for the life of the world. "The cutting with the lance signifies that he was led like a lamb[12] to the slaughter, and remained silent like a lamb before its shearers." "The wine and the water are [Greek *esti,* sing.] blood and water that came from his side. . . . For this lance is in place of the lance that pierced Christ on the cross." "The bread and the chalice are truly an imitation of the mystical meal at which Christ took the bread and wine and said: 'Take, eat and drink, all of you; this is my body and my blood,' and thereby showed that he wished to give us a share in his death and resurrection."[13]

At the very beginning of the liturgy, then, the sacrificial symbolism calls for ritual expression. At the same time, however, those who want to interpret the statements of Germanus concretely as the earliest testimony to an actual preparation of the gifts at the beginning of the liturgy[14] must explain why Germanus mentions the actions of the prothesis again before the Great Entrance and summarizes them there. It may be due to a systematization of interpretative motifs in which the author bases his explanation of the liturgy of the word on "the predictions of the prophets" and "the coming of the Son of God" (in parallel with the history of salvation) and then moves on to the passion, death, and resurrection only in connection with the Great Entrance.

The Barberini Codex clearly shows the prothesis coming at the beginning of the liturgy.[15] Moreover, the rapid development of this rite is clear from the oldest Latin translation[16] of Germanus' commentary:

"Therefore the priest receives the sacrificial bread on the discos from the deacon or subdeacon, takes the lance, cleans it, and makes an incision in the form of a cross, saying as he does so: 'Like a lamb he was led to sacrifice and was silent like a little lamb before its shearers.' (After saying this and placing the prosphora on the sacred discos, he points to it and says:) 'He does not open his mouth; in his humiliation his judgment is taken away; who shall fathom his generation? His life is taken away from the earth.' After these words the priest takes the sacred chalice and, as the deacon pours wine and water into it, says: 'From his side came forth blood and water, and he who saw this bears witness to it, and his testimony is true.' Then he places the sacred chalice on the table of God, points, in the bread, to the slaughtered Lamb and, in the wine, to the blood shed, and continues: 'There are three that bear witness: the Spirit, the water, and the blood, and these three are one now and for ever and for eternity.' Then he takes the censer and while incensing says the prayer of presentation."[17]

In determining the point to which the prothesis (also called "proscomide") had developed at the beginning of the ninth century, the witness usually invoked is the account (attributed to Gregory of Decapolis) of the miraculous conversion of a Saracen.[18] We read there:

"When the priest had begun the divine proscomide and had taken the bread in order to accomplish the unbloody sacrifice, the Saracen saw the priest taking a little child in his hands and slaying it as he mixed its blood in the chalice and broke its body, which he laid on the discos. . . . And when the time for the sacred Entrance came, the Saracen again, and even more clearly, saw the child divided into four parts on the discos and its blood in the chalice."[19]

According to the accompanying text the cruciform incision in the bread for sacrifice has a representational value that is determined not so much by the death on the cross (which is what is properly being signified) as by the Old Testament slaying of the Passover lamb and, above all, by the incarnation and birth. The figural-symbolic presence of the body of Christ on the discos is experienced as that of a little child born only shortly before. If we find unsatisfactory the psychological explanation that the human body present in such a small space as a discos is readily imagined to be that of a little child, then we should probably see in this description a graphic popular parallel to the incarnational principle[20] in accordance with which the Greek Fathers compare the rendering present of Christ at the epiclesis with the incarnation that took place by the power of the Holy Spirit descending on Mary.

The Lamb of God symbolism of the sacrificial bread thus is also conceived as a symbolism relating to the incarnation, but it need not be linked to notions such as those expressed in the vision I cited a moment ago. This is clear from the wording of the offertory prayer at the prothesis of the eighth/ninth-century Liturgy of Chrysostom, a prayer that is modeled almost verbatim on the eucharistic epiclesis.[21] The customary prothesis prayer in both liturgies today (a prayer that at the time was peculiar to the Liturgy of Basil[22]) has a similar content.

The development of the eleventh-century prothesis in particular will be determined by the idea that the rites of the prothesis must symbolize not only the incidents attendant on the sacrificial death but also those attendant on the birth, in order to justify the status of the gifts as images (*antitypa*) of the body of Christ[23] and to make possible further symbolic actions in connection with them.

C. THE LITURGICAL COMMENTARY OF PATRIARCH GERMANUS

The entire liturgical development of the age, as well as its connection with the church's conception of images, is reflected in the liturgical commentary I have cited several times in the last few pages. Its author is considered to be the iconophile Patriarch Germanus (d. 733), who at the beginning of iconoclasm (730) was deposed because of his public defense of images.[1] But the attribution of the commentary (entitled *History of the Church and Contemplation of the Mysteries—Historia ekklêsiastikê kai mystikê theôria*[2]) is by no means unanimous. The manuscripts name Basil more often than Germanus, and more rarely Cyril of Jerusalem.[3] But the attribution to Basil and Cyril can only be a way of attesting the commentary's fidelity to tradition and ensuring its authority. And in fact since the eighth century the work has often been copied or printed along with liturgical formularies,[4] although in the process it has often been adapted to the current state of the liturgy by means of interpolations.

The surest basis for an approximate dating of the commentary is the Latin translation made in 869–870 by Anastasius Bibliothecarius during his stay in Constantinople. He sent it to Charles the Bald (d. 877) along with sections of the *Mystagogy* of Maximus the Confessor.[5] In an accompanying letter Anastasius describes the contents of the packet: "Some of what Blessed Maximus wrote regarding the mystical celebration of the Catholic Church . . . and others which, according to the Greeks, are the views of Germanus, of esteemed memory, former head of the Church of Constantinople."[6] In light of the efforts made to keep this kind of work as up to date as possible, the evidently widespread, but seemingly not completely certain ("according to the Greeks"), attribution to Germanus at least supplies us with an earliest possible date. But the latest possible date would seem to be fairly close to the earliest, and this for several reasons. The text Anastasius had before him had been in circulation for a long time and had been interpolated. Furthermore, Theodore of Studites seems to refer to the commentary.[7] And, finally, the commentary's attestation of the prothesis is the earliest we have and perhaps goes back even to the period before the development of the ceremony at the beginning of the liturgy.[8] In view of these facts, the only period of origin that seems at all likely, apart from the time of Germanus himself, is the first decades of iconoclasm. Yet no traces of the iconoclast controversy can be seen in the commentary. It seems justified then to speak of "the liturgical commentary of Patriarch Germanus."

A restoration of the Greek text to its original form long seemed impossible, but Nilo Borgia has probably come close to it by drawing on two manuscripts[9] that make clear both the interpolations and the lacunae in the text used by Anastasius. A comparison of the texts shows immediately that large sections of the material peculiar to Anastasius' translation are foreign bodies. Thus seven sections on the garb of monks, included by Anastasius in his translation, were evidently not part of the original text, which is an explanation of the liturgy that certainly was not composed with the monastic situation in mind. In addition, these sections unduly separate the description of the priest's vestments from the description of the prothesis (including sacrificial bread, wine, water, and lance). Similarly, the sequence of explanations after the Great Entrance is disturbed by three sections from the *Mystagogy* of Maximus that have made their way into the text.

Conversely, the description in the text used by Anastasius breaks off suddenly after the Thrice Holy (Sanctus), and a makeshift ending is supplied by borrowing two passages on communion from Maximus. The text tradition introduced by Borgia, on the other hand, carries the interpretation to its conclusion in a harmonious way. We may therefore regard this tradition as authentic, even though it is attested only by two manuscripts of the fourteenth and sixteenth centuries.

As a vivid example of developments in the period between the composition of the commentary and its translation by Anastasius, 150 years at most, we may take the interpretation of the censer. On the occasion of the incensation at the Alleluia before the gospel, the text originally said: "The censer stands for the humanity of Christ and the fire for his divinity, and the sweet-smelling cloud proclaims the fragrance of the Holy Spirit."[10] Anastasius, on the other hand, has before him the following tasteless expansion of the original:

"Or, on the other hand, the belly of the censer is to be looked upon as the womb of the Virgin, which carried the divine coal, that is, Christ, in whom the entire fulness of the godhead dwells . . . or, again, the belly of the censer represents the baptismal font, since in receiving the coal with its divine fire it also receives the sweet-smelling, Spirit-wrought, gracious divine sonship . . . and spreads its fragrance."[11]

These passages show not only the lack of concern with which the text was expanded, but also how taste and the conception of symbolism had developed since the time of Germanus. While in the original text the symbolism of the incense may be seen to echo christological comparisons of the patristic age and the Areopagite's interpretation of the incense, a reification of symbolism has gained the upper hand in the expanded text. The same process has admittedly made headway in Germanus himself. The natural meaning of liturgical actions and their function in the liturgy as a whole are neglected in Germanus' explanation as he ascends to a higher symbolic meaning. On the basis of purely external similarities, liturgical forms and symbols are reinterpreted as images of salvation-historical and heavenly realities.

The parallelism with the contemporary development in iconography, and especially in the image of Christ, is unmistakable. Symbolic representation is replaced by portraitlike image in which the higher reality becomes accessible to direct vision. Liturgical interpreters all too easily overlook the fact that possibilities of representation available to iconography or mystery drama are not available to the liturgy. Above all, these explanations risk losing sight of the real human community that stands before God listening and praying, offering sacrifice and thanking him. This community can hardly be given its due place in a liturgy that is interpreted in a purely pictorial way, whereas this is not difficult when the liturgy is understood as symbolic.

As Theodore of Studites says, an icon of Christ may be called "Christ."[12] But if one calls bishop, priests, and deacons "Christ," "apostles," and "angels," respectively,[13] exaggerations are almost unavoidable. As a matter of fact, the author of our commentary rather frequently identifies liturgical symbols, which are conceived as a kind of image, with that which they designate,[14] but without determining more specifically the connection between the two[15] and without doing justice to the earthly reality as a special situation of salvation that has been appointed by God.

The transformation of liturgical symbols into images is striking in the interpretation of the priestly vestments:

"The priestly garment corresponds first of all to the robe of Aaron that reached his feet. Above all, however, it gives the appearance of fire, in accordance with the prophet's words: 'He makes the winds his messengers and flames of fire his servants,' and again: 'Who is this that comes from Edom, in blood-red garments from Bosrah? Why is your robe red like the garments of those that tread the winepress?'—this last being a reference to the bloodsoaked garment of Christ's flesh on the cross. And because, in addition, Christ wore a purple cloak during his passion, the priest's vestment shows who the high priest is whose badge he wears."[16]

The symbolism of the vestments not only refers back to the history of salvation but also upward to heavenly realities. These too are represented in an extreme portraitlike manner:

"The priests image forth the seraphic powers by wearing garments that are covered as it were with wings; by singing the hymn with two further wings: their lips; by holding Christ, the divine and spiritual coal, and carrying him to the altar in their hands. The deacons for their part are images of the angelic powers and with the delicate wings that are their linen oraria they hold themselves everywhere in readiness, like ministering spirits sent to serve."[17]

Finally, the bands around the cuffs (epimanikia) of the sticharion represent the manacles Christ wore when led to Caiaphas and Pilate. The epitrachelion (stole) represents the rope around his neck, while the bishop's woolen omophorion represents the strayed lamb whom the Good Shepherd took on his shoulders.[18]

Fortunately the commentary is not concerned solely with the interpretation of such individual symbols. It also bears witness to the more important symbolic contents that were finding expression in the iconography and liturgy of this period. Like Maximus before him, Germanus devotes a part of his commentary to the description and explanation of the church, as we would expect from the title: *History of the Church and Contemplation of the Mysteries* (with its echo of Maximus' *Mystagogy*). Germanus' thoughts here are fully consistent with the evidence derived directly from church architecture and iconography, according to which, as we saw, the church is a cosmos embracing heaven and earth and ruled by the Pantocrator. Thus we read in Germanus:

"The church is heaven on earth, and in it the God who is exalted above the heavens dwells and abides. It depicts the crucifixion, burial, and resurrection of Christ. It is exalted above the tabernacle of the testimony of Moses . . . prefigured in the patriarchs, announced in the prophets, founded on the apostles, adorned by its bishops, and brought to perfection in its martyrs."[19]

The description cannot but remind us of the cruciform, domed Byzantine church with the dome above the nave representing heaven, and with its pictorial decoration. The groups of saints mentioned by Germanus are the same as those listed by Photius in his description of the Nea, with the addition of the bishops, whose images do in fact adorn the church in the fully developed Middle Byzantine system of decoration.

"The apse corresponds to the grotto at Bethlehem in which Christ was born, and to the cave in the rock in which he was buried."[20] Accordingly, the altar stands for the grave, and the ciborium (baldacchino) for the hill of Calvary which in fact was a short distance from the tomb. But in a kind of symbolic shorthand one and the same spot represents the crucifixion, the burial, and the resurrection. Thus the altar at the same time represents the table of the Last Supper.[21]

We are not told in any clear detail how the Bethlehem symbolism of the apse was developed. But in reality it is only the altar that can have been involved, and of this we are told: "It was prefigured by the ark of the covenant in which the manna was kept: the manna is Christ, the bread that came down from heaven."[22] In the eleventh century the function of symbolizing the event at Bethlehem would be assigned chiefly to the table of preparation.[23]

The altar is also the throne of God, on which he sits in his Cherubim-drawn chariot.[24] This interpretative motif is a more direct inspiration than the text of the Cherubikon for the representation of the Cherubim in the dome of Hagia Sophia.

The bema, or sanctuary, is the place where Christ is enthroned with his twelve apostles. But the bema also represents the second coming, when Christ will appear on his throne of glory to judge the world.[25] The enclosing wall around the bema signifies that priests alone have access to the place. Such a wall is also found at the Holy Sepulcher in Jerusalem.[26]

"The ambo for its part represents the shape of the stone at the holy tomb, on which the angel sat after moving it and from which, there close to the entrance, he announced the Lord's resurrection to the myrrh-bearing women."[27] The ambo, located near the royal doors, is the place from which the deacon carries out his functions during the major part of the liturgy, especially when he proclaims the litanies and summons the congregation to pray. The above-quoted interpretation of the ambo signifies that the function of the deacon here is not simply like that of an angel, as it is generally, but specifically like that of the angel who proclaimed the message of the resurrection. Consequently, to the extent that the liturgy derives its character from the deacon as he issues his proclamation from the ambo, it could not but appear as bathed in the brilliance of the resurrection.

This aspect of the interpretation is admittedly not maintained consistently. The symbolism proper to the ambo is actuated, strictly speaking, only at one point in the liturgy when, some time after the gifts have been deposited on the altar, the deacon raises aloft the aer (veil), which has previously enclosed the gifts as in a tomb, and with a triple exclamation signifies the resurrection that took place on the third day.

This rite is part of a symbolic cycle that includes the whole liturgical event from the transfer of gifts, or Great Entrance, to the beginning of the anaphora. In the mind of Germanus it is probably this part of the liturgy that most clearly shows both church and liturgy to be a proclamation of the death, burial, and resurrection of Christ and a pictorial representation of it. (Proclamation and pictorial representation amounted to the same thing at this period.) Let me quote the very characteristic reflections of this section of the commentary, beginning with the Great Entrance:

"The Cherubikon manifests, via the deacons who lead the way and via the ripidia [fans] with their representations of the Seraphim, the entrance of all the saints and the just who go before the cherubic powers and the hosts of angels. These in turn invisibly hasten on before Christ the great King, carried in the hands of corporeal beings, as he advances to his mystical sacrifice.[28] With all of these the Holy Spirit also proceeds in the bloodless spiritual sacrifice. He is visible to the eyes of the mind in fire and incense and in smoke and fragrance; the fire shows his divinity, the fragrant smoke his presence, as he descends invisibly and fills us with fragrance through the mystical and lifegiving bloodless sacrifice. The spiritual powers and the choirs of angels join us in crying 'Alleluia' as they see the cross and death which complete the economy, the victory over death, the descent into the underworld, and the resurrection after three days.[29]

"What follows is in imitation of the burial of Christ when Joseph took the body down from the cross, anointed it and wrapped it in a clean cloth, and with the aid of Nicodemus buried it in a new tomb hewn out of rock. The sanctuary is a likeness of the holy sepulcher, and the altar is the resting place where the spotless and all-holy body was laid."[30]

The discos stands for the hands of Joseph and Nicodemus, and the chalice for the vessel in which the blood of Christ was collected. The veil over the discos covers his face as the handkerchief did in the tomb. Finally, the aer symbolizes the stone that sealed the tomb.[31]

"See, Christ is crucified, Life is buried, the tomb is closed, the stone sealed. The priest comes up, he comes with the angelic powers; he stands no longer as in an earthly place but as at the heavenly altar before the throne of God, and gazes upon the great inexpressible and unfathomable mystery of Christ; he confesses grace, proclaims the resurrection, and seals the faith.[32] The white-robed angel comes to the stone, rolls it away with his hand, shows himself in the form of the deacon and cries aloud through the voice of him who proclaims the resurrection on the third day while raising the aer aloft[33] and saying: 'Let us stand aright' (see, the first day); 'Let us stand in awe' (see, the second day); 'In peace let us offer [the anaphora]' (see, the third day). The people cry out, confessing the grace of Christ's resurrection: a mercy of peace, a sacrifice of praise. The priest instructs the people in the knowledge of the triune God that has come to us through the grace of Christ."[34]

The dialogue before the Preface follows, climaxing in the invitation to give thanks to the Lord, because it is right and just that we should raise the eyes of our spirit to the heavenly Jerusalem and direct thither our hymns of thanksgiving. At this point the chapter and a main section of the commentary end at the same time. From the text, however, one could hardly infer that the called-for thanksgiving consists in the anaphora that follows at this point and is the real sacramental embodiment of the remembrance of Christ that has just been described in images.

In the passages that I have cited, the symbolism based on the life of Christ was to some extent combined harmoniously with a symbolism based on the heavenly liturgy; the manner is reminiscent of Theodore of Mopsuestia. From this point on, however, the symbolism of the heavenly liturgy takes over completely. The first part of the anaphora is interpreted wholly in the light of the Thrice Holy (Sanctus) that has been sung in union with the Cherubim and Seraphim.

Thus the priest is said to stand between Cherubim (represented by the deacons with their ripidia[35]) and devote himself to the holy vision of God. Germanus' typical failure to distinguish adequately between symbol and reality, between exemplar and image or copy, leads him in this description to anticipate the glory of heaven in a way that almost conceals the earthly condition of the celebrant. But at least it is only the priest who, like Moses on the mountain, stands at the altar, far removed from the people, and there "contemplates (*katopteuôn!*) the glory of God with unveiled face."[36] "The ripidia and the deacons meanwhile render visible the six-winged Seraphim and the many-eyed Cherubim."[37] "The fact that one of the Seraphim was sent carrying in his hand a coal which he had removed with tongs from the altar signifies that the priest holds in the tongs of his hand the spiritual coal which is Christ and that with this coal he sanctifies and purifies those who receive communion."[38]

The redaction of the commentary that Anastasius used in his translation breaks off a few lines after this. On the other hand, the text provided by N. Borgia explains the remainder of the anaphora, the Our Father, and the communion, but the explanation follows the liturgical text so closely that even in this redaction the strictly symbolic explanation ends with the Thrice Holy.

I should indicate here the symbolism attached to the liturgy of the word; it is a symbolism based essentially on the incarnation. Thus "the antiphons are the predictions of the prophets and announce the coming of the Son of God."[39]

"The entrance of the gospel reveals the coming of the Son of God and his entry into this world. . . . In addition, the bishop's vestment shows forth the red and bloodied vestment of the flesh of Christ which the incorporeal Logos donned and which is as it were soaked through with the spotless blood of the Mother of God, the Virgin. Thus he took upon his shoulders the lost sheep, that is, the race of Adam—he, the Good Shepherd, who with the staff of his cross leads the new Israel to pasture."[40]

The Trisagion hymn, for its part, reminds us of the glorious manifestation of the angels at Christmas.[41] The ascent of the bishop to his throne in the apse shows "that the Son of God took both the mortal flesh in which he had robed himself, and the sheep which he had lifted upon his shoulders (that is, the race of Adam, signified by the omophorion [pallium]), and carried them beyond all the Principalities, Virtues, and Dominations among the heavenly powers and offered them to God the Father."[42] "The holy gospel signifies the presence of the Son in which God revealed himself to us; he spoke to us no longer from the obscurity of a cloud and in hints . . . but appeared visibly to all as a real human being and was seen. . . . Through him God the Father has spoken to us face to face."[43]

The liturgy is thus a representation not only of the death, burial, and resurrection, but essentially also of the incarnation. This last is seen most clearly in the Little Entrance, in the bishop's vestments, and in the liturgy of the word, especially the proclamation of the gospel. The Little Entrance is the solemn procession of the bishop to the altar (and no longer his initial entrance into the church); the book of the gospels is carried in this same procession, so that Germanus can speak of the "entrance of the gospel." In the reference to the bread for the sacrifice, on the other hand, and in the description of the prothesis,[44] there is hardly any symbolic reference to the incarnation. Here, and above all from the Great Entrance to the beginning of the anaphora, the explanation looks to the cross, tomb, and resurrection.

All in all, then, Germanus allots far more space to symbolism relating to the life of Jesus than do Maximus and Dionysius. In fact, he even goes beyond Theodore of Mopsuestia in this respect, since he relates a good many details of the liturgy to externally similar details in the life of Jesus, without, however, making consistent application of a unified principle of interpretation, as Theodore does.

In the eleventh century Theodore of Andida will successfully attempt to organize the many interpretative motifs found in Germanus. He will do this by synchronizing the entire liturgy, from prothesis to communion, with the life of Jesus.

The Complete Liturgical Depiction of the Mystery of Christ in the Age of the Comneni

In the rites of the prothesis, the Byzantines of the eighth century, with their delight in images, had given graphic expression to the mystery of Christ in the liturgy. After the triumph of sacred images and of the theology behind them, the liturgy began to appear increasingly as a copy of the entire work of redemption; this was in keeping with the idea, explicitly set forth in the liturgical explanations of the time, that Christ's command to "remember" him be implemented in a pictorial way. The same approach finds expression in the pictorial program for the church building, in the form of the cycle of pictures of the mysteries, which attains its full development in the eleventh century.

Until this time the prothesis had symbolized only the death of the Lord and the opening of his lifegiving side. Now a new symbolic action was added: the placing of the asterisk [a cruciform metal stand with a small pendant star] over the gifts in memory of the Lord's birth and the star of Bethlehem. As a result, the beginning of the liturgy became symbolic of the incarnation and birth, and this in turn suggested that the following parts of the liturgy should be interpreted as relating to the later phases of the life of Jesus. What Theodore of Mopsuestia had begun long ago, Nicholas of Andida now carried to the extreme when he adopted as a principle for his commentary on the liturgy the idea that every phase in the life of Jesus, from incarnation to ascension, must be represented in the celebration of the eucharist. He regarded the pictorial decoration of the church as an explicit confirmation of this approach.

A. THE CHURCH BUILDING AS PLACE OF THE MYSTERY-PRESENCE
In the Middle Byzantine period the meaning assigned to the church building found expression in its pictorial decoration. Thus the Nea had appeared as a hierarchically ordered cosmos ruled by Christ, the angels, and the saints. A church thus conceived was evidently a

sacred place of worship, but the specifically sacramental events accomplished therein, and in particular the celebration of the eucharist, did not find adequate expression. After all, the author of the discourse against Caballinus had considered the mysteries of baptism and eucharist to be sufficiently conveyed by images of the crucifixion and resurrection.

Without ceasing to respect the hierarchic order and to render present individual sacred personages, the most representative churches of the eleventh century succeeded in showing the cosmos of the church to be one whose character is determined by the salvific meaning of the events of Christ's life. This effect was achieved by reintroducing scenic pictures, although these were chosen in accordance with strict principles.

In the convent church of Hosios Lukas (beginning of the eleventh century)—the earliest of the three Greek churches that have already been mentioned several times—the new cycle of pictures contains eight representations. The first four of these correspond to the cycle of Christmas mysteries (annunciation, nativity, presentation, and baptism) and are placed in the corner niches beneath the base of the dome.[1] The other four pictures represent events of the passion and Easter (washing of the feet, crucifixion, resurrection, appearance of the risen Jesus to Thomas) and are arranged in the narthex or vestibule. In addition there is a representation of the Pentecost event in the dome over the bema.[2]

The church of Nea Moni on Chios (about the middle of the eleventh century) displays an expanded cycle of scenic representations, while the number of pictures of individuals is less than in Hosios Lukas. In the eight niches beneath the base of the dome and in the nave are depicted the annunciation, nativity, presentation, baptism, transfiguration, crucifixion, descent from the cross, and resurrection. On the walls of the narthex are the raising of Lazarus, the entry into Jerusalem, the washing of the feet, and another scene now unrecognizable, while in the vault the ascension and the sending of the Spirit are represented.[3]

In the church at Daphni (end of the eleventh century), there are twelve scenes in the niches beneath the dome and in the niches of the nave alone; among them is the nativity of Mary. Other scenes are placed in the narthex.[4]

The representations I have listed are usually described as "festal pictures," but the name does not do full justice to the facts. Most of the pictures do in fact correspond to the major feasts of the liturgical year. There are, however, some among them (e.g., the pictures of the washing of the feet, the descent from the cross, or the appearance of Christ to Thomas) that can be regarded as festal pictures only in a very attenuated sense, since they represent events that are not properly the object of a festal celebration, even if commemoration is made of them on important days of the liturgical year (the three given as examples are commemorated on Holy Thursday, Good Friday, and the Sunday after Easter).

On the other hand, in many of the cycles, especially the earlier ones, there is no proper representation of important major feasts. Moreover, even if we assume that the later obligatory number of twelve major feasts[5] (along with Easter) had not yet achieved canonical status,[6] the divergences in the various cycles of pictures remain unexplained as long as we continue to make the festal calendar the sole norm for the choice and presentation of the pictures.

As a matter of fact another principle was at work. What was being represented in the cycles was not simply a collection of individual major feasts, but rather the mystery of Christ in its entirety, as this is made present in the liturgico-sacramental life of the church and in the liturgical year, but especially in the celebration of the eucharist, the administration of the sacraments, and the proclamation of the gospel. Thus the pictures express in their own manner that the church building is a place where the mystery is present; moreover, by representing the mystery they help to render it present. The cycle of pictures is therefore aptly called a "liturgical cycle."[7]

Since the church building is above all the place where the eucharist is celebrated, we must think of the cycle of pictures of the various mysteries as being also an explanation of the liturgy, and in particular an implementation of the words of the anamnesis: "Mindful of all that was done for our salvation." Just as the words of the anamnesis—"the cross, the tomb, the resurrection on the third day, the ascension, the session at the right hand, and the second coming in glory"[8]—are intended not as a complete list but as a description of the entire event of salvation by means of representative moments in it, so too the pictures of the mysteries represent the entire mystery of Christ, regardless of the precise number and choice of pictures in the cycle. The cycles are the pictorial counterpart of Germanus' statement about the church building: "The church represents the crucifixion, burial, and resurrection."[9]

Despite the constant enrichment of the pictorial program, the cycle of pictures of the mysteries was brought increasingly into line with the festal calendar, while the mystery of the eucharist found expression in new iconographic themes that were outside the cycle. The growing influence of the festal calendar is already clear at Daphni, where the cycle of scenes depicted is enlarged by inclusion in the nave of the nativity of Mary, and in the narthex of still other scenes from her life. The description, "cycle of pictures for the feasts," now becomes more appropriate than it would have been earlier, while the description "liturgical cycle" makes no distinction between the traditional pictures based on the gospel accounts and such newly added liturgical subjects as the communion of the apostles and the heavenly liturgy.

B. THE EXPLANATION OF THE LITURGY
AS A SUMMATION OF THE SAVING WORK OF CHRIST
The testimony that the later, more fully differentiated cycle of festal pictures offers with regard to the conception of the liturgy finds its exact counterpart in the commentary of Nicholas and Theodore of Andida and in the richly illustrated scroll of texts that is listed as ms *Staurou 109* of the patriarchal library in Jerusalem.[1] Theodore of Andida lived in the eleventh or twelfth century; his exact dates are unknown.[2] On paleological and iconographical grounds the liturgical scroll is to be regarded as a work from the end of the eleventh century.[3] It originated in Constantinople, probably between 1092 and 1118,[4] and was intended for use in a church of St. George[5] in that city.[6]

The two documents have this in common, that they relate the representations of the mysteries in the picture cycles of their time to the liturgy by identifying the content of an individual picture with the meaning of some part of the liturgy.

This coordination of picture content and individual liturgical rite represents a conscious approach to the interpretation of the liturgy, even in the case of the liturgical scroll. It did not result, therefore, simply from an effort to illustrate all parts of the text equally. In what follows, I shall endeavor to prove these statements from the character of the illustrative material itself and from the striking correspondence between this material and the interpretative motifs used by Nicholas and Theodore of Andida.

1. A Liturgical Commentary in Pictures
Among the illuminated liturgical scrolls[7], scroll *Staurou 109* in the patriarchal library of Jerusalem is exceptional both for its choice of pictures and for their execution.[8] The illustrations refer in almost

every instance not simply to individual words but also and above all to the meaning and function of the prayers and actions in question.

From among the subjects depicted in contemporary monumental painting,[9] the scroll contains individual representations of Christ, Mary, angels, and saints (Paul, John the Baptist, Basil and Chrysostom, Constantine and Helena), as well as pictures of the mysteries of the annunciation, nativity, baptism, presentation in the Temple, transfiguration, raising of Lazarus, entry into Jerusalem, prayer in the Garden of Gethsemane, crucifixion, and resurrection, and of Mary's entry into the Temple and her passing.[10] Interestingly enough, the scroll also contains representations that were not yet customary in church monumental painting at this time but were gradually making their way in: Chrysostom officiating at the altar (a picture that later develops into the "Liturgy of the Church Fathers"), the communion of the apostles, the heavenly liturgy (here in a very early form that resembles the communion of the apostles and anticipates a subject that would not become widespread until the fourteenth century), the hospitality of Abraham, and, finally, the eucharistically interpreted vision of Peter of Alexandria (which is attested in monumental painting only from the fourteenth century on). These representations are, as it were, precursors of the pictorial program of the Palaeologue period, and will be discussed in this connection in the next chapter.

The correlation between the twelve pictures of mysteries and the prayers of the liturgy is especially instructive with regard to the eleventh-century conception of the liturgy.[11]

The first two mystery pictures, the annunciation and the nativity of the Lord, are connected with the first prayer of the scroll, the silent prayer at the Little Entrance. In the left margin of the text the picture of the birth forms the letter *D* of the opening word of the prayer *Despota Kyrie* ("Ruler, Lord . . ."),[12] while the annunciation appears opposite, in the right margin. The choice of pictures is not determined by individual words in the text, but is intended rather to reveal the meaning and position of the Little Entrance in the liturgy. That is, just as the incarnation introduces the work of salvation, so the Little Entrance introduces its liturgical re-presentation and thus resembles or even becomes an image of the incarnation.

Maximus the Confessor had already expressed a comparable idea: "The first entrance of the high priest into the church for the celebration of the sacred synaxis is an image and likeness of the first coming of the Son of God, our redeemer, in the flesh into this world."[13] But in Maximus the symbolic reference of the Little Entrance was not limited to the incarnation and nativity. It looked beyond these, although not with the same detailed clarity, to the entire work of salvation[14] as the act whereby all earthly things are brought home to God. As a result, the second phase of the total entry, the actual ascent to the altar, could already symbolize the entry of Christ into the heavenly holy of holies.

Germanus had assigned a less comprehensive symbolism to the Little Entrance, seeing this as an image of the incarnation and nativity. Moreover, despite his usual tendency to divide the symbolic content of the liturgy into as many separate symbols as possible, even he did not manage to introduce further differentiation into this initial event. It would seem at first sight, therefore, that when our scroll places the pictures of the mysteries of the annunciation and nativity beside the text of the Little Entrance, it is to be interpreted along the lines of Germanus.

It is possible, however, to interpret the scroll in another way. In the time of Germanus the Little Entrance was preceded only by the antiphons; now, however, the already highly developed order of the prothesis stood at the beginning of the liturgy. Thus the further away the Little Entrance is from the actual beginning of the liturgy, the less suited it seems for symbolizing the very beginning of the work of redemption at the moment of the incarnation. On the other hand, in an episcopal liturgy (and it was for such that the scroll was meant), the Little Entrance still represents a beginning insofar as at this moment the bishop himself solemnly assumes active presidency of the liturgy.

It is also clear, however, that this action of the bishop is far more suited, by reason of its vividness, to symbolize the entrance of Christ into a visible existence among men (that is, his birth)[15] than it is to symbolize the annunciation and conception at Nazareth, which were accomplished in silence and seclusion. A much more suitable liturgical re-presentation of the event at Nazareth would seem to be the beginning of the prothesis, which is accomplished in the silence and seclusion of the prothesis chamber. For this reason Theodore of Andida, our chief witness to the eleventh/twelfth-century conception of the liturgy, says in his explanation of the prothesis: "The deacon who separates the divine body [the reference is to the "lamb"] from the bread of sacrifice, represents the angel who greeted the Virgin with 'Hail!.' "[16]

Such a conception of the prothesis may also be behind the choice of the picture of the annunciation in our scroll. Since the scroll, meant for an episcopal liturgy, needed to contain only the text from the Little Entrance on, and since therefore it was not possible to place the picture of the annunciation next to the text of the prothesis, it may be that even in the place where it now stands the picture refers back to the preceding prothesis. This would explain why it does not serve as an initial but stands opposite the first initial (supplied by the picture of the nativity),[17] whereas all the other mystery pictures in the scroll do serve as initials and in this way are more clearly related to the nearby text.

The next mystery picture is located at the silent prayer for the second litany of the faithful. The initial, a *P* at the beginning of the words *Palin kai pollakis* ("Once more, and over and over . . ."),[18] along with two figures in the right-hand margin of the text, form a picture of the presentation of Christ in the Temple; the subject is identified by a caption *Hypapantê* ("Meeting"). As in the prayer at the Little Entrance, so in this silent prayer there is no word that could have suggested the illustration. Once again, therefore, the motive for the choice of the picture is not to be sought in the text but in the position of the prayer within the liturgy as a whole. In fact, the concluding doxology of the prayer immediately precedes the Cherubikon, the solemn song accompanying the transfer of gifts, in which Theodore of Mopsuestia had already seen Christ advancing to his sacrifice.

The picture of the presentation in the Temple is a happy choice, since it explains the meaning of the liturgical action from two points of view. On the right, Joseph and Mary bring their gifts and thus remind us that the bread and wine that are being transferred are our human gifts and attest to our personal spirit of sacrifice. In the group of figures that form the initial, Christ, carried in the arms of Symeon and Anna, consecrates himself to the Father, thus showing that he himself is the real sacrificial gift in the liturgy and is already symbolized as such by the bread and wine at the Great Entrance.

The initial for the *Oudeis axios* ("No one is worthy . . ."),[19] the silent prayer at the Great Entrance, shows Christ in a mandorla, blessing the bishop (the possessor of the scroll and present celebrant of the liturgy) who stands opposite in the right-hand margin. In view of what is said in the prayer about the unworthiness of the celebrant to perform the sacred sacrificial action that is now beginning, the blessing seems especially imperative.

Beneath the prayer there is a representation of the heavenly liturgy,[20] and it offers a further interpretation of the transfer of gifts as the real beginning of the sacrificial action proper. In the picture we see Christ at the altar; angels with ripidia stand to the right and the left; behind, on either side, are six apostles, whose attitude shows that the present picture has its origin in the picture of the communion of the apostles. Another angel appears as a fellow minister; he is swinging a censer, and his figure forms the initial of the subsequent silent prayer. He is evidently directing the fragrant smoke of the incense to the sacrificial gifts that his counterpart, an angel functioning as a deacon, is bringing in (with his right hand he holds the discos above his head, and with the left holds the chalice before his breast). The scene is recognizably a representation of the Great Entrance.

This picture provides a needed complement to the mystery picture of the Hypapantê, since it shows Christ as priest, whereas the picture of the Hypapantê shows him as victim. Thus there is expressed in images that which the last sentence of the prayer immediately above the picture of the heavenly liturgy expresses in words: "You yourself are the sacrificing priest and the sacrificial gift; you yourself accept the sacrifice and are at the same time the sacrificial food, Christ our God. . . ."

The fourth mystery picture of the scroll, a representation of the anastasis (resurrection), interprets the first part of the anaphora, that is, the part preceding the Thrice Holy. The picture forms the initial *A* in the words *Axion kai dikaion* ("It is fitting and right . . .")[21]. Christ stoops to Adam, still a prisoner in the underworld, so that their heads almost touch; he takes Adam by the hand and pulls him up to share in the resurrection. In the right-hand margin of the text we see David and Solomon.

The choice of this picture may have been occasioned by the words of the anaphora, "You raised us up when we were fallen,"[22] but at the same time the picture conveys the meaning of the entire prayer, a meaning that is summed up in the quoted words. For the anaphora is a "eucharistic" prayer, that is, a thanksgiving for the redemption that reaches its climax in the resurrection. But in addition, the anaphora is a prayer of consecration and anamnesis and as such proclaims the death and resurrection of the Lord to be efficaciously present, as can be seen from all anamnesis formulas and from the expanded commemoration "command to repeat" in the anaphora of Basil.[23] Of all the mystery pictures, that of the anasatasis is the most impressive proclamation of redemption, since redemption is summed up in the resurrection (which means the conquest of death and salvation for all the children of Adam).[24] The scroll's choice of picture is here, then, a most happy one.

The redemption that found its expression as completed reality in the picture of the anastasis is made concrete for the individual believer in the picture that accompanies the next part of the anaphora: the picture of the raising of Lazarus. By means of this miracle Jesus gave credibility to the words he had spoken to Martha: "He who believes in me, though he die, yet shall he live" (Jn 11:25). It may be that the similarity of this text to another passage that is cited in the anaphora,[25] "so that every one who believes in him should not perish but have eternal life" (Jn 3:16), favored the choice of this picture. Of course, the miracle in question (by which Lazarus received a new life on earth and not eternal life) is only a promise that the cited words, based on the death and resurrection of the Lord, will be fulfilled. For this reason the picture of the raising of Lazarus can express the meaning of the anaphora only when it stands in a relation of subordination to the picture of the anastasis.

Christ's words of institution, which like all the texts spoken aloud by the priest are written in capital letters, are decorated with a representation of the communion of the apostles.[26] Elsewhere it is only the prayers read silently and written in small letters that have accompanying illustrations. The picture here has two parts. In the left margin we see Christ giving the sacred bread to a group of six apostles with Peter at their head. In place of a title the opening words of institution, *Labete, phagete* ("Take, eat . . .") stand over this part of the picture. In the right margin the giving of the chalice is depicted, and over it are the words *Piete ex autou* ("Drink from this . . ."). The communion of the apostles is evidently in its proper place here, since the words being illustrated, "Take and eat," refer to communion.

The initial for the text of the anamnesis is formed by a picture of the baptism of Christ. The scene is not directly related to the object of the anamnesis, which is largely identical with the object of the thanksgiving prayer and therefore has already been represented in the picture of the anastasis. What the picture of the baptism does, in keeping with its position between words of institution and anamnesis, is to illustrate in a sensible way the fact that the words of institution have their liturgical effect through the invocation (epiclesis) of the Holy Spirit.

Byzantine iconography had two available ways to indicate the action of the Holy Spirit on the gifts by depicting his descent. It is understandable that the decision here was to show the descent of the Spirit at the baptism rather than the sending of the Spirit at Pentecost. Why? Because the purpose was to give visual expression to the idea that the Holy Spirit descends on the bread and wine as "images" of the body of Christ, thus turning them into the very reality of the body of Christ. The representation of Christ in the picture of the baptism refers the viewer both to the "images" of the body of Christ prior to the consecration and especially to the real presence of Christ after the consecration.[27]

This liturgical interpretation of the baptism is underscored in the picture by the fact that the two angels present at the event have adopted the attitude of celebrants. In contrast to the rest of the iconographic tradition, one of the angels is shown not with hands veiled but as making the gesture with which priest and deacon point to the sacred species at the words of institution and epiclesis.[28]

Homage is paid to the Lord now present, just as it was paid to him long ago at his entry into Jerusalem. And just as at that time the hour of sacrifice and glorification had struck for Christ (Jn 12:23), so now the liturgy gives a share in his sacrifice and glorification. For this reason the artist uses a picture of the entry of Christ into Jerusalem in order to illustrate the epiclesis prayer, which begins with the words *Eti prospheromen* ("Once again we offer you this spiritual and bloodless sacrifice . . .").[29] In this picture the disciples with their palm branches and garments form the initial, while Christ and his apostles enter from the right side.

The ultimate recipients of the sacrifice and the primary givers of the graces won by the sacrifice are the persons of the Most Holy Trinity. In Byzantine iconography the three can only be depicted in the form in which they showed themselves to Abraham long ago. They are depicted in this manner before the text of the next prayer, in which the Church asks for "the fellowship of the Holy Spirit and the fullness of the heavenly kingdom" for all who will receive the sacred gifts in communion.[30]

The commemoration of the saints in the final section of the anaphora is illustrated by pictures of John the Baptist and George, while the prayer for the living and "for the city in which we dwell"[31] is illustrated by pictures of Constantine and Helena and of the walls of Constantinople.

In the prayer before the Our Father we ask that we may share in the sacred banquet for the sake of inheriting the kingdom of heaven and not for judgment and condemnation.[32] The illustration here is provided by a representation of the vision of St. Peter of Alexandria and of his beheading. This subject and its relation to the eucharist will play an important role in church painting from the fourteenth century on [33]; for this reason it deserves mention here as well.

The life of this saintly bishop of Alexandria, who was beheaded as a martyr by Maximinus in 311, reports that when the condemned man was in prison Christ appeared to him in the form of a twelve-year-old boy who was in a pitiable state and dressed in torn clothing. To the saint's astonished question: "Lord, who has torn your tunic?" Christ answered:

Arius has torn me (!); be on guard not to admit him to communion. For some will come and plead for him. Be careful not to listen to them. And get word to Achilla and Alexander not to receive him, for after your departure they will shepherd my Church, for which I became a little child and died, though I live eternally."[34]

The words: "became a little child and died, though I live eternally," are given a eucharistic interpretation in Byzantine iconography,[35] for Peter is represented as a liturgical celebrant, while Christ stands on an altar in front of Peter as a twelve-year-old boy (or else as a little child just old enough to stand) dressed in torn garments. The words of their conversation are often written on the painting in an abridged form.

The use of the picture of the vision and beheading of Peter as an illustration for the prayer of preparation before communion is intended as a reminder. Like Arius, who sinned against Christ by schism and heresy, any ill-disposed person is excluded from communion and from fellowship with Christ. On the other hand, like Peter, who was faithful to the Lord even unto martyrdom and who was deemed worthy of communion with Christ when he was in prison and especially as he was about to die, so everyone who loves Christ receives a special share in him through communion.

Of the five remaining festal pictures, two relate to the reception of communion, two others to the effects of the reception of communion, and the final one to the completion of the liturgy.

The words of the prayer said with bowed head: "May the sacred sacrificial gifts become a blessing for us,"[36] refer to the communion that is to follow. The prayer is therefore illustrated by a picture that serves as a type of the reception of communion. The picture is an expanded representation of the presentation of Mary in the Temple (November 21). It shows Mary, aged three years, being received into the temple by the high priest and nourished with heavenly food by a descending angel. The picture is based on the story in the apocryphal Protogospel of James.[37]

The prayer at the elevation of the sacred species is associated with a representation of the Koimesis (dormition of Mary), which focuses primarily on the appearance of the Lord at Mary's death.[38] The picture thus corresponds to the words: "Look down upon us from your glorious throne and come to sanctify us."[39]

A picture of Christ and the apostles in the garden of Gethsemane has been chosen to illustrate the prayer of thanksgiving after communion.[40] The choice becomes understandable if we recall Christ's warning to watch and pray lest we fall into temptation (Mt 26:41). In fact, over the group of the apostles to the right of the text stand the words: "So, could you not watch with me one hour?" (Mt 26:40). The illustration thus reflects the request in the litany that is being recited at this point: "That the entire day (and our entire life) be holy . . . and sinless."

The prayer behind the ambo is illustrated by a picture of the transfiguration. The idea being expressed is evidently that in communion we share in the transfigured body of Christ. In the liturgical texts, admittedly, the idea occupying the foreground is of the resurrection as an effect of communion. But since the scroll had already assigned the picture of the resurrection to the anaphora, it seemed reasonable to choose instead a picture of the transfiguration. In addition, the latter was made more appropriate by the words in the prayer: "Sanctify all who love the splendor of your house, and glorify them by your divine power."[41]

At the end of the scroll stands a picture of the crucifixion, occasioned here by the words of the final prayer before the last blessing: "Christ, our God, you yourself are the fulfillment of the Law and the Prophets. You have accomplished the entire plan of salvation as determined by the Father."[42] Although the thought is not clearly spelled out any further in the text, these words suggest by their position at the end of the ceremony that the completion of the liturgy is seen as an allegory of the fulfillment of the divine plan of salvation in the life of Christ. In the eleventh century a liturgical action as allegory easily became a liturgical action as picture. Consequently the picture of the crucifixion at the end of the scroll may be deliberately set over against the pictures of the incarnation at its beginning, with the intention of signaling that the liturgy is from beginning to end a pictorial representation of the memorial of Christ.

The collection of mystery pictures in this scroll corresponds in its iconography rather closely to the cycle of festal pictures in the monumental painting of the time, and therefore it gives us reliable information about the liturgical function of this cycle and about the comparable motifs in liturgical interpretation. At the same time, however, there is an important difference between the two types of pictures. The mystery pictures of monumental painting have the purpose of rendering present, in a quasi-sacramental way, the events of the history of salvation; the miniatures of the scroll, on the other hand, illustrate the full, many-leveled meaning[43] of liturgical texts and actions. In many instances the historical scene in the illustration serves simply as a parabolic garb for what is real or to be realized solely in the here and now. Thus, for example, the picture of the baptism of Christ is not meant to proclaim the event at the Jordan (or its general saving significance) but rather the Spirit-effected presence of Christ under the appearances of bread and wine. The scene on the Mount of Olives points to the permanently valid admonition of Christ to watch and not fall into temptation.

Yet what makes this scroll so characteristic of the conception of the liturgy at this period is that these meanings are embedded, as it were, in the salvational-historical symbolism of the liturgy. Thus the scroll bears witness, although not as directly as the cycle of festal pictures in monumental painting, to a conception of the liturgy that sees the eucharistic celebration as basically a reproduction of the saving work of Christ. It is a conception that Nicholas of Andida expounds in a very emphatic manner.

2. The Liturgical Commentary of Nicholas and Theodore of Andida
The most liturgically informative document from this period is the *Summary Meditation on the Symbols and Mysteries Accomplished in the Divine Liturgy,*[44] or *Protheoria*, which Bishop Nicholas of Andida composed at the urging of Bishop Basil of Phyteia, and which one of Nicholas' successors, Theodore, revised. Nicholas follows deliberately the interpretative method of Germanus,[45] but endeavors to give it a theological basis and reduce it to a unified system.[46] To this end he relies above all on arguments from the doctrine on images. This can be seen right at the beginning of the commentary in the threefold justification he gives for his main concern: the representation of the *entire* work of salvation in the eucharistic celebration.

"Many who exercise a priestly office know and profess that what is accomplished in the Divine Liturgy is a copy of the passion, burial and resurrection of Christ our God. I am unable to say, however, why they are ignorant (or so they seem to me) that the liturgy also denotes all the manifestations which accompanied his entire saving life among us in the flesh: his conception, his birth, his life in the first thirty years, the activity of his precursor, his public debut at his baptism, the choice of the apostles, and the three-year period of miracles which roused envy and led to his crucifixion.

"Moreover, that which possesses only a head and lacks feet, hands, and other members can hardly be called a body. But learn from Christ's own words that what was sacrificed was a true body; for he says: 'Take and eat. This is my body.' "[47]

In support of his main thesis, that the sequence of the individual parts of the liturgy depicts the life of Christ from the incarnation to the ascension, the *Protheoria* appeals to the words of Christ, "This is my body," with which, of course, the commission of remembering is connected.

A more detailed justification might be offered for the analogy here asserted between the wholeness of the Lord's body and the completeness of the memorial of his life. After all, Christ describes his body as "given" and his blood as "poured out," so that the consecration of the gifts cannot be separated from the reality-filled memorial of his death. But the memorial of his death expands to include "all that was accomplished for our salvation." Furthermore this "body," which is Christ's saving work and which at the consecration of the gifts becomes sacramentally present in virtue of the words of institution cited by the *Protheoria*, calls for pictorial "embodiment" in the liturgy.

Yet the *Protheoria* does not proceed in that way. The authors comment that everyone recognizes the liturgy as being a rendering present of the death and resurrection, but they do not turn this fact into an undisputed premise from which to draw further conclusions consonant with their conception of the liturgy. They are not concerned to give a theologically nuanced evaluation of the individual liturgical words and actions in accordance with their degree of causality. Rather, they understand the entire liturgy as a kind of icon, or rather a cycle of pictures of the life of Christ. The similarity, which they regard as obvious, between the liturgical event and the prototypical event that is Christ's life, or, better, the transparency of the former in relation to the latter, necessarily excludes any imperfection in the depiction. If the Fathers of the Trullan Synod had already seen in every icon of Christ an anamnesis of the entire work of redemption,[48] how much truer must this not be of the liturgy, which is no ordinary icon but contains the very reality of Christ?[49]

The following arguments in particular show that the Andidans' interpretation of the liturgical reality of Christ derives from the categories of pictorial thinking. A biography written by a human being requires that the life be described from its beginning and without arbitrary omissions. Therefore "the faithful picture of the lifegiving body" that the Holy Spirit draws certainly cannot be so incomplete as to lack a member.[50]

The sacred scriptures, too, present a complete and unabridged picture of Christ. But authentic liturgy must be coextensive with the gospels in its content. The holy Fathers, chief among them Basil and Chrysostom, also understood Christ's words, "Do this in remembrance of me," as calling for an unabridged presentation, and they organized the celebration of the liturgy accordingly. For this reason, too, they attributed great importance to the custom of the fermentum, since only in leavened bread can Christ's body be correctly represented as ensouled and united with the divinity.[51]

As a third argument the *Protheoria* appeals to the evidence of the sacred icons: "For in them the devout person contemplates all the mysteries of the economy of Christ our God, from the coming of the archangel Gabriel to the Virgin Mary, down to the Ascension and return of the Lord."[52] Gregory the Theologian, too, in his preaching at Christmas and again at Easter, had presented the festal event not in isolation but as part of the complete work of redemption.

The *Protheoria* sums up: "Therefore every believer must realize that through the mysteries accomplished in it the celebration of the Divine Liturgy as a whole reveals in symbolic form the entire economy of the saving descent of our true God and Redeemer Jesus Christ."[53] But in numerous instances diverse actions of Christ must be expressed by a single symbolic action of the liturgy. Events that in their time occurred in various places must now be brought together at the table of preparation and the altar. According to Theodore, the table of preparation becomes the place where the events of Bethlehem and Nazareth are exhibited, while the events that once took place in Jerusalem occur now at the altar. Since Jerusalem, as the place where the most pivotal event in world history occurred, is the center of the earth and at the same time stands midway between heaven and earth, the holy Fathers arched the baldacchino over the altar as an image of the heavens, and the altar itself stands on an elevation between the four pillars that support the baldacchino.[54]

Now the celebration of the mysteries can unfold at the table of preparation and the altar and in the area between the two. The celebration is begun by the deacon, who thus resembles the archangel who greeted the Virgin.

"The Body of the Lord is separated from the bread of the eulogy and prosphora as it once was separated from the womb of the Virgin. . . . This is done by the deacon (for such is the custom in the Great Church) by means of an icon instrument known as the lance (though the time has really not yet come for using such an instrument). Having been removed from the center of the prosphora, the Body of the Lord is offered separately. The deacon who does this, at the same time prepares the Blood of the Lord which later on, at the time of the passion, will be consecrated by the descending Holy Spirit. He leaves it on the table of preparation, while the priest utters the appropriate prayer."[55]

"Thus the Body of the Lord now remains on the table of preparation as at Bethlehem, where Christ was born . . . but also, and at the same time, as at Nazareth. . . . To sum up the matter: the table of preparation represents the entire period of thirty years and the life of Christ before his baptism."[56]

"The priest who accomplishes the opening part of the liturgy is an image of John the Baptist, who began the proclamation by saying: 'Do penance; the kingdom of heaven is at hand,' and by baptizing all who came to him. Once the liturgy has begun in this way, the first intercession is offered and after this the series of verses from the prophets which we call the antiphons."[57]

The *Protheoria* goes on to give the three litanies and antiphons that are already found in the Barberini Codex and that have been in use ever since. On the other hand, it describes the external liturgical form in a somewhat arbitrary manner because of the concern to relate the form to a higher order of things. In its statement that the antiphon shows us, first, that "it is good to praise the Lord who was born for the salvation of the human race," we recognize the first antiphon, Psalm 91 (numbering according to the Greek Bible), which is thus related to the content of the prothesis. The text cites as the beginning of the second antiphon the words, "The Lord is king" (Ps 92). The words, "At the intercession of the Mother of God [or: of the saints], deliver us!" are added to the antiphons. After the second antiphon the hymn *Ho monogenês*, composed by the blessed Emperor Justinian, is sung; "it fits in well with the symbols of the Lord's birth."[58] The praise of "one of the Most Holy

Trinity," which resounds in Justinian's hymn, is completed after the Little Entrance by the Trisagion, the song of praise in honor of the entire Blessed Trinity.

The entrance of the bishop stands for Christ's manifestation at the Jordan, for "up to this point, the bishop, like Christ, was not recognized by all."[59] In the Great Church the patterns in the marble floor, called "rivers" (*potamoi*), refer to the Jordan. The priest who began the liturgy now yields place to the bishop, just as John did when he said, "His honor must increase, mine must decrease." The words of the third antiphon, which accompany the Entrance ("Come now! Let us sing praise to the Lord!"), are reminiscent of the first meetings of the Lord with the apostles.[60]

Immediately after the Entrance and the singing of the Trisagion the bishop ascends to his cathedra, thus symbolizing the passage from law to grace. Further signs of the new covenant are preceded by the prokeimenon (literally, "that which lies before"), which according to our Andidan commentators derives its name from this position. The blessing for the reading and the reading itself symbolize the calling and sending of the apostles, along with their commission to compile the sacred scriptures and proclaim the message; at the same time blessing and reading also represent the fulfillment of the commission, of which we are told in the Acts of the Apostles and the apostolic letters.[61] The authors here forestall the objection that they are anticipating later events and remind the reader that it is impossible always to follow the same order of parable, symbol, and reality when dealing with persons, places, and times.

The holy gospel proclaims Christ's sermons, commandments, and miracles, as well as his suffering, burial, and resurrection.[62] The incensation during the Alleluia signifies the grace of the Holy Spirit that was given to the disciples when the Lord sent them out to heal sicknesses.[63] The intercessions after the gospel refer to the further teaching activity of the Lord as well as to the preparation of the catechumens for baptism.[64]

"The transfer of the holy symbols of the Body and Blood of the Lord from the table of preparation and their removal to the altar during the singing of the Cherubikon manifest the entry of the Lord into Jerusalem from Bethany. On that occasion, with meditative voices a great throng of people and the children of the Hebrews sang a hymn to him as King and Victor over death. At the same time, though in a manner incorporeal, the angels joined the Cherubim in singing the Thrice Holy. The deacons carry scepters and swords as signs of royal dignity, as well as ripidia in imitation of the Cherubim. The Cherubikon, which is sung meanwhile, is an admonition to all to persevere with alert minds from now until the end of the liturgy and to set aside all earthly thoughts as befits those who are to receive the great King in communion."[65]

After the sacred gifts have been placed on the altar the bishop prays for himself and for the people and asks God the Father to find pleasing the sacrifice of his Son which is being offered."[66] Soon after, the *Protheoria* explains the cry of the deacon: "Let us stand in orderly fashion and in fear of God! Let us be attentive to the holy anaphora!"[67]

"What is the 'anaphora'? It is, of course, the gaze directed at the prototypes of the symbols being accomplished. For the name 'anaphora' is referential and parabolic. Therefore we stand trembling and weeping, convinced that we now see the God-Man himself as he suffers for us. Let us therefore stand recollected and unmoved so that as we offer this sacrifice in peace and undistracted by the lower senses, we may become worthy to see his divine resurrection and be filled with joy by it—especially those who, as the holiness of the place requires, participate in his body, for they suffer with him, are buried with him, and rise again with him."[68]

In this idiosyncratic explanation of the anaphora Theodore plays upon the various meanings of the verb *anapherein*. This can mean "to trace something back to," that is, in this case to relate the antitypes (of the liturgical anaphora) to the prototypes (in the passion of Christ). It can also mean to "endure," and therefore, in this passage, can be a reminder that we must make the suffering of Christ our own and bear it with him. But according to its original meaning in liturgical use the word has the same sense as *prospherein*, that is, to "offer" and "sacrifice." But this last meaning remains very much in the background, at least as far as a liturgical co-offering by the faithful is concerned. It is not accidental that Theodore cites the summons of the deacon in a form in which nothing is said of a *prospherein* by the faithful and in which the verb *prosechein* probably means nothing more than to meditate attentively.

"The closing of the doors, the drawing of the curtain hung before them, as is customary in monasteries, and the covering of the divine gifts with the so-called aer signifies, it seems to me, the night in which the disciple betrayed Jesus. . . . For why should this veil be called *aer*, that is "misty air," if not because it represents the

94

darkness of that night? . . . The removal of the aer and the opening of the curtain and the doors are an image of the morning when they led Christ away and handed him over to Pilate."[69]

"But what is to be said of the ripidia which the deacons hold in their hands meanwhile and which move back and forth, as though trembling, over the sacred gifts?"[70] The Andidans protest that it is almost presumptuous to speak of this, but they say that with God's help they want to persevere even here in the task they have accepted. Their interpretation takes for its starting point the pictures of the Cherubim on the ripidia themselves: Angels always and everywhere accompanied Christ, especially during that night when he was betrayed and on the following day when he was crucified. But when they saw the Lord suffering, they were seized by deep consternation. Now they hid their faces and turned away; now, filled with awe at his divine majesty, they turned back to the Lord. This continued until the crucifixion. But when they saw the wonders that took place at the moment of his death, proving his godhead anew, their consternation ceased. This is why the deacons wave the ripidia until the elevation of the species, an act that signifies Christ's exaltation on the cross. The reverence with which the angelic powers adored the Lord's divinity finds expression meanwhile in the singing of the Thrice Holy.

"After the ekphonesis comes the Thrice Holy hymn and, after that is sung, the prayer of Basil the Great or of divinely inspired Chrysostom, which begins with the divine nature and moves forward to the incarnation. And after the entire work of salvation has been described, the celebrant cries in a loud voice: 'Take and eat.'

"There seems to be a problem here in the fact that the word 'all' is lacking in 'Take and eat,' but then appears in the 'Drink from it.' I answer that the word 'all' has a historical meaning and a spiritual meaning: a historical meaning because of the cunning of the betrayer in connection with these mysteries, and a spiritual meaning for the apostles and the holy Fathers. For whereas the apostles received the divine bread in their hands from the hand of Christ and communicated with faith and fear of God, Judas alone hid the bread he had received, showed it to the Jews, and thus betrayed the mystery to them. For this reason (it is said) the words 'Never will I betray the mystery to your enemies' were added to the prayer 'In your holy supper.'[71]

"On the other hand, the betrayer was unable to hide the divine blood, which all received from the chalice with lips and mouth;

instead he drank like all the others. Knowing this in advance, the Lord omitted the word 'all' in connection with the bread, but added it to the words about the chalice."[72]

Another reason why Christ said "Drink of this, all of you," in connection with the chalice was the spiritual meaning he intended for later times. He wanted all who receive the sacred body to drink the holy blood as well. He did not add "all" when speaking of the bread in order to indicate that those who would approach the holy Supper must first examine themselves. "But the words, 'As often as you eat this bread and drink this cup,' show that those who can should eat and drink every day."[73]

The *Protheoria* devotes only a few sentences to the epiclesis. The different versions of the epiclesis formula in Basil (ending with the words "shed for the life of the world") and in Chrysostom ("transforming them through your Holy Spirit")[74] do not demonstrate any opposition. Chrysostom, the *Protheoria* says, wanted to emphasize the special property of the lifegiving Spirit, while Basil wished to stress more the *ousia* and *energeia* common to the three divine persons.[75]

The two liturgies also differ in the commemoration, but this time in the way it is introduced.

"For Basil, a man filled with God, introduces the commemoration of the saints by saying: 'In order that we may find mercy and grace together with the holy Fathers, the patriarchs and all the other just.'[76] Chrysostom, however, as is written at this point, judges that the sacrifice is appropriately being offered for them as well.[77] And legitimately! . . . For at that time one man died for all. . . . And we profess that in the liturgy we gaze precisely on that death and on the resurrection. For it is clear that what happened at that time is now fulfilled in those who offer the sacrifice in a fitting manner.

"Let no one say: How can the bishops intercede for such saints? For, since the bishops have been deemed worthy to act in the person of Christ, the High Priest, they are able to offer such intercession."[78]

In general, the bishops do and say a great many things in the liturgy that are beyond the natural powers of a human being, as, for example, when they cry out Cherubic and Seraphic hymns. Thus the great Dionysius emphasizes the point that the liturgy is accomplished in imitation of the heavenly powers and their various orders, which are imaged forth in the various classes of celebrants. In keeping with this view he calls the deacon "purifier," the priest "illuminator," and the bishop "perfector." Consequently, among the things done and said by the bishop during the liturgy there are those that he does as mediator among men, others that he does in imitation of the heavenly powers, and still others that Christ our God accomplishes through him.[79]

When, therefore, during the commemoration of the saints he remembers, "above all, our utterly holy and pure Lady and Mother of God, who is praised above all other creatures,"[80] he does so in the person of Christ, as he expressly says in another prayer: "You it is who offer and are offered."[81]

The *Protheoria* explains in detail why the various just persons and saints are named in the liturgy. Next comes the commemoration of the hierarchy, the other living, and the dead. Mention is also made of those "for whom the sacrifice is offered."[82] Such an offering of the sacrifice in behalf of particular living and dead persons found new pictorial expression in Nicholas' and Theodore's time in the offering of particles of bread from the special prosphoras at the prothesis.[83]

After the Our Father comes a prayer said with bowed head. The following "elevation of the venerable Body images forth the elevation on the cross, the death on the cross, and also the resurrection."[84]

"At this point a small vessel of warm water is brought, and some of it is poured into the chalices or mixing flagons on the altar so that the blood and water may come forth warm as they did from the lifegiving wellspring in the divine side. The warm water, poured in at communion time, thus makes the image complete, so that when the communicants touch the rim of the chalice they touch as it were the divine side."[85]

After the elevation "the celebrant undertakes the division of the divine body. But although it is divided, the God-Man remains undivided and indivisible in each piece of the divided bread. And although he had been subject to suffering and death, his flesh did not experience corruption in the lower world."[86]

"The reception [of the holy mysteries] signifies the distribution of the bread at the Supper before his death, and also of the common cup, of which our Redeemer said: "I will not drink from it again until I drink it new in the kingdom of my Father." And in fact he did drink of it again in an unusual and marvelous way after his resurrection; he did so, not because his body still had need of nourishment, but in order to convince the disciples of his resurrection."[87]

"Then comes the prayer of thanksgiving and the removal of the remaining divine food; this signifies the taking of our Lord and God into heaven." The prayer behind the ambo is, as it were, the summation of all prayers and of the victories they represent![88]

The *Protheoria* thus continues to the end to interpret the liturgy in terms of the life of Christ. Germanus, on the contrary, had dropped this approach at the beginning of the anaphora and replaced it with a description of heavenly glory that was modeled on an Old Testament vision in the Temple.

C. THE PROTHESIS RITE AND THE STAR OF BETHLEHEM

The development of the prothesis symbolism from the eighth to the eleventh centuries becomes perfectly clear if we compare the interpretations of the preparation of the gifts in Germanus and the *Protheoria*. Of course, the Andidans' desire to find the entire life of Christ symbolized in the liturgy had already prepared them to see in the prothesis a manifestation of the incarnation. But in addition, by his time ritual expansions of the prothesis already provided points of contact for such an interpretation. The fruitful basis for the interpretation was the consciousness that the gifts, being "likenesses" of the body of Christ, contained an anamnesis of the incarnation, as indeed did every picture of Christ. This consciousness found expression in Germanus as it did in the two prothesis prayers of the Barberini Codex, although it had not as yet been given a specific expression in ritual.

The first real quasi-pictorial expression of incarnational symbolism to which the Andidans could appeal legitimately was provided by the cutting of the central, sealed part of the prosphora from the rest of the sacrificial bread.[1] Patriarch Nicholas Grammaticus (1084–1111) speaks of the rite of excision as follows:

"The first prosphora is that of the Lord (*despotikê*). He who offers it must with the lance inscribe a cross on the prosphora and say the (corresponding) verse. Then he is to insert the lance and separate out the seal, whether this be square or circular, and say these words: 'The Lamb of God, the Son of the Father, who takes away the sins of the world, is offered in sacrifice.'"[2]

If the seal is to be regarded as the Lamb, then its separation from the prosphora must be interpreted either as the separation (begun in the incarnation) of Christ the sacrificial Lamb from the rest of the human race or as a direct symbol of the birth from the Virgin. In keeping with their style of interpretation Nicholas and Theodore opted for the second alternative, although it is much less consonant with the context provided by the prothesis symbolism as a whole. The extreme interpretation of the rite that the *Protheoria* followed would not ultimately win out, just as the custom attested by it of having the deacon perform the prothesis[3] (thus suggesting the symbolic interpretation of the deacon as an archangel[4]) would very soon be abandoned and contested bitterly in its final manifestations.[5]

In the eleventh century we already find particles being cut from the sacrificial bread in commemoration of Mary, the saints, the living, and the dead, and being laid on the discos alongside the Lamb. This shows that the sacrificial bread was now seen as representing the entire human race and not so much Mary in particular.

At the same time, however, a further new rite provided full justification for the Andidans' mode of explanation. From the eleventh century on, the inventories of various churches and monasteries list the "asterisk,"[6] which, as the name suggests, probably had from the very beginning a more than purely practical meaning. Germanus had already said of the discos that it is "also interpreted as the circle of the heavens which accepts within its circumference Christ, the spiritual sun which appears in the bread."[7] In keeping with this, the asterisk seems initially to have simply continued the general celestial symbolism of the discos. The oldest texts accompanying the placing of the asterisk over the blessed bread agree[8] in citing Psalm 32:6: "By the word of the Lord were the heavens made, by the breath of his mouth their entire host." Nonetheless it was but a short step from this to the explicit interpretation of the asterisk as referring to the Star of Bethlehem. The step was doubtless taken long before the diataxis (ordo) or ceremonial of Philotheus (d. 1379),[9] in which the formula now used is given: "And the star came and stood above the place where the child was."

Here the symbolism of the incarnation found unmistakable expression. At the same time, however, in thus focusing on historical circumstances accompanying the birth of Christ, this incarnation symbolism could only with difficulty be brought into intellectual harmony with the passion symbolism in the rest of the prothesis.

Chapter Six

Liturgical Standardization and Reflection
in the Age of the Paleologues

Ever since the time of the iconoclasts the liturgy had been regarded
increasingly as a pictorial representation of the mysteries of Christ's
life. The ultimate consequences of this conception revealed themselves in the development of the prothesis as an image of the incarnation and birth and in the interpretative method of the *Protheoria*.
At the same time, however, this development and this method radically exhausted the possibilities of the liturgy as representation of
the mysteries. It is true that in the later period a few further
touches were added or some points were made clearer, but the
overall shape of the liturgy remained essentially unchanged.

As a result, the codification of the rubrics that Philotheus Kokki-
nus (d. 1379), later patriarch, undertook when he was hegumen of
the Great Laura on Athos,[1] was at the same time the first codification of the definitive liturgical order. There would still be considerable divergences in the various liturgical manuscripts, but the use of
printing gradually led to a high degree of unification, even if not to
the complete standardization that has characterized the Latin liturgy with its papally approved "typical" editions.

Now that liturgical development was essentially closed, the explanations of the liturgy could claim all the greater authority. And
in fact the liturgical writings, dating from this period, of Nicholas
Cabasilas, lay theologian and mystic (d. after 1363), and of Symeon,
metropolitan of Thessalonica (d. 1429), acquired a reputation that is
unsurpassed in Orthodoxy even today.

The new flowering of liturgical interpretation was matched by a
new liturgical iconography. The Middle Byzantine system of decoration had reached its fullest form with the development of the festal cycle. The pictures of the mysteries of Christ's life were an
expression of the liturgical anamnesis, and the representation of the
Pantocrator in the dome, surrounded by angels, showed the liturgy
to be a heavenly event. As an iconographical rendering present of

what they represented, these pictures were themselves part of the liturgy, and the standardization of the liturgical order meant at the same time that this pictorial program had reached its fullest possible embodiment.

If, then, artistic creativity was to find an acceptable outlet in new iconographic pictorial themes, it could no longer do so within the existing canon, but had to adopt a decisively new perspective. Just as liturgical creativity could no longer operate unrestrictedly in shaping the liturgy but had to find its outlet rather in liturgical interpretation, so too the new liturgical themes in iconography manifested a reflective cast. Artists dealt in their representations not only with the content of the liturgy, that is, the mystery of Christ, but also with the liturgical form of the Church's rituals. Their intellectual perspective was thus no longer that of the original texts but of the liturgical commentaries and of certain liturgical hymns such as the Cherubikon.

A. THE LITURGICAL THEMES OF LATE BYZANTINE ICONOGRAPHY AS INTERPRETATIONS OF THE LITURGY

The iconographic themes of the Middle Byzantine system of decoration continued to have their place in Late Byzantine churches. But they no longer set the tone in an exclusive way. The pictorial program was also enriched by representations of a new kind,[1] while at the same time the program as a whole was internally transformed.[2] If we compare the new pictorial types with those of the Middle Byzantine period, we discern in them an element of reflection such as we would have expected to find earlier only in illustrations for texts. In these new pictures the reality represented is seen not as it revealed itself historically and is attested in sacred scripture, but in the ahistorical forms in which it presents itself to religious speculation and mystical experience.

This meant a departure from the classical doctrine on images, which had refuted all the iconoclastic objections to the possibility of representing the divine by referring to the historically visible revelation of God in Jesus Christ. As a result of the new outlook, we even find in one of the most representative Greek churches of the fourteenth century a picture of God the Father,[3] who in the eyes of the theologians of images was the utterly "indescribable." Admittedly, such pictures are relatively few, and in the seventeenth century a Synod of Moscow would expressly ban them in Russia.[4] There were fewer hesitations about the equally revolutionary depiction of

Christ in angelic form as the angel of the mighty plan[5] and of John the Baptist in the semblance of an angel.[6]

The ahistoricity of this iconography and its failure to distinguish between visible and invisible are, of course, understandable in an age that was dominated by Palamism, since one of the main theses of this teaching is that the uncreated light of Tabor can be experienced in a bodily manner.[7] Mystical experience, which is considered attainable by every believer, will normally have its origin in liturgical experience. Correspondingly, liturgical themes play the most important role among those that are specific to Late Byzantine iconography.[8] Among these, in turn, eucharistic themes have pride of place.[9] Of these the communion of the apostles,[10] the liturgy of the church Fathers, and, somewhat later, the heavenly liturgy become obligatory parts of the decoration of churches. The communion of the apostles has its place in the apse beneath the picture of the Theotokos; the liturgy of the church Fathers appears either beneath the communion of the apostles or in the prothesis chamber; and the heavenly liturgy is represented in the dome (beneath the picture of the Pantocrator or that of the angelic orders), in the apse (directly beneath the Theotokos and above the communion of the apostles), or in the prothesis chamber.

Given the reflective character of the new iconography and its departure from the classical conception of images, it was only natural that some of the new themes should first become known through illustrations in manuscripts and then make their first appearance in monumental painting in the peripheral areas of the church building. Illustrations were not liturgical pictures and therefore were from the outset essentially unrestricted in their choice of subjects. Thus the eleventh-century scroll from Constantinople, which we saw in the preceding chapter, already brought together in advance (although in simple modes of representation) the most important of the Late Byzantine liturgical themes.[11]

As far as monumental painting is concerned, the two most important metropolitan churches of the Slavic world, the Sophia churches of Kiev (1037) and Ohrid (c. 1050) (both of them dedicated to Divine Wisdom, like the Great Church of Constantinople), played a trailblazing role in the spread of the new liturgical themes. The splendid mosaic in the apse of the cathedral at Kiev shows the communion of the apostles. Also in the apse we find the powerful full-length figures of the church Fathers, who gaze unwaveringly at the altar of the church and serve as models for the later liturgy of the church Fathers. Various Old Testament scenes and depictions of New Testament miracles, all related to the eucharist, and, above all, legends of the saints told in detail make it even clearer how very much this pictorial decoration differs from the pictorial program of Greek churches of the era.[12]

The Ohrid church of Hagia Sophia also depicts the communion of the apostles, although in a less common form, since it shows the apostles prior to the actual moment of the reception of communion. It also has the church Fathers; St. Basil celebrating the liturgy; a representation, in several parts, of the sacrifice of Isaac; and still other pictures relating to the eucharist.[13]

1. The Communion of the Apostles

The apse of the church of Hagia Sophia at Kiev represents the communion of the apostles in the form that would subsequently become quite typical. We see Christ giving the holy bread to the apostles[14] at the left side of a baldacchino-covered altar, and giving them the sacred cup at the right side of the same altar. Behind the Lord in both instances stands an angel wearing a white sticharion and holding a liturgical fan or ripidion.[15] On the altar we see a discos with the consecrated bread already broken into small pieces for distribution, a cross, an asterisk, a lance, and a sponge. The words of institution are given in full above the scene.

Such a representation is evidently quite alien to the principles of the doctrine on images. According to the latter, the communion of the apostles can only be represented in the historical form of the Last Supper; in addition, the emphasis would be on the continuing significance of this saving event for the present time. The Supper presented in a heavenly mode or even the truth that Christ is present at the eucharistic celebration as host of the meal ought not to find iconographic representation in a church, since the heavenly mode and Christ the host cannot be seen by earthly eyes. Even in the church's liturgy only the priest is visible; Christ is present invisibly (and therefore cannot be represented).

The special character of this new iconography shows precisely in the fact that it hurdles the barrier between visible and invisible, time and eternity, symbol and reality, and gives expression to the mystically experienced unity of the two. And in fact the way in which the communion of the apostles is represented does not permit the question of difference to be raised; that is, the question of whether that which is represented is the ecclesial liturgy with its participation in eternal life through grace or, on the contrary, the heavenly reality itself that is being seen through the medium of the ecclesial liturgy. The two coincide, and since the heavenly event is experienced in all the details of the church's liturgy, everything in the Kiev picture of the communion of the apostles is shown with equal affection and in equal detail: the altar, the ripidia, the cross, the asterisk, the lance, and the sponge.

The parallels between such a mode of representation and the explanations of the liturgy are easy to see. Even in the age of iconoclasm there had arisen an extensive identification of sign and signified in ecclesial symbolism. This outlook showed in the fact that the knife could be called "lance," the bread, "Lamb," and, above all, the deacon, "angel."

Germanus, in particular, had cultivated this kind of language and had pushed the similarity between liturgy and heavenly event to the point that the predicates belonging to each could be interchanged. Thus, for example, in speaking of the symbolism of the resurrection he says: "The white-robed angel advances, rolls away the stone . . . and cries."[16] Elsewhere he says that during the anaphora the priest stands before the throne of God between two cherubs.[17] As the form of the liturgy came increasingly to be regarded as a picture of heavenly reality (just as the icon of Christ was regarded as a picture of Christ), it was inevitable that in time the heavenly liturgy should in turn be represented iconographically in the forms proper to the earthly liturgy.

This interpretation of the communion of the apostles is shown to be justified especially by subsequent representations of the theme and by the representations of the heavenly liturgy, which developed out of the communion of the apostles. In the early communion of the apostles at Kiev the ritual element is not yet heavily emphasized. True enough, the altar and all its furnishings are depicted in painstaking detail, but Christ himself does not yet appear in episcopal vestments, as he will later on.[18] His liturgical activity is in any case limited to the giving of the bread and the cup; correspondingly, the encounter with the Lord that is expressed in the picture is specifically that which occurs in the reception of communion during the liturgy. We can still perceive the reference back to the Supper and the connected indication that consecration and communion are of divine institution in greater degree than the rest of the liturgy. These two points are also made by placing the words of institution above the scene in capital letters.

At Ohrid, however, it is already clear that in such representations communion and the encounter with the Lord that occurs specifically therein need not be unconditionally emphasized. For at Ohrid

Christ stands at the center of the altar and holds in his left hand the still undivided consecrated bread; the large, round loaf-form of the bread is unique to this picture and was probably inspired by the dispute over unleavened bread that had just broken out. The Lord's right hand is raised in blessing (or in a rhetorical gesture). The apostles are shown in a posture of reverence; Peter, at their head, is even bending his knee.[19]

The Ohrid fresco shows a close resemblance to the illustration, described earlier,[20] for the prayer *Oudeis axios* in the liturgical scroll from the patriarchal library in Jerusalem. In the illustration, however, Christ holds in his left hand a scroll and not the consecrated bread, while an angelic deacon brings discos and chalice, thus showing the representation to be of the Great Entrance. If we imagine this scene to have no apostles but instead a still larger number of gift-bearing angels, we have the pattern for the representation of the heavenly liturgy, which extends the identification of earthly and heavenly liturgies to the Great Entrance and thus in principle to the church's liturgy in its entirety. In monumental painting this manner of depicting the heavenly liturgy prevails from the fourteenth century on.

Since the early examples of the heavenly liturgy in monumental painting also contain elements from the liturgy of the church Fathers, let me describe this latter pictorial type before dealing with the pictures of the heavenly liturgy in greater detail.

2. The Liturgy of the Church Fathers

The liturgy of the church Fathers is part of the fixed program in Late Byzantine church painting, where it occupies the lower region of the apse, beneath the communion of the apostles. Once again, the Sophia churches of Kiev and Ohrid provide good early examples of the type. The reader will recall the principle which we saw at work in Hosios Lukas: that the saints, bishops, and deacons are to be represented, as far as possible, in the sanctuary or close to it. In a clarification of this principle the Sophia church of Kiev depicts eight sainted bishops[21] near the windows of the apse; they wear liturgical vestments and, with the archdeacons Stephen and Lawrence, stand full-size, facing both the altar and the viewer. The picture at Ohrid is almost identical. In addition, this church has, on the side wall of the apse, a fresco unique in the monumental painting of the period. It depicts the Liturgy of St. Basil and makes it clear that the bishops represented in the sanctuary were now regarded as, so to speak, heavenly concelebrants in the church's liturgy. In keeping with this idea the pictures of bishops in the apse underwent gradual development during the next two centuries.

The fresco in the apse of the church of the Mother of God in the Serbian monastery at Studenica, founded by King Stephan Ne-manja, may serve as a representative example of the state of development at the end of the twelfth and beginning of the thirteenth centuries.[22] The bishops no longer gaze fixedly at the real altar of the church, but are turned instead to a central point in the curving apse, as though in place of a window there is an altar there at which they are concelebrating. In the window niche, half turned to the supposed altar, half to the concelebrating bishops, stand the archangels Michael and Gabriel; they are acting as heavenly deacons, for they are wearing liturgical vestments and with uplifted orarion are summoning the congregation to prayer. The bishops, meanwhile, are reading their silent prayers from scrolls. Basil and Chrysostom occupy the first places to the right and left of the altar. The texts in their scrolls are from the silent prayers at the Great Entrance ("No one is worthy") and the prayer at the prothesis ("God, our God").[23] Unfortunately, these prayers give us no information about the course of the liturgical celebration here represented, since they are rather attributes of these church Fathers.

A century before Studenica, a curious fresco in an apse at Boiana (Bulgaria) anticipates the further development of the liturgy of the church Fathers in a symbolic representation.[24] Here four bishops, Basil and Chrysostom first among them,[25] bow down before an altar on which stand a chalice and a discos. The altar itself has an unusual round shape, similar to that of the stone at the tomb of Christ as usually represented in the Easter picture of the myrhh-bearing women. Apparently the artist chose this way of signifying that the altar is the Lord's tomb. We are reminded at the same time of Germanus' method of interpretation, for in his explanation of the symbolism of the burial he likewise makes no distinction between the invisible symbolic content and the real ritual action, but says in this context: "The place where the spotless and holy body of the Lord is laid is the altar."[26]

At Boiana only the symbolism of the altar is illustrated directly. Later representations of the liturgy of the church Fathers, however, give visible form to the very sacrifice that is offered at the altar. Thus the frescoes in the monastery of Sopoćani, which were painted shortly after the middle of the thirteenth century and are regarded as the artistic high point of Serbian church painting, show, in the apse, ten celebrants who are depicted in the style of

106

Studenica and are gathered now at a painted altar beneath the window.[27] On the altar are chalice and discos. The sacrifice is depicted as in midcourse, for on the discos we see the sacrificial gift: Christ himself in the form of a small child who is covered with the veil over the discos.

Like the Saracen in the miracle reported by Gregory of Decapolis,[28] anyone contemplating this picture and at the same time spiritually experiencing the liturgy will see the child lying in the discos. The only difference is in the moment being depicted: in the story the time is that of the prothesis and the Great Entrance, whereas in the picture the bishops are shown in the act of concelebrating. As a fresco in an apse, this picture shows what is happening at the altar; more specifically, it shows Christ as sacrificial gift during the time from the epiclesis to the breaking of the bread. No particular moment in this part of the liturgy is singled out in the fresco at Sopoćani, whereas the fresco in the monastery of St. Nikita at Čučer probably refers to the epiclesis: Basil and Chrysostom hold their scrolls closed in their left hand, while with their right hand they bless the sacrificial gift, their fingers forming the monogram of Christ.[29]

The fresco in the apse of the royal church built at Studenica by King Miljutin helps us to a closer interpretation of the liturgy of the Fathers. In it we see an altar painted in the usual manner in a small niche between two tall episcopal figures; at the altar two angels in diaconal vestments reverently wave their fans over the child Jesus.[30] Above the altar are the words: "The Lamb of God is sacrificed and slain for the life of the whole world."

This inscription resembles rather closely the formula for the slaying of the Lamb at the prothesis[31] and is at the same time very like the formula for the breaking of the bread before communion.[32] In both rites the sacrificial gift called the "Lamb" is symbolically sacrificed and dissected: at the prothesis by having a deep cruciform incision made in it, and before communion by being broken,[33] first into four parts, and then into many parts depending on the number of communicants. In keeping with the inscription, the representation is given the name "Lamb" or also "Melismos" (= dissection, division).

Since "melismos" was originally the technical liturgical expression for the "fraction" or breaking of the bread before communion, a picture called "Melismos" should, of course, represent the sacrifice of the Lamb that is symbolized by the breaking of the bread. As a matter of fact, however, in the pictures thus far described what is represented is not the dividing of the bread but rather the state of the victim as established by the consecration, but prior to the fraction.

The actual act of dividing (melismos) the Lamb, in the form not of the fraction but of the symbolic slaying at the prothesis, is represented with almost repulsive vividness in the frescoes of the prothesis chamber in the Serbian churches of Ljuboten and Mateič (fourteenth century).[34] Here we see one of the two celebrants driving the lance into the side of the child on the discos, while the other blesses. The fact that the rite being depicted is the prothesis is made univocally clear by the use of the lance and by the place chosen for the picture, namely, the prothesis chamber. The two frescoes thus correspond exactly to the miracle story told by Gregory of Decapolis.

At this period the event recorded probably seemed miraculous less by reason of *what* was made visible to the Saracen, and indeed visible to his very senses, than by reason of the privilege being granted to a man who was not disposed for conversion. The general prevalence of the Hesychast ideal makes it difficult to doubt that at this period a sensible grasp of the sacramental and symbolic content of the liturgy was regarded as a mystical experience very worth striving for.[35] It is in this sense that Gregory Palamas is to be understood when, referring in his Easter sermon to the appearances of the risen Lord and to our own encounter with Christ in the liturgy, he says:

"The house of God in which we are is a real symbol of the tomb. . . . For behind the curtain there the house has an interior room in which the body of Christ is laid and which also contains the holy altar. . . . Those therefore who hasten to draw near to the divine mystery and the space containing it and who persevere to the end . . . will undoubtedly see the Lord himself with the eyes of their mind and even, I claim, with their bodily eyes. For anyone who gazes with faith on the mystical banquet and the bread of life that is given in it sees under the species the divine Word himself who became flesh for us and dwells in us as in a temple."[36]

In harmony with the usual explanation of the liturgy, Gregory sees this manifestation of the risen Lord to the bodily eye in communion as very closely connected with the liturgical burial after the Great Entrance. In this context he cites almost verbatim a characteristic passage from the commentary of Germanus.[37] But what holds

108

for the burial symbolism should also hold for the symbolism of the prothesis, since Nicholas and Theodore of Andida's informative interpretation of the latter had long since found a place in the interpolated and widely used versions of the commentaries of Germanus and Pseudo-Sophronius.[38] Anyone who takes this interpretation seriously will "with the eyes of the mind and even with bodily eyes" see on the table of preparation and later on the altar the bread that came down from heaven, and he will see it in the form it took in the manger at Bethlehem.

Since, according to the commentaries, the event of Bethlehem is accomplished first and foremost on the table of preparation, it is not surprising that in the pictorial decoration of the apse in the prothesis chamber, the iconography of this period should likewise depict the Lamb on the discos in the form of a little child. These representations of the Bethlehem symbolism (but without the sacrificial rites accompanying it in the prothesis frescoes at Ljuboten and Mateič) are found as frequently as the already described representations of the Lamb in the main apse. Moreover they completely resemble the latter, although, of course, without the large number of concelebrating bishops that is customary in the main apse. Usually, however, the two principal celebrants, Basil and Chrysostom, do appear in the prothesis chamber frescoes; ripidia-carrying angels are often shown as well,[39] although they are really appropriate only at the time of the anaphora. Conversely, the symbolism of the prothesis exercised an even greater influence on the frescoes of the main apse, in which the painted altar resembles a table of preparation. The prothesis symbolism, which evidently served as a model for this depiction of the altar, seems to have played a determining role in the whole iconography of the Lamb.

At the time when the prothesis was being developed, its symbolism was felt to be a pictorial imitation of the sacramental event that takes place in the anaphora.[40] It is typical of this new period, however, that subjective participation in the sacramental event should be determined by the intensity of the experience at the prothesis and the Great Entrance.[41]

The burial symbolism, which Gregory Palamas, following Germanus, emphasizes in his sermon and connects with the bodily vision of the Lord, likewise finds its iconographic representation in the picture known as the liturgy of the church Fathers. But this variant of the latter theme is by no means as frequent in church painting as the Lamb variant, even though the liturgical burial had been a favorite theme in liturgical interpretation ever since the time of

Theodore of Mopsuestia and, even more importantly, is clearly attested in the liturgical texts themselves.

We may regard the fresco in the exonarthex of the church of the Mother of God in Studenica as an early preliminary stage in the iconography both of the burial and of the sacrificial Lamb (and as, at the same time, a further development of the picture at Boiana).[42] In the Studenica fresco, Basil and Chrysostom stand at a baldacchino-covered altar that looks like something halfway between a table and a bier. Near the back edge of the altar is a discos with the round, sealed loaf of sacrificial bread and, to its right, a chalice. Christ lies outstretched on the altar, his loins covered with a black veil; he is in the form of an approximately twelve-year-old child. He is not a corpse, however, but (like the little child on the cradle-shaped discos in the picture of the Lamb) has raised himself up slightly; he looks out with wide open eyes and is giving a blessing with his right hand. Basil and Chrysostom, too, are making a gesture of blessing with their right hand; this is reminiscent of the epiclesis, as it is in the depiction of the Lamb at Čučer.

Three frescoes at Dečani show clearly the liturgy of the Fathers at the moment of the burial. Christ lies there dead, eyes closed, a bearded man who has died in his maturity; he wears a loincloth as in the usual representations of the cross and is stretched out on an altar that is covered with black. The fresco in the narthex is distinguished by showing a four-winged cherub over the altar[43] while the other two frescoes, which are located in side chapels and are like the first in all other respects, show angel-deacons with ripidia standing by the altar and facing the church Fathers.[44]

The representation in the prothesis chamber of the Rumanian church of St. Nicholas at Curtea de Argeş (ca.1340–1360) is an entirely independent conception. Christ lies on a bierlike altar, closely wrapped in graveclothes; the curtains of the baldacchino are drawn. Two angel-deacons stand at the altar with their ripidia, while to the side of them are throngs of angels in an attitude of mourning. Beneath the altar are two angels holding candlesticks with candles, while two others bring smoking censers. I. D. Ştefanescu, who gives a full description of this picture,[45] interprets the liturgical details (ripidia, drawn curtains, incense) as pointing clearly to occurrences during the anaphora.

The representations on the epitaphios are also to be interpreted as expressions of the eucharistic-liturgical symbolism of the burial and also as representing the commemoration of the burial on Good Friday. The epitaphios is an embroidered icon of the dead Lord or of his burial.[46] Nowadays it is seen chiefly when priests carry it in solemn procession at vespers on Good Friday as a way of representing the burial of Christ; it is subsequently deposited in a place that has been prepared for it in the middle of the church and is known as Golgotha or the Holy Sepulcher.[47] But originally in the fourteenth century, the epitaphios also served as an aer and was carried during the Great Entrance.[48] The same symbolism also finds expression today in the pictorial decoration of the antimension. The well-known fourteenth-century epitaphios from Salonica, now in the Byzantine Museum at Athens,[49] brings out in a striking way the eucharistic reference of the burial symbolism, for to the left and right of the burial are the two scenes making up the communion of the apostles.

3. The Heavenly Liturgy
In the iconographic development of the communion of the apostles and the liturgy of the church Fathers, we saw the number of angels steadily increasing. This is indicative of a tendency in the treatment of these themes to regard the Supper, the incarnation, the sacrifice, and the burial less and less as the historical events which had originally been cosignified in the measure possible to liturgical representation, and increasingly as eternally present heavenly realities. It was in this context that the picture of the heavenly liturgy was developed, with artists using for the purpose representational elements from the other liturgical themes. It was not accidental that the heavenly liturgy, inspired as it was by the Cherubikon, should be represented as taking the form of a Great Entrance; the result was to confirm iconographically that the Great Entrance was indeed the focal point of liturgical symbolism.

In the course of the fourteenth century it became practically obligatory to depict this theme somewhere in the church building. The dome was regarded as a suitable location for it or, secondarily, the sanctuary or the prothesis as the place where the Great Entrance starts in the liturgy.[50]

As the miniature, described earlier, in the eleventh-century liturgical scroll showed, it was possible for the pictorial type known as the heavenly liturgy to emerge from the further development of the communion of the apostles. But early examples of the heavenly liturgy in Serbian monastic churches show that the representations of the angels in the dome and the pictures of the liturgy of the Fathers played an even greater part in the development of this theme.

The painting in the dome of the Serbian monastery of Chilandri on Athos[51] shows a circle of Cherubim and Seraphim surrounding the Pantocrator. Beneath is a second circle of angels in the vestments of deacons and priests. They are carrying candlesticks, ripidia, and altar vessels, and are proceeding from an altar depicted on the western side of the dome (probably the table of preparation) to a similar altar on the eastern side. There is no other representation of Christ in addition to the Pantocrator at the top of the dome, and consequently the procession of angels as well as the choir of Cherubim and Seraphim above it are seen to be in the service of the Pantocrator. This representation of the heavenly liturgy differs, therefore, from the Middle Byzantine program of dome painting only insofar as the angels who serve the Pantocrator are wearing liturgical vestments, carrying liturgical furnishings, and facing a heavenly altar.[52] At the same time, however, this small superficial alteration betrays the Late Byzantine tendency whereby pictorial themes that are based on the Bible and salvation history (for example, the pictures of angels seen in prophetic visions or in the story of the Ascension) are modified into timeless symbolic representations in liturgical form.

The liturgy of the church Fathers, which gives special place to those bishops who in their lifetime were particularly active in matters liturgical, initially had a historical point of reference. The addition of angelic assistants, however, gave the theme an increasingly timeless dimension, and we even find it now and then completely absorbed into the theme of the Heavenly Liturgy. Thus, for example, in the apse (painted c. 1370) of the monastery of St. Mark in Skoplje, we see Christ as celebrant at the altar and an entrance procession that includes church Fathers as well as angels. In this procession Basil and Chrysostom carry chalices, and two other bishops carry the cross and the book of gospels.[53]

In the Church of Our Lady (painted c. 1330) at Péc in the Serbian patriarchate, the heavenly liturgy, which directly surrounds the Pantocrator in the dome,[54] does not display the episcopal celebrants from the liturgy of the Fathers, but it does include their sacrificial victim, the Lamb, as one element in the representation. On the eastern side of the fresco, directly beneath the huge book of gospels that the Pantocrator holds in his left hand, we see the table of preparation, on which, as in the liturgy of the church Fathers, the child Jesus lies, in this case under a large asterisk. The baldacchino-covered altar is depicted opposite, on the western side of the dome. Behind the table of preparation a cherub stands guard. At both sides of the table, hosts of angels, instead of liturgical celebrants,

112

bow in reverence; they are dressed in the robes worn by archangels in Middle Byzantine painting. The sacred gifts are thus thought of as still on the table of preparation at this moment of the Great Entrance; meanwhile the first of the ripidia-carrying angelic celebrants has already reached the main altar. Since the Pantocrator is present and illuminating the procession, there is no representation of Christ as celebrant at the altar; as sacrificial victim he appears on the table of preparation in the manner described.

The two aspects of Christ as *prospherôn* (offering) and *prospheromenos* (being offered) (to use the language of the prayer *Oudeis axios* before the Great Entrance) find expression in the so-called Paten of Xeropotamou.[55] At an altar (which we must imagine as matched by a table of preparation) Christ is twice represented as high priest in episcopal vestments: to the left of the altar, as he sends the procession on its way, and to the right as he welcomes the leader of the procession. The representation thus corresponds exactly to the actual course of the Great Entrance, for after the bishop, the principal celebrant, has given the sacred gifts and the vessels on the table of preparation to his fellow celebrants, he does not himself take part in the procession, but stands at the royal doors, in front of the altar, and waits for it there. In this picture, then, the head of the procession has already reached Christ. First come the angels with candlesticks, incense, and ripidia, then angelic deacons and priests with discos and chalices. The next-to-last angel carries in his hands the episcopal omophorion,[56] and the last angel carries on his back the great veil known as the aer.

As *prospheromenos* Christ appears as he does in the liturgy of the church Fathers and specifically in representations of the liturgical burial; he is not wearing a loincloth, however, but is covered with a small veil. The picture thus incorporates the burial symbolism into the performance of the Great Entrance itself. As a matter of fact the same thing actually takes place in the liturgy as a result of carrying the epitaphios in the procession.

In pictures of the Heavenly Liturgy the epitaphios is sometimes huge in size. On the Paten of Xeropotamou it is indeed only the size of the Latin shoulder-veil used in blessings with the eucharist, and it is carried on the back of but a single angel. But the very beautiful and early picture of the heavenly liturgy in the prothesis chamber of the Peribleptos church at Mistra already shows an epitaphios that is carried by three or four angels,[57] while in the Sophia church at Mistra four angels are likewise shown carrying the epitaphios.[58]

This expansion of the Great Entrance directly corresponds to the symbolism attested by Germanus when he has the angels sing the Alleluia of the Cherubikon, "because they see Christ's victory over death, his descent into the underworld, and his resurrection on the third day."[59] Above all, the carrying of the epitaphios at the Great Entrance makes it possible to turn the immediately following veiling of the gifts into a real picture of the burial and then, later on, to proclaim the subsequent resurrection of the Lord by the removal of the veil and its display by the deacon in the ambo.

B. THE LITURGICAL COMMENTARIES

This era possessed in Nicholas Cabasilas and Symeon of Thessalonica the two most important Byzantine commentators on the liturgy.

Nicholas was connected closely with the most influential ecclesiastical circles in the empire, but he himself in all likelihood never held an office in the church. His uncle, Nilus Cabasilas, a respected theologian and teacher in the capital, saw to Nicholas' education. Uncle and nephew enjoyed a close relationship with Emperor John Cantacuzenus (1347–1354). Toward the end of his life Nilus became metropolitan (probably in 1361) of his native city, Thessalonica; he died in 1363. This is also the last year for which we have sure information regarding Nicholas.

The first certain information on Symeon as metropolitan concerns the year 1425; he died in 1429. His writings display in a quite special manner the stamp of their time of origin, for theological polemics, along with canonical and narrowly rubrical considerations, occupy a large place in them. I shall first discuss the liturgical writings of Symeon as being an instructive witness to the liturgical forms and liturgical interpretation of that period. I shall then close with an appreciation of the theologically more profound work of Cabasilas, which provides the occasion for some basic reflections on Byzantine interpretation of the liturgy.

1. Symeon of Thessalonica: The Collection
and Canonization of Symbolic Interpretative Motifs

Just as Philotheus' codification of the rubrics more or less marks the end of liturgical development and the canonization of the forms developed up to that time, so the writings of Symeon of Thessalonica represent the canonization of liturgical interpretation in the manner of Germanus and the Andidans, which had by now become customary in Byzantium. The inculcation of this tradition is the purpose both of the metropolitan's principal work, a kind of manual

114

for the clergy,[1] in which chapters 79–100 on the eucharist[2] are of concern to us here, and of a separate work entitled *Explanation of the House of God, of the Functions Exercised Therein by Priests, Deacons, and Bishops, of the Sacred Vestments Which Each of Them Wears, and of the Sacred Mystagogy, with the Reason for Each of Its Divinely Accomplished Rites.*[3]

The first of these two works is in the form of a dialogue in which a cleric asks brief, modest questions, and a bishop gives detailed and authoritative answers. Dionysius, regarded as a disciple of the apostles, is repeatedly cited as the most important witness to tradition.[4]

The second work, which I shall discuss first, is a kind of catechism containing over 100 short questions and answers[5] that deal with all aspects of the themes listed in the title. Symeon's intention is simply to let the tradition speak. He states explicitly that he has taken his explanations from the writings of the holy Fathers, "not adding anything new to what they have handed on, and not changing this tradition in any way but preserving it undistorted as we do the holy profession of faith."[6] The liturgy is celebrated as it was instituted by Christ, with bishops and priests concelebrating or priests alone concelebrating with one another.[7] This fact is attested by Dionysius, the "disciple of the apostles," as well as by the holy Fathers Basil and Chrysostom, "proclaimers of God," whose instructions and prayers teach us how the Church practices "the first and second entrances and the other parts of the sacred celebration."[8]

Other witnesses to the prevailing tradition are Gregory the Great,[9] Isidore of Pelusium,[10] and, above all, Maximus, "who carefully explains the whole mystery of the sacred liturgy which the Church celebrates."[11] Germanus is not expressly named, although the author makes extensive use of him. It is probably that Symeon knew Germanus' *History of the Church* as the work of Basil. Of course, Symeon makes use of many interpretative motifs that are familiar to him as "tradition" but that in fact have no connection with the authorities he cites; he even regards the order of the liturgy as apostolic. Nonetheless his appeal to Isidore of Pelusium, Dionysius, and Maximus is to be taken as representing a real literary dependence.

We are reminded of Maximus at the very beginning of the explanation of the church, where the division of the latter into two parts (sanctuary and nave) symbolizes the two natures in Christ as well as body and soul in the human person. Nonetheless it is also possible to regard the church as divided into three parts, as a sign of the Most Holy Trinity: sanctuary, nave, and narthex; these signify respectively the supracelestial world of God, the heavens, and the earth.[12]

The altar is the throne of God and the tomb of Christ[13]; the incense is the fragrance of the grace of the Holy Spirit[14]; the ambo is the stone that was rolled away from the tomb,[15] for the "early morning" gospels (Eôthina[16]) are proclaimed from the ambo by the deacon in the liturgy and by the priest in orthros. In all this it is Germanus who is speaking, as he does so often in Symeon.

As often as priests, deacons, and even the faithful sing the sacred hymns, they represent the various orders of angels.[17] On the other hand, only the celebrants who may enter into the sacred sanctuary represent the heavenly powers by their actions.[18] The bishop for his part is an image of Christ.[19] His likeness to Christ is already evident from the mandyas, the copelike mantle that the bishop wears as he enters the church. As a sign of the bishop's teaching authority, the mandyas has wavelike stripes (potamoi, "rivers"), which start from two squares (pômata) representing the Old and New Testaments.[20]

Symeon gives a detailed description and explanation of all the vestments and cites the prayers, still customary today, that are to be used at the donning of each vestment. These prayers are among the last ones added to the order of the liturgy. The deacon has two vestments, the sticharion and the orarion. The brightly colored sticharion shows his similarity to the angels, while the orarion symbolizes wings by reason of its choice material and the way in which its two ends hang from the shoulders.[21] It is for this reason that the triple Hagios (Holy) is embroidered on the orarion.

A priest wears five vestments: sticharion, epitrachelion, girdle, epimanikia, and phelonion.[22] A bishop has seven vestments, however, comparable to the seven gifts of the Holy Spirit.[23] In addition to the priestly vestments he wears the epigonation and the omophorion. The epigonation hangs like a sword from the priestly girdle; this last already symbolizes virtue and strength,[24] and the epigonation heightens the symbolism, because it signifies the strength of Christ and his victory over the power of the evil enemy.[25] But it is the omophorion more than anything else that shows the bishop to be an image of Christ. It is made of wool and represents the strayed sheep, our human nature, which the Logos took upon himself in the incarnation.[26]

Symeon turns next to the explanation of the liturgical action itself:

"The bishop, when about to celebrate the sacred liturgy, descends from this throne, thus manifesting the descent of the divine Logos to us. Robed in the sacred vestments, he symbolizes the incarnation. The fact that he comes from his throne as far as the doors of the church represents the coming of the Lord to earth and his visible life among us until his death and his descent to the underworld. This last is symbolized by the bishop's progress westward to the doors. Once the liturgy has begun at a sign from the bishop (for without the bishop nothing can be undertaken), the priests within [in the sanctuary] pronounce the prayers, thus symbolizing the angelic orders in heaven."[27]

"Once the bishop has finished praying outside [i.e., outside of the sanctuary], he remains there. The deacons assist him, thus representing not only the apostles but also the angels who served the Lord in his saving actions. The descent of the priests after finishing their prayers within proclaims the descent of the divine angels for the resurrection and ascension. The bishop then prays together with the priests that the angels may enter in with them and join in celebrating the liturgy. By the bowing and raising of his head the bishop makes the resurrection visible to all. The deacon does the same when he elevates the book of the gospels . . . and cries aloud: "Wisdom! Stand erect!" . . . The words, "Come, let us adore the Lord!," sung in a clear voice, and the acclamation that follows also symbolize the resurrection and the ascension of the redeemer.[28]

"But the bishop also images forth the risen Lord who has been taken up into heaven. That is why I said that the entire nave of the church is an image of earth, while the holy bema is an image of heaven."[29]

The voice behind this explanation is evidently that of Maximus in his *Mystagogy*. The fact that in the fourteenth century (unlike the seventh) an entire section of liturgy now intervened between the first entrance of the bishop into the church and the Little Entrance into the sanctuary is very useful to Symeon, because it makes possible a better development of Maximus' symbolism of the incarnation as ordered to the ascension. Since, moreover, the bishop does not enter the church through the main door together with the faithful (as he did in the time of Maximus) but comes from the sanctuary, Symeon has an opportunity to concretize the interpretative motifs of Maximus by making the bishop's entrance a symbol not only of the Logos' coming to earth but also of his descent from heaven.

On the other hand, given this interpretation, it is now more difficult to take account of the prothesis as well and to combine its symbolism of the gifts with the previously indicated symbolic references to persons that is found in the *Mystagogy* of Maximus. In this work Symeon simply omits the prothesis just as Dionysius in his time had omitted an interpretation of the transfer of the gifts because the bishop played no part in it. Only at the conclusion of the work, in connection with the distribution of the antidoron, does Symeon say, seemingly to excuse himself, that he had intended to explain the prothesis as well, but the Fathers, to whom he owes his entire explanation, had done this in such detail that it did not seem he should repeat it.[30]

In the remainder of the explanation Symeon likewise follows Maximus closely. Thus the readings symbolize the preaching of the apostles after the Lord's ascension, and the gospel prepares the way for the parousia that will occur when the Good News has been proclaimed to the whole world. At the end the Lord will send his angels to separate the wicked from the good. The church already effects this separation when by means of the deacon's summons she separates the faithful from the catechumens. Under the term "catechumens" Symeon includes not only the unbaptized but also those who had committed some serious crime and in the early church would have been excommunicated.[31]

"The transfer and entrance of the venerable gifts is marked by splendor . . . and renders visible the return of Christ when he shall come in glory. For this reason the pallium embroidered with the cross also comes at the head of the procession, just as the sign of Jesus will appear in heaven and Jesus will reveal himself. Next come the deacons who take the place of the angels. Then come those who carry the sacred gifts, and after them everyone else, including those who carry the holy veil above their heads, thus symbolizing the naked and dead Christ."[32]

Thus the Great Entrance symbolizes the coming of the reign of God:

"The kingdom of God is Christ himself and the vision of his work of salvation in which he humbled himself to the point of accepting death; he sacrificed himself and allowed his sacrificed, lifegiving and divine body to be seen with its wounds. Having become immortal, he also ensured our victory over death by offering us im-

118

mortality, life, and divinization from his wounds . . . and giving himself to us as the bread of life. . . . For this reason the Great Entrance symbolizes both the parousia of the Redeemer and his burial."[33]

In the essential features of his explanation Symeon thus repeatedly follows the *Mystagogy* of Maximus, but he also inserts the very concrete interpretative motifs of Germanus. As in Maximus' explanation of the Great Entrance, so here the historical work of salvation is to be seen from a heavenly vantage-point in its supratemporal and eternal existence. It was, however, much easier for Maximus to take this approach, since he saw the correspondence between, on the one hand, the liturgical event with its basis in the history of salvation and, on the other, eternal life, as consisting much more in the interior grace of redemption within believers than in the concrete symbolism of the liturgy. For that matter, out of all the rites in the liturgy between the Great Entrance and communion Maximus offered an explanation only of the kiss of peace, the profession of faith, the Thrice Holy, and the Our Father.

When Symeon now inserts into the external framework of Maximus' explanation all the concrete pictorial symbolisms developed by Germanus and Theodore of Andida, he bursts the framework apart. In the final analysis he retains only Germanus and Theodore, whose identification of symbol and reality now reappears in an even more extreme form; at the same time he includes the heavenly reality at every point in the course of the liturgy. Symeon's explanation is the first complete literary counterpart to the iconography of the heavenly liturgy. In fact, the two appear at almost exactly the same historical moment.

Symeon continues his explanation by justifying the manifestations of respect by the people at the Great Entrance. These are given, first, because of the intercessions of the priests at the sacrifice, but secondly also out of reverence, this being due to the gifts as images of the body and blood of Christ. Those who refuse this reverence or speak of the gifts as "idols" are worse than the iconoclasts. "For if we show reverence (*timê kai proskynêsis*) to sacred images, how much more should we show it to the gifts, which, as Basil the Great says, are images and sacrificial gifts which are destined to become the body and blood of Christ."[34] They undergo this change at the epiclesis: "The bishop calls down the grace of the Holy Spirit on himself and on the gifts being offered, in which, once they have been made perfect by the sign of the cross and the invocation of the Spirit, he immediately see Jesus lying alive before him."[35]

In his explanation of the elevation, division of the bread, and commingling of the elements, Symeon follows the Andidans:

"The elevation of the bread manifests the raising of Jesus on the cross. . . . The bishop now divides the bread into four parts, arranges these in the form of a cross, and sees in them the crucified Jesus. . . . He then takes the upper part, makes a sign of the cross with it, places it in the chalice, and thus accomplishes the unification of the mysteries. . . . He next pours warm water into the chalice. He does this to attest that the body of the Lord, even when dead and separated from the divine soul, remains lifegiving, not deprived of its divinity, and not separated from the efficacy of the Spirit."[36]

As in Nicholas and Theodore, the transfer of the gifts to the table of preparation after the communion of the faithful symbolizes the ascension. This explanation had meanwhile became part of the liturgical text itself, which Symeon quotes exactly: "Exalt yourself above the heavens, O God, and let your glory fill the earth."[37]

Symeon gives a detailed explanation of the prothesis in his other work, the manual for the clergy. In fact, it accounts for approximately half of the entire explanation of the liturgy in this book, although the longest sections are devoted to the question of unleavened bread and the controversies with the Armenians. The prothesis is accomplished by the highest in rank of the priests concelebrating with the bishop, for it is the task of this priest "to perform the introductory part of the sacred sacrificial action." In doing this and in speaking the words of Isaiah and the other prophets about the sacrificial death of Christ, he himself resembles the prophets and in particular the Precursor of the Lord.[38]

The prothesis contains a multiplicity of symbolisms. The discos represents the heavens, "for it is round and receives the Lord of heaven." The asterisk symbolizes the stars and in particular the star of Bethlehem. The veils signify the firmament, but also the swaddling clothes and the graveclothes. The table of preparation symbolizes the cave of Bethlehem and the manger.[39]

The priest performs the rites of the prothesis after he has received the blessing of the bishop and has donned the sacred vestments (in the same order as is customary today). When he makes the cruciform incision in the seal, "he announces the crucifixion of

Christ." "And by accomplishing the commemoration as Christ commanded he images forth what Christ suffered for us."[40]

Since the sacrificial bread is a symbol of Christ, it must contain yeast, which symbolizes his soul, water, which signifies his baptism, and salt, which signifies the teaching of the Logos. The chalice, for its part, must contain wine and water in accordance with the words spoken as these are poured in.[41]

Symeon then enumerates the particles that are removed from the remaining prosphoras with the lance and are placed next to the seal on the discos. The first particle is offered "to honor and commemorate" the Mother of God. As the seal is an image of the body of Christ, so the first particle stands "in place of" the Mother of God and has its place on the discos in accordance with the words of the psalm: "The queen stands at your right hand . . ." (Ps 44:10).[42] A particle must also be offered for the angels "because they assisted in the work of salvation and were united with us and because together we form one Church."[43] Then come the particles for the Precursor, the prophets, the apostles, and the other saints

"because the saints too take part in this awesome mystery as cooperators of Christ. . . . These particles, however, are not changed into the body of Christ or into the saints themselves, but are only sacrificial gifts . . . which in the course of the sacred action are sanctified through union and communion with the Lord and allow a healing power to pass to those for whom they are offered and, through the saints, into us."[44]

Finally, the priest offers other particles for the bishops, the clergy, the ruler, the founders of the church, the community, those who have died in Christ, and every Christian soul of good will.

"The particles offered for the saints are thus offered for their glory and honor, for the increase of their dignity (!), and for a great acceptance of divine enlightenment; the particles for the faithful and specifically for the deceased, are offered for the forgiveness of their sins and for their union with divine grace. Those offered for the living, assuming that these live their lives in a spirit of repentance, will be advantageous for the remission of punishments, the forgiveness of sins, and the hope of everlasting life."[45]

While it is beneficial to offer particles for those who are worthy, it is dangerous and harmful to offer them for the unworthy. For if such particles come in contact with the body of the Lord and are taken from the chalice in drinking the sacred blood,[46] they become a source of condemnation, comparable to an unworthy communion. The priest for his part must avoid playing a part in this condemnation and possibly being condemned himself.

At communion the priest must be careful to give the faithful a share not simply of the particles but of the body of the Lord. For although everything in the chalice is soaked in the sacred blood and thus the latter is received in receiving a particle, it is nonetheless prescribed that each believer receive both the body and the blood of the Lord.[47]

When the offering of the particles is finished, the priest puts incense in the censer and incenses the star (asterisk). He then places the latter on the discos with the words: "And behold, the star came and remained over the place where the child was," "thus showing in a symbolic way what had happened at the birth."[48] "Then he takes the veil, which together with the other veils signifies the swaddling clothes, and says the words of the psalm: 'The Lord is king . . .' (Ps 92), which announce the incarnation."[49] Then he covers the discos and the chalice.

"Finally, having incensed, he places over discos and chalice the aer, which symbolizes both the firmament in which the star shone, and the gravecloth. For this reason the aer goes several times around the anointed, dead Jesus, and is called an epitaphios. As clearly as though written on a tablet it teaches the whole mystery: that the Lord was announced as Lamb by the prophets; that he came from heaven and was born, according to the flesh, in a cave and a manger. Moreover the mysteries of the passion are also symbolized even at his birth. For the star which stood over him made him known to the wise men. But Herod then persecuted him, and Simeon took him in his arms and proclaimed him to be the sign that would be contradicted. . . . This is why the circumstances of the passion are also shown in this manner."[50]

The priest recites the prayer of oblation and

"tracing the form of a cross, incenses the gifts, the altar, the sanctuary, and the priestly ministers. We know of some who even incense the entire church and the congregation, in keeping with what Saint Dionysius says: that before the liturgy the whole church is incensed beginning from the sanctuary and ending at the altar again."[51]

With regard to the order of the prothesis, Symeon says finally that all the priests and deacons offer particles. The deacons may not do this independently, however, but only through the mediation of a priest,[52] since the offering of particles is a priestly sacrificial action; this is a principle that unfortunately is not heeded in many places, including even Athos.

As this last precept shows, Symeon is very much concerned that at every point a hierarchic order should be observed among the celebrants. The principle comes from Dionysius, who is constantly appealed to as a source. The influence of the Areopagite is much more visible in this work than in the one discussed earlier. For the entire discussion of the sacraments that makes up the second part of his manual, Symeon has evidently chosen as his model the Areopagite's *Ecclesiastical Hierarchy*, which is similar in its conception.

In keeping with the emphasis on hierarchic order, Symeon also gives in this work precise details on the rules for concelebration. The bishop is the head of the group of concelebrating priests, as Christ is head of the apostles.[53] The bishop's blessing is requested by the others before they don the sacred vestments[54] and before each incensation.[55] He alone of the celebrants is incensed first and last on each occasion.[56] His signal marks the beginning of the liturgy,[57] the whole course of which is governed by the principle: "Apart from me you can do nothing."[58]

But the priests in their own rank are also fully active. They perform the sacrificial rites of the prothesis[59]; like the bishops they may sit on priestly thrones during the readings[60]; they place the sacred vessels on the altar. All of these are acts forbidden to deacons. The priests offer the same prayers as the bishop,[61] although they need not actually say them since the bishop says them aloud in the name of all.[62] As true priestly concelebrants they stand with the bishop at the altar during the anaphora, although their subordination to the bishop is always respected. For this reason Symeon says:

"The first bishop (*archhiereus*) approaches the altar, touches it, and offers the mysterious sacrifice, in which he represents him who was sacrificed for us; the others take part in it through him as a mediator. Therefore unlike the first bishop the other bishops (*episkopoi*) and priests in the sanctuary do not draw near to the altar when they are concelebrants (*sylleitourgoi*). The other ordained ministers have a still lesser rank[63] and may not say the same words[64]; they also come last to holy communion, along with the deacons."[65]

In connection with communion Symeon says: "The bishop alone communicates first and directly, just as among the archangels the first have the first share, and through them those of middle rank, and through these in turn the rest, as Dionysius says. Thus the bishops and the priests receive from the bishop, and through the priests the other priests and deacons."[66] The subdeacons, lectors, monks, and people communicate outside the sanctuary.

The abundance of interpretative motifs used by Symeon, as well as the variety and multiplicity of his sources, shows that the writer has been extremely faithful to the tradition as known to him and has in fact brought together everything that might help explain the liturgy. Down to the present time, therefore, the liturgical writings of Symeon have been respected, passed on, and copied repeatedly as being a compendium of liturgical interpretation and an inventory of all the interpretative motifs approved by the church. But while Symeon was indebted to the traditional explanation of the liturgy, especially since Germanus, and while there can be no doubt of his subjective fidelity to the entire ecclesial tradition, even the oldest, it is a fact that his age had little real knowledge of the ancient history of the liturgy. According to Symeon's own principles his reflections have such value as tradition gives them. But the traditions upon which he draws for his explanation differ in age, dissemination, and objective validity. The very fact that he tries to do justice to them all in the same degree makes large sections of his explanation both ambiguous and confusing.

2. Nicholas Cabasilas: Concentration on the Essential

A Commentary on the Divine Liturgy by Nicholas Cabasilas occupies a special place among the explanations of the liturgy after Germanus.[67] It is an intellectually independent and carefully developed work that constantly relates the meaning of the many liturgical symbolisms to the sacramental event proper of the eucharistic celebration; in addition, this sacrament is given a comprehensive dogmatic treatment.

As a treatise on the sacrifice of the mass Cabasilas' work has always been of great interest to western theologians.[68] At the Council of Trent it was cited as a valuable witness to ecclesial tradition. Cervini, one of the theologians of the Council, commissioned a translation of it and thus allowed it to become more widely known.[69]

And yet as an explanation of the Byzantine liturgy and especially in terms of its place among the other commentaries, the work has thus far received little attention beyond occasional references and citations.[70] Nonetheless a comparison with Germanus, the Andidans, and, above all, Symeon will be of interest from the standpoint of liturgical history.

The opening sentences of the work already give evidence of an unusual, almost scholastic, conceptual clarity:

"The essential act in the celebration of the holy mysteries is the transformation (metabolê) of the elements into the Divine Body and Blood; its aim is the sanctification of the faithful, who through these mysteries receive the remission of their sins and the inheritance of the kingdom of heaven. As a preparation for, and contribution to, this act and this purpose we have prayers, psalms, and readings from Holy Scripture; in short, all the sacred acts and forms which are said and done before and after the consecration of the elements. While it is true that God freely gives us all holy things and that we bring him nothing, but that they are absolute graces, he does nevertheless necessarily require that we should be fit to receive and to preserve them."[71]

This santification comes about in two ways. First, the prayers, psalms, readings from scripture, and actions of the liturgy raise us up to God. But

"there is another way in which these forms, like all the ceremonies of the Holy Sacrifice, sanctify us. It consists in this: that in them Christ and the deeds he accomplished and the sufferings he endured for our sakes are represented. Indeed, it is the whole scheme of the work of redemption which is signified in the psalms and readings, as in all the actions of the priest throughout the liturgy; the first ceremonies of the service represent the beginning of this work; the next, the sequel; and the last, its results. Thus, those who are present at these ceremonies have before their eyes all these divine things. The consecration of the elements—the sacrifice itself—commemorates the death, resurrection, and ascension of the Savior, since it transforms these precious gifts into the very Body of the Lord, that Body which was the central figure in all these mysteries, which was crucified, which rose from the dead, which ascended into heaven. The ceremonies which precede the act of sacrifice symbolize the events which occurred before the death of Christ: his coming on earth, his first appearance and his perfect manifestation. Those which follow the act of sacrifice recall the 'promise of the Father,' as the Saviour himself called it: that is, the descent of the Holy Spirit upon the apostles, the conversion of the nations which they brought about, and their divine society. The whole celebration of the mystery is like a unique portrayal of a single body, which is the work of the Savior."[72]

This introduction already makes quite clear what it is that Nicholas has in common with the traditional explanation of the liturgy and what it is that distinguishes him from this tradition. He retains the idea, current since Theodore of Mopsuestia, that the several parts of the liturgy symbolize the parts of the life of Jesus. This idea had meanwhile left a decisive mark on the liturgy itself, so that now no commentator on the Byzantine liturgy could ignore it. In adopting this approach Nicholas regards it as important that events follow the same sequence in the life of Jesus and in the liturgy. This emphasis links him with Theodore of Mopsuestia (although the latter was satisfied to see in the liturgy a depiction of the life of Jesus from the beginning of the passion to the appearances of the risen Lord), but especially with the Andidans. Maximus and Germanus had seen the symbolic reference to the life of Jesus as operative only in certain sections of the liturgy, while Symeon follows the temporal sequence less exactly. Nicholas' description of the liturgy as a portrayal of the work of the Savior is also reminiscent of the Andidans.[73]

And yet the very comparison with the Andidans shows Cabasilas' independence. His explanation is limited deliberately to the work of redemption, while, contrary to the Andidans, any symbolization of the great deeds and miracles is expressly excluded. Thus, in explaining the beginning of the prothesis, Cabasilas says that when the priest makes a cruciform incision in the sacrificial bread with the lance and speaks the words: "In commemoration of our Lord and God and Savior Jesus Christ," his words refer not only to the bread but to the entire celebration, in accordance with the Lord's command at the institution. Cabasilas then asks which actions of Christ are to be commemorated.

"That he raised the dead, that he gave sight to the blind, that he ruled the tempests, that he fed thousands with a few loaves, thus showing himself to be God Almighty? By no means. Rather, we must remember those events which seem to denote nothing but weakness: his Cross, his Passion, his Death—these are the happenings which he asks us to commemorate."[74]

That is how Paul understood the command. And when the Lord said at the Supper: "This is my body," he did not add "which worked miracles," but rather "which will be broken for you," and at the blood: "which will be shed for you." For it is suffering and death that effect our redemption, and without them a human being cannot reach the resurrection. The miracles, on the other hand, were performed in order to arouse faith.

For Nicholas, then, the liturgical symbolization of the life of Jesus clearly reaches its climax in the sacramental anamnesis of Christ's death at the consecration. The special position of the sacrifice proper, which Nicholas emphasized in the very first sentence of his commentary, is never lost sight of for a moment. It is precisely this unambiguous theological emphasis that is missing in the other liturgical commentaries since Germanus. In fact, the Andidans reduced the importance of the anaphora to a dangerous degree, while none of the commentaries attempted to highlight the difference between a properly sacramental and a merely symbolic rendering present of the mystery. The symbolism of the prothesis and the Great Entrance had frequently been presented in so realistic a manner, that it was hardly possible for any symbolism to have a more profound impact in the anaphora.

Nicholas brings theological clarity in this area. For while he allows the symbolism of the prothesis and the Great Entrance to have its just place, at the same time he makes this uncompromising remark in connection with the prothesis.

"As long as it remains in the *prothesis* the bread thus separated from the rest is still only bread. But it has acquired a new characteristic—it is dedicated to God; it has become an offering, since it represents our Lord during the first phase of his life on earth, when he became an oblation. Now this happened at the moment of his birth."[75]

And, correspondingly, at the Great Entrance: "If any . . . adores them [the gifts] as if they were the Body and Blood of Christ, and prays to them as such . . . he is confusing this ceremony with that of 'the entry of the presanctified,' not recognizing the differences between them."[76]

The quality that most distinguishes Nicholas' commentary from the traditional explanations of the liturgy, however, is his respect for the original structures of the liturgy and for the natural meaning of the individual texts and actions. In his introduction, as we saw, he insists that the prayers, psalms, and readings should first of all (in keeping with their literal meaning) convert us to God. Only secondarily do they also remind us of Christ. The relation of natural to higher meaning is explained in connection with the vestments: the natural meaning or function of garments is to clothe the body; to the extent that there are differences among garments, they indicate the profession, rank, and dignity of those who wear them.[77]

The same holds for the liturgical actions. These are performed because of a present need, but then also to symbolize actions of Christ:

"For example, we have the bringing of the Gospel to the altar, then the bringing of the offerings. Each is done for a purpose, the one that the Gospel may be read, the other that the sacrifice may be performed; besides this, however, one represents the appearance and the other the manifestation of the Saviour; the first, obscure and imperfect, at the beginning of his life [at his baptism]; the second, the perfect and supreme manifestation [at the entry into Jerusalem]. There are even certain ceremonies which fulfil no practical purpose, but have only a figurative meaning; such as the action of piercing the Host, and tracing thereon the pattern of a cross, or again the fact that the metal instrument used for this perforation is shaped like a lance; there is also the ceremony which takes place near the end, of mixing a little warm water with the wine."[78]

Nicholas goes on to apply this principle in explaining the individual parts of the liturgy. The prothesis has for its purpose to prepare and dedicate the gifts. Bread and wine are the first fruits of human toil. They signify the life they nourish, and the surrender of them to God signifies the surrender of our own lives.[79] In relation to Christ they symbolize his sacrifice of himself that began at his birth and was completed by his death on the cross. That is why the seal is cut out of the sacrificial loaf: because Christ separated himself from the midst of the human throng and dedicated himself to God.[80] So too the Lord's death is, as it were, already inscribed in the bread in anticipation of the anamnesis of his death at the consecration.[81] The gifts are covered because the life of the Lord remains hidden until his baptism.[82]

The explanation of the enarxis with its ektenes and antiphons is primarily a treatise on prayer. At the same time, however, in accordance with their meaning as signs, the antiphons are shown to be prophecies of the birth and hidden life of the Lord.

The Little Entrance introduces the liturgy of the word. The book of the gospels, which is raised on high and visible to all, signifies the Lord who from this point on will reveal himself in his word.

"What do the readings from Holy Scripture at this point in the liturgy signify? I have already told you their practical purpose; they

128

prepare and cleanse us in readiness for the great sanctification of the holy mysteries. Their significance, however, is this: they represent the manifestation of the Saviour, by which he became known soon after his showing. The first showing of the Gospel, with the book closed, represents the first appearance of the Saviour, when, while he himself remained silent, the Father made him manifest. . . . But that which is represented here [i.e., in the proclamation of the scriptures] is his more perfect manifestation, during which he mingled with the crowd and made himself known not only by his own words, but also by that which he taught to his Apostles. . . . That is why the Epistle and Gospel are read."[83]

The Great Entrance, too, takes place, first of all, in order to meet a need. That which is to be offered on the altar must be brought to the altar, and this in a reverent and careful way.[84] At the same time, however, the Great Entrance also signifies the final public appearance of Christ at his entry into Jerusalem.[85] There is no symbolic explanation of the placing of the gifts on the altar and of their veiling, but in compensation there is a detailed explanation of the literal meaning of the dialogue.

After repeating the words of institution,

"the celebrant prostrates himself and prays, while applying to the offerings these words of the Only-Begotten, our Saviour, that they may, after having received his most holy and all-powerful Spirit, be transformed—the bread into his holy Body, the wine into his precious and sacred Blood.

"When these words have been said, the whole sacred rite is accomplished, the offerings are consecrated, the sacrifice is complete; the splendid Victim, the Divine oblation, slain for the salvation of the world, lies upon the altar. For it is no longer the bread, which until now has represented the Lord's Body, nor is it a simple offering, bearing the likeness of the true offering, carrying as if engraved on it the symbols of the Savior's Passion; it is the true Victim, the most holy Body of the Lord, which really suffered the outrages, insults and blows; which was crucified and slain, which under Pontius Pilate bore such splendid witness; that Body which was mocked, scourged, spat upon, and which tasted gall. In like manner the wine has become the blood which flowed from that Body. It is that Body and Blood formed by the Holy Spirit, born of the Virgin Mary, which was buried, which rose again on the third day, which ascended into heaven and sits on the right hand of the Father."[86]

In his discussion of the epiclesis Cabasilas shows that a simple enunciation of the words of institution is not enough for the consecration; in fact, even the Latins do not claim this, since they regard the intention of the priest as a condition for validity. Nicholas evidently assumes that such an intention must also find expression through image and word in the sacramental sign itself. He therefore considers the prayer *Supplices te rogamus* ("We suppliantly beseech you . . .") in the Latin canon to be part of the consecration and, in fact, to be the Latin form of the epiclesis.[87]

The pouring of some hot water into the Precious Blood is taken by Nicholas as a sign of the descent of the Holy Spirit upon the church. The Spirit came upon the church at Pentecost in order to complete the saving work of Christ; he descends in the liturgy in order to complete the sign-character of the consecrated sacred gifts.

"The whole scheme of Christ's work, as we have seen, is depicted in the Host during the liturgy; there we see the symbol of the infant Christ, of Christ led to death, crucified, and pierced with a lance; then we see the bread transformed into the most holy Body which actually endured these sufferings, and rose from the dead, and ascended into Heaven, where it sits at the right hand of the Father. So it is fitting that the later fulfilment of all these events should be symbolized, that the celebration of the liturgy may be complete, the final effects being added to the work of redemption."[88]

In this symbolism the water symbolizes the Holy Spirit, since the water has received the heat of the fire and since the Holy Spirit descended in tongues of fire. The mysteries themselves (the body and blood of Christ) signify the church, which draws its nourishment from them.

This explanation stays close to the original symbolism of the Zeon. It tacitly makes the descent of the Holy Spirit on the gifts its point of departure[89] (a descent that was expressed in the epiclesis and had for its effect to turn the gifts into the living, lifegiving, and immortal flesh and blood of the Lord). Now, with the reception of communion about to take place, his explanation considers that descent in relation to the faithful.[90]

The symbolization of the historical work of salvation is completed by the symbolism of the Zeon. From the viewpoint of the *intensity* of symbols, Nicholas distinguishes clearly between the symbolism coming before and after the anaphora, these being comparable to representations on tablets, and the properly sacramental rendering present of the death on the cross through the real presence of the body of Christ. Of this latter presence he expressly says that it is no longer a likeness or a representation on a tablet, but pure reality.

With regard to the degree of *pictoriality*, Nicholas, in the passage just referred to (Chap. 37) describes the symbolism of the prothesis with expressions that are reminiscent of the popular iconographic representations of the Lamb and of the unnuanced approach of Germanus, Nicholas and Theodore of Andida, and Symeon. Elsewhere in Cabasilas liturgical symbolism is a matter not so much of picturing as of conveying a meaning in a sensible way. In taking this view, Nicholas harks back to an earlier understanding of symbolism such as had most recently been found in Dionysius and Maximus. This is especially clear in his explanation of the entrances, the symbolic character of which is found not so much in an external likeness to the manifestation of Christ as in the similarity of meaning that exists between the inauguration of the liturgy of the word or, as the case may be, of the sacrifice, and the beginning of the public teaching ministry of Jesus or his passion.

Nicholas is thus able to coordinate the course of the liturgy with the phases of the historical work of salvation, without leaving out of account the formal structure of the liturgical celebration. On the other hand, he manages this synchronization only by subordinating the symbolism of the cross to the symbolism of the incarnation at the prothesis and by avoiding the usual interpretation of the deposition of the gifts as symbolizing the burial of Christ. Again, there is no reference to the words, "Exalt yourself above the heavens,"[91] which are spoken before the remaining elements are carried back to the table of preparation, and which were part of the liturgy at this time.

The presence after the Great Entrance of the burial symbolism that would subsequently find clear expression in the troparion, *O Noble Joseph,* immediately renders impossible any attempt at a consistent synchronization. Even in Theodore of Mopsuestia the symbolic burial at this point can be fitted to some extent into the explanatory system only as an anticipatory reference to what should properly come after the account of institution. In Germanus the symbolic references to the life of Jesus last in any case only until the anaphora. The *Protheoria,* on the other hand, goes beyond the burial symbolism at this point and interprets the darkness that lies over the now veiled gifts as referring to the night of the betrayal.

Nicholas is likewise able to integrate the prothesis into a synchronizing interpretation of the liturgy only by explaining the Bethlehem symbolism of the asterisk as a pictorial-symbolic rendering present and the symbolism of the death on the cross as a representation of the destiny that the gifts will fulfill only at a later point. In other words he must postulate diverse modes of symbolization for two actions that are in fact equally pictorial.

In keeping with his rather "Antiochene" method of interpretation and his christocentric devotional outlook, Nicholas shows himself very reserved toward the symbolism of the heavenly liturgy. In the fourteenth century this symbolism was elsewhere emphasized to an exaggerated degree and had found expression in the liturgy especially in the Cherubikon, the prayers at the Little Entrance, and the Trisagion. Nicholas' explanation here is more sober than the liturgical text itself. The deficiency is certainly a pardonable one, since the author's primary concern is to render the symbolism of the liturgy transparent in relation to its properly sacramental nucleus and especially in relation to the anamnesis of the death and resurrection of the Lord. Since Cabasilas is far more successful in this attempt than any of the Byzantine commentators before him, his explanation deserves to be highly esteemed.

Conclusion

The Byzantine liturgical commentators from Maximus to the Andidans were explaining a liturgy that was still undergoing major development. They reflected in their writings the forces that in their day were inspiring this development; it is primarily from this point of view that they are of interest. Behind the explanations of Nicholas Cabasilas and Symeon of Thessalonica, on the other hand, stands a liturgical order that is practically complete. Consequently, in discussing these last two men the question arises of the liturgical appropriateness and abiding value of their commentaries.

Symeon attempts to do justice to the original meaning of the individual liturgical texts and actions by collecting the various testimonies offered in the tradition and juxtaposing these as though they were of equal value. He does not realize that these testimonies were historically conditioned; instead he attributes the greatest possible antiquity and authority to all parts of the liturgy and all principles of interpretation. As a result, the really original liturgical structures are often concealed from him by secondary traditions; at times these also hide rather than manifest the essence of the eucharistic celebration.

Nicholas, on the contrary, takes the essence of the eucharistic celebration as his point of departure, and from this vantage point exercises a masterful control over the individual interpretative motifs. He is independent of the earlier commentators; he evaluates the various parts of the liturgy according to their theological significance and their function within the eucharistic celebration as a whole.

At the same time, however, both commentaries in quite different ways make it clear that only historical study can bring to light the original meaning of the individual liturgical texts and actions. The development from the early liturgy of Constantinople to the Byzantine liturgy in the age of Symeon took a full 1,000 years, and in the various periods of that millennium the symbolism based on the life of Jesus and the symbolism of the heavenly liturgy, the two main currents that shaped the Byzantine liturgy, imposed themselves in quite diverse ways.

The life-of-Jesus symbolism was applied especially in the rites of the prothesis, the fraction and commingling, the deposition of the gifts on the altar, and in the custom of the Zeon. The symbolism of the heavenly liturgy found expression in the Cherubikon, the prayers of the Little Entrance, and the Trisagion. The two symbolisms often intermingled, as, for example, in the organization of the entrances. The life-of-Jesus symbolism exerted its dominance most unilaterally between the eleventh and fourteenth centuries: in the symbolism of the asterisk and in the words, "Exalt yourself above the heavens," but above all in the explanation of the *Protheoria* and, in a more serene manner, in the commentary of Nicholas Cabasilas. But the attempt, made especially in this period, to synchronize the temporal sequence of liturgical actions with the various phases of the life of Jesus was defeated by the more ancient symbolism of sacrificial death in the prothesis and the symbolism of burial and resurrection after the Great Entrance. The presence of such symbols at these points meant that the same memorial of the Lord's death and resurrection that takes place sacramentally in the anaphora was also being proclaimed in other and quite diverse parts of the liturgy.

In view of this symbolism and of the predominantly "Areopagitic" forces that have shaped the history of the Byzantine liturgy, we may describe the structure of Byzantine liturgical symbolism as follows. The sacramental Christ-event of the anaphora manifests itself in the Byzantine liturgy in various concentric strata of symbols that give pictorial expression to this event in ever new ways. The intensity of the symbolic power at work decreases in a hierarchical series of stages as the distance from the sacramental center increases. Dionysius in his time had seen all the symbolic actions of the liturgy, beginning with the first incensation, as depicting the ways followed by God in his sacramental work of salvation. Similarly, in the later history of the Byzantine liturgy, and especially under the influence of thinking about images, the "mystery of God's love for us" unfolds concretely in the form of a heavenly liturgy and as a commemoration of the mystery of the death and resurrection of Christ "in a varied abundance of sacred symbolic ceremonies" and even condescends to accept "pictorial representation" in the remote preparatory actions of the prothesis and the beginning of the liturgy.

As a result, the encounter with the mystery of Christ in the liturgy takes place in a series of actions: first, in the greeting given to the sacred icons, among which are found representations of the mysteries of redemption; then, in the symbolic rites of the prothesis and in the liturgy of the word that is solemnly introduced by the Little Entrance; next, in the Great Entrance and in the subsequent symbolic actions that prepare for the anaphora. Finally, the encounter takes place no longer in images but in the reality of the body of Christ himself and in the sacramental memorial of his redemptive work, which, however, is in turn vividly attested in the symbolic actions that take place between the account of institution and the communion.

Thus its history and its present reality show that the Byzantine liturgy is, in its symbolic form, a pictorial development of the sacramental eucharist.

Part Two

New Contributions

Chapter One

The Byzantine Rite and Its Development
into the Rite of the Entire Orthodox World[1]

When the up-and-coming patriarchate of Constantinople adopted
as its own and developed further the ancient liturgical heritage of
Antioch, a move that finds exemplary expression in the person of
John Chrysostom, it was not adopting a purely local tradition.
Rather it was participating in the most important creative power liturgically that had emerged since the postapostolic period. Antioch
was a world metropolis and major center of early Christianity. Not
the least proof of this is the theological clarity and immense influence of the early Christian and Antiochene tradition of eucharistic
prayer.[2]

The intellectual power of Alexandria, on the other hand, was not
exercised in the liturgical sphere. As for Rome, the most important
third-century testimonies to its liturgical life (e.g., the *Apostolic Tradition* of Hippolytus) still depended upon the Antiochene heritage,
while the native Roman developments of the fourth century—in,
for example, the form of the Roman canon—were dependent
largely on North African and, indirectly, Alexandrian influences.[3]

The heritage proper to Jerusalem could not develop on its home
ground once the city was destroyed in 70 A.D. Elements reflecting
its very early, Jewish-Christian character would emerge later, for
example in the Quartodeciman celebration of Easter in Asia Minor,[4]
or undergo a new development in East Syrian Christianity, chiefly
outside the boundaries of the empire. Only as a result of Constantine's actions did Jerusalem once again exercise an influence on the
church at large; at Nicea in 325 it was given the honors of a patriarchate (initially "leaving untouched the privileges of the Metropolitan of Caesarea"[5]).

In this same fourth century, as a result of the crowds of pilgrims
from the entire Christian world who flocked to the holy places and
to the churches that represented them, Jerusalem exerted a strong
liturgical influence on the other churches of the East. This was es-

pecially true of the celebration of the liturgical year there, since this city had the unique advantage that the liturgical rendering-present of the events of salvation could occur in the holy places themselves, in accordance with the biblical accounts, and in a manner "suitable to the place and the day,"[6] and thus be intensely memorable. At the beginning of this century the celebration of the liturgical year was still limited to Easter (with Pentecost) and a few memorials of local martyrs.[7] By the end of the fourth century, however, it had undergone extensive development in the most important Christian metropolises, while in Rome and Constantinople it had become almost a reflection of the celebration in Jerusalem. Symbolic of this development at Rome was the conversion of two principal churches (Holy Cross and St. Mary Major) into a Roman Jerusalem (*Ad S. Crucem in Jerusalem*) and a Roman Bethlehem (*S. Maria ad praesepem*).[8]

In achieving its subsequent position as *the* Orthodox liturgical order and its expressiveness as the most important form of liturgical tradition for the church at large, the Byzantine rite was helped by the readiness it showed (extensively after the age of iconoclasm) to integrate all the important impulses from Jerusalem with its own Antiochene heritage and, at the same time, to win for these impulses a new, worldwide sphere of influence. In regard to celebration of the liturgical year (and of the daily prayer of the hours, which received a decided impress from the liturgical year) this "all-Byzantine" rite stood rather in the light shed by Jerusalem,[9] but as far as the celebration of the eucharist went, it emerged rather as the rite of the Great Church and the representative of the imperial city. In fact, the order followed in the "Great Church," that is, Hagia Sophia, heavily influenced the development of the eucharistic liturgy on certain points. Thus the rise of the enarxis (the opening section of the liturgy with its doxology and three series of ektenes and antiphons)[10] was strongly influenced by local customs,[11] while the development of the relation of the prothesis to the Great Entrance and the final preparation of the gifts before the beginning of the anaphora was influenced in no less a degree by the structural layout of the Great Church.[12]

Local conditions, then, did contribute to the emergence of the final form of the liturgy. More important, however, than any of these contributions were the reciprocal relations between the liturgy and the major overall developments that occurred in the areas of dogma, culture, and ideas, both within the Byzantine empire and in the inhabited world of the time.

Two centuries before the end of the Byzantine empire and the close of the independent development by the Byzantine patriarchate, this liturgical order became the rite of the entire Orthodox world. The development was attributable to the dependence of the ancient patriarchates of Antioch and Alexandria, which had been reduced to a small number of faithful by the Monophysite movement of the fifth century and by later Arab domination, and to the weakness, sealed by the Crusades, of the Jerusalem patriarchate. But in a canonical report the current Antiochene patriarch, Theodore Balsamon (d. 1214), then resident at Constantinople, says that the new status of the Byzantine rite has long since been achieved in fact. He writes as follows: "All the Churches of God must follow the custom of the New Rome and celebrate the liturgy according to the tradition of those great Church Fathers and beacons of piety, St. John Chrysostom and St. Basil.[13]

Even though Balsamon also appeals to codified imperial law, which states that in the absence of special written legislation to the contrary the custom of the New Rome is to be followed,[14] his reference to the great teachers and beacons of piety represents more than a set of ornamental epithets used in describing the two liturgical formularies.

The liturgy of the Byzantine patriarchate had also acquired a representative character from the standpoint of the history of the faith, and this undoubtedly made the reception of that liturgy as the liturgy of the entire Orthodox world seem an internally consistent development.

Chapter Two

The Byzantine Anaphora as Development
of the Early Christian Eucharistic Prayer[1]

The celebration of the eucharist is, of course, at the center of the liturgical life of Orthodoxy, so much so that in patristic usage and that of the Eastern churches the word "liturgy," when used without qualification, refers to the eucharistic liturgy.[2] The central action and linguistic nucleus of the eucharistic liturgy, in turn, is the anaphora ("sacrifice"). But despite the preference shown since the Byzantine era[3] for this word for the eucharistic prayer, instead of the ancient word "eucharistia" (thanksgiving), the linguistic structure of the early Christian prayer of thanksgiving has remained undisturbed. This important continuity amid an otherwise rapidly developing liturgical order deserves consideration, especially in our own time when in reforming its own eucharistic prayer Rome has felt obliged to look for and find continuity with the models provided by the early church.

A. THE PRESERVATION AND DEVELOPMENT OF THE EARLIEST
STRUCTURE: THANKSGIVING AND EXPRESSION OF FAITH
When the two Byzantine anaphoras are directly compared with the early Christian eucharist, it is clear that they embody the earliest structure known for the eucharistic prayer and that they are authentic witnesses to the faith when judged by the norm of the earliest tradition. The early Christian eucharist in question is attested for the early third century in the *Apostolic Tradition* of Hippolytus,[4] and for the middle of the second century (at least for its structure and most important contents) by Justin, the philosopher and martyr.[5] The latter two documents presuppose a liturgy that is acclimated to Rome but has behind it a Syrian heritage. The Latin language and the native Roman character began to impose themselves from the middle of the third century on[6] and point to North African and, ultimately, Alexandrian influences (this accords with the North African origins of Latin theology).[7]

142

The eucharistic prayer of Justin is characterized by being in its entirety an act of thanksgiving for creation and redemption. Like the "blessings" ("eulogies") and "eucharists"[8] in the letters to the Ephesians and Colossians (especially Col 1:12–20), Justin's prayer is formulated in strictly theological and christological terms. In Justin we already find as well the reflection that is generally customary in the later eucharistic prayers: that the Lord's legacy to the church is celebrated by means of a constitutive action (which must be described as a sacrifice) on the bread and wine, with an accompanying thanksgiving for the work of redemption.[9] Apparently Justin thus already presupposes in the structure of the eucharistic prayer an element that from Hippolytus on is always expressed (after the account of institution) in a special part of the text that is known as the anamnesis and that is formulated in dependence on 1 Corinthians 11:26.[10] In the anamnesis the memorial of the Lord is described as the accomplishment of a sacrifice, accompanied by thanksgiving.[11]

It seems that Justin had already developed a historico-salvational vision and that in his view the Lord's words were recited as those spoken by Jesus at the Last Supper, and therefore required for their liturgical actualization here and now a special prayer of petition.[12] This interpretation is rendered probable by the fact that the entire prayer, and not the historical words alone, gives a character apart, "eucharistizes," the gifts that are to be shared in communion. Viewed in the perspective of Justin, then, the anaphora of Hippolytus would represent a consistent embodiment of the most ancient Christian vision, not only inasmuch as it expresses thanksgiving, remembrance, and sacrifice, but also inasmuch as it contains the first recorded special prayer for sanctification (epiclesis) in connection with the eucharistic gifts.[13]

In addition to its general character as a thanksgiving that is focused on the history of salvation, Hippolytus' eucharistia is set apart by two traits: (1) the motifs of the thanksgiving are strictly soteriological and from the New Testament and are embedded in an overall trinitarian conception, and (2) in its contents the prayer is analogous to the baptismal confession with its comprehensive expression of the Christian faith. Until the end of the fourth century the confession of faith of the candidate for baptism was followed by the immersion, which was unaccompanied by a special formula of administration. At this period the confession took the form of a threefold "I believe" response to the three questions of the minister regarding the faith of the candidate; taken together the three questions include, in Hippolytus, almost the entire content of the later Apostles' Creed.[14] The only real difference is that, as compared with the third part of the Apostles' Creed, the third baptismal question is extremely concise: "Do you believe in the Holy Spirit in his holy Church?"[15] But this primitive version also reveals the perspective in which the later additions in the third part of the Apostles' Creed, especially the phrases "communion of saints" and "forgiveness of sins," are to be read, namely, in a pneumatological and ecclesiological context and, more specifically, as designations for the sacraments of baptism and confirmation, which are constitutive of the church.[16]

In the third century, then, the belief in the operation of the Holy Spirit in the church, which becomes "one body and one spirit" (Eph 4:4) through the eucharist, has not yet been related to the eucharist in the baptismal profession of faith. And yet the expression of this belief is already fully developed in the third part of the eucharistic prayer![17] (Similarly, the "descent into the realm of death," which later assumes an important role in its christological and soteriological setting in the Apostles' Creed, likewise does not occur in the baptismal profession of faith in Hippolytus but does have its place in his anaphora.[18]

In the tradition of eucharistic prayer, the two Byzantine anaphoras advanced consistently along the way marked out by Justin and Hippolytus (and, in the final analysis, already indicated in Ephesians and Colossians). In the Rome liturgy, which was already acquiring its characteristic stamp in the fourth century, the thanksgiving (in the narrower sense of the term) was being limited to the preface and made to depend for its specific content on the period of the liturgical year; the canon proper, for its part, was being fragmented into prayers for the acceptance of the sacrifice and reflections on the offering being made. Meanwhile, the Syrian and Byzantine anaphoras were developing the structures attested in Justin and Hippolytus. This development mirrored contemporary developments in the history of dogma in connection with the first two ecumenical councils and led to a clearer reflection on the doctrine of the eucharist and on the conception of the consecration.

The result was an even greater emphasis on the comprehensive expression of soteriological faith that had marked the early Christian anaphora. Any specification of individual saving acts corresponding to the feasts of the church (such as is characteristic of the Roman prefaces) was avoided. All in all, the witness of faith given by the anaphora, like that of the baptismal professions of faith and the symbols of Nicea and Constantinople, was one that always embraced the whole object of faith. Furthermore, the pneumatological and ecclesiological vision continued to put its stamp on the third part of a composition that as a whole had a trinitarian structure. The result was to provide a basis for an ecclesiology,[19] a sacramental theology, and a theology of office that during the first millennium did not call for any dogmatic definition, but that were implicit in the soteriological content of faith as aspects in which this soteriology worked itself out.[20]

The following characteristics of the two Byzantine anaphoras show how, while preserving the original structures, these compositions developed the early Christian eucharistic prayer and gave it greater precision:

1. the expanded salutation of God, which is structured as a synthesis of apophatic and kataphatic theology (in the Liturgy of Chrysostom: "You are God, the inexpressible, the unfathomable, the invisible, the incomprehensible. In you is the fullness of everlasting life, and yet you remain immutably the same . . .");

2. the expansion of the salutation of the Father into a salutation of the Son and the Holy Spirit as well (the passage just quoted continues: "You and your only-begotten Son and your Holy Spirit . . .");

3. the addition of thanksgiving for creation, with a transition to the hymn of the angels (Is 6), the Thrice Holy, which was still lacking in the early Christian anapahora;

4. the further specification of the anamnesis;

5. the explication of the consecratory effect of the epiclesis;

6. the addition of intercessory prayers to the prayer for the church that is built up by the sacramental koinonia (see below in connection with Basil);

7. the new form of the doxology, based on the dogma of Trinity and naming the three divine persons as equals (on the conflict over the doxology see the following section in connection with Basil).

These various expansions do not impair the structural identity with the early Christian anaphora, as unmistakably expressed in the common characteristic sequence of thanksgiving (geared to the history of salvation and including thanksgiving for the Last Supper), anamnesis, epiclesis, prayer for the church, and trinitarian doxology.

B. THE ORIGINALITY OF THE ANAPHORA OF BASIL
AND THE THEOLOGY OF THE SAINT

If we compare the two Byzantine anaphoras, especially with an eye
to the consistent development of the early Christian vision and its
focus on the dynamics of salvation, we find in the anaphora of Basil
an originality that is not due solely to the temporal priority of this
anaphora but rather corresponds to the authentic theological conception of the great Cappadocian (pp. 4f.).

The special theological character of the anaphora of Basil, as compared with that of Chrysostom, may be seen (apart from its greater
fullness) in the following elements in particular:

1. The more nuanced description, based on a theology of revelation, of the relation of the *Son to the Father* and of the *Holy Spirit to
the Son*, as well as of the Spirit as the source of sanctification and vitality for every spiritual creature.

Consider, for example, the particularization in the address to
God:

"Father of our Lord Jesus Christ,
   of our great God and the Redeemer in whom we hope!
He is the image of your goodness,
   the seal of likeness which manifests you as Father.
He is the living Word: True God.
He is eternal wisdom,
   life, holiness, power, and true light.
He made known the Holy Spirit,
   the Spirit of truth,
   the gracious gift of sonship,
   the pledge of the future inheritance,
   the earnest of eternal blessings,
   the power that gives life,
   the wellspring of sanctification.
Strengthened by him, every rational creature serves you
   and praises you unceasingly. . . ."

2. The especially detailed thanksgiving, which begins with the
creation of human beings and their gracious guidance through the
Law and the prophets and leads via praise of the incarnation
(praise that has been rewritten in strikingly christological terms) to
an exposition of the saving work of Christ. In this thanksgiving the
following points are noteworthy as signs of greater originality.

3. The soteriological emphasis, greater than even in Hippolytus,

146

on the inner unity of death and resurrection; this is achieved by introducing the theologoumenon of the descent into the realm of the dead:

"He gave himself as a ransom to death
  in which we were shackled, having been sold to sin.
In order to fill everything with himself
  he descended from the cross into the realm of the dead
  and assuaged the pains of death.
On the third day he arose from the dead
  and prepared for all flesh
  the way to resurrection from the dead,
  for corruption could not overcome
  the author of life.
He became the firstborn of those who have fallen asleep,
  the firstborn from the dead, so that in all things he might go on
  before. . . ."

4. The linking (even in the thanksgiving) of the salvation-historical economy and its continuation in the sacraments, as when it is said in connection with the baptism in the Jordan (and later in connection with the legacy of the Supper):

"He acquired us as his chosen people, as a royal priesthood, as a
  holy people.
He washed us clean in water and sanctified us through the Holy
  Spirit."

(Before the account of institution:)

"As a memorial of his saving passion
  he left us the signs of remembrance,
  which we, in accordance with his command, have offered."

5. The liturgical expansion of the account of the Supper ("He took the cup with the fruit of the vine . . . mixed it, gave thanks, blessed and sanctified it. . . .") and the inclusion of the Pauline explication (1 Cor 11:26) in Christ's command to remember him.

6. The clear reference in the anamnesis back to the giving and offering of the gifts, which themselves are already perceived as a pictorial representation of the actions at the Supper (see the words, "the signs of remembrance, which we . . . have offered," which come just before the account of institution).

7. The vision of salvation working itself out in the effects of the epiclesis:

"May your Holy Spirit come upon us and upon these gifts; may he bless and sanctify them, and reveal this bread to be the precious body . . . and this cup to be the precious blood of our Lord and God and Redeemer, Jesus Christ.

This approach, with its preference for the term "sanctify," corresponds to Basil's doctrine of the Trinity as nuanced in terms of a theology of revelation (see item 1).

8. The prayer for the church (in the second part of the epiclesis), which, in a manner linking it especially close to the early Christian vision of things, describes the church as being built up by the eucharist so as to become the community that is one body in the one Holy Spirit (in accordance with 1 Cor 10:16f.; 12:12f.; Eph 4:4): "unite all of us, who share in the one bread and the one cup, in the fellowship of the one Holy Spirit."

9. The ecclesiological continuation of the epiclesis prayer in the intercessions:

"Lord, be mindful also of your holy, catholic, and apostolic Church, which reaches from one end of the world to the other. You acquired it for yourself with the precious blood of your Christ: therefore grant it peace and preserve your holy house until the end of time."

All these characteristics of the anaphora of Basil correspond in a special way to the saint's theological views as these emerge from his writings and with special clarity from his work *On the Holy Spirit*.[21] This book, although based on liturgical sources, turned out to be the saint's mature presentation of his overall trinitarian vision; parts of it give the impression of being not only a justification for the form of the doxology that Basil preferred,[22] but also the inspiration for the structure and viewpoint of whole passages in the anaphora that bears his name.

It is not surprising that the work of formulating the entire anaphora, as distinct from the doxology alone, should not be directly echoed in the writings of the saint. We must bear in mind that at this period the concrete formulation of the thanksgivings and intercessions was still left, in a certain measure, to the individual bishop. In the overall text, on the other hand, the stereotyped elements, such as the dialogue before the anaphora and the doxologies, were the earliest to take a more or less set form. Furthermore, while a certain variability was still permitted in the doxologies, the situation of dogmatic conflict inevitably led to a clear preference for

148

a particular form or even to a settlement on a particular form as a sign by which one's orthodoxy could be recognized.[23]

Among the characteristic traits of the anaphora of Basil that in fact are confirmed in the writings of the saint is the exemplary correspondence between the conception of the Trinity and the conception of the church.[24] This correspondence had already marked the early Christian eucharistic prayer, and Basil retained it despite the fuller development of his christology and his doctrine of the Spirit. He even showed later ages a path of reconciliation that preserves unchanged the statement in the Symbols of Nicea and Constantinople on the "procession of the Spirit from the Father" (which the Orthodox churches strictly maintain) but also makes room for the vision of the economy of salvation that characterizes the early Christian baptismal confessions and eucharistic prayers, in which every confession of the Trinity retraces the path of the fulfillment of salvation in the Spirit "who is revealed by the Son."[25]

Like John in his summarizing testimony (15:26: "But when the Counsellor comes, whom I shall send to you from the Father, even the Spirit of truth, who proceeds from the Father, he will bear witness to me"), Basil's focus is not solely on the identity or nature of the divine Persons, to whom equal adoration and glory are given in the doxology, but, in fidelity to revelation, on the vision both of the processes of the intratrinitarian life and of the communication of salvation in baptism and eucharist.

In the text of the anaphora, too, the being and manifestation of the Spirit are described from the vantage point of the Son (and ultimately also from that of the primal ground of divine being, the Father). The Spirit is proclaimed to be lifegiving power and the source of all sanctification; these statements are explicitly not restricted to the temporal and earthly sphere. The theological train of thought nonetheless continues to emphasize the dynamics of salvation in the action of Christ and the time of the Church: "He washed us clean in water" (by the example [typos] of his baptism in the Jordan and his saving presence in the sacrament of baptism) "and sanctified us through the Holy Spirit."

In this trinitarian vision that is based on a theology of revelation, the eucharistic event—the way in which those "signs of remembrance of his saving passion, which he left for us," actually contain sacramental reality in our midst—could not be better expressed than in the petition, "May the Holy Spirit come upon the gifts; may he bless and sanctify them and reveal them," as the body and blood of Christ.

149

In particular, the petition for the building up of the church by "the one bread and the one cup into the koinonia of the Holy Spirit" shows how pneumatological ecclesiology and eucharistic ecclesiology inseparably condition one another. Basil thus becomes the main authority for the ecclesiology, derived from the New Testament and the early Fathers, which modern Orthodox theology calls "eucharistic ecclesiology" and which has already proved itself as a theological basis for a new ecumenical encounter of the churches.[26]

C. ST. JOHN CHRYSOSTOM AND THE CHRYSOSTOM ANAPHORA

When it came to relating the anaphora of Chrysostom in tradition-historical terms to the life and activity of the saint himself, the state of research at one time made it no more than probable that the anaphora bearing Chrysostom's name, together with its decisive characteristics, was known in Constantinople prior to its use by Nestorius. On the other hand, Nestorius found already in place a uniquely pointed form of the invocation (epiclesis) of the Spirit and of the entire reflection on the action of consecration; these seemed difficult to imagine before the Council of 381. In addition, other traits of this anaphora showed that some time had elapsed since the period when the anaphora of Basil originated. It could therefore be said that internal criteria pointed to an origin in the period when Chrysostom himself was archbishop of Constantinople. Nonetheless the patrologists and most historians of the liturgy denied the saint's authorship of the anaphora bearing his name.

The proof of actual authorship was a somewhat lengthy process. Among other things, it had still to be shown that at least the naming of Chrysostom as author in the liturgical manuscripts, beginning with the Barberini Codex of the eighth century, was a clear reference to a complete formulary by this saint and that this naming was in turn to be explained by a still older tradition of attribution. In addition, new groupings and comparisons of the surviving manuscript material were needed. Above all, however, the same kind of proof had to be attempted that had been successful with the anaphora of Basil: the proof that theological and stylistic traits found in both the anaphora and the writings of the saint were such that they could not be explained by someone's subsequent use of these writings but only by the liturgical activity of the saint himself. Such a proof required in turn a new examination of Chrysostom's homilies, which are filled to overflowing with liturgical references, and of the saint's entire literary production.

150

All of these immense tasks have in fact been carried out in the last fifteen years. F. van de Paverd supplied a more complete collection and more precise analysis of the liturgy-related passages in Chrysostom and was able to make a careful reconstruction of the course of the liturgy which the saint's writings presuppose in Antioch, on the one hand, and in Constantinople, on the other.[27] As far as the development of eucharistic doctrine is concerned, the analysis of Chrysostom's statements with regard to the Lord's words and to the epiclesis[28] provided new criteria for placing this anaphora in the history of tradition. (This holds true even if one does not accept the author's concluding summary in favor of assigning the full consecratory effect to the Lord's words as spoken in the liturgy.) Unfortunately, van de Paverd did not relate the objective of his work in any special way to the anaphora of Chrysostom and to the possibility of attributing this to the saint.[29]

In regard to the manuscript materials for the text of the anaphora, A. Jacob has done decisive preliminary work since 1963.[30] The grouping of the manuscripts, first, according to the number and completeness of the special prayers of the priest in the Liturgy of Chrysostom[31] and, second, according to region of provenance,[32] has shown that in the tradition of the Constantinopolitan formulary the textual material described as "Chrysostomic" was handed on as a complete ordo beginning with the prayer for the catechumens.[33] This was true even in a period when the actual course of the liturgy required further prayers for the priest during the prothesis and the liturgy of the word; for this purpose the "Basilian" texts were chosen or else a group of texts of varying eastern origins[34] that now and then were likewise attributed to Chrysostom.[35]

As G. Wagner has been able to show in greater detail,[36] when the three indications of Chrysostom as author in the Barberini Codex are viewed in the light of Jacob's results, they no longer give the impression of arbitrariness. Instead, beginning with the prayer for the catechumens, they state that the group of texts that follows each indication, and thus the formulary as a whole, is the work of Chrysostom. Now, it is easy to understand that the series of intercessions and priestly prayers for catechumens and faithful that closes the liturgy of the word should be regarded as a single whole (and placed under a single indication of authorship). But some further explanation is required of the fact that a single indication of authorship that refers directly to the "prothesis (later called proscomide) prayer" immediately before the anaphora should also extend to include the incomparably more important and independently meaningful anaphora. In fact, the history of the meaning of the term "proscomide" shows that in the patristic age it was synonymous with "anaphora" (= offering, sacrifice).[37] Moreover, in the Syrian liturgies the prothesis-proscomide prayer before the dialogue that begins the anaphora was understood to be the first in the series of prayers of the eucharistic sacrifice.[38] Consequently, the indication of the author, given at the prothesis prayer, could embrace the anaphora (in the narrower sense) as well.

"Prothesis" thus has its ancient meaning of "anaphora" in the codices that have survived from the eighth century, that is, from a time when the shift of the word's meaning to "preparation of the gifts" had already taken place and when its reference was now to the beginning of the liturgy. Such an anachronism can only be explained by its having been taken at this point from an older textual tradition as part of a set of traditional, stereotyped rubrics or indications of authorship, as the case might be. And in fact it is possible to trace a fixed version of the prothesis rubrics back as far as the Justinian code of law.[39] We may therefore assume that the name of Chrysostom was also transmitted as part of an older rubrical tradition.

By a direct comparison of the anaphora and the writings of Chrysostom, G. Wagner has succeeded impressively in doing what can only be done with probability by further extending the range of positive external testimony. He has proved that important characteristics in the formulation of the Chrysostom anaphora—a formulation that gives particular shape to an already rather ancient heritage—go back in fact to the age and the thinking of the saint. The most likely explanation of these characteristics, therefore, is that he was the author or, as the case may be, editor of the anaphora.[40]

The following characteristic traits, which distinguish the anaphora of Chrysostom from comparable texts, match exactly the theological outlook and dogmatico-historical situation of Chrysostom and even formulations that are peculiar to him:

1. The four apophatic expressions used in the salutation to God are found, in the same sequence, in Chrysostom's third homily "On the Divine Incomprehensibility," which was directed against the Anomoeans, the rationalist wing of the Arian party.[41]

2. The expression of trinitarian faith in the lapidary form of a naming of the three divine persons (connected only by the conjunction "and") is repeated three times; it is found repeated elsewhere

only in the anaphora of Theodore of Mopsuestia, a friend of Chrysostom from his student days in Antioch. Such a repetition fits in perfectly with the situation of conflict in which Diodorus and Flavian (the former was subsequently a teacher of John and Theodore; the latter was their bishop!) made this formulation of the trinitarian faith a watchword of Orthodoxy.[42] Theodore also emphasized this formulation of the anaphora in his eucharistic catechesis.[43] Basil, who was no less concerned than they to maintain the equal dignity of Son and Holy Spirit with the Father, had developed the address to the trinitarian God in a more nuanced way.

3. The offering of thanks "for graces of which we know but also for those we do not suspect; for graces known or unknown to us," is striking in view of the objective kind of statement proper to an anaphora. It can be explained only as an utterance of private devotion; such an origin is available in the prayer that Chrysostom cites as a "prayer of a holy man whom I know."[44]

4. The summation of thanksgiving for redemption in a single statement based on John 3:16 ("You so loved your world that you gave your only-begotten Son, in order that everyone who believes in him may not be lost but may have everlasting life") is strange when compared with Basil and the rest of the older tradition of eucharistic prayer. Its brevity is justified only if the statement is felt to be not a shortening but a very dense and comprehensive vision of the Lord's self-giving in the history of salvation and in the eucharist. In fact, references to John 3:16, accompanied by this kind of reflection on its relation to the eucharist, are frequent in Chrysostom's writings.[45]

5. The formulations of individual elements in the anamnesis, which A. Baumstark noted as being singular and conspicuous (p. 9, nn. 41–43) also have parallels in the writings of the saint and are evidently to be explained as stylistic peculiarities.[46]

6. There is no direct correlate in the writings of Chrysostom for an element that is particularly characteristic of the epiclesis in the anaphora. I refer to the additional clause that follows the petition for the transformation of the gifts: "by transforming (these gifts) through your Holy Spirit."[47] Although *metaballein*, the term for the change, was already current in the early Fathers, Chrysostom does not use it in a eucharistic context, but has instead the verbs *metarrhythmizein* and *metaskeuazein*.[48]

The added clause in the anaphora hardly comes, then, from Chrysostom. It does, however, belong to his time and reflects a new development: the anaphora is no longer experienced as a sin-

gle totality, and the naive early Christian vision, in which the salvation-historical thanksgiving is regarded as consecratory, has
dimmed; instead, individual phases of the anaphora, the Lord's
words and the epiclesis, are beginning to have their independent
meaning.

7. There is a striking parallelism between the language of Chrysostom and a turn of phrase that is characteristic of this anaphora:
the offering "for" the saints and for "all who have been perfected
in faith." The expression is already rare in other anaphoras from
the same period and is avoided in the Liturgy of Basil. Chrysostom
himself, on the other hand, occasionally expresses in this form the
idea that through the eucharistic presense of his sacrifice, Christ
causes the church in its entirety to participate in salvation.[49]

The results of this textual comparison allow us to say of the anaphora, and probably also of the priestly prayers directly surrounding
it, that "they must have been transmitted essentially in the form in
which they were spoken by John Chrysostom when he was bishop
of Constantinople."[50]

D. THE NEW EMPHASES IN THE ANAPHORA OF CHRYSOSTOM
AS A MIRROR OF LITURGICAL DEVELOPMENT
The most clearly defined new emphases in the Chrysostom anaphora—the differentiation introduced into the anamnesis and epiclesis, with the expanded list of objects of remembrance in the
former and the emphasis on the transformation worked by the latter—do not reflect simply the development of christology and of
the doctrine of the Holy Spirit. They reveal at the same time new
emphases in the Christian experience of salvation and a new as-
sessment of the symbols that mediate this experience, but therefore
also of the entire role of the church.

1. The Early Christian Ethos and the New Outlook on Symbols
In the eucharistia of Hippolytus the church is still, as it were, the pilgrim hastening to her eternal goal. In her thanksgiving she praises
God for all the great saving deeds of history, but she knows that
amid the tribulation and persecutions of this world she can experience this salvation only in the Spirit and through signs whose full
"reality" will be revealed only in eternity. As a result she celebrates
the memorial of the Lord in an extremely concentrated form, although she does reflect briefly on the implications of following

Christ for her own ethos and on the celebration of the Lord's Supper in signs (the celebration is based on the giving of food and the offering[51] of the community). The actions and gifts of the community acquire a new reality through the Spirit, yet "the holy things" (*ta hagia*) continue to be the "image" (*antitypon* and *homoiôma*) of the body of Christ and are not thought of as identical with either the salvation-historical or the eschatological presence of Christ.[52] Through participation in "the holy things" and through the fellowship of the Spirit, the Church begins now to sing the praise of God that will lead to eternal praise of him.[53]

The expanded text of the anamnesis and the corresponding explanation of the liturgy in Chrysostom (and especially in Theodore of Mopsuestia) show that the consciousness of salvation as historically acquired by the Lord and now bestowed on the church by the Spirit was no longer regarded as sufficient. The history of salvation was now experienced as portrayed in a re-presentational and at times even re-historicizing way (pp. 14–20). Symbols were felt to be pictorial and, inasmuch as they were sacramental, as already "reality" in their own right. Thus while the early Fathers could apply the concepts of *antitypon* and *homoiôma* as sacramental designations even to the eucharistic body of Christ, they were now related to the symbolic representations as such, and especially to the gifts of the sacrifice, the liturgical accomplishment of which was already being seen as a pictorial representation of the action at the Supper.[54]

Thus even before the account of institution (which is put in the past tense), Basil too speaks of "the memorial signs of the saving body, signs which we have offered in accordance with his commission"; in the anamnesis (before the invocation of the Spirit), he speaks of the offering of the "antitypes of the body and blood of Christ," whereas after the epiclesis these same gifts are called simply the "body and blood of Christ." At a later date and in response to the erroneous interpretation by the iconoclasts, the Seventh Ecumenical Council will not allow the expression "antitypes" to be applied in any way to the real body and blood of Christ.[55] In support of this decision it appeals expressly to Basil, whom it certainly understands correctly.[56]

Like the realities of salvation history, eschatological realities also become "visible" in the liturgical mysteries. The liturgical signs, which had been regarded as types and pledges, become images. Thus Theodore of Mopsuestia in particular understands *typos* and *semeion* as synonyms for *eikôn*.[57]

This new way of looking at liturgical and ecclesial reality was connected with the history of dogma, but surely it was to an even greater degree a reflection of an ecclesial situation that had changed radically since the time of Constantine and Theodosius. It was now possible to organize the world along sacral lines, turning earthly things into mirror-images of divine reality and incorporating dimensions of the kingdom of God into earthly history. This is the path that the Byzantine empire and Byzantine culture would travel until the destruction of the empire in 1453. In the process, this most astonishing (but at the same time utterly illusory) conception of empire[58] would be accompanied by a flowering of Christian culture that has no parallel in history. The Byzantine liturgy shared in this cultural development and (without being absorbed into it) became its most distinguished element.

2. Development of the Anamnesis and New Emphases in Understanding the Feast of Easter

Within the overall liturgical development that occurred in this period, the expansion of the anamnesis in the anaphoras of Basil and Chrysostom was associated closely with the differentiation of the one memorial of Christ into the multiplicity of the liturgical year. The Byzantine rite as a whole received its character as much from the dramatic unfolding of the liturgical year as it did from the eucharistic liturgy, and the differentiation of the one, all-inclusive memorial of the Lord into the feasts of the liturgical year as celebrated in Jerusalem at the end of the fourth century best illustrates the way in which the contemporary development and filling out of the eucharistic anamnesis gave new influence and effectiveness to the tradition.

The only annual feast of redemption known to the early Christians was the feast of Easter. The Easter sermon of Melito of Sardis shows that, in addition to various key moments in the Old Testament history of salvation, the memorial did include the incarnation and birth of the Lord (later made separate feasts and celebrated on Christmas, Epiphany, and March 25), but also that the memorial culminated in the remembrance of the death and resurrection as an inseparable unity.[59] The various positions taken in the dispute over the date of Easter give no hint at all of any disagreement on the content of Easter in the various churches.[60] The Quartodeciman dating of Easter on the fourteenth of Nisan was dictated by the date of Jesus' death, but the controlling vision was still that of John's "theology of exaltation."[61] The alternate choice of a Sunday for the annual feast of redemption (independently of the Jewish calendar) likewise reflected a Pauline and Johannine focusing on the "passage from death to life."

In the Easter vigil as celebrated in Jerusalem at the end of the fourth century, tradition was maintained to the full, but there was in addition a separate focus on one phase in the memorial of the death-resurrection. The remarks that Egeria makes specifically on the Easter Vigil[62] are few but nonetheless give a clear picture of the Vigil celebration in the Martyrium basilica, since she says that what is usual in the rest of the universal church is also done here, [63] and of the ensuing celebration in the rotunda of the Anastasis, since she has already described the regular Sunday vigil held in Jerusalem at cockcrow.[64]

The Jerusalem liturgy was unique in that it not only could render present and remember events that had happened there of old, but could do so in places drenched in history and meaning and at the very hour of the day when they had originally occurred. As a result, the church of Jerusalem learned not only to carry out the memorial of Christ's saving deeds because these had an abiding significance for our salvation, but also to let itself be affected by the symbolic power of the locality and the hour and thus be absorbed into a kind of mystical contemporaneity with the events of the life of Jesus.

Thus during the night of Easter, after the Vigil celebration of the word, baptism, and eucharist with its anamnesis focused on Easter (as determined by the sacraments being administered), the community went to the Anastasis and the place of the empty tomb. They went like "the myrrh-bearing women" who hastened to the tomb "in the early morning of the first day"[65] and were deemed worthy of receiving the Easter message. They went in order that they too might once again hear the gospel of the resurrection and be able to interiorize its message in a way befitting this unique liturgical celebration of it. But this celebration in the Anastasis likewise received the seal of the eucharist at the end, thus focusing the remembrance once more on its objective center.

The memorial of the death and burial of Jesus and, more generally, the stational liturgies were all organized in accordance with the same principle of rendering present "the place and the hour." The stational liturgies in particular, which began with the Saturday of the raising of Lazarus and with Palm Sunday, made it possible for the liturgical celebration to become an "image" of the biblical events.[66]

3. Possibilities and Limits of Representational Symbolism

The whole of the Byzantine liturgy and Byzantine piety was profoundly influenced by the model that the celebration of the liturgical year in Jerusalem provided. There can be little doubt that Theodore of Mopsuestia's explanation of the liturgy harks back to experiences of this kind. The fourteenth-century Byzantine liturgy will organize the Great Entrance, with its transfer of the "images of the body of Christ"[67] (according to Theodore's explanation), as a representation of a procession for the burial of the Lord; the great veil (aer) that is carried in this procession takes the form of a gigantic embroidered icon of the lamentation over Jesus (epitaphios).[68] Moreover, even today the deposition and veiling of the gifts is followed by the recitation of the troparion *O Noble Joseph* that is sung on Good Friday during the burial ritual at hesperinos (vespers) and during the orthros (matins) procession. Of the numerous Easter stanzas added to this hymn, in many places the verse: "Christ, giver of life . . . showed you his tomb," has been generally accepted.[69]

Of course, this interpretation of the transfers of the gifts as found in Theodore of Mopsuestia already suggests the question of how, once a particular phase of the life of Jesus has been singled out from the integral original symbolism and given this kind of pictorial interpretation, it can again become an integral part of the sacramental celebration. And is the danger of disintegration perhaps further increased when the visualization of a later phase in the life of Jesus (here, his burial) is made to anticipate in time the sacramental rendering-present of his death (and resurrection)?

Theodore's explanation of the liturgy evidently yields a unified series of symbols. Its members (at the Great Entrance and the deposition of the gifts the members in question are the way of the cross and the burial) fit in each with the others, but only in their polarity and their overall unity and completeness do they reflect the content of the sacramental event (death and resurrection) as an integral whole. This method of organizing symbols in a concentric system (it is characteristic of the overall structure of the Byzantine liturgical form) runs less danger of reducing the unique importance of the *sacramental* action of the anaphora and allowing the latter to be absorbed in a sequence of liturgical actions that simply imitate *symbolically* the phases of the life of Jesus.

Even though many interpreters of the liturgy in fact succumbed to this danger,[70] the developing liturgy itself did not yield to it in an excessive degree. Theodore of Mopsuestia did not pave the way for this kind of deterioration. Above all, such a tendency found no support in John Chrysostom. His symbolism often does come across as pictorial[71] and at times it extends to peripheral details, but it constantly relates these back to the essential. Even when judged by the high standard of the ethos and sacramental piety of the early Christians, his anaphora and the explanation of the eucharistic event in his writings show no loss of the essential but only a constant and manifold enrichment.

Centrifugal tendencies (that begin in the liturgical history of this period) are admittedly already reflected in the anaphora of Chrysostom. They do not exert their possible effect in the anaphora itself, however, since they are always counterbalanced. Thus the strong emphasis on the effect of the epiclesis is balanced by a high esteem for the efficacity also possessed by the Lord's words as spoken at the Supper and in the liturgy.[72] And because these two emphases balance each other, they do not rupture the unity of meaning in the anaphora as a whole, in which the sacramental event is always viewed from the vantage point of salvation history and of its actualization in the form of thanksgiving.

The anamnesis, for its part, is formulated in a uniquely contrapuntal way, since it both summarizes and develops what it commemorates.[73] The intercession gives the impression of being really archaic, since it is organized from the ecclesiological standpoint of "offering for" the ecclesial community (of the saints and "those made perfect in faith"); nonetheless, as compared with the intercession in the anapahora of Basil, it allows greater prominence than before to subjective and hierarchic concerns in the development of its details.[74]

On the whole, then, the anaphora of Chrysostom is the natural center (and at the same time a reflection in its individual formulations) of a liturgical ordo that was faithful to tradition but also advanced in relation to its times. It is therefore rightly at the center of the life and piety of a church that is accustomed even today to looking upon its faith as articulated less in doctrinal definitions than in its liturgical tradition, which is indeed respectful of the old and yet possessed of ever new vitality.

Chapter Three

The Entrance of the Bishop
and Its Liturgical Form

In the time of St. John Chrysostom and until late into the fifth century the liturgy began with the proclamation of the word. Nonetheless great attention was already being paid to the entrance of the bishop at the beginning of the liturgy. It was his presence that turned the congregation into a New Testament community of prayer and sacrifice. Ignatius of Antioch had already thought of the bishop presiding over the eucharist as "the bishop who presides in place of God" and of the priests as "the presbyters who are in place of the apostolic council."[1] Chrysostom, too, regards the first ascent of the bishop "to the holy bema"[2] as important, especially because this marks the actual beginning of the liturgy and because by his opening greeting of peace, the bishop unites the community in the peace of Christ and in the power of the Holy Spirit.[3]

When the beginning of the liturgy was interpreted in this manner it inevitably called for further expansion. And by the end of the fifth century the opening phase already included song and prayer and an incensing of the entire church by the bishop. Dionysius the Areopagite gives a mystical interpretation of this opening event with reference to the meaning of the liturgy as a whole and to the ways in which God communicates his grace.

The Trisagion, the oldest entrance song of the Byzantine liturgy, goes back to before the middle of the fifth century, and until today has retained its place before the beginning of the readings. But in its role as song accompanying the bishop's entrance it was replaced during the first part of the Justinianic era by the hymn *Only-begotten Son*, which had been composed by the emperor himself. Both hymns originated in periods of dogmatic conflict: the Trisagion around the time of the Council of Chalcedon (451) when the Monophysite movement first got out of hand, and Justinian's hymn in the early years of the emperor's reign when he followed a policy of reconciliation with the Monophysites and anticipated the direction to be taken by the Second Council of Constantinople (553).

By means of his edition[4] and analysis[5] of the Typikon of the Great Church, J. Mateos has been able to explain in a highly interesting way the liturgical function of these two hymns. As a further result of his explanation, the subsequent rather forlorn position of the hymn *Only-begotten Son* in the second antiphon of the enarxis ceases to be disconcerting.

A. THE TRISAGION HYMN

The Council of Chalcedon provides the first testimony to the existence of this hymn. Its singing in the context of the Council suggests that it was regarded as a song of victory over the followers of Dioscurus and Eutyches. The text itself, however, and the subsequent liturgical use of the song can hardly be explained entirely in that light.

The legend concerning the origin of the hymn conceives it as an expression of humble prayer that pleads for the mercy of God, here praised as "Thrice holy"; the legend may be regarded as supplying valid information regarding the character of the hymn and its period of origin. The use of the hymn at Chalcedon supposed, in fact, that the text was already known and in widespread use. Its originally penitential character is suggested by its use at Constantinople in intercessory processions (this we know to be an ancient custom)[6] as well as by the tenor of the prayers at the Trisagion,[7] which are likewise far older than the manuscript witnesses to them (these go back to the eighth century).

The disputes over the christological versus trinitarian interpretation of the hymn and in particular over its "theopaschite" expansion, which determines both the form and the interpretation of the text in all the "Monophysite" churches down to our own time, elicited hardly any echo in the context of the strictly liturgical use of the hymn at Byzantium. The tradition of dogmatic interpretation, as represented by John Damascene, unconvincingly divided the three acclamations, "Holy One," "Strong One," and "Immortal One" among the three divine hypostases. On the other hand, the liturgical context (the accompanying prayer and doxology) and its parallel (the prayer for the approach to the altar before the anaphora) manifest the same outlook as does the Thrice Holy (Sanctus) of the angels within the anaphora. That is, the hymn is addressed to the Triune God who even in the anaphora (where the salutation of the prayer is directed first to the Father) is praised in the doxology as "the Father and the Son and the Holy Spirit." The text of the Trisagion was therefore derived from the Sanctus and was evidently given its form with the aid of an insert from Psalm 41:3 (LXX).[8]

The closeness of the Trisagion to the Sanctus, in regard both to the history of its origin and to its text, also enables us to gain a clear understanding of its function as a song accompanying the entrance of the bishop for the liturgy. When Chrysostom discusses the significance of the bishop's entrance, he already places the emphasis on the ascent to the holy bema. Maximus the Confessor (d. 662) will later see this action as symbolizing the entrance of Christ the High Priest into the heavenly holy of holies and will interpret the entire liturgy in this light. But what could be a more appropriate accompaniment for the entry into the holy of holies and the presence of God than another echoing of Isaiah's vision, which had already set its stamp, via the Sanctus, on the anaphora?

The special Byzantine manner of singing the Trisagion—with its repetition after a "Glory be to the Father" and (in the case of a pontifical liturgy) its additional psalm-verses, sung antiphonally before and after, and its alternation of celebrants and choir—displays the characteristic way of performing a processional chant. In the ancient celebration of baptism this kind of antiphonal singing of Galatians 3:27 along with verses from Psalm 31 (LXX) accompanied the procession of the neophytes from the baptistery to the church, where the (eucharistic) liturgy was immediately begun.[9] Even today Galatians 3:27 is sung in place of the Trisagion on what were in olden times the days appointed for baptisms, while in every celebration of baptism the same chant provides the transition from baptism and anointing with myron to the ensuing eucharist, which begins with the readings from scripture.

In the early days of its use, the Trisagion originally came into its own as a processional song, accompanied by numerous psalm-verses, especially on days with a stational liturgy and preceding rogation procession.[10] Soon, however, it was used for the entrance of the liturgy even on other days. In the sixth and seventh centuries, however, new combinations of psalm-verses and troparies came into use as processional and entrance songs; they have survived to the present time in the form of the third antiphon. Thus the Trisagion was sung only after a new entrance ritual; in the seventh and eighth centuries two more antiphons separated the Trisagion even further from the actual beginning of the liturgy.

In a pontifical liturgy the Trisagion still accompanies, not indeed the entrance of the bishop into the church, but his ascent to the bema or sanctuary. Nowadays, moreover, a solemn blessing[11] serves as a reminder of the simple greeting of peace that marked the first ascent to the bema in the days of Chrysostom.

B. THE HYMN "ONLY-BEGOTTEN SON"

As may be inferred from the Typikon of the Great Church, the hymn composed by Justinian was likewise used originally as an entrance song.[12] As a response in a processional song it could be joined to Psalm 94 in the ferial order as late as the tenth century; Psalm 94 is the psalm still sung at the Little Entrance on most days, although it now has for a response "Save us, Son of God . . . for we sing Alleluia to you"[13] (this psalm is now the third antiphon of the enarxis).

Antiphonal psalmody using Justinian's hymn or the troparion proper to a given feast day[14] became the new form for the Little Entrance in the sixth century. By comparison the present-day first and second antiphons are a secondary development. The singing of three antiphons was originally peculiar to stational processions or, as the case might be, the interim liturgies celebrated in the Forum or in one of the churches that were located on the processional route from Hagia Sophia to the stational church. The antiphon sung at the Little Entrance in the stational church itself had, on the other hand, a clearly different function. But in the tenth century the practice of singing three antiphons began to exert an influence on the liturgy of Sundays and other days on which there was no procession. As a result, the antiphon that was already part of the set liturgical order (for the now ritualized Little Entrance) came to be preceded by two further antiphons, during which, however, the bishop and clergy do not yet enter the sanctuary.[15]

The content of the later first and second antiphons shows that these are subordinate to the antiphon for the Little Entrance. For the choice of Psalms 91, 92, and 94 (LXX) is to be explained by Psalm 94:2 in particular ("Let us come before the Lord with thanksgiving") with its directly "eucharistic" reference, whereas Psalm 91 (v. 2: "to proclaim your mercy in the morning") has the orthros for its primary setting, and Psalm 92 is suitable in a general way for any liturgical use "in the house of the Lord."[16]

Chapter Four

The Great Entrance: The Transfer of Gifts
and Its Relation to the Offering of the Faithful
and the Offertory Procession

To the Justinian age with its immense influence on the whole of
Byzantine culture, the Byzantine rite owes not only the organization of the Little Entrance with the aid of the emperor's own dogmatic hymn. It owes even more the form of the procession with the
gifts at the beginning of the sacrificial liturgy, a form that sets its
stamp on the entire liturgy. Maximus speaks of this procession as
the "entrance of the sacred mysteries"; it has in every age profoundly influenced popular piety.

A. THE CHERUBIC HYMN

R. F. Taft has made a comprehensive study of the history and significance of the Great Entrance and its accompanying chants in the
context of the preanaphoral rites of the eucharistic celebration.[1] I
have room here for only a few points from the inexhaustible store
provided us by the fruits of his research.

The specific meaning of the words, the original manner of execution, and the prehistory of the hymn of the Cherubim, or Cherubikon, which is such an important expression of Byzantine liturgical
symbolism, are now explained. It is also clearer now in what way it
provided new stimuli for the interpretation of the liturgy.

Is this hymn to be identified as the one that Patriarch Eutychius
found to contain the "foolish" assumption that at the moment
when it is sung "the king of glory is led in"? Or if the Cherubikon
was not in fact the song to which Eutychius was referring, did its
introduction at least cause this idea to prevail?

The role that Psalm 23 played in the transfer of gifts in the liturgical traditions of Jerusalem and the Armenians suggests that the patriarch's criticism was directed at the use of Psalm 23:7–10.[2] And in
fact there is an echo of such a use in Byzantine sources. It is perhaps to be found less in those late witnesses that introduce Psalm

23:7 and 117.26a as a dialogue between priest and deacon at the entrance of the gifts into the sanctuary—and which probably for the first time enrich the Late Byzantine burial symbolism with the aspects of descent into hell and resurrection[3]—and is to be seen rather in the entrance ritual of the procession with the relics at the dedication of a church, in which the singing of Psalm 23:7 can in fact be traced back to the time of Eutychius.[4]

It is clear that in the sixth century the Alleluia was sung as an antiphon to Psalm 23:7–10. It was then adopted as a conclusion for the Cherubikon (and parallel texts) and (in accordance with the practice of antiphonal singing that would continue for centuries) alternated with the entire hymn as an antiphon with individual psalm-verses.[5]

It is not clear whether the coarse symbolism (or even complete confusion of the unconsecrated gifts with the consecrated), which Eutychius insinuates in connection with the use of Psalm 23:7–10 at the transfer of the gifts, was really attached to the liturgical practice he was denouncing, or whether on the contrary he misunderstood what was going on. In any case the text of the Cherubikon, introduced a short time later, is not only more nuanced but also takes very careful account of the structures of the subsequent sacramental action.

If the Cherubikon's exhortation to "lay aside all worldly care" refers, like a similar passage in Cyril of Jerusalem, to the "Lift up your hearts" (or, in the Antiochene usage of Chrysostom, "Lift up your minds and hearts"!) in the dialogue before the anaphora,[6] then the reference to the Thrice Holy that we sing "to the Trinity who create all life" is a clear reflection of the Sanctus and its Seraphim (Is 6:3). This is because it is expressly stated in the introduction to the Sanctus in the Byzantine anaphora that this song is sung by both the Cherubim and the Seraphim.

Above all, however, justice is probably best done to the text of the Cherubikon in those interpretations of the liturgy that see the words *ton basilea tôn holôn hypodexomenoi* as referring directly to the reception of communion (rather than expressing simply a symbolic openness to a sacramental completion of the "reception").[7] The *Protheoria* already gives this interpretation (pp. 35–39). The words should therefore be translated: "to receive the King of all" or—in order to preserve the undoubtedly symbolic view taken of the action as a whole (as well as to preserve the element of the already-present in this form of the future tense)—"to prepare to receive the King of all."

B. THE GREAT ENTRANCE AND THE OFFERING OF THE GIFTS

The Cherubikon looks ahead in an appropriate way to the further action that will take place in the anaphora; moreover, its implicit symbolization of the gifts as "images of the body of Christ" had long since been justified by the Antiochene Fathers. Nonetheless, the question exists whether the hymn's words and symbolism—which already shed the radiance of the Thrice Holy over the transfer of the gifts—bring out for the transfer and for the preanaphoral rites and texts as a whole the meaning that is so clearly expressed in the *prospheromen* statements of the anamnesis. These statements relate to the offering of the gifts and are found in the early Christian *eucharistia* of Hippolytus and the two Byzantine anaphoras.[8] Hippolytus' statement ("remembering his death and his resurrection we offer you bread and wine") and its consistent development in Basil and Chrysostom show that, according to the earliest liturgical tradition, the eucharistic sacrifice developed out of the offering of gifts with its original symbolism of sacrifice and self-giving. Despite the heavy emphasis that Chrysostom in his writings places on the priest's authority to offer sacrifice, the basic anaphoral statement that the entire people forms a sacrificing community (in its thanking, remembering, and offering) remains unchallenged.

Yet this aspect, the offering of gifts, does not appear in the songs of the Great Entrance, any more than it does in the liturgical commentary of Theodore of Mopsuestia. It is questionable whether in its preanaphoral rites and texts the Byzantine liturgy has anything that can be compared to the Roman offertory. We must therefore inquire, first of all, whether any indications can be found in the prehistory of the transfer of the gifts that the transfer by the deacons and its interpretation by Theodore of Mopsuestia, which no longer suggest any act of offering by the faithful, may in fact have suppressed or, as the case may be, absorbed such an act.

Reputable scholars thought at one time that they could show precisely where and when a procession with gifts, serving as an act of oblation by the faithful, was suppressed and replaced by a diaconal transfer of the gifts. Thus A. M. Schneider interpreted the Syrian *Didascalia* of the third century as still referring to "an offertory procession of the faithful who bring bread and wine to the altar."[9] On the other hand, the mention in the *Apostolic Constitutions* of a simple bringing of the gifts by deacons, together with the first establishment at that time of pastophoria at the sides of the sanctuary, seemed to Schneider to indicate the precise point in time when the change from old custom to new took place. This date, he thought, could be confirmed by archeologists depending on the presence of pastophoria.[10]

Detailed examinations of the Syrian sources by Hanssens, van de Paverd, and Taft[11] have shown, however, that the assumption, based on western liturgical history, of an eastern "offertory procession of the faithful to the altar" is an unverifiable postulate. True enough, the obligation of the faithful to supply the gifts for the common celebration of the eucharist holds for the East as well. But insofar as the sources are not completely silent about the concrete liturgical fulfillment of this obligation, the only visible preanaphoral form of lay participation in the eucharistic sacrifice which they attest is the simple giving of gifts to the deacons at the entrance to the church.

The *Didascalia* and the *Testamentum Domini* do nonetheless show in a very precise way the link in meaning between the giving of gifts by the faithful (at the beginning of the liturgy) and the anaphoral action that is constitutive of the sacrament and that the anamnesis so clearly shows to be the accomplishment of the memorial of Christ in the form of thanksgiving and the offering of bread and ·wine. The *Didascalia* speaks of one of the deacons as assigned to be present at (and to regulate) the gift-giving of the faithful, while both deacons "afterwards, when you [the bishop] offer" are to "minister together in the Church."[12] The bishop thus completes what began with the offerings of the faithful.

The *Testamentum Domini* clearly describe the oblatory activity of the faithful as one that springs from baptism and is to be exercised accordingly: "A presbyter and the proto-deacon are to sit with the readers (in the place for the commemoration) and write down the names of those who offer oblations or the names of those for whom they offer them."[13]

Yet the witnesses are in agreement that the deacons are responsible for bringing the gifts needed for the eucharist to the altar before the anaphora, an activity which receives its first detailed symbolic interpretation from Theodore of Mopsuestia. What is noteworthy here is not that deacons transfer the gifts nor that even before their consecration the gifts are regarded as symbols of the body of Christ. What is noteworthy is that the entire passage of the gifts from their being given by the faithful to the anaphoral act of eucharistic offering is so strongly marked from the beginning by a consciousness of Christ's presence and so little by the surrender of the offerers' lives, even though Romans 12:1 requires this as a basic presupposition for any spirit of worship in Christian life.

In his day, Hippolytus, who bears witness to the earliest liturgical tradition on Roman soil, had not only shown the transfer of the gifts to be firmly anchored in the structure of liturgy; he had also expressed the meaning of this transfer in the prayer for the ordination of deacons.[14] But the corresponding prayer of ordination in the *Apostolic Constitutions* (VIII, 17–18) contains no reference to this point and in fact gives evidence of a different view of things.

In Chrysostom's anaphora the statement of offering is formulated according to Romans 12:1, but he does not make use of this heritage for a theology of the eucharist. The phrases "spiritual sacrifice" and "unbloody sacrifice" are used of the eucharist in a rather formulaic way[15] and, contrary to their biblical and liturgical meaning, are applied only to the celebrant and to the sacrificial action that takes place, as it were, at his hands. The giving of gifts by the faithful plays but a small role in Chrysostom, the transfer of the gifts none at all.[16] His attention is focused entirely on the sacrifice of Christ, the presence of which is experienced through remembering.

With regard to an understanding of the Great Entrance in the Byzantine liturgy, it follows from what has been said that it did not suppress an earlier offertory procession of the faithful nor eclipse the idea of an offertory that might earlier have been connected with the transfer of the gifts. There had never been an offertory procession of the faithful to the altar in the Syro-Byzantine liturgical tradition, although there was of course, a giving of gifts by the faithful in view of the anaphora. But the element of sacrificial offering contained in this gift-giving was not brought out by the Greek Fathers of the fourth century in connection with the diaconal transfer of the gifts. As compared with what Chrysostom and Theodore have to say, the Great Entrance represents an impressive development of the rite as far as liturgical organization is concerned. But as far as interpretation is concerned, the specifically Byzantine Cherubikon is far more reserved than Theodore (or the parallel texts in the Liturgy of James) and simply reflects without distortion the authentic liturgical structure of the anaphora.

Until into the second millennium the deacons were responsible for the transfer of the gifts at the Great Entrance. Such is the testimony of the liturgical commentary of Patriarch Germanus. And when the euchologies of the tenth to the twelfth centuries give the following caption to the silent prayer at the Great Entrance, "Prayer said by the priest while the sacred gifts are being brought in," they show clearly that the priest (or at least the principal celebrant) is not the one who had to accomplish the transfer of the gifts.[17] The procession is described in a particularly vivid way in the translation by Leo Tuscan (between 1173 and 1178) of a Constantinopolitan source:

"During the prayer for the catechumens they go to the loaves that have been offered and carry them to the sacred altar, while the archdeacon goes on before with the censer. The deacons follow, carrying the patens with the sacred bread: first, the deacon who had sung the gospel; second, the one who had led the Insistent Litany; third, the one who had prayed for the catechumens; and finally, the rest in their proper rank and carrying the sacred chalices. They all sing this hymn: 'We who mystically represent the cherubim. . . .' When they reach the holy doors of the chancel the archdeacon enters in and incenses the altar, and is followed by the priests in order. After the sacred bread has been deposited on the altar in the form of a cross and the aer has been spread over it, the archpriest says to the priests standing around the altar: 'Pray for me, holy priests.' "[18]

But as early as the sixth century priests occasionally took part in the transfer of the gifts, as is shown by a scholion of John of Scythopolis (before 550) on the passage in which Dionysius the Areopagite says: "The privileged members [= the deacons] of the group of celebrants, in conjunction with the priests, place the holy bread and the cup of blessing on the altar of God."[19] John understands this as referring to a participation by priests in the actual transfer, and he explains it by saying: "This is done everywhere where there is a limited number of deacons."[20] But priestly participation is found often enough in the sources of the eleventh to the thirteenth centuries even where the reason given did not apply; this was especially the case in pontifical liturgies.[21] It was probably a manifestation of a growing esteem for and ritual development of the procession with the gifts. In the fourteenth century priests always took part in the Great Entrance and carried the chalices.[22]

Only of the bishop did it remain true (as it is today) that his first contact with the gifts came when the procession, in which he took no part, entered the sanctuary. Thus it is precisely the two entrances, so characteristic of the Byzantine liturgy, that, when seen in a pontifical liturgy, still display clearly the structure of the liturgy in the sixth century.

The lack of an offertory procession and of the corresponding interpretative motifs in Syro-Byzantine liturgical history still leaves open
the question whether the offering idea finds expression in the
prayer said by the priest between the Great Entrance and the anaphora, somewhat as it does in the Roman *Oratio super oblata* (prayer
over the offerings). Dionysius the Areopagite had turned his attention to the matter of gift symbolism only when he came to the activity of the priestly celebrant. It would be quite possible, therefore,
for a retrospective interpretation of the offering of gifts by the faithful to find expression in a special prayer before the anaphora, as
the priest was beginning his own sacrifical role. Such a retrospect
would have to be found in the "prothesis prayer," the counterpart
(or earlier version) of which in the *Apostolic Constitutions* leads directly from the transfer of the gifts to the anaphora.[23]

In Theodore of Mopsuestia and the later Byzantine liturgy this
prayer retained its place after the transfer of the gifts, even though
the transfer itself had been moved to the beginning of the entire
sacrifical liturgy and was now followed by the kiss of peace (and
washing of the hands) that had formerly inaugurated the sacrificial
liturgy (after the prayer of the faithful).[24] In addition, since the sixth
century the profession of faith has also separated these rites from
the anaphora, which rites are by their nature related to the anaphora.[25]

By its position, then, the Byzantine prayer of offering seems connected more with the transfer of the gifts than with the anaphora.[26]
By its content, however, it is a prelude to the anaphora, and in it
there is hardly any reference back to the offering of the faithful and
the transfer of the gifts.

The researches of J. Mateos and R. E. Taft[27] have shown that the
original function and basic idea of the prothesis prayer in the Chyrsostom formulary correspond to those of the prayer that the priest
says in the East and West Syrian liturgies as he approaches the altar
for the sacramental sacrifice. Thus the prothesis prayer is a reflection of the anaphora during the stage of priestly preparation for the
latter. It does not contain, however, a verbal summation of and a
reflection on the symbolism and peculiar meaning of the offering of
bread and wine by the faithful, such as are found in the most representative examples of the Roman *Orationes super oblata*.

Characteristic of the prothesis prayer is a passage that in translations is often referred to as the "acceptance of the prayer at the

heavenly altar," but that in fact should be read as follows: "Lead (us) to (this) your holy altar."[28] The prayer speaks indeed of "these gifts and spiritual sacrifices" and twice mentions the whole people, not however as a sacrificing community but rather as a community for which the priest offers the sacifice and upon which God's blessing is asked. The gifts and spiritual sacrifices are, in passing, located in the context of (human) offering and (divine) sanctification. There is, however, no real reflection on their meaning for the accomplishment of the sacramental sacrifice. Rather, they are part of the concrete intention with which the altar of sacrifice is approached, and they help describe this approach. All the same, the emphasis on the sacrifice as "spiritual" and as "sacrifice of praise"[29] strikes a sympathetic chord and does not suggest a technical approach to or vocabulary of sacrifice.

The prothesis (proscomide) prayer, then, does not express the idea of an offertory as understood in the West. Its later title (in which the word "proscomide" has its original sense of "anaphora") means "sacrificial prayer." To indicate the distinction from the text of the anaphora itself (and in accordance with a title that occurs once for a parallel text in the Liturgy of James), it should be translated: "Prayer (at the beginning) of the sacrifice."[30]

The prayer of offering or prothesis prayer in the Liturgy of Basil does concretize the petition for acceptance of the sacrifice by invoking "the gifts of Abel, the sacrifice of Noah, the holocaust of Abraham, the priestly service of Moses and Aaron, the peace offering of Samuel." It thus refers explicitly to the gifts in their present (unconsecrated) state and to the offering as an expression of a sacrificial attitude. But even here the offering of the sacrifice by the priest is the entire focus of attention,[31] as can be seen from the petition that God would accept the gifts "as you accepted this true liturgy from the hands of the apostles," and that the priest himself might be deemed worthy of reward "as a faithful and prudent steward on the terrible day of your just recompense." In fact, the precise function of this prayer within the overall structure of the liturgy has already been defined right at its beginning: "Receive us in your overflowing mercy as we approach your holy altar, so that we may be worthy to offer this spiritual and bloodless sacrifice."

As we try to evaluate the Great Entrance and its interpretation in the Cherubikon, both forms of the prothesis prayer—which, after the anaphora, probably belongs to the oldest stratum of priestly prayers—provide confirmation that in the Byzantine liturgy of the sixth century, this part of the ceremony does not distance itself from eucharistic symbolism. On the contrary, it expresses a vision that is characteristic at least of the age of John Chrysostom, in which the presence of Christ's own sacrifice is the basic theme of the eucharistic celebration and is reflected, in a manner comparable to that of the anaphora, in all the basic actions and texts of the celebration.

Chapter Five

The First Byzantine Explanation of the Liturgy: A Synthesis of Dogmatic, Liturgical, and Mystical Tradition

Maximus the Confessor (d. 662) was connected closely with the spiritual and cultural life of the capital by his birth and by the civil offices he filled in his early life. He subsequently became a monk, a witness to the tradition of the Roman church, and a precursor of the Sixth Ecumenical Council (680–681). In his work as a whole, and especially in his *Mystagogy*, he also achieved an astonishing synthesis of the various realms of the mind.[1] He united in his person the various currents of the ascetical and mystical tradition that originated in Basil and Evagrius; he combined the world vision of a Dionysius the Areopagite, the dogmatic heritage of Chalcedon (but not without influences from Neo-Chalcedonianism), and, not least, the experience of the symbolic wealth of the post-Justianianic liturgy.

By comparison with later Byzantine explanations of the liturgy, Maximus' original synthesis and spirituality did not lead to the kind of work that becomes popular or is written to meet the permanent catechetical needs of the clergy. That role was left to be filled by the commentary of Patriarch Germanus (d. 733) and ultimately by the compendiumlike liturgical explanation of Symeon of Thessalonica. And yet Symeon's real (although often concealed) conception of the liturgy would have been unthinkable were it not for Maximus. Moreover, Maximus had an important role in the continuing influence of Dionysius the Areopagite.

In 1966 R. Bornert published a detailed study of the Byzantine liturgical commentaries (of which Maximus' was the first), in which these were examined from several points of view: philology, literary history, and history of theology.[2] The study yielded important insights into Maximus in particular and a new approach to his *Mystagogy* (probably written in 628–630)[3] in the light of his work as a whole and of the various traditions on which he drew.

It became clearer than before that the *Mystagogy* is not a commentary properly speaking and in fact does not even belong primarily to the liturgical tradition. Its place is at least as much in the history of mystical and ascetical literature. The *Mystagogy* combines the sacramental symbolism of Dionysius with the contemplation of human nature as found in Evagrius (the symbolic structure of which he tries to co-opt for mystical contemplation) into a synthesis that may be called a "liturgical *theôria*."[4] It is not possible, for example, to understand the excessively long fifth chapter (of the first seven in the *Mystagogy*) except in the light of Evagrius (but also as a corrective of his picture of the spiritual life as an ascent to a *theôria* that leaves behind every *praxis*, even one that is accomplished in *agapê*[5]). For while this chapter yields very little by way of a liturgically functional interpretation of the church building, it does formulate very clearly the doctrine of ascent that is characteristic of Maximus by contrast to Evagrius:

"He said then that the five essential pairs recognizable in the soul are situated in the one essential pair that points to God. These essential pairs are: spirit and consideration, wisdom and prudence, contemplation and action, knowledge and virtue, everlasting insight and faith. The pair that reveals God, however, is truth and goodness, and if the soul is impelled onward by these it will be united to the God of all things."[6]

The choice of liturgical actions that Maximus will interpret is not governed simply by the principle that he does not want to repeat Dionysius. Rather his own ascetico-mystical intention of bringing to light the meaning hidden in the liturgy causes him to pass over precisely those central texts that show most clearly the specifically sacramental way in which the eucharistic mystery is actualized. It causes him to concentrate instead on the interpretation of many visible actions, which in addition to their strictly liturgical function offer further possibilities of spiritual ascent to the source from which issue divine revelation and the communication of salvation. "As for Origen, so for Maximus the liturgical mystagogy is less an initiation into the mystery of the liturgy than a way into the mystery with the liturgy as a point of departure."[7]

Yet Maximus does not indulge in arbitrary allegorizing. He is a qualified exegete and dogmatic theologian. This means that in showing how liturgical realities mediate knowledge and salvation,

174

he uses categories that reflect the paths followed by revelation and the operation of grace in the history of salvation.

His concept of *mystêrion* accords with the New Testament outlook (1 Corinthians, Ephesians, Colossians), and he follows the Fathers before him in applying it to the liturgical mysteries. The mystery manifests itself as revelatory and sanctifying, and is experienced, with increasing intensity: first in type or foreshadowing (proper to the Old Testament time of salvation); then in "images of future realities"; then in visible form (peculiar to the New Testament time of salvation) or, as the case may be, in symbols (proper to the experience of the New Testament reality of salvation in the liturgical mysteries); and some day in its unveiled truth.[8] The content of the liturgy is the reality of salvation as given in the New Testament, and therefore the *symbolon* has the same objective value as the *eikôn*. It even seems that there is a complete correspondence between Maximus' use of *symbolon* in the *Mystagogy* and his use of *eikôn* in his exegetical writings, and that the preference given to *symbolon* in the second part of the *Mystagogy*, where an interpretation of the liturgy is provided, is due to the influence of Dionysius.[9]

The image (*eikôn*) reproduces the form (*morphê*) of the future archetype and gives a participation in the latter, but it does not yet contain it in its complete form (eidos).[10] For this reason the symbolism of the liturgy does not mean, in Maximus' mind, any lessening of sacramental realism but is rather the specific form in which this realism is actualized.[11] Such a vision does work, however, against a location of sacramental reality in isolated actions in the course of the liturgy.

Maximus' concept of image is thus grounded in his conception of the theology of revelation and the history of salvation. This continues to be true in his explanation of the church. The first chapter, which deals with the living church as a reflection and actualization of the divine process of salvation, is not simply a kind of prefixed introduction. Rather it shows that even in the following six chapters, however much the interpretation may repeatedly take as its point of departure the spatial elements of choir (*hierateion*) and nave (*naos*), the realities symbolized—universe, human being, and scripture—are not simply reflected there in a static manner. On the contrary, even where the point is not directly made, the church building (in the functioning of its parts) is an image of the living church and its actualization of salvation; consequently, it is, as tradition says, the "*domus ecclesiae*" (house of the church).[12] Thus the

175

duality-in-unity of *hierateion* and *naos* can be adopted as the focal point of interpretation in the properly liturgical chapters of the *Mystagogy* and shown to advantage in the key function that the two entrances have in the structure of the liturgy as a whole: "the first entrance of the high priest into the holy church" (chapter 8) and "the entrance of the holy mysteries" (chapter 16).

The individual parts of the liturgy are explained from two points of view[13]: that of salvation history and eschatology, which corresponds to the journey of the church in its entirety to its heavenly goal, and that (on which Maximus especially dwells) of ascetical purification and the ascent of the soul to mystical unity with God. Maximus, ascetic and mystic, thus provides an interpretation of the liturgy that is intended to be, before all else, a spiritual guide for monks.[14]

In determining the shape of the Byzantine liturgy itself, the two entrances played as characteristic a role as they do in Maximus' system of explanation. Thus in connection with the "entrance of the people with the high priest into the church," interest is increasingly focused on "the advance of the high priest to the sacred choir and his ascent of this to the priestly throne." This description in Maximus corresponds exactly to the emphasis placed on the bishop's entrance in the "Basilian" entrance prayer as compared with the earlier vision of things that marks the prayer assigned to the Liturgy of Chrysostom in the Barberini Codex.[15] The bipolarity of the Little Entrance as seen in Maximus also corresponds to the doubling of entrance songs as early as the sixth century, as the Trisagion, the ancient entrance song, now becomes the song sung after the entrance of the bishop into the sanctuary, while the (third) antiphon (with troparies) functions as an entrance song.

The revelational and apocalyptic character of the Great Entrance, so much stressed by Maximus, finds even sharper expression in the "Prayer at the beginning of the sacrifice" than it does in the symbolism of the Cherubikon. In the liturgy of the sixth and seventh centuries (where it is separated from the anaphora by the kiss of peace and the profession of faith), this prayer has the effect rather of a prayer "after the entrance of the mysteries." In the Liturgy of Basil, which was determinative for Constantinople, the prayer speaks of the "way of liberation which you have shown us" and of the "unveiling of the heavenly mysteries" and ends with a glance at the "terrible day of your just retribution." Whether or not Maximus' interpretation was inspired by this prayer,[16] the Orthodox, in their high regard for the Great Entrance, would pay increasingly less heed to the clear reference to the anaphora that is contained in the words of a Cherubikon and would instead make the entrance a key experience of the eucharistic mystery.

Chapter Six

Development of the Liturgy to Its Complete Form after the Age of Iconoclasm

The symbolism of the as yet unconsecrated eucharistic gifts of bread and wine had emerged in the high patristic period. In the age of Justinian, with its liturgical creativity, this symbolism received its organized development in the Great Entrance, while in the age of iconoclasm, which was so highly sensitive to all pictorial connections, it produced new results in the form of preparatory rites that already called attention to it.

The preparation of the gifts, accomplished in symbolic actions in the prothesis,[1] was henceforth not simply a preparatory part of the liturgical order. It was also the clearest expression of the peculiarly Byzantine way of experiencing the mysteries. Moreover, especially from the eleventh century on, it so inspired liturgical interpreters and iconographers that they sometimes failed to recognize its function of preparing for and reflecting the anaphora and were tempted to turn it into a mystery-event in its own right. In addition to the great value set on it in the liturgical commentaries, miracle stories became associated with it[2] and iconographic representations of it intensified its symbolism to the point of bloody realism.[3]

Nonetheless the very ancient element of offering and intercession that had been associated with the gift-giving of the faithful continued to have its place in the overall symbolism of the prothesis and especially in the concluding priestly prayer. In like manner, the custom that grew up in the eleventh century of placing on the discos, alongside the Holy Lamb, particles of the sacrificial bread in memory of the saints and in intercession for the living and the dead meant that the idea of the *koinonia tôn hagiôn*, the communion of saints arising out of participation in the holy gifts, was preserved in an illustrative form at a time of decreasingly frequent communion and of diminishing awareness of the social nature of Christ's ecclesial body. It also meant that the custom of offering loaves (now restricted to the prosphoras, in accordance with the ritual) received a new stimulus.

The place of the prothesis (later called "proscomide") at the beginning of the liturgy calls for an explanation. Why should this set of rites, the later name of which, proscomide, originally meant the same as "anaphora" and is still connected with the sacrificial prayer after the Great Entrance, have developed before the liturgy of the word? What is the relation, in this history of development, between proscomide-prothesis and enarxis? The development of the enarxis with its antiphons and ectenies presupposes, after all, that it has a real introductory function, and yet this development reached completion only at a time when the initial actions of the liturgy had already taken the form of the prothesis.

These rival developments—a beginning with the liturgy of the word and a beginning with a process that is part of the sacrifice, with the proscomide-prothesis actually coming first—can be easily explained in light of the diverse liturgical roles of bishop, priests, and deacons. One deacon (or, as the case may be, one priest and one deacon) can already be engaged with the gifts in the prothesis chamber, before another priest and deacon begin the liturgy for the congregation. And even this second beginning can be described as preliminary, until the bishop himself at the Little Entrance makes the liturgy fully what it is meant to be: the liturgy that unites all classes in the church, from the bishop with his presbytery down to the catechumens and penitents.

The enarxis, too, with its three antiphons and prayers (and the parallel litanies subsequently attached to all three prayers) was absorbed by the comprehensive pictorial thinking that marked the understanding of the liturgy at this period. Unlike the prothesis and the deposition of the gifts on the altar, however, the prayers and the singing of the antiphons provided little opportunity to see reflected in them the sacrificial action of the anaphora. On the other hand, the contemporary tendency to see the individual phases of Christ's life depicted in the course of the liturgy could be exercised even on the enarxis.

Thus Germanus sees in the psalms that serve as the antiphons of the enarxis the Old Testament preparation for the self-manifestation of the Logos. An interpreter might, however, desire to avoid a reference back to the Old Testament. Then, since the prothesis already presented the birth and childhood of Jesus and since the liturgy of the word had to represent his public teaching ministry, the interpreter was thrown back, for the enarxis, chiefly on a symbolic reference to the proclamation of the Lord by his Precursor. This is, in fact, what we find in the *Protheoria* of Nicholas and Theodore of Andida, where it lends dramatic effect to the shift of roles from priest to bishop at the passage from enarxis to Little Entrance.

Among the various interpreters of the liturgy from Germanus to Symeon, archbishop of Thessalonica (in whose time the development of the liturgy itself was almost fully completed), only Nicholas Cabasilas also concerns himself with the original point of each part of the liturgy. He alone considers it advisable to offer remarks on a theology of prayer in connection with the enarxis.

A. PROTHESIS: A SYMBOLIC REPRESENTATION
OF THE MYSTERY OF CHRIST

The earliest witness to prothesis rites[4] at the beginning of the liturgy is in the commentary of Patriarch Germanus. It raises the question whether the preparation of the gifts at this point is something entirely new, even though it had a basis in the ancient offerings of the faithful at the beginning of the liturgy, or whether the new rite simply develops further a preparation of the gifts that, it is to be assumed, originally took place immediately before their transfer to the altar. The location of the rite at the beginning of the liturgy would then be the result of a shift to that position, which could have taken place only after the institution of the catechumenate had disappeared and the discipline of secrecy (the *arcanum*) maintained toward the catechumens had lost its purpose.[5]

The assumption of such a relocation of the preparation of the gifts fits in nicely with the words of Patriarch Eutychius who, in his rejection of the symbolism of the gifts, speaks of the "newly mixed chalice." A further question arises: should we assume that there was also a prayer just before the transfer of the gifts that had the same function as the concluding prayer of the prothesis, and which we might be tempted to identify with texts in the vicinity of the Great Entrance or at least to discover in traces it has left?

The text that follows upon the Great Entrance and was called "prothesis prayer" in earlier liturgical usage is certainly not suited to the earlier phase of a preparation of the gifts. It is, rather, directly preanaphoral in character, for it lacks precisely the reference, so characteristic of the Roman *oratio super oblata*, to an offering by the faithful in the form of an offertory procession. Even though the custom of offerings by the faithful was maintained in the East, there was no offertory procession there and therefore no original set place for an expression of this act of oblation in a specific prayer

180

of the priest. In addition, in the fourth and fifth centuries the transfer of the gifts by the deacons varied in its position relative to the fixed order of priestly prayers and might take place either before or after such elements in the liturgy of the faithful as the kiss of peace, the washing of hand, and the diptychs.[6]

The fact that the prothesis prayer, which in the eighth century stands at the beginning of the Byzantine liturgy,[7] is found in manuscripts of the Liturgy of James from the ninth century on[8] in an offertory-like position before the profession of faith provides no argument that such was its original position in the Byzantine liturgy. The reason is that the texts of the Liturgy of James were strongly influenced by the Byzantine liturgy at this period. But, since the Liturgy of James had no comparable prothesis at the beginning of the liturgy in which to insert the prayer in question, it was able to insert it at another point.[9]

Is it possible, however, that the present-day (but not universal) custom in pontifical liturgies of having the bishop place commemorative particles of the sacrificial bread on the discos just before the Great Entrance and recite the usual concluding prayer of the prothesis[10] is an echo of an earlier prothesis at this point in the liturgy? After all, the organization of the two entrances in the pontifical liturgy does retain the clarity of an older structure.

As a matter of fact, however, in the present instance the greater originality of the episcopal liturgy consists solely in the fact that today, as of old, the bishop receives the gifts only when they arrive at the sanctuary for the properly sacrificial action of the liturgy. All the preceding actions with regard to the gifts have their roots in the complex function exercised by deacons in the patristic period, when it was the responsibility of the deacons to receive the gifts from the faithful, make a selection from them, and see to their transfer.

The only point of contact for a priestly prayer that would express the idea of a preanaphoral oblation is the offering by the faithful that, in the East, is made visible only at the beginning of the liturgy. This is equally true, moreover, for an episcopal liturgy and its prayer of offering as it is for a priestly liturgy. These two points are brought out in a tenth-century witness that is highly instructive for the entire structure of the liturgy. According to this testimony, the bishop completes the giving of gifts by the faithful (this latter action itself being evidently held in high esteem) and says the concluding prothesis prayer, but he has not on this account already officially taken the leadership in the community's liturgy, which first manifests itself as such at the Little Entrance:

"First of all, the gifts that have been arranged and prepared by those in charge of the oblations are presented to the patriarch, after he and the clergy next in rank have put on their church vestments. The patriarch places the gifts on the patens, and while incensing them recites this prayer: 'Lord, our God, you sent us the Bread from heaven . . .' [= the prothesis prayer]. Then, prior to the entrance of the bishop, the presbyter and deacon enter the church and stand before the chancel while the presbyter with bowed head silently recites the following prayer: 'Lord, our God, ineffably great is your power . . .' [= prayer of the first antiphon].''[11]

This passage shows with admirable clarity the decisive presupposition for a structural understanding of the entire section of the liturgy that was introduced, beginning in the sixth century, before the Little Entrance. That presupposition is the interplay of various liturgical roles and the existence of various venues for activity. A problem in understanding or, as the case may be, organizing the logical sequence of rites and texts that make up this liturgical order arises only when the ranks of the celebrants are reduced from three to two (priest and deacon) or even to a priest alone. It arises, above all, when the scenes of activity—at the altar and in the nave, and, in addition, at the prothesis altar, which belongs in the skeuophylakion or in a side-apse—are likewise finally reduced to one, namely, the sanctuary.[12]

The liturgical order followed in the Great Church, in which the skeuophylakion was separated from the main body of the building and had its own entrances, makes a prothesis rite before the beginning of the liturgy of the word seem an entirely natural solution. It seemed natural because it arose from the need of regulating the oblations of the faithful and from the course followed by the procession of the patriarch into the church. The order followed in this case renders meaningless the question why there was a preparation of the gifts even before the liturgy of the word began.

The cooperation of the patriarch in the action did not, however, extend to the preparation of the chalice. This raises the question whether this action may have been the business of the deacons, to whom in fact the Great Entrance was exclusively entrusted even in periods when the prothesis had already attained a high degree of development. In any case, the participation of the patriarch in the prothesis does not seem to have become a permanent tradition at Constantinople, nor does a similar role for the bishop seem to have become a widespread practice.

182

In the eleventh century, down to the twelfth, which was when the prothesis reached its highest development, most of the sources assign the rite to the deacon[13] and reserve only the concluding prayer to the priest[14] (and sometimes not even this[15]). The notion that this practice represents a more recent tradition arising out of increased interference on the part of the deacons has not been shown likely.[16] The fact is rather that the custom of the city of Constantinople (along with influence exerted by the Greeks of Italy[17]), which reserved an increasingly greater share of the prothesis to the priest, did not prevail in the other liturgical regions, although in other respects these other regions zealously followed Constantinople in expanding the prothesis rite.

Characteristic of this development is the lengthy and scrupulous list of questions that a priest-monk of Crete sent to his own metropolitan, who was staying in Constantinople in the time of Patriarch Nicholas III Grammaticus. The monk desired to obtain precise information on the customs followed by the Great Church in celebrating the prothesis. With regard to the participation of the deacons, the questioner wonders "who is to do the offering and cutting of the sacrificial bread when a deacon celebrates along with a priest: is it the priest, with the deacon standing by, or the deacon? And if the deacon, is the priest present or not?" Furthermore, if, as often happens, the deacon performs the prothesis, does he do it all using the same words as the priest would use? When he mixes wine and water in the chalice, does he also say the words: "One of the soldiers . . ."? May he also bless the Zeon? And so on.[18] But despite uncertainty on these various points, the concluding prayer is regarded as always reserved to the priest.[19]

The answers given by the metropolitan are short and concise: in the Great Church the priest is always present at the prothesis and performs the rite himself. The deacon simply transfers the gifts to the altar. "In the other Churches, however, it is the deacon who performs the prothesis, and the priest then immediately pronounces the prayer of blessing over the gifts."[20]

The prothesis prayer recited by the priest is the oldest prayer of the prothesis ritual and the authentic expression of its original meaning. It echoes the old offering of gifts by the faithful, for it expresses the idea of gift-giving as a sign of the human disposition for self-sacrifice. It expresses, that is, the same idea that in the early Christian period had acquired its fixed place at the very heart of the anaphora and that still today shows the celebration of the eucharist to be a movement from the offering of gifts to the accomplishment of a sacrifice in which these gifts are used.

Just as the statement of sacrificial offering in the anaphora follows upon the anamnesis, so too the echo of this statement in the prothesis prayer follows upon an anamnetic passage: "God, our God, you sent us the Bread from heaven, the food for the life of the entire world. . . ." And as in the anaphora, so here the statement of offering is followed by an epicletic petition, "Do you yourself now bless this sacrifice and take it to your heavenly altar," a formulation reminiscent of the prayer *Supplices te rogamus*, which is the ancient equivalent of the epiclesis in the Roman Canon.[21] The intercessory prayer that is connected with the action of pointing to the gifts has reference, of course, to the offerers: "In your love for us, be mindful of all those who have offered this sacrifice, and of all for whom we offer it." A further petition that the priest might perform his service with a pure heart leads into the concluding doxology.

In summary, the prothesis prayer voices the same basic idea found in the actions and prayers making up the Roman offertory.[22] Like the offertory, the prothesis is a reflection of the anaphora, with the emphasis on the *prospheromen* statements of the latter.

B. THE WAYS OF LITURGICAL EXPLANATION AND THE
UNDERSTANDING OF IMAGES IN THE SEVENTH
ECUMENICAL COUNCIL

The Byzantine veneration of images and the understanding of the liturgy as a kind of icon had a powerful influence on liturgical development. This influence can be seen at work not only in the development of the prothesis rites themselves, but also in the principles of interpretation that are applied in the liturgical commentaries. Nonetheless, while the various commentaries written from the eighth to the fourteenth centuries all express the ideas of the Seventh Ecumenical Council, they differ considerably among themselves in their intellectual level and in the internal consistency with which they apply pictorial categories to the liturgy and the sacraments.

1. The Historia Ekklesiastikê of Patriarch Germanus (d. 733):
Saving Event as Visual Representation
The liturgical commentary of Patriarch Germanus takes us into the liturgical situation that arose with the outbreak of iconoclasm. The numerous forms in which the text has come down to us and the numerous attributions of authorship in the tradition left the ques-

tion of authorship unresolved for a long time; only very recently has that question been fully answered.[23] External testimony, reconstruction of the original form of the text and, finally, a meticulous stylistic comparison with the other works of the patriarch point to the time of Germanus as the period of origin and to the man himself as the author.

The oldest known witness to this authorship is Anastasius Bibliothecarius, who had an interest in history and the opportunity to gain information from the archival and library personnel of the Byzantine capital at the time of the Council of 869–870. But in the eyes of the hierarchy and the people of that day, and all the more in the eyes of later centuries, this liturgical commentary had behind it a venerable tradition that was regarded, like the liturgy itself, as originating in Basil the Great. Most of the manuscripts preserved from the tenth century on bear the name of Basil as author.[24] Moreover, the commentary was included, together with the Liturgies of Chrysostom and Basil, in the early printed editions of the liturgical texts. Its vast diffusion and its identification with tradition in this area explain its subsequent history of interpolations.[25] The latter serve as a mirror of liturgical development.

It is a fact, of course, that in later times some independent works did stand out in this interpretative tradition; that of the two bishops, Nicholas and Theodore of Andida, for example, and, above all, the great theological mystagogy of Nicholas Cabasilas. But the *Protheoria* of the bishops of Andida became the preferred source of material to be interpolated in Germanus.[26] Moreover, it was not Cabasilas but Symeon of Thessalonica (d. 1429)[27] who was regarded as the great canonical authority and the transmitter of the traditional interpretative motifs to the following centuries. Although Symeon was strongly influenced by Dionysius and Maximus in his overall conception, it was Germanus above all whom he followed in the majority of his concrete interpretative motifs.

The traditional Byzantine interpretation of the liturgy is thus mapped out in advance in the work of Germanus. This author seems to have possessed a great sensitivity to the representational element in the liturgy and a boundless veneration for it. Such an approach to the liturgy is apt to promote a still further pictorialization of the actions of the liturgy.

The very title of Germanus' work (*historia ekklesiastikê kai mystikê theôria*) is characteristic of his method of interpretation. *Historia*, the key word, comes from the biblical theology of the Fathers.[28] The concept expressed in it looks specifically to the history of salvation as centered in the incarnation. In Germanus' use, however, the emphasis is on the liturgical actualization of the saving event, and the word refers in particular to the representational liturgical concretization of that event. Thus the word *historia* occurs in the commentary itself in the sense of "depiction, reproduction."[29] The first two words (*historia ekklesiastikê*) of the title therefore mean the concrete, pictorial self-representation (or representational meaning) of the ecclesial-liturgical event in which the history of salvation, with its center in the incarnation, renders itself present through remembrance and becomes visible.

The complete title might therefore be translated, not as "Church History and Mystical Contemplation" (as in Part I of this book), but rather as "Ecclesial Representation of Salvation and Mystical Vision." On the other hand, the element of *theôria*, of the "spiritual" meaning of liturgical actions (a sense having to do with the soul's life of grace and its eternal fulfillment), on which Maximus had so much concentrated in his time, is almost completely lacking in Germanus. It is not surprising, therefore, that the word *theôria* is often lacking in the title of the surviving manuscripts.[30]

The application of *historia*, a concept referring to the salvation history of the gospels, to the representational and ritual action of the liturgy reflected a basic idea of the theology of images, namely, that the pictorial representation given in icons is parallel to the representation of the events of salvation in sacred scripture. Image and word were conceived as being comparable factors in the church's proclamation and communication of salvation, and in the heat of the battle against the iconoclasts the image was often given priority.

This attribution of equal and even superior value to images as compared with the words of scripture appears in the theoretical writings of the iconophile theologians only in the second phase of iconoclasm, in the work of Patriarch Nicephorus (d. 828) and Theodore of Studios (d. 826).[31] It seems not to have been derived from icons in themselves nor from the function of painted images within the liturgy, but rather to have been reached originally by direct inference from a pictorial understanding of liturgical actions. The reason for saying this is that when comparisons were made between, on the one hand, the word of scripture and gospel and, on the other, images, the word was considered not in itself but primarily in its liturgical proclamation.

G. Lange has studied carefully the development of the theology of images with a view to determining in particular the series of stages in the understanding of the relation between proclamation in

186

word and proclamation in image. He finds that, typically enough, the attribution to icons of the same high value set on the pictorialization of the gospel (the latter being a chracteristic of the explanation of the liturgy in the *Historia ekklesiastikê*) occurs not in the writings of Patriarch Germanus on the theology of images, but in those of his later successor, Nicephorus.[32] The latter exaggerates the incarnational basis of icons of Christ to the point of maintaining that the kenosis of the Logos continues in his images.[33] And yet, although Nicephorus is here taking the theology of images far beyond what John Damascene and the Second Council of Nicea would accept, he is in fact only applying to reflection on images as such what had already been said with regard to the representational actions of the liturgy.

Naturally, the systematic theology of images exercised an influence in turn on the representational understanding of the liturgy. This is especially true of the ideas of Theodore of Studios, the "scholastic theologian" of images and their unyielding champion. The primary focus of his thinking is the identity of the represented with its pictorial manifestation. In his view, prototype and reproduction are one in hypostasis (although not essentially so), as may be seen from the veneration paid to the image of the emperor in place of the emperor himself and from the complete similarity of a reflection and its original.[34]

Not only does the prototype suffer no loss of individuality through being reproduced. It is even the case that the peculiar nature and power of the prototype are to be seen precisely in the possibility, and even need, it has of being manifested through reproduction. As a seal bears the sealing image in itself but remains ineffective unless it is used for sealing,

"so if Christ does not manifest himself in an artistic image, he remains to this extent inactive and ineffective. . . . The sealing image shows its proper dignity only when it is impressed on many and varied materials. The same is true of the image of Christ. We believe, of course, that because he has assumed human form, he has his image in himself. But we praise his glory all the more when we see his image represented in various materials."[35]

Although at first glance these comparisons may seem quite remote from the gospels, in the final analysis Theodore is not simply giving free rein to speculation. His intention is rather to trace the ways followed in the economy of salvation, and to this starting point his thinking returns constantly.

In Theodore's view, the dynamic power of the prototype in its individuality consists in its ability to effect a "hypostatic unity of original and copy." He applies the same thought to the historically unique redemptive situations reported in the gospels. Although in this context he focuses on the cross of the Lord in particular,[36] he does not seem to understand the cross as the archetypal model for speaking of the redemptive event as present in its images. Rather he describes the reproductive power peculiar to any and every prototype (even one in the form of a historical event) in such general terms[37] that there seems to be no difference, with regard to the capacity of the represented to render itself present, between the strictly liturgical-anamnetic conception in the *Discourse against Caballinus* (pp. 51–56) and the cycle of anamnetic mystery pictures of the Middle Byzantine period.

2. The Protheoria of Nicholas and Theodore of Andida

In light of the mutual influence that image theology and liturgical explanation exerted on each other, it is understandable that the commentary of Nicholas and Theodore of Andida, which most clearly reflects the victory of Orthodoxy,[38] should pay heed to the scholastic side of the doctrine of images, rather than to the implications of this doctrine for the theology of proclamation. Thus it is the abbot of the monastery of Studios who seems to speak through the mouth of the bishop of Andida when the *Protheoria* states, as the basic principle of the commentary, that the identity of the eucharistic and historical bodies of the Lord makes it impermissible to let any phase of his life go unrepresented in the liturgy. Were we to allow such omissions, we would not be fulfilling the Lord's command to remember him; we would rather be amputating limbs from the body of Christ.

R. Bornert has shed some light on the obscurity surrounding the historical location of the author and his work.[39] The manuscripts diverge notably in attributing the work now to Bishop Theodore, now to Bishop Nicholas, both of Andida. This time, however, the divergence is not evidence of an uncertain transmission, as in the commentary of Germanus and its interpolated versions, which have such a mystifying tradition of authorial attribution. The fact is that the difference in attribution to Nicholas or Theodore is matched by a difference in the form of the text. A comparison yields the following picture: the name of Nicholas is associated with a version of the text that is longer and also less polished in structure and grammar; the name of Theodore is associated with a shorter version in which all the signs point to a later revision of Nicholas' text, but which at the same time reflects a situation that on the whole has changed but little.[40]

Among the indications that argue for the priority of the longer version by Nicholas two are most important. One is the presence, in the title, of the name of Bishop Basil of Phyteia (to whom the work is dedicated). The other is a formulation, in the explanation of the prothesis, which hints that during the period between the two redactions there had been a change in the prothesis ritual in the normative practice of the Great Church, with a priest replacing the deacon in the excision of the sacred Lamb from the sacrificial bread. According to Nicholas it is "not surprising" that a priest too should perform this action, since such is the practice in the Great Church. The custom is evidently still recent, and knowledge of it is not universal (to say nothing of the practice itself not being imitated in the other churches). For Theodore, on the other hand, this function of the deacon, although still made the basis of the explanation, is only something "that used to be the custom" in the practice of the Great Church.[41]

As for the date of Nicholas' version, Bornert argued that a passage that probably presupposes the outbreak of the unleavened bread controversy[42] points to 1053 as the earliest identifiable date, whereas the abundant use made of the commentary by Michael Psellus in his didactic poem for the imperial princes,[43] which was composed in 1067 at the latest, provides a later point of reference.[44] Other indications that the eleventh century was the period of composition are the clash with the Bogomils[45] and a statement in connection with the rite of the Zeon that corresponds exactly to the contemporary iconographic representation of the death on the cross, in which blood and water are seen flowing from the side of Christ as a lifegiving source.[46]

More recently, J. Darrouzès, in his edition of the same Nicholas' *Discourse on Offering Azymes in the Divine Liturgy*, composed sometime before 1100, has shown that this treatise not only confirms Nicholas' authorship of the pristine redaction of the *Protheoria*—he himself says he wrote it—but also provides new historical points of references leading Darrouzès to conclude that Nicholas probably composed his Protheoria while in Constantinople between 1095 and 1099.[47]

This dating, of course, applies only to the commentary in the form in which it came from Nicholas. The situation reflected in Theodore's recension is on the whole unchanged. His version cannot therefore be notably later in its date of origin, and Theodore himself must be regarded as the immediate successor of Nicholas or at least one of the next few bishops of Andida.[48]

3. The Influences of Representational Thinking
on the Theology of Proclamation and Sacramental Theology:
The Liturgical Commentary of Nicholas Cabasilas

After Germanus and the *Protheoria* of Nicholas and Theodore of Andida, a third name must be mentioned in the context of pictorial thinking: Nicholas Cabasilas.[49] These three commentaries present most clearly the Antiochene conception of the liturgy that became the characteristic heritage of the Byzantine church. On the other hand, a comparison of Nicholas' commentary with the earlier two shows that he applies the concept of image in a much more sublime and nuanced way. Like the *Protheoria*, Nicholas insists that the entire, unabridged mystery of Christ is represented and sacramentally actualized in the liturgy. But this does not require, in his view, an unbroken sequence of rites representing historical details; it means rather that the entire series of liturgical actions is to turn the mind to the event that takes place in the anaphora and that is no longer susceptible of iconographic representation. For in the anaphora the words of the Lord and the epiclesis effect the actual presence of the central mystery of Christ: his death and resurrection.[50]

The importance of icons and representational rites is not lessened thereby. However, these are viewed in terms of their most primordial function and theological basis. Their function is liturgical; their basis is in the theology of proclamation. In the comparison between image and gospel that runs through the entire theology of icons, the ultimate focus is on rendering-present and representation in the service of the saving event that continues to exert its effectiveness. The determining point of reference is the liturgical proclamation of the gospel and the sacramental presence of salvation. However, the gospel does not communicate its contents in the form of a historical report; rather it interprets them in the context of the festal event being celebrated in the liturgy and translates them into ecclesial reality.[51]

This liturgical orientation of the authentic theology of icons (with its constant appeal to the economy of salvation) had already found expression in the *Discourse against Caballinus*, which so closely reflected the mind of St. John Damascene. It found its practico-theological embodiment in the precept of veneration of icons at the Seventh Ecumenical Council, which ranked images alongside the crucifix, the book of the gospels, and the liturgical furnishings,[52] and which compared images with the elements of the sacrifice as antitypes of the body of Christ and treated them as the equals of the elements in this respect.[53] Although the precept of icon veneration is expressed in broad terms as far as iconographic content and use are concerned, the comparisons made show nonetheless whence the Council derives its dogmatic concept of image and the perduring norm for its actualization. That source is the liturgy; that norm is the liturgy's own sacramental mode of actualization.

The superior theologian of images, the one who most consistently applies the dogmatic concept of image, is not the author of the *Protheoria*, who explicitly invokes iconography and the veneration of images, but Nicholas Cabasilas, who draws his inspiration wholly from the liturgical tradition.

Nicholas does indeed venture to say that "the whole celebration of the mystery is like a unique portrayal [*eikon*] of a single body, which is the work of the Saviour." However, this statement is not based solely on the similarity between the representational rites and the mysteries of the life of Jesus. It is based rather on the indivisibility of the mystery of Christ, the presence of which is given in the presence of the Lord's own body.[54] The depictive rites have power to represent and render present, not from themselves, but from the continuing efficacy of the redemption, an efficacy that is experienced in the sacramental anamnesis and reflected in the representational rites.

This position of Nicholas can be seen with special clarity in the interpretation of the prothesis and in the symbolism proper to the sacrificial gifts once the prothesis has taken place. Thus (he says) "the whole scheme of Christ's work . . . is depicted" for the faithful "in the Host [as on a tablet, *pinax*] during the liturgy."[55] But of the act of consecration he says that the Victim on the altar "is no longer the bread, which until now has represented the Lord's Body, nor is it a simple offering, bearing the likeness [*eikon*] of the true offering, carrying as if engraved on it the symbols of the Saviour's Passion; it is the true Victim, the most holy Body of the Lord, which really suffered the outrages, insults and blows."[56]

The symbolic actions that take place before communion can complete the presence of the sacrifice as far as symbolic representation is concerned. They cannot, however, ignore the anaphora and simply continue the series of preanaphoral symbolic rites. Nicholas here eliminates the mistaken conclusion drawn from the theology of images, a conclusion that the *Protheoria* had erected into a principle but that had already been detectable in Germanus. I am referring to the postulate that all the phases of the life of Jesus, including his miracles, must be represented in liturgical ritual. It was a misunderstanding that came disturbingly close (even if from an entirely contrary starting point) to the basic principle of the iconoclasts, who wanted to make the concepts of eucharist and image coextensive.

Prospect: Nicholas Cabasilas as Witness to the Ecumenical Faith

The theologically important liturgical commentary of Nicholas Cabasilas demands recognition not only in the context of thinking about images but in its own right as a comprehensive witness to the faith. Shortly before the period when the Byzantine liturgy reached its definitive form, it found in this commentary an empathetic explanation that, after an almost thousand-year-long, rambling history of symbolization and interpretation, once again gave the central liturgical event the authentic place it had in the early Christian and Antiochene heritage and in the concept of the mysteries that had been developed by Cyril of Jerusalem, Basil, and John Chrysostom.

It was not an accident, then, that the Fathers of the Council of Trent, despite their attachment to scholastic theology and to the Roman liturgical tradition, heard the voice of the earliest tradition speaking in Cabasilas' commentary and recognized the ecumenical importance of his testimony. In view of contemporary reflection on the essential structures of tradition, that importance has only increased and must be at least briefly indicated here.

I have already shown the value of Cabasilas' liturgical commentary for an understanding of the basic structure of the liturgy in its primary ritual and linguistic aspects, and of what might be called the hierarchic gradient of intensity and importance, from the sacramental sacrifice and meal proper to the pictorial-symbolic elements of a multileveled total liturgical form. But special mention ought to be made of his tradition-inspired understanding of the liturgy as an integral expression of the faith and the nature of the church, an expression that takes shape in the liturgical action and becomes concretely legible there.

Just as St. Basil's teaching on the Trinity is not conceptual speculation but an interpretation of the way in which God brings salvation to pass and of the way set down for human experience of the divine,[1] so too Cabasilas sees the structure of sacramental actualization as corresponding to the witness to the trinitarian faith that is given in the anaphora. He is very careful to bring out the decisive moments within the liturgical and sacramental event and, in particular, the relation of the words of institution to the change (*metabolê*) of the elements. Nonetheless he sees the full meaning of the Lord's words as manifested precisely in their actualization by the Holy Spirit, as petitioned in the epiclesis. Like John Chrysostom, Cabasilas compares the words of institution with the creative power of God's words, "Be fruitful and multiply,"[2] and thus shows that the liturgical epiclesis does not detract from the power of Christ's words at the Supper but represents rather an application of them, since it is the Spirit who continues the Lord's saving work and brings it to fulfillment.

Cabasilas correctly feels that even the Roman Canon does not simply identify Christ as celebrant of the Supper and the Church's priest who repeats the words of the Supper. Instead, in keeping with the basic laws governing the human encounter with God, the Canon has the priest humbly ask that the consecration take place; in the original structure of the Canon this petition is especially clear in the prayer *Supplices te rogamus*.[3] Cabasilas thus transcends the polemics of the dispute over the epiclesis. He becomes an ecumenist by drawing on older and deeper sources than do the supposed spokesmen for the Roman and Byzantine traditions, men who can understand their own liturgical tradition only as opposed to that of others, instead of as an equally valid expression of possibilities offered to all in common.

In his theology of sacrifice, Cabasilas likewise already transcends (as far as the essential problematic is concerned) the opposed positions in later Catholic teaching on the sacrifice of the mass and in the Catholic-Protestant controversy. Cabasilas asks, in very precise terms, how the liturgy can truly be a sacrifice. He answers that it is not a sacrifice insofar as it is an offering of bread and wine, for this is only a type of the real sacrifice. "Yet on the other hand it seems impossible that it can be the Lord's Body which is sacrificed. For this Body can no longer be slain or stricken, since, now a stranger to the grave and to corruption, it has become immortal. . . . Yet if he is sacrificed at every celebration of the mysteries, he dies daily."[4] Such a daily death is impossible, since having been sacrificed once for our sins, he dies no more. The *ephapax* (once for all) of the letter to the Hebrews appears three times in this passage.

And yet a sacrifice does take place, and this not simply in sign

194

and image; there is a real sacrifice. "The bread," which is not itself the victim offered,

"is changed from ordinary unsacrificed bread into that very Body of Christ which was truly sacrificed. . . . Under these conditions, it is not necessary that there should be numerous oblations of the Lord's Body. Since the sacrifice consists, not in the real and bloody immolation of the Lamb, but in the transformation of the bread into the sacrificed Lamb, it is obvious that the transformation takes place without the bloody immolation. Thus, though that which is changed is many, and the transformation takes place many times, yet nothing prevents the reality into which it is transformed from being one and the same thing always—a single Body, and the unique sacrifice of that Body."[5]

Cabasilas thus pinpoints the sacramental actions of the liturgy. Yet by no means does he isolate these from the course of the liturgy as a whole, either in relation to the wealth of image and symbol that makes up the form of the liturgy or in relation to the religious and ethical aspect of the structure of the action, an aspect that is decisive for an understanding of the eucharistic sacrifice that will be faithful to the scriptures. In this context it is clear that as the structure of the anaphora requires, Cabasilas takes fully into account the aspect of the "sacrifice of petition and thanksgiving" that is accomplished in prayer.[6]

More clearly, perhaps, than his model, John Chrysostom, Cabasilas also highlights the primordial call, in Romans 12:1, for a Christian attitude of sacrifice; this is the same Pauline passage that supplied the phrase *logikê latreia* (reasonable service) in the anaphora of Chrysostom. It is true that Cabasilas, too, relates the passage in its eucharistic actualization to the sacrifice of Christ himself and understands it as referring to the linguistic side of the action.[7] But elsewhere he also consciously makes his own the existential meaning of Paul's words, according to which they embrace the whole of Christian life. He does this in connection with the offering of the gifts of bread and wine, which are both lifegiving gifts from God and the first fruits of human toil. Since these gifts denote human life as such, the offering of them expresses the liturgical community's faith-inspired sacrificial attitude.

By and large Cabasilas lays special emphasis on the ecclesiological aspect of the eucharistic action. Thus his interpretation of the ancient and venerable call to communion (already anticipated in the

Didache 10,6): "Holy things to the holy!" is marked by the depth characteristic of the New Testament.[8] In accordance with 1 Corinthians 10:16f., the holiness of the church and membership in the body of Christ are made dependent on participation in the eucharistic body, but there is also a reciprocal conditioning. Similarly, the rite of the Zeon becomes an occasion for a more profound reflection on the action of the Spirit in the church.[9]

The church as *koinonia tôn hagiôn*—the community of the holy (*communio sanctorum*) that is built up by the eucharistic gifts (the *sancta* or "holy things")[10]—and, inseparable from this first aspect, the Church as *koinonia of the Spirit*,[11] these are central focuses of liturgical interpretation that, once the high patristic age had passed, were not found again in this genre of theological literature in the concentrated form given them in Cabasilas. They are also focuses that alone will enable us to bring out fully all the perspectives operative in the texts of the anaphora.

Eucharistic ecclesiology and the rediscovery of the pneumatological aspect of the eucharistic action have already become juncture points for the contemporary ecumenical encounter of the Orthodox, Catholic, and Evangelical churches.[12] Nicholas Cabasilas may well serve as a guide on the path along which this new kind of theological reflection is leading us.

Glossary

aer: large veil covering chalice and paten.

anaphora: eucharistic prayer.

antidoron: see eulogy.

antimension: consecrated corporal or "portable altar," with relics in one corner.

asterisk/star: cruciform stand made of two pieces of curving metal with a small star or cross hanging from the point of junction; placed over paten to keep the veil from touching the bread.

bema: raised platform for the clergy; the sanctuary.

discos: paten.

ecphonesis: doxological ending of a prayer; it derives its name ("exclamation") from being proclaimed aloud.

eiliton: corporal.

ektene: insistent litany after the gospel.

enarxis: the part of the liturgy between prothesis and Little Entrance, comprising three litanies, silent prayers, and antiphons.

epigonation: stiff square of material with an embroidered image, hanging from left waist of a priest, under the phelonion, or attached to sakkos of a bishop.

epimanikia: cuffs worn to keep the sleeves of the sticharion in place.

epitrachelion: stole.

eulogy: bread blessed but not consecrated, and distributed after mass "in place of the eucharist" (antidoron).

hesperinos: vespers.

iconostasis: screen, decorated with icons, separating the sanctuary (bema) from the rest of the church.

mandyas: mantle worn by bishops.

narthex: antechamber (vestibule) to the nave, separated from latter by columns, railing, or wall.

omophorion: pallium (but worn by all bishops).

orarion: narrow stole that deacon wears over left shoulder.

orthros: matins.

pastophoria: side rooms off the sanctuary, serving as sacristies, etc.

phelonion: chasuble.

prokeimenon: responsorial psalmody before the epistle.

proscomide: a term in Germanus referring to the preparation of the gifts or prothesis; prayer of *accessus ad altare* before the anaphora.

prosphora: bread and wine "offered" for use in the eucharist.

prothesis: rite of preparation of the gifts (also referred to as proscomide); prayer said during this rite; altar and chapel where the rite is performed.

ripidion: liturgical fan (a circle of decorated metal with a wooden handle).

sakkos: dalmatic.

skeuophylakion: sacristy.

sticharion: alb.

Abbreviations

Altaner-Stuiber	B. Altaner and A. Stuiber, *Leben, Schriften und Lehre der Kirchenväter.* Freiburg, 1978.[8]
ALW	*Archiv für Liturgiewissenschaft.* Regensburg, 1950ff.
Beck	H. G. Beck, *Kirche und theologische Literatur im byzantinischen Reich* (Byzantinisches Handbuch II, 1). Munich, 1959.
Betz	J. Betz, *Die Eucharistie in der Zeit der griechischen Väter I/1. Die Aktualpräsenz der Person und des Heilswerkes Jesu im Abendmahl nach der vorephesinischen griechischen Patristik.* Freiburg, 1955.
Betz II	II/1. *Die Realpräsenz des Leibes und Blutes Jesu im Abendmahl nach dem Neuen Testament.* Freiburg, 1964.
BM	*Benediktinische Monatsschrift.* Beuron, 1919ff.
Borgia	N. Borgia, *Il commentario liturgico di S. Germano patriarca constantinopolitano e la versione latina di Anastasio bibliothecario.* Grottaferrata, 1912.
Bornert	R. Bornert, *Les commentaires byzantins de la Divine Liturgie du VIIe au XVe siècle* (Archives de l'Orient Chrétien 9). Paris, 1966.
Botte	B. Botte, *La Tradition Apostolique de saint Hippolyte* (LQF 39). Münster, 1963.
Br	F. E. Brightman, *Liturgies Eastern and Western* I. *Eastern Liturgies.* Oxford, 1896.
ByZ	*Byzantinische Zeitschrift.* Leipzig, 1892ff.
Byzslav	*Byzantinoslavica.* Prague, 1929ff.

Chalkedon	A. Grillmeier and H. Bacht (eds.), *Das Konzil von Chalkedon. Geschichte und Gegenwart*. 3 vols. Würzburg, 1951–1954.
COD	J. Alberigo, et al. (eds.), *Conciliorum oecumenicorum decreta*. Bologna, 1973.[3]
CSHB	Corpus Scriptorum Historiae Byzantinae. Bonn, 1828ff.
DACL	F. Cabrol and H. Leclercq (eds.), *Dictionnaire d'archéologie chrétienne et de liturgie*. Paris, 1924ff.
DOP	*Dumbarton Oaks Papers*. Cambridge, Mass., 1941ff.
DS	H. Denzinger and A. Schönmetzer (eds.), *Enchiridion symbolorum*. Freiburg, 1963.[32]
ECQ	*Eastern Churches Quarterly*. Ramsgate, 1936ff.
ELit	*Ephemerides Liturgicae*. Rome, 1897ff.
EO	*Echos d'Orient*. Paris, 1897ff.
Eucharisties	B. Botte et al., *Eucharisties d'Orient et d'Occident* II (Lex Orandi 47). Paris, 1970.
Funk	F. X. Funk, *Didascalia et Constitutiones Apostolorum*. 2 vols. Paderborn, 1905.
GCS	Die griechischen christlichen Schriftstellar der ersten drei Jahrhunderte. Leipzig, 1897ff.
Hanssens	J. M. Hanssens, *Institutiones liturgicae de ritibus orientalibus*. II–III. *De missa rituum orientalium*. Rome, 1930–1932.
Jacob, *Formulaire*	A. Jacob, *Histoire du formulaire grec de la liturgie de saint Jean Chrysostome* (Diss., Catholic University of Louvain, 1968).
Jacob, *Recherches*	A. Jacob, *Recherches sur la tradition manuscrite de la liturgie de saint Jean Chrysostome* (Lic.-Diss., Catholic University of Louvain, 1963).
Jacob, "Tradition"	A. Jacob, "La tradition manuscrite de la liturgie de S. Jean Chrysostome (VIIIe–XIIe siècles)," in *Eucharisties* (Paris, 1970), 109–138.

Jacob, "Uspenski"	A. Jacob, "L'Euchologe de Porphyre Uspenski. Codex Leningr. gr. 226 (Xe siècle)," *Museon* 78 (1965) 173–214.
JEH	*Journal of Ecclesiastical History*. London, 1950ff.
JLH	*Jahrbuch für Liturgie und Hymnologie*. Kassel, 1955ff.
JLW	*Jahrbuch für Liturgiewissenschaft*. Münster, 1921–1941.
JÖBG	*Jahrbuch der österreichischen byzantinischen Gesellschaft*. Vienna, 1951ff.
JTS	*Journal of Theological Studies*. London, 1899ff.
Jungmann	J. A. Jungmann, *The Mass of the Roman Rite: Its Origins and Development (Missarum Solemnia)*, tr. by F. A. Brunner. 2 vols. New York, 1951, 1955.
LQF (LF)	Liturgiewissenschaftliche Quellen und Forschungen. Münster, 1957ff. (from 1919: Liturgiegeschichtliche Forschungen; from 1928: Liturgiegeschichtliche Quellen und forschungen).
Mansi	J. D. Mansi, *Sacrorum conciliorum nova et amplissima collectio*. Florence, 1737ff.; Paris, 1899ff.
Mateos, Le Typicon	J. Mateos, *Le Typicon de la Grande Eglise. Ms. Sainte-Croix No. 40. Introduction, texte critique et notes*. 2 vols. OCA 165–166. Rome, 1962–1963.
Mateos, La célébration	J. Mateos, *La célébration de la patrole dans la liturgie byzantine*. OCA 191. Rome, 1971.
MD	*La Maison-Dieu*. Paris, 1945ff.
ND	J. Neuner and J. Dupuis (eds.), *The Christian Faith in the Doctrinal Documents of the Catholic Church*, rev. ed. Staten Island, N.Y., 1982.
OCA	Orientalia Christiana Analecta. Rome, 1935ff.
OCP	*Orientalia Christiana Periodica*. Rome, 1935ff.
OrChr	*Oriens Christianus*. (Leipzig) Wiesbaden, 1901ff.

Ostkirchen-kunde	E. von Ivanka, J. Tyciak, and P. Wiertz (eds.), *Handbuch der Ostkirchenkunde*. Düsseldorf, 1971.
OstkSt	*Ostkirchliche Studien*. Würzburg, 1951ff.
Paverd, van de	F. van de Paverd, *Zur Geschichte der Messliturgie in Antiocheia und Konstantinopel gegen Ende des 4. Jahrhunderts. Analyse der Quellen bei Johannes Chrysostomos*. OCA 187. Rome, 1970.
PE	A. Hänggi and I. Pahl (ed.), *Prex Eucharistica. Textus e variis liturgiis antiquioribus selecti* (Spicilegium Friburgense 12). Freiburg, 1968.
PG	J. P. Migne (ed.), Patrologia Graeca. Paris, 1857–1866.
PL	J. P. Migne (ed.), Patrologia Latina. Paris, 1878–1890.
PO	R. Graffin and F. Nau (eds.), Patrologia Orientalis. Paris, 1903ff.
PrOrChr	*Le Proche-Orient chrétien*. Jerusalem, 1951ff.
RAC	T. Klauser (ed.), *Reallexikon für Antike und Christentum*. Stuttgart, 1941 (1950) ff.
REB	*Revue des études byzantines*. Paris, 1946ff.
RGG	*Die Religion in Geschichte und Gegenwart*. Tübingen, 1957.[3]
RivAC	*Rivista de archeologia cristiana*. Rome, 1924ff.
ROC	*Revue de l'Orient chrétien*. Paris, 1896ff.
SC	Sources chrétiennes. Paris, 1941ff.
Schulz	H.-J. Schulz, *Ökumenische Glaubenseinheit aus eucharistischer Überlieferung*. Paderborn, 1976.
Schulz, "Opfer"	H.-J. Schulz, "Liturgischer Vollzug und sakramentale Wirklichkeit des eucharistischen Opfers," OCP 45 (1979) 245–266; 46 (1980) 5–19.
SE	*Sacris Erudiri*. Bruges, 1948ff.
Storf	*Griechische Liturgien*, tr. by R. Storf (Bibliothek der Kirchenväter). Kempten, 1912.

StPL	K. Gamber, *Studia Patristica et Liturgica*. Regensburg, 1967ff.
Taft	R. E. Taft, *The Great Entrance. A History of the Transfer of Gifts and Other Preanaphoral Rites of the Liturgy of St. John Chrysostom*. OCA 200. Rome, 1975; 2nd ed., 1978.
TG	*Theologie und Glaube*. Paderborn, 1909ff.
ThRev	*Theologische Revue*.
TLZ	*Theologische Literaturzeitung*. Leipzig, 1878ff.
Tonneau-Devreesse	R. Tonneau and R. Devreesse (eds.), *Les homélies catéchétiques de Theodore de Mopsueste* (Studi e Test 145). Vatican City, 1949.
TU	Texte und Untersuchungen zur Geschichte der altchristlichen Literatur. Leipzig-Berlin, 1882ff.
Wagner	G. Wagner, *Der Ursprung der Chrysostomusliturgie* (LQF 59). Münster, 1973.
ZKG	*Zeitschrift für Kirchengeschichte* (Gotha) Stuttgart, 1876ff.
ZKT	*Zeitschrift für katholische Theologie*. (Innsbruck) Vienna, 1877ff.

Notes

PREFACE TO THE FIRST EDITION

1. J. A. Jungmann, *The Place of Christ in Liturgical Prayer*, tr. by A. Peeler from the 2nd German ed. (Staten Island, N.Y., 1965).

2. P. de Meester, "Les origines et les développements du texte grec de la liturgie de saint Jean Chrysostome," in *Chrysostomika. Studi e ricerche intorno a S. Giovanni Crisostomo* (Rome, 1908), 254–357; idem, "Grecques (Liturgies)," *DACL* 6:1591–1662.

3. J. M. Hanssens, *Institutiones liturgicae de ritibus orientalium*. II–III. *De missa rituum orientalium* (Rome, 1930–1932).

4. In Russia, at the end of the last century, N. F. Krasnosel'chev. A. A. Dmitrievski, and others also brought historico-liturgical research to full development, but they devoted themselves chiefly to the study of liturgical mss, and only a few of these go back to the first millenium.

INTRODUCTION

1. Letter *Anno ineunte* on the occasion of the visit of Pope Paul VI to the Phanar on July 25, 1967; text in T. F. Stransky and J. B. Sheerin (eds.), *Doing the Truth in Charity*. Statements of Pope Paul VI, Popes John Paul I, John Paul II, and the Secretariat for Christian Unity (Ecumenical Documents I; New York, 1982), 186–187. On the concept of "sister Churches" see E. Lanne, "Schwesterkirchen—Ekklesiologische Aspekte des Tomos Agapis," in Stiftung Pro Oriente (ed.), *Auf dem Weg zur Einheit des Glaubens. Koinonia* (Erstes ekklesiologisches Colloquium zwischen orthodoxen und römische-katholischen Theologen, April 1974 in Wien. Referate und Protokolle; Innsbruck, 1976), 54–82; henceforth cited as *Koinonia*.

2. On the original doxological orientation of dogma and on the ecumenical relevance of this fact see E. Schlink, "Die Struktur der dogmatischen Aussage als ökumenisches Problem," in his *Der kommende Christus und die kirchlichen Traditionen* (Göttingen, 1961), 24–46. See also H.-J. Schulz, "Die Liturgie als Interpretationsprinzip der Dogmenentfaltung im Dialog mit den Orthodoxen," *Königsteiner Studien* 25 (1979) 35–45.

3. On the eucharistic celebration of the local church as the most representative expression of ecclesial faith see H.-J. Schulz, *Ökumenische glaubenseinheit aus eucharistischer Überlieferung* (Paderborn, 1976); henceforth cited as Schulz.

4. See the argument for the sacramentality of the episcopal office from the ordination texts of the earliest liturgical tradition as given in the Constitution on the Church *(Lumen Gentium)* 21, as well as the emphasis on the eucharistic dimension of the episcopal office, ibid., 26 and frequently. See also H.-J. Schulz, "Das liturgisch-sakramental übertragene Hirtenamt in seiner eucharistischen Selbstverwirklichung

nach dem Zeugnis der liturgischen Überlieferung," in P. Blaser (ed.), *Amt und Eucharistie* (Paderborn, 1973), 208–255.

5. On these three aspects of office and on its two degrees, episcopal and presbyteral, see Schulz 87–122.

6. Thus the prayer for the ordination of a bishop in Hippolytus (B. Botte, *La Tradition Apostolique de Saint Hippolyte* [LQF 39, Münster, 1963], 6–10, henceforth cited as Botte) became the presently valid prayer of episcopal consecration in the revised Roman Pontifical, *De ordinatione Diaconi, Presbyteri et Episcopi* (Rome, 1968); English translation, *The Rites of the Catholic Church* II (New York, 1979), 25–108. The first of the new Eucharistic Prayers (*Prex Eucharistica* II) was based on the anaphora of Hippolytus (Botte 10–16), and the baptismal confession of faith (in the form of questions and answers, just before the act of baptism) was filled out in accordance with the detailed baptismal question in the *Apostolic Tradition* (Botte 48–50), where it includes almost the whole second part of the later Apostles' Creed.

7. I. Ortiz de Urbina, *Nicée et Constantinople* (Histoire des conciles oecumeniques 2, ed. by G. Dumeige; Paris, 1963), 53ff.

8. N. Afanassieff, N. Koulomzine, J. Meyendorff, and A. Schmemann, *The Primacy of Peter*, tr. by K. Farrer et al. (Westminster, Md., 1963), may be regarded as the principal statement of a eucharistic ecclesiology. For the reflection of a eucharistic ecclesiology in the documents of Vatican II and in Reformed theology see B. Forte, *La chiesa nell'eucaristia* (Naples, 1975); for its relevance to the contemporary Catholic-Orthodox dialogue see *Koinonia*, with statements in favor of it by Metropolitan Damaskinos Papandreou (86f., etc.), J. Klinger (115–126), J. Ratzinger (134), P. Duprey (87, 158), and E. Lanne (68, 87, 132).

9. Decree on Ecumenism (*Unitatis Redintegratio*), 11.

10. See Schulz 8–10.

11. On the connection of the two aspects see P. Evdokimov, "Fundamental Desires of the Orthodox Church vis-a-vis the Catholic Church," in H. Küng (ed.), *Do We Know the Others?* (Concilium 14; New York, 1966), 66–76, and the theologically normative basis for it in the text of the epiclesis (clearest in Hippolytus and Basil).

12. Text of the statement in G. Müller-Fahrenholz (ed.), *Eine Taufe. Eine Eucharistie, Ein Amt. Drei Erklärungen* (drawn up and authorized by the Commission on Faith and Order), 13–20 (reprinted from Beiheft 27 of *Ökumenische Rundschau*; Frankfurt, 1976[2]). The view taken in this document is close in substance to the structure and wording especially of the anaphora of Chrysostom; see H.-J. Schulz, "Orthodoxe Eucharistiefeier und ökumenisches Glaubenszeugnis. Zur Eucharistie-Erklärung der Kommission fur Glauben und Kirchenverfassung des Ökumenisches Rates der Kirchen," *Der christliche Osten* 34 (1979) 10–15; idem, "Die Theologie der Ostkirche als ökumenischer Impuls," in G. Kaufman (ed.), *Tendenzen der katholischen Theologie nach dem Zweiten Vatikanischen Konzil* (Münster, 1979), 95–111.

13. Resolutions of the 2nd and 3rd Panorthodox Conferences in Rhodes (2nd conference, September 1963; report in *Kirche im Osten* 8 [1965] 185; 3rd conference, November 1964; report in *OstkSt* 14 [1965] 68–82 at 77). On the two principles cited see H.-J. Schulz, *Wiedervereinigung mit der Orthodoxie? Bedingungen und Chancen des neuen Dialogs* (Münster, 1980).

14. See the list of abbreviations pp. 199–203, for the principal works of the authors named.

15. The footnotes indicated by an asterisk and attached to the chapter titles of the "New Contributions" refer to the almost unchanged original book. The page references in the text of the "New Contributions" are also to the original book.

16. But the heavily systematized index of subjects cannot (and is not meant to) turn this little book into an introduction or a manual. Readers desiring the latter are referred to the relevant works of Hanssens, Janeras, Onasch, and the *Handbuch der Ostkirchenkunde* (332–385; Schulz, 386–443; Dalmais), as well as to the notations in books of liturgical texts (espec. Edelby, "Pour une restauration de la liturgie byzantine," *PrOrSyr* 7 [1957], 97–118).

PART ONE

CHAPTER ONE

Introduction

1. *"Ta presbeia tês timês"*: canon 3 (*COD* 28).
2. Beck, *Kirche und theologische Literatur im byzantinischen Reich* (Byzantinisches Handbuch II, 1) (Munich 1959), 30; henceforth cited as Beck.
3. Ibid.
4. *COD* 75f.
5. See P. de Meester, "Grecques (Liturgies)," *DACL* 6:1596.

Section A

1. The prayers peculiar to each are the first and second prayers of the faithful, the prayer over the gifts, the prayer at the litany for the presentation of the gifts, the prayer of inclination, the prayer of thanksgiving after communion, and the concluding prayer (after the prayer behind the ambo).
2. The Divine Liturgy of our holy Father Basil the Great is now celebrated on only ten days of the year: the saint's own feast day (January 1), the Sundays of Lent (except for Palm Sunday), Holy Thursday and the vigils of Easter, Christmas, and Epiphany. On the other days (but only on Saturdays during Lent) the Divine Liturgy of our holy Father John Chrysostom is celebrated. On Wednesdays and Fridays of Lent and on the first three days of Holy Week the celebration of communion from the presanctified gifts is joined to vespers. Until the eleventh century the Liturgy of St. Basil was the one more frequently used. In the oldest mss it comes in first place.
3. This is the Vatican Codex Barberinus graecus 336, which is printed in F. E. Brightman, *Liturgies Eastern and Western. 1. Eastern Liturgies* (Oxford, 1896), 309–344; henceforth cited as Br.
4. See below, p. 8.
5. J. D. Mansi, *Sacrorum conciliorum nova et amplissima collectio* (Florence, 1737ff.), 11: 956; henceforth cited as Mansi. Cf. J. M. Hanssens, *Institutiones liturgicae de ritibus orientalibus. II–III. De missa rituum orientalium* (Rome, 1930–1932), n. 1485; henceforth cited as Hanssens.
6. Beck 473.
7. PG 86:1368C.
8. Text in Hanssens n. 671.
9. *Tractatus de traditione divinae missae* (PG 65:849–852). This text was circulated widely when the Byzantine liturgies were first printed (1560).
10. See, e.g., O. Bardenhewer, *Geschichte der altkirchlichen Literatur* IV (Freiburg, 1924), 207.
11. F. J. Leroy, "Proclus, 'de traditione divinae Missae': Un faux de C. Palaeocappa," *OCP* 28 (1972) 288–299.

12. See, e.g., J. A. Jungmann, *The Mass of the Roman Rite: Its Origins and Development (Missarum Solemnia)*, tr. by F. A. Brunner (2 vols.; New York, 1951, 1955), 1:35, henceforth cited as Jungman; and Hanssens, nn. 673, 658.

13. This view may still be seen in H. Lietzmann, *Mass and Lord's Supper*, tr. by D. H. G. Reeve (London, n.d.). On p. 108 Lietzmann writes: "Our further investigation will show that the developed Eastern liturgies of later times, in particular Ba. and Ja., have drawn their prefaces from the complete text of the preface of A.C."

14. See Jungmann, 1:35.

15. A. Baumstark, *Die Messe im Morgenland* (Sammlung Kösel; Kempten, 1906), 72.

16. H. Engberding, *Das Eucharistische Hochgebet der Basileiosliturgie* (Münster, 1931).

17. Ibid., lxxiv, lxxvi.

18. Jungmann, *The Place of Christ in Liturgical Prayer*, 176–185; M. J. Lubatschiwskyj, "Des heiligen Basilius liturgischer Kampf gegen den Arianismus," *ZKT* 66 (1942) 20–38.

19. Engberding lxxv.

20. Ibid., lxxvi.

21. B. Capelle, "Les liturgies 'basiliennes' et saint Basile," in J. Doresse and E. Lanne, *Un témoin archaïque de la liturgie copte de s. Basile* (Bibliothèque du Muséon 47; Louvain, 1960), Appendix.

22. Ibid., 51f.

23. Ibid., 55f.

24. Ibid., 57ff.

25. See Hanssens n. 1484 where the mss are cited in which the liturgy of St. Basil comes first.

26. *Euchê katêchoumenôn pro tês hagias anaphoras tou Chrysostomou* (Br 315).

27. *Euchê tês proskomidês tou hagiou Joannou tou Chrysostomou meta to apotithênai ta hagia dôra en tê hagia trapezê* (Br 319).

28. *Euchê opisthambônos tou Chrysostomou* (Br 343).

29. The prayer over the catechumens is, moreover, the first in the order of prayers as long as the liturgy begins with the readings (that is, until the fifth century). Hanssens thinks (n. 1490) that in the Barberini codex this prayer is the first in the order proper to the Chrysostom formulary, since the preceding prayers are missing in other mss and by and large did not win permanent acceptance.

30. Apart from the liturgy of the word and the anaphora this applies to a prayer after the anaphora, another after communion, and another at the dismissal.

31. I. E. Rahmani, *I fasti della chiesa patriarcale antiochena* (Rome, 1920), XXVI–XXXI. Idem, *Les liturgies orientales et occidentales étudiées séparément et comparées entre elles* (Beirut, 1928), 388, 403, 712.

32. H. Engberding, "Die syrische Anaphora der Zwölf Apostel und ihre Parallel-texte," *OrChr*, 3rd ser., 12 (1937) 213–247.

33. Ibid., 245.

34. A. Baumstark, "Zur Urgeschichte der Chrysostomosliturgie," *TG* 5 (1913) 299–313 at 312.

35. Ibid., 302–308.

36. See the following passages characteristic of C (in agreement with Ne) in the texts of C and Ne that Baumstark gives in parallel columns, or in Brightman where the special character of C as compared with Ba is easily recognizable. The following footnotes refer to these passages in C as given in Brightman.

37. Br 322, 5f.

38. Br 322, 13ff.

39. Br 322, 21.

40. Br 322, 23ff.

41. Br 328, 30.

42. Br 328, 30.

43. Br 329, 2.

44. Baumstark "Zur Urgeschichte," 308.

45. In a review of Lietzmann's *Messe und Herrenmahl* in *OrChr*, 3rd ser., 6 (1931) 114, Baumstark gives his final opinion: "The actual evolution of the text took . . . the form of an increasingly rich development of an originally very brief nucleus. It is precisely at this point that Engberding's study of Ba brings clarity and great precision and thus will block, once and for all, the false trail which I myself traveled in my attempt to prove the priority of the Nestorian liturgy over the liturgy of Chrysostom."

46. In his review of A. Raes, "L'authenticité de la liturgie de s. Jean Chrysostome" (*OCP* 24 [1958] 5–16) in *ALW* 7 (1961) 253, O. Heiming indicates the possibility that Chrysostom himself may have used the Liturgy of the Apostles, but he also mentions the many still unverified presuppositions needed for such a demonstration.

Section B

1. J. A. Jungmann, *The Place of Christ in Liturgical Prayer*, tr. by A. Peeler from the 2nd German ed. (Staten Island, N.Y., 1965), 144ff.

2. Ibid., 172ff.

3. Ibid., 175.

4. Ibid., 176.

5. J. Betz, *Die Eucharistie in der Zeit der griechischen Väter I/1. Die Aktualpräsenz der Person und des Heilswerkes Jesu im Abendmahl nach der vorephesinischen griechischen Patristik* (Freiburg, 1955), 128; henceforth cited as Betz.

7. Botte 16.

8. Br 328f.

9. Br 328, 20ff.

10. Br 328, 1.

11. Br 328, 10f.

12. H. Engberding, *Das eucharistische Hochgebet der Basileiosliturgie* (Münster, 1931), 24, 1–3.

13. Ibid., 25, 1–5 = Br 327, 19–23; cf. B. Capelle "La procession du Saint-Esprit d'après la liturgie grecque de s. Basile," *OrSyr* 7 (1962) 72.

14. Betz 290ff., 334ff.

15. This view of the Fathers is not the same as the identification, by the fourteenth-century Byzantine theologians, of the *moment* of consecration with the epiclesis. In the mind of the Fathers, the special epiclesis shows that it is because of its epicletic character that the anaphora enables the words of institution to exercise their efficacy. Cf. Betz 330ff.

16. Betz 391.

17. *Ad Serapionem epistulae* 1, 31 (PG 26:605A). See Betz 391.

18. Tr. in Br 287–288. See Betz 337.

19. B. Botte, "L'épiclèse dans les liturgies syriennes orientales," *SE* 6 (1954) 48–72 at 56.

20. On the term *hagiazein* cf. Betz 302ff.; on *anadeiknumi* see E. Peterson, "Die Bedeutung von *anadeiknumi* in den griechischen Liturgien," in *Festgabe A. Deissmann* (Tübingen, 1927) 320–326, and the review by A. Baumstark, *JLW* 7 (1927) 357.

21. The communion call, *ta hagia tois hagiois,* was in general use in the fourth century. For Jerusalem cf. Br 466, 24 (Cyril); for Antioch Br 475, 12 (Chrysostom) and Br 24, 20 *(Apostolic Constitutions).* On the expression *ta hagia tôn hagiôn* in the Alexandrian Fathers, see Betz 304.

22. Botte, "L'épiclèse," n. 19, 54ff., where the epiclesis texts in Ba, Ja, and C are compared and analyzed. In the process of expansion the original ending, *ta hagia tôn hagiôn,* was lost.

23. *Cat. myst.,* 5, 7 (in J. Quasten, *Monumenta eucharistica et liturgica* II [Florilegium Patristicum 7], 101). See Br 465f.

24. "*Metabalôn tô pneumati sou tô hagiô*" (Br 330, 5f.).

25. H. Engberding, "Die syrische Anaphora der Zwölf Apostel und ihre Paralleltexte, "*OrChr,* 3rd ser., 12 (1937) 213–247 at 226.

26. Botte, "L'épiclèse," 61.

27. A. Baumstark's claim (in his *Comparative Liturgy* [London, 1958], 48) that the special epiclesis of the Spirit would not have been possible before 381 is not defensible in this unqualified form (cf. ibid., the restrictive comment of the editor, B. Botte), but it is certainly valid for the more explicit formula of the concluding part of the epiclesis in C (see O. Heiming, *ALW* 5 [1957] 114).

Section C

1. Mt 26:29; Mk 14:25; Lk 22:16.

2. E. Peterson, *The Angels and the Liturgy,* tr. by R. Walls (New York, 1964), offers a theology of the Thrice Holy in the Christian liturgy.

3. On the epiclesis as liturgical form of the eucharistic incarnation see Betz 318ff.

4. Clear echoes of this passage are to be found in the Byzantine liturgy in the prayer before the elevation of the species and the breaking of the bread: "Look down upon us, Lord Jesus Christ. . . . You are enthroned above with the Father and are invisibly present with us as well. Graciously extend your mighty hand to us and give your pure body and precious blood to us and, through us, to your entire people" (Br 341; see Br 393).

5. *In Matt. hom.* 50, 3 (PG 58:507). Betz 103.

6. Ibid., 82, 5 (PG 58:744). Betz 103.

7. *Hom. de beato Philogono* 6 (PG 48:753). Betz 296.

8. The term used here, *ta teloumena,* refers to the entire ritual celebration of the liturgy (O. Casel, *JLW* 6 [1926] 153; G. Fittkau, *Der Begriff des Mysteriums bei Johannes Chrysostomos* [Theophaneia 9; Bonn, 1953] 180; Betz 296). It was used in this sense by various Fathers (Betz 220) and the later Byzantine commentators on the liturgy.

9. *In Matt. hom.* 82, 1 (PG 58:739). Betz 220.

10. *De sac.* VI, 4 (PG 48:681).

11. G. Fittkau, *Der Begriff des Mysteriums bei Johannes Chrysostomus.* Theophaneia 9 (Bonn, 1953) 87.

12. Ibid., 83.

13. Ibid., 89.

14. Ibid., 88.

15. In passages in which *mysteria* means the eucharistic celebration it occurs sixty-one times with a qualifying adjective, the latter being in twenty-eight instances some term expressing the idea of "terrifying" (Fittkau 125). These expressions, which appear first in Basil but then occur especially in Chrysostom, Cyril (or John) of Jerusalem, and Theodore of Mopsuestia (Betz 126), have received close attention from

students of liturgical history. E. Bishop was the first to see in them a manifestation of a devotional shift in the fourth century; they were then extensively studied by J. A. Jungmann in his *Die Stellung Christi im liturgischen Gebet* (Münster, 1925), 217–222; cf. now the translation of the revised 2nd ed., *The Place of Christ in Liturgical Prayer*, 244.

16. Fittkau 125.
17. Ibid., 126.
18. *Contra eos qui subintroductas habent virgines* 10 (PG 47:509).
19. Ibid., and *In I. Cor. hom.* 35, 5 (PG 61:313D).
20. *In II. Cor. hom.* 2, 6 (PG 61:399B).
21. *In Hebr. hom.* 17, 5 (PG 63:133A); *In illud: Vidi Dominum hom.* 6, 3 (PG 56:138D).
22. *In I. Cor. hom.* 40, 1 (PG 61:348B).
23. *De prod. Jud. hom.* 1, 6 (PG 49:382B).
24. Fittkau 126f.
25. *De prod. Jud. hom.* 1, 6 (PG 49:380). Betz 104.
26. *Hom. cat.* 15, 19 (R. Tonneau & R. Devreesse, [eds.], *Les homélies catéchétiques de Theodore de Mopsueste* [Studi e Testi 145; Vatican City, 1949], 495; henceforth cited as Tonneau-Devreesse). Betz 136.
27. Ibid., 15, 15 (Tonneau-Devreesse 487). Betz 132.
28. "We must think of the man who stands now at the altar as an image (*eikôn*) of that high priest. . . . For he carries out, in a kind of image (*eikôn*), the liturgy of this ineffable sacrifice" (*Hom. cat.* 15, 23; Tonneau-Devreesse 497). Betz 231.
29. Theodore is here echoing especially Lk 22:43.
30. *Hom. cat.* 15, 25 (Tonneau-Devreesse 503–505).
31. They "also have a garment (*schêma*) which corresponds to the reality, for their outward dress is more illustrious than they themselves are; on their left shoulder they wear the orarion, which hangs down at equal length on both sides." This last point is explained in detail (*Hom. cat.* 15, 23; Tonneau-Devreesse 501).
32. *Hom. cat.* 15, 26 (Tonneau-Devreesse 505).
33. Ibid., 16, 26f. (Tonneau-Devreesse 507).
34. *Epist.* I, 123 (PG 78:264D–265A). Betz 235.
35. Br 379.
36. *Hom. cat.* 16, 16 (Tonneau-Devreesse 557).
37. Ibid., 16, 11 (Tonneau-Devreesse 551–553). Betz 233.
38. Ibid., 16, 17 (Tonneau-Devreesse 559).
39. Ibid.
40. Ibid., 16, 26 (Tonneau-Devreesse 575–577).
41. See the description in Hanssens n. 1390–1395.
42. "*Eis plêrôma Pneumatos Hagiou*" (Br 341, 20).

CHAPTER TWO

Introduction

1. Even the saintly bishops of Constantinople, Gregory of Nazianzus and John Chrysostom, had to put up with interference from Alexandria. In fact, Bishop Flavian became a martyr as a result of mistreatment by Dioscurus.
2. For information on the disputes after the Council of Chalcedon and their significance in the history of theology see the extensive work of A. Grillmeier and H. Bacht (eds.), *Das Konzil von Chalkedon* I–III (Würzburg, 1951–1954).

Section A

1. Mansi 6:936C. See Hanssens n. 884.
2. Hanssens n. 886, especially p. 115.
3. Ibid., n. 891ff.
4. See below, p. 29.
5. *De fide orth.* III, 10 (PG 94:1020AB).
6. Beck 372; see Hanssens n. 885.
7. *De fide orth.* III, 10 (PG 94:1021AB).
8. *De hier. eccl.* 3, 7 (PG 3:436C). J. Stiglmayr, *Des heiligen Dionysius Areopagita angebliche Schriften über die beiden Hierarchien* (Bibliothek der Kirchenväter; Kempten, 1911), 133.
9. Hanssens n. 1136.
10. *De hier. eccl.* 3, 2 (PG 3:425B). Stiglmayr 120.
11. Marcellinus Comes, *Chronicum ad ann. 512* (PL 51:937–938). Hanssens n. 896.
12. Eustratius, *Vita S. Eutychii* 10, 92 (PG 86:2377C).
13. Appealing to Eustratius, Brightman includes this notice: *ho hiereus thymia tēn ekklēsian* in his Appendix O: "The Byzantine Liturgy before the Seventh Century" (527, 10).

Section B

1. J. Stiglmayr (*ZKT* 33 [1909] 383–385) and Hanssens (n. 684) have expounded the identity of the liturgy of Dionysius with the Syrian liturgy. Especially striking is the prominence given to the profession of faith which was introduced by Peter Knapheus in 476 at the earliest.
2. PG 3:424–445; J. Stiglmayr, *Des heiligen Dionysius Areopagita angebliche Schriften über die beiden Hierarchien* (Bibliothek der Kirchenväter; Kempten, 1911), 117–145.
3. See, e.g., Maximus, *Mystagogia*, Preface (PG 91:660) and Symeon of Thessalonica, *De sancta liturgia*, Preface (PG 155:253), and many other passages.
4. E. von Ivanka, *Dionysius Areopagita. Von den Namen zum Unnennbaren* (Sigillum 7; Einsiedeln, n.d.), 13.
5. Ch. 3, 3 (PG 3:428D–429B; Stiglmayr, *Dionysius Areopagita*, 124f.).
6. For the "uninitiated," Dionysius even gives an explanation of the synaxis as a community celebration that is based entirely on the natural structure of the liturgy (PG 3:428B; Stiglmayr, *Dionysius Areopagita*, 121f.).
7. Br 361.
8. Ch. 3, 11 (PG 3:440C; Stiglmayr, *Dionysius Areopagita*, 138).
9. See Jn 16:8. Gregory of Nyssa also refers to this passage of scripture in explaining his idea of redemption: *Or. cat.* 22 (PG 4560C).
10. H. Koch, *Pseudo-Dionysius Areopagita in seinen Beziehungen zum Neuplatonismus und Mysterienwesen* (Mainz, 1900).
11. This point is expressly made by H. U. von Balthasar, *Kosmische Liturgie. Das Weltbild Maximus' des Bekenners* (Einsiedeln, 1961), 40.
12. Betz 99, 105, etc.
13. Citations from Dionysius appear first in the writings of Patriarch Severus of Antioch (512–518; d. 538), a moderate Monophysite, and were known to the Orthodox in their discussions with the Severian bishops.

CHAPTER THREE

Introduction
1. Beck 425ff.
2. Ibid., 260f.
3. Ibid., 285f.
4. Ibid., 372.
5. Ibid., 376.
6. Ibid., 388.
7. "Only-begotten Son and Word of God [the Father], though immortal you willed for our salvation to take flesh of the holy Mother of God, Mary ever-virgin. Abiding unchanged, you became man and, nailed to the cross, O Christ our God, you destroyed death by your death. Do thou, one of the Holy Trinity and glorified equally with the Father and the Holy Spirit, rescue us!" (Br 365f.).
8. V. Grumel, "L'auteur et la date de la composition du tropaire *Ho monogenês*," *EO* 22 (1923) 398–418.
9. PG 86:995C = PL 69:227C.
10. Grumel; see Beck 54, 388.
11. PG 108:477B.
12. Br 33; 116 (James and Mark); cf. Br 365f. (Byz.).
13. C. Moeller, "Le chalcédonisme et le néochalcédonisme en Orient de 451 à la fin du VIe siècle," *Chalkedon* 1:637–720.
14. Beck 378.
15. L. H. Grondijs, *L'iconographie byzantine du Crucifié mort sur la Croix* (Leiden, 1941) = Grondijs I; idem, *Autour de l'iconographie byzantine du Crucifié mort sur la Croix* (Leiden, 1961) = Grondijs II. See the rejection of a connection between the Zeon and Aphthartite docetism in the reviews by A. Michel, *ByZ* 50 (1967) 164–167, and A. Mayer-Pfannholz, *ALW* 1 (1952) 389f.; also A. Grillmeier, *Der Logos am Kreuz. Zur christologischen Symbolik der älteren Kreuzesdarstellung* (Munich, 1956).
16. The decisive text for Grondijs' argument is from Nicetas Stethatos: There is no lifegiving power in the unleavened bread because it is dead, but in the bread that is the body of Christ "there are three living elements which bestow life on all who eat it worthily: the Spirit, water and blood. The same was manifested in the crucifixion of the Lord when the wounding of his flesh with a lance caused water and blood to flow from his pure side. For at that time the living Holy Spirit remained in his divinized flesh. When we eat it in the bread that has been transformed by the Spirit and has become this flesh, we live in him because we eat a living and divinized flesh. And when we drink the living and very warm blood together with the water that flowed from his pure side, we are cleansed from all sins and filled now with the Holy Spirit, for as you see we drink it *warm* from the chalice, *just as it flowed from the Lord's side.* For from the warm flesh of Christ that remained living through the power of the Spirit, blood and water flowed forth for us" (Grondijs II, 87f.; see Grondijs I, 46ff.).
17. Grondijs II, 89 = *ByZ* 51 (1958) 344: "I have shown the probability that the enrichment of the Byzantine eucharistic rites by the addition of the Zeon in the sixth century reflected Aphthartodocetic teaching, which both Justinian and the prelates of the capital had accepted. . . . The speedy rejection of this teaching then . . . removed the sole dogmatic basis for the new rite. . . . At this point Nicetas appealed to the action of the Holy Spirit. . . . He assumed that the Spirit did not abandon the

corpse of Christ after the soul had separated from the body and the Word had loosened his bonds with the man Jesus to the extent required for death to be possible."

Grondijs assumes that down to the eleventh century the prevailing view among theologians was that the separation of soul from body in the death of Christ presupposed a similar separation of the Logos from the body; and that Nicetas has the Holy Spirit replacing the Logos as the latter disengages himself (in whole or in part). But Grillmeier (*Der Logos am Kreuz* 11ff.; "Der Gottesohn im Totenreich," *ZKT* 71 [1949] 1–53, 184–203, espec. 187–194) and Michel (art. cit., 164f.) have shown that after Chalcedon no one maintained a separation of the Logos from the body. Leontius of Byzantium and John Damascene, whose tradition Nicetas continues, expressly teach the continuing union of the Logos with the soul on the one hand and with the body on the other.

18. "Some passages in Symeon of Thessalonica suggest that the teaching of Nicetas still had adherents at that time" (Grondijs II, 99). See pp. 119–120.

19. See below, pp. 39ff.

20. Beck 376f.

Section A

1. For the history of Hagia Sophia: A. M. Schneider, *Die Hagia Sophia zu Konstantinopel* (Berlin, 1939), and J. P. Richter, *Quellen der byzantinischen Kunstgeschichte* (Vienna, 1897) 12–101.

Hê megalê ekklêsia was the official name of the capital's principal church, which had been begun by Constantine and was consecrated in 360. At the beginning of the fifth century the name *Hê Hagia Sophia* was also current.

2. On the history of the construction of Justinian's church of Hagia Sophia, especially the initiatives taken by the emperor, the legendary miracles, and the help given by an angel, see Richter, no. 52 (pp. 23–49), where a synopsis is given of F. Combefis (*Originum rerumque Constantinopolitanarum variis auctoribus manipulus* [Paris, 1664]), Anonymus Banduri (A. Banduri, *Imperium Orientale sive Antiquitates Constantinopolitanae* [Paris, 1711, and Venice, 1729], where an anonymous eleventh-century topographical description of Constantinople and a description of the church of Hagia Sophia—usually cited as Anonymus Banduri—are given), and Kodinos (Topography of Constantinople: PG 157:613–633).

3. Schneider 13.

4. PG 157:628C. See Schneider, and Richter, no. 52 (p. 49).

5. John Cantacuzenus, *Historia* 4, 4 (CSHB 25:29).

6. "This unrivalled . . . church of 'Divine Wisdom' was henceforth as it were the heart of the Rhomaic empire, and its fortunes and misfortunes accurately mirrored those of the realm. Within its precincts all important acts of state were accomplished: here new emperors were crowned and deceased ones were mourned; here famous victories were proclaimed and triumphs were celebrated after successful wars; here too the apprehensive populace gathered when armed savage hordes beset the walls of the city. It was proudly shown to foreign ambassadors, travellers and pilgrims; on the occasion of the signing of important treaties it was festively decorated. In keeping with its importance it was populated by a throng of the clergy; at the beginning of the seventh century it was prescribed that there should be 600 of them. They were needed not only for liturgical functions but also for the solemn ceremonial of the court which at other times was secluded in the Sacred Palace. Then the solemnly majestic interior of the church became the theater in which the Eastern Roman

Empire displayed its theocratic dignity to its subjects in the blinding splendor of a magnificent display such as one associates with fairy tales" (Schneider 18).

7. While Dionysius maintains the hierarchic distance of the Church's celebrants from the angelic celebrants in heaven even during the celebration of the liturgy, Maximus emphasizes the "angelic" dignity of the faithful during the celebration of the eucharist (see below, pp. 48ff.).

8. The uniquely shallow and broad shape of the dome of Hagia Sophia was not imitated, but a dome of some kind did become obligatory.

9. Even the early Christian basilica was in a way an "image" of heaven, less however through *imitation* (e.g., of the cosmic heaven) than through *symbolization*, namely as house of the holy community (house and community alike were called *ekklêsia*), as property of Christ the Basileus (for the use of the terms *basilikê* and *oikos basileios* in Eusebius see L. Voekl, *RivAC* 29 [1953] 49–66), and as throne room of God. See E. Sauer, in J. A. Jungmann (ed.), *Symbolik der katholischen Kirche* (Symbolik der Religionen 6; [Stuttgart, 1960], 58ff.)

10. See J. Lassus, *Sanctuaires chrétiens de Syrie* (Paris, 1947), 98f.; T. Klauser, "Ciborium," *RAC* 3:85.

11. Chrysostom, *In ep. I. ad Cor. hom.* 36, 5 (PG 61:313).

12. *De aedificiis* I, 1 (CSHB 45:177; Schneider 12); tr. in C. Mango, *The Art of the Byzantine Empire 312–1463. Sources and Documents* (Englewood Cliffs, N.J., 1972), 75.

13. Ibid. (CSHB 45:175; Schneider 10); Mango 74.

14. Ibid. (CSHB 45:179; Schneider 13); Mango 76.

15. In his discourse at the dedication of the basilica of Tyre (314), Eusebius (*Historia ecclesiastica* 10, 4; GCS 9:862–883) explains the functions of the parts of the building by relation to events and happenings in the mystical body of Christ. Thus the windows of the basilica are symbolic of the enlightenment of the community by the divine light of grace.

16. C. Schneider, *Geistesgeschichte des antiken Christentums* (Munich, 1954) 100.

17. PG 86:2119–2158; Richter, nos. 61, 81, 92; partially tr. in Mango 80ff.

18. A. M. Schneider 13; Richter, nos. 56–61.

19. A. M. Schneider 13; Richter, nos. 62–64.

20. Verses 686ff. (PG 86:2145); Richter, no. 81 (p. 74); tr. Mango 87.

21. Verses 717ff.; tr. Mango 88.

22. K. Holl, "Die Entstehung der Bilderwand in der griechischen Kirche," in his *Gesammelte Aufsätze zur Kirchengeschichte* II (Tübingen, 1928) 225–237.

23. Particulars and recent literature on the origin of the iconostasis in W. Felicetti-Liebenfels, *Geschichte der byzantinischen Ikonenmalerei* (Olten-Lausanne, 1956), 73–75, and K. Onasch, "Bilderwand," *RGG* I, 1276.

24. This is especially emphasized in the interpretation of the church building given by Maximus in his *Mystagogy* (see p. 43); there too the term "entrance" occurs for the first time (see p. 46).

25. Cf. O. Treitinger, *Die oströmische Kaiser- und Reichsidee nach ihrer Gestaltung im höfischen Zeremoniell* (Darmstadt, 1956²), espec. 49–84; C. Schneider, "Das Fortleben der gesamten Antike in der griechischen Liturgie," *Kyrios* 4 (1939) 185–221 at 205f. An especially characteristic example: the picture of the Ruler of the Universe accompanied by a spear-carrying bodyguard of angels (Cherubikon).

26. The kontakion, which was the hymnic genre especially cultivated in the sixth century, is in its content "a versified sermon which relies very heavily on the dramatic devices of a rhetoric that makes use of interjections, questions, apostrophes, and so on" (Beck 264). On the relations between this literature and dramatic per-

formances see G. La Piana, *Le rappresentazioni sacre nella letteratura bizantina dalle origini al secolo IX* (Grottaferrata, 1912).

27. K. Onasch, "Der Funktionalismus der orthodoxen Liturgie," *JLH* 6 (1961) 1–48.

28. P. Trembelas, "L'audition de l'anaphora." In *1054–1954. L'Eglise et les Eglises* 2 (Chevetogne, 1955), 207–220 at 211. The loud voice was henceforth used only for the words of the introductory dialogue, the transition to the Thrice Holy, the words of institution, the words at the elevation of the species and at the remembrance of the Mother of God and the hierarchy, and for the concluding doxology.

Section B

1. *Mystagogia* 16 (PG 91:693).

2. Kedrenos, *Ad ann. Justini* 9 (PG 121:748B).

3. "Hoi ta cheroubim mystikôs eikonizontes kai tê zôopoiô triadi ton trishagion hymnon prosadontes tên biôtikên apothômetha merimnan. Hôs ton basilea tôn holôn hypodexamenoi tais aggelikais aoratôs dorupheroumenon taxesin. Allêlouia, allêlouia, allêlouia."

4. *Hom. cat.* 15, 25 (Tonneau-Devreesse 505).

5. Ibid. (Tonneau-Devreesse 503).

6. Same view in K. Onasch, *Einführung in die Konfessionskunde der orthodoxen Kirchen* (Berlin, 1962), 116: "[The Cherubikon] gives especially striking expression to the Areopagite's conception of the earthly liturgy as imitating the heavenly." See also idem, "Der Funktionalismus der orthodoxen Liturgie," 25ff.

7. PG 3:425C; J. Stiglmayr, *Des heiligen Dionysius Areopagita angebliche Schriften über die beiden Hierarchien* (Bibliothek der Kirchenväter; Kempten, 1911), 120.

8. PG 3:437A; Stiglmayr 134.

9. PG 3:437C; Stiglmayr 136.

10. PG 3:440B; Stiglmayr 137.

11. Hanssens (n. 1190) lists various codices of the Liturgy of James that have this hymn as the regular song at the Great Entrance.

12. Br 45, 25ff.: *Sigêsatô pasa sarx.* This hymn, too, is called "Cherubikon" in the mss.

13. The following utterance cannot be located in the second period of Eutychius' reign (577–582).

14. *De Pasch. et S. Euch.* 8 (PG 86:2400f.); English translation in R. Taft, *The Great Entrance. A History of the Transfer of Gifts and Other Preanaphoral Rites of the Liturgy of St. John Chrysostom.* OCA 200 (Rome, 1975; 2nd ed. 1978); henceforth cited as Taft.

15. Thus, e.g., Hanssens n. 1114. Brightman (532, 17f.) says: "Both of the existing Cherubic Hymns *Hoi ta cheroubim* and *Sigêsatô* are open to this criticism, and one of them may be, inaccurately, referred to."

16. The corresponding words in the hymn *Sigêsatô* are: "Basileus tôn basileuontôn" ("King of all who exercise kingship").

17. But Brightman observes (573) with regard to the hymn *Nun hai dynameis* that "this may be the form alluded to 532, 9 (Eutychios '. . . Basilea doxês . . .'), in which case it must have been used at first in the ordinary liturgy." But he does not take into account the Easter Chronicle for 615.

18. PG 92:989AB.

19. Br 346, 13.

20. Br 348, 16.

21. Br 348, 21ff.

22. *Protheoria* 18 (PG 140:441B).

23. M. Tarchnišvili, *Die byzantinische Liturgie als Verwirklichung der Einheit und Gemeinschaft im Dogma* (Würzburg, 1939), 27, describes the Great Entrance as follows: "This sacred dance frequently takes such moving and enchanting forms that many of the faithful cast themselves to the floor and remain lying there. The procession advances over the outstretched 'corpses' and completes its sacred course at the altar, while the choirs repeat the song of the angels, the Cherubikon, . . . that had been begun even before the procession, and sing it to the end."

24. *Commentary on the Divine Liturgy*, tr. by J. M. Hussey and P. A. McNulty (London, 1960), 65 (italics added).

25. On the controversy over leavened bread between the Byzantines and the Latins see Hanssens nn. 230–261 and A. Michel, *Humbert und Kerullarios* (Paderborn, 1930); for the same controversy between the Byzantines and the Armenians see Hanssens nn. 262–282; on the Jacobite custom of using salt and oil in the preparation of the sacrificial bread and on the resultant controversies with the Byzantines and the Armenians, see Hanssens nn. 281–295, and W. de Vries, *Sakramententheologie bei den syrischen Monophysiten* (Rome, 1940), 155–162.

26. See Hanssens nn. 400–479.

27. Ibid., nn. 442,448.

28. Ibid., n. 442.

29. Ibid., n. 446.

30. Ibid.

31. De Vries 157.

32. Canon 32 (Mansi XI, 956–957).

33. This testimony implies that the rite of the Zeon had become universal in the sixth century. See, e.g., Grondijs 83ff.; Hanssens n. 410; Beck 242.

34. PG 132:1249S. For the ms tradition of the *Narratio de rebus Armeniae*, which probably originated in the eleventh century, and for the various attributions of it see Grondijs 83 and Beck 532.

35. Mansi XI, 956–957.

36. The passage in Chrysostom (PG 58:740A) reads as follows: "Why did the risen Lord drink no water but only wine? Since there are some who are accustomed to use water in the mysteries, he wanted to show that he established the mysteries using wine, and therefore when he rose from the dead he set the customary table with wine." Chrysostom is here opposing certain heretics who attempted to celebrate the Eucharist with water. See Hanssens nn. 391–399.

37. Hanssens n. 444.

38. Ibid., n. 473.

39. See the argument of the Trullan Synod (Canon 32) and, among the Jacobites, e.g., George, "Bishop of the Arab Tribes" (d. 724); in Hanssens n. 473 and de Vries 162.

40. Trullan Synod, Canon 32 (Mansi XI, 956–957).

41. See pp. 19–20.

42. *Hom. cat.* 16, 17 (Tonneau-Devreesse 559). See J. P. de Jong, "Le rite de la communion dans la messe Romaine dans ses rapports avec les liturgies syriennes," *ALW* 4 (1955) 245–278 at 261ff.

43. An accompanying formula, initially a simple blessing, appears for the first time in the translation of the liturgy by Leo Tuscus, who was active at the court of Emperor Manuel I (1143–1180). See Grondijs 90. The customary thirteenth-century formula, *Zesis Pneumatos Hagiou* (Fervor of the Holy Spirit) (see Grondijs 91ff.) closely imitates the formula of the commingling.

44. Codex Barberinus gr. 336: Br 309–344.

45. Ibid., 341.

46. Nicephorus, Canon 30, 13 (in J. Pitra, *Juris ecclesiastici Graecorum historia et monumenta* II [Rome, 1868], 330): "A priest must not celebrate the liturgy without warm water, unless there is a large congregation and no warm water is to be found anywhere."

47. This is how Theodore of Mopsuestia at any rate sees the resurrection proclaimed. See Betz 233f.

Section C

1. PG 91:657–717; English translation in J. Stead, *The Church, the Liturgy, and the Soul of Man: The Mystagogia of St. Maximus the Confessor* (Still River, Mass., 1982).

2. PG 91:660D–661A).

3. Chap. 2: "How and in what manner the holy church of God is an image of the universe, which consists of visible and invisible beings" (PG 91:668C).

4. Chap. 4: "How and in what manner the holy church of God represents the human person in a symbolic way, and how it in turn is represented by human beings as a human being" (PG 91:672A). See Chap. 5: The church and the soul.

5. Chap. 6: "How and in what manner even holy Scripture is called a human being" (PG 91:684A), and Chap. 7: "How the world is called a human being, and in what way the human being in turn is called a world" (PG 91:684D).

6. PG 91:668D–669A.

7. DS 294, tr. in ND, no. 612. Leo's formulation was adopted by the Sixth Ecumenical Council (DS 557).

8. "Maximus was . . . the soul of the Lateran Synod" of 649 and thus the crucial forerunner of the Sixth Ecumenical Council.

9. PG 91:669AB.

10. *Mystagogia* 8 (PG 91:688).

11. "Lord and Master, our God! You have appointed the orders and armies of angels and archangels for the liturgy of your glory in heaven. Grant that as we enter the holy angels too may enter to celebrate the liturgy with us and glorify your goodness" (Br 312ff., after the Barberini Codex from the end of the eighth century).

12. *Mystagogia* 9 (PG 91:689).

13. Ibid., 10–12 (PG 91:689).

14. Ibid., 13–14 (PG 91:692).

15. Ibid., 16 (PG 91:693).

16. Ibid., 17 (PG 91:693).

17. Ibid., 18 (PG 91:696).

18. Ibid., 19 (PG 91:696).

19. Ibid., 20 (PG 91:696).

20. Ibid., 16 (PG 91:693).

21. Ibid., 21 (PG 91:696).

22. Ibid., 22 (PG 91:697).

23. Ibid., 23 (PG 91:697C).

24. Ibid., 24 (PG 91:701D).

25. Ibid. (PG 91:704D). Here, in contrast to chapter 21, there is explicitly question of communion.

26. Ibid., 23 (PG 91:700D).

27. Ibid., 24 (PG 91:704C).

218

28. *Ambigua* (an explanation of obscure passages in Gregory of Nyassa and Dionysius) (PG 91:1308A).
29. *Commentarium in Johannem* 19, 1 (PG 14:536D).

CHAPTER FOUR

Section A
1. Basic for an understanding of this program are: E. Giordani, "Das mittelbyzantinische Ausschmuckungssystem als Ausdruck eines hieratischen Bildprogramms,"
JÖBG 1 (1951) 103–134, and O. Demus, *Byzantine Mosaic Decoration* (London, 1947).
2. For the change in the program of decoration in the fourteenth century see
pp. 100f.
3. See pp. 56ff.
4. See pp. 77–78ff.
5 PG 95:309–344;
6. But on the date of death see Beck 477.
7. Beck 488.
8. This patriarch's loss of the iconoclast emperor's favor is mentioned in the text
(PG 95:333A). Beck 488–following J. M. Hoeck, "Stand und Aufgaben der Damaske-
nos-Forschung," *OCP* 17 (1951) 5–60 at 26, and M. B. Melioranskij, *George of Cyprus and
John of Jerusalem, Two Little-known Battlers for Orthodoxy in the Eighth Century* (in Russian; St. Petersburg, 1901)—gives 764 as the actual year for the composition of the
discourse and says that the version that has survived originated in Byzantium around
the time of the Seventh Council.
9. PG 95:313C–316B.
10. Ibid.; 325C–328A.
11. Thus Theodore says: "Those who look at the icons see Christ in them" (ibid.,
429A); "An icon of Christ is nothing else than Christ, except for the difference
in nature" (425D); "We call icons of Christ 'Christ' " (337C). See L. Koch, "Zur
Theologie der Christusikone," *BM* 20 (1938) 168–175 at 170. All of Koch's essays under the same title (ibid., 19 [1937] 375–387; 20 [1938] 32–47, 168–175, 281–288, 437–
452) are fundamental for understanding the theology of images. According to John
Damascene, images "are filled with God's power and grace, because the name of
him whom they represent is invoked upon them in a kind of epiclesis" (Beck 301).
12. Definition of the Seventh Ecumenical Council (Nicea II) (DS 600; ND 1251).
13. Ibid. Even more explicit is the formula of the Fourth Council of Constantinople
(869–870): "We decree that the sacred image of our Lord Jesus Christ, the liberator
and Saviour of all men, must be venerated (*proskyneisthai*) with the same honor as is
given to the book of the holy Gospels" (DS 653; ND 1253).
14. It was precisely at this council that the concept of "unwritten tradition" (*para-
dosis aggraphos*) was worked out and set alongside that of "written tradition" (*para-
dosis eggraphos*) (DS 611).
15. God was the first to make an image of himself, namely, his Son (John Damascene, PG 94:1345AB); the incarnation grounds the representational character of the
image of Christ; Christ himself instituted images when he sent his image to Abgar.
Finally, images have divine legitimation due to the supernatural origin of many
of them. On the image sent to Abgar and other images "not made by human hands"
(*acheiropoiêta*), see E. von Dobschütz, *Christusbilder* (Leipzig, 1899). The reports of
miracles found their way even into the acts of the councils.
16. "For, as though the language of the words contained in this book [the Gospels]

219

all can reach salvation, so, due to the action which these images exercise by their colours, all, wise and simple alike, can derive profit from them. For, what speech conveys in words, pictures announce and bring out in colours. It is fitting, in accordance with sane reason and with the most ancient tradition, since the honour is referred to the principal subject, that the images derived from it be honoured and venerated, as is done for the sacred book of the holy Gospels and for the image of the precious cross" (DS 654; ND 1253). Nicephorus and Theodore of Studios even give images priority over the word, because they are less open to misinterpretation, but especially because they bring us closer to the eschatological vision (see Beck 304).

17. Theodore of Studios praises John the Spatharios, who had chosen an icon of St. Demetrius as a sponsor in a baptism, and he takes the occasion to compare the presence of the saint in his icon with that of Christ in his word when he healed the centurion's servant: "There the divine word took the place of the Lord's bodily presence; here the material icon took the place of its original. There the great Logos was present in his word, invisibly accomplishing the great miracle of healing by the power of his divinity, and here the venerable martyr was spiritually present in his image in order to hold the child in his arms" (PG 99:961BC).

18. The common view was that the authentic features of Christ were made known in the Abgar image and the other *acheiropoiêta*.

19. The traditional features of the icons of Christ correspond to the original, even after the ascension and at the second coming. The correspondence is guaranteed by the words: "This Jesus, who was taken from you into heaven, will come in the same way as you saw him go into heaven" (Acts 1:11). Therefore the picture of the Pantocrator is identical with the typical Christ of the ascension icons.

20. Therefore the sight of the image of Christ is a foretaste and guarantee of the eschatological vision. One cannot reject the former without excluding oneself from the latter: "If then any one does not venerate the image of Christ the Savior, let him not see him when he comes in the glory of his Father . . . but let him be separated from communion with him and from his glory" (DS 655).

21. On the connection between icon painting and ancient Egyptian portraiture see W. Felicetti-Liebenfels, *Geschichte der byzantinischen Ikonenmalerei* (Olten-Lausanne, 1956), 15. The depiction of the individual saints, which has remained unaltered in Byzantine iconography through many centuries and is determined by books of rules, is based on the conviction that it conveys the true features of the persons portrayed. The depiction of the princes of the apostles goes back in fact to a very ancient iconographic tradition.

22. Sources for the Nea: J. P. Richter, *Quellen der byzantinischen Kunstgeschichte* (Vienna, 1897), nos. 948–961 (pp. 352–359).

23. Photius, *Description of the New Church of the Most Blessed Mother of God:* in George Kodinos, *Excerpta* (CSHB 16, 199f.); tr. in C. Mango, *The Art of the Byzantine Empire 312–1453. Sources and Documents* (Englewood Cliffs, N.J., 1972), 186.

24. Mansi XIII, 252C.

25. God the Father cannot be represented since he is by nature "uncircumscribable." It is due to the incarnation that Christ can be represented. The Holy Spirit can be represented only in the forms in which he has revealed himself: as a dove at the baptism in the Jordan, and as fiery tongues at his descent upon the apostles. Regarding icons of the Trinity see L. Ouspensky and V. Lossky, *The Meaning of Icons*, tr. by G. E. H. Palmer and E. Kadloubovsky (Boston, 1969), 202–207.

26. On the possibility of representing the angels, see below, pp. 59ff.

27. Discourse against Caballinus 3 (PG 95:313C).

220

28. Mansi XI, 977–980.

29. On the icon of Christ as an anamnesis of redemption, and especially of the incarnation, see Koch 281–288, 437–452.

30. On the eschatological aspect of the icons of the ascension see Ouspensky and Lossky 198. On the other hand, the image of the Pantocrator seems to be an abbreviated version of the ascension icon and is used in place of the latter in the dome. See Demus 20.

31. The second coming is also mentioned as an object of remembrance in the anamnesis. The Fathers of the Eighth Council (Constantinople IV) make the vision of Christ at his second coming depend on veneration of his icons now (DS 655).

32. See Demus 54.

33. This is described by Paul the Silentiary: "In the midst . . . has been placed a shining silver orb, and a cross surmounts it all" (Richter, no. 81, p. 75; PG 86:2145, vv. 736ff.; Mango 88).

34. Nicephoras Gregoras gives exact measurements in describing the restoration of the Pantocrator image in the dome after the earthquake of 1346 (CSHB 40, 255). The medallion has a diameter of 11.6 m; the height of the head is 6,44 m. These are very close to the proportions of the Pantocrator image preserved in the church of Daphni; see A. M. Schneider, "Die Kuppelmosaiken der Hagia Sophia zu Konstantinopel," *Nachrichten der Akademie der Wissenschaften in Göttingen, Phil.-Hist. Kl.* (1949), 345–355 at 350).

35. Restorations of the church and/or the dome occurred in 869 and 986–994 (A. M. Schneider 355).

36. See J. Pascher, "Der Christus Pantokrator in der Liturgie," *Jahresbericht der Görres-Gesellschaft 1939* (Cologne, 1940), 42ff.

37. The Platytera (*platytera ton ouranon*) may be regarded as a later extension of the pictorial type known as the Blachernitissa (the image venerated in the church of St. Mary at Blachernae). The representation in the Nea corresponds to the Blachernitissa. See Felicetti-Liebenfels 49f. and Plate 6 on 44. For other representations widely used in Byzantium see the iconographic index, Felicetti-Liebenfels 128.

38. Thus the opening stanza in particular: "O Mother of God, I, your City, freed now from danger, dedicate to you, the champion and leader, thanksgivings for victory."

39. See H.-J. Schulz, "Die 'Höllenfahrt' als 'Anastasis,' " *ZKT* 81 (1959) 1–66 at 10ff.

40. Discourse against Caballinus 11 (PG 95:328BC).

41. The Fathers of the Seventh Council appeal to the apparitions of angels as the basis for their acceptance of icons of angels: "Patriarch Tarasius said: 'The Father [John of Thessalonica, whose work had just been read] thus shows that the angels too are to be painted since they are circumscribed beings and many of them have appeared to human beings.' The Holy Synod said: 'So it is, Lord!' " (Mansi XIII, 164f.). There is evidently a reference here to angelic apparitions in the New Testament and not to the prophetic visions of the Cherubim and Seraphim.

42. See Dionysius, *Hierarchia caelestis* 2 and 15. Of course, there is question here of the imaged *language* of scripture and not of iconographic representations. The prophets do not draw pictures of the angels but offer symbols that require anagogical interpretation in order that "we may not be so impious as to believe, with the crowd, that celestial and godlike spirits are provided with many feet and faces, that they are formed as stupid like oxen or ferocious like lions, or that they have curved beaks like eagles or shaggy feathers like birds. Nor are we to imagine that they are fiery wheels above the heavens, or material thrones on which the Thearchy may rest, or

many-colored horses, or spear-carrying war-leaders, or whatever else the scriptures have conveyed to us in sacred images and a medley of richly meaningful symbols" (ch. 2; J. Stiglmayr, *Des heiligen Dionysius Areopagita angebliche Schriften über die beiden Hierarchien* [Bibliothek der Kirchenväter; Kempten, 1911], 6). Imaged language is used even of God and Christ in the scripture (Stiglmayr 15). The scriptures use conflicting symbols, lest we "cling to the types as though they were true in themselves" (Stiglmayr 16). Chapter 15 (Stiglmayr 73–86) interprets the symbols in detail.

43 See n. 41.

44. The first triad of angelic orders includes the Seraphim, Cherubim, and Thrones (*Hierarchia caelestis* 7); the second triad, Dominations, Virtues, and Powers (ch. 8); the third, Principalities, Archangels, and Angels (ch. 9).

45. This is the date given by A. M. Schneider 355 for the representations of the Cherubim. There were restorations in 869 and 986–994.

46. This emerges from the poems of Nicetas Stethatos (CSHB 41:783) and George Phrantzis (CSHB 19:289), which probably allude to one of the songs for the dedication of Hagia Sophia. See A. M. Schneider 353f.

47. The most famous example of a representation of the ascension in a dome from this period is the mosaic in the dome of the church of Hagia Sophia in Salonica. See A. M. Ammann, *La pittura sacra bizantina* (Rome, 1957), 65, 90, fig. 1.

48. *Hierarchia caelestis* 12: "It is therefore . . . not at all out of place that the word of God should call our hierarch too an 'angel,' since by the power that is special to him he shares in the interpretative function of the angels and, as far as is possible for a human being, is elevated to the rank of proclaimer like them" (Stiglmayr 63).

49. See Giordani 132.

50. Ibid., 125.

51. Ibid.

Section B

1. Theodore of Studios, *Kephalaia* (PG 99:489B).

2. See the same argument in John Damascene (Beck 301). Therefore no one who rejects images can have a share in the redemption (DS 655).

3. Koch 447.

4. Dread of interfering with the traditional organization, even while engaged in creative liturgical effort, led to the addition of ever new supplementary rites of preparation and conclusion. As a result, the original beginning of the liturgy at the Little Entrance had prefixed to it, one after another, the individual parts of the enarxis (since the seventh century), the rites and prayers of the prothesis, the set prayers at the donning of the liturgical vestments, and the prayers before the iconostasis (as late as the fourteenth century). Similar phenomena can be observed in all the liturgical families.

5. Mansi XI, 977–980. See above p. 57.

6. Basic here: M. Mandalà, *La protesi della liturgia nel rito bizantino-greco* (Grottaferrata, 1935), and Hanssens nn. 782–795.

7. PG 86:2400-1. See above, p. 38.

8. See Hanssens n. 1111.

9. For this dating see below, pp. 67f.

10. N. Borgia, *Il commentario liturgico di S. Germano patriarca costantinopolitano e la versione latina di Anastasio Bibliotecario* (Studi Liturgici 1; Grottaferrata, 1912), 28; henceforth cited as Borgia.

11. This is Hanssens' view, n. 787.

12. From this time on, at the latest, the bread for the sacrifice or, as the case might be, its sealed middle section has been called "lamb." After the consecration the name "lamb" reappears at the fraction.

13. Borgia 19f.

14. See Borgia 7 and Mandalà 60ff.

15. Br 309. Even though the concluding prayer of the priest at the prothesis is the only text in the codex, it does not exclude extensive preparatory actions by priest and deacon (as well as accompanying words not included in the order of prayers in the Euchologion).

16. The translation made by Anastasius in 869–870 is based on an interpolated redaction of the commentary that had been in existence for some time (see below, pp. 68f.).

17. Borgia 20f.

18. Thus according to Hanssens n. 788 and Mandalà 60ff. The attribution to Gregory of Decapolis is disputed, however; the manuscript tradition does not go back beyond the fourteenth century (Beck 579). The ritual actions mentioned in this account (cruciform incision with the lance, thus dividing the lamb into four parts, and the subsequent pouring of wine and water) are also attested in the commentary translated by Anastasius. But the type of vision by which the Saracen is converted fits in better with fourteenth-century ideas that play a part especially in the iconography of that period.

19. PG 100:1201C–1203C.

20. Betz 277–300.

21. Br 309: "Lord, our God . . . look on us and on this bread and this cup, and make the bread your undefiled body and the cup your precious blood for participation by souls and bodies."

22. Ibid.

23. In its rejection of the iconoclast thesis (presented at the iconoclast synod of 754) that there is only *one* authentic image of Christ, namely the eucharist, the Seventh Council expressly declares that the eucharist is not an "image" but the "reality" of the body of Christ, but that before the consecration the bread and wine may rightly be described as "images" (*antitypa*) of the body of Christ (Mansi XIII, 265BC).

Section C

1. Beck 473f.

2. Under this title an extensively interpolated redaction became very widely known when joined to the first printed editions of the liturgical formularies (Rome, 1526; Paris, 1560) (= PG 98:383–454). There is a list of the various editions in S. Pétridès, "Traités liturgiques de saint Maxime et de saint Germain," *ROC* 10 (1905) 287–313, 350–364, at 293f. Two English translations of the work are now available: *Historia ecclesiastica. The Contemplation of the Divine Liturgy by Our Father among the Saints Germanus I, Patriarch of Constantinople*, D. Sheerin (trans.), icons written by M. Melone (Fairfax, Va., no date), which provides a translation as edited by Borgia; and P. Meyendorff (ed.), *St. Germanus of Constantinople on the Divine Liturgy. The Greek Text with Translation, Introduction, and Commentary* (Crestwood, N.Y., 1984), which contains a reedition of Borgia's reconstruction of the Greek text.

3. Pétridès 292f. and Borgia 2 list the attributions of the individual mss.

4. See n. 2 and Borgia 2, n. 3.

5. Pétridès 287ff.

6. Ibid., 296f.

7. See above, p. 62. F. E. Brightman, "The *Historia mystagogica* and Other Greek Commentaries on the Byzantine Liturgy," *JTS* 9 (1908) 248–267, 387–398, assumes that Theodore used Germanus. The symbolisms that Theodore assumes as familiar can be documented in Germanus as follows: "hê hagia trapeza (the holy table) = Borgia 11, lines 7f.; *hê longkê* (the lance) = Borgia 19, lines 30f.; *to eilêton* (the eiliton or corporal) = Borgia 28, lines 23f.

8. See above, p. 65.

9. Vat. gr. 790 (fourteenth century) and Neap. gr. II B 2 (1526). See Borgia 2 and 7f. Borgia gives the text of these mss and the translation of Anastasius (after Petrides) in parallel columns.

10. Borgia 25.

11. Ibid., 26.

12. PG 99:337 (see above, p. 54,n.11).

13. The deacons are practically called angels when the commentary says at the Thrice Holy: "the priest being between the two cherubim" (Borgia 33, line 26), since the "cherubim" are obviously the deacons with their ripidia (fans), or when at the description of the symbolism of resurrection "the white-robed angel" is said to perform the deacon's actions.

14. This kind of identification is expressed by the verb "is" (*esti*): e.g., "the gospel is the parousia" (Borgia 26, line 15), or "the wine and water is the blood . . . that came forth" (Borgia 19, lines 26ff.). It is true, of course, that even before the author undertook his explanation, many liturgical objects and names belonging properly to the higher realities signified: *hê longkê* (the lance), *ho aêr* (the veil), etc.

15. But a determination does seem to be at least hinted at in the frequently recurring verb *emphainei* (make visible, allow to be seen, reveal). Liturgical forms would accordingly have to be regarded as fully transparent media for the manifestation of higher (salvation-historical and heavenly) realities. See H.-J. Schulz, "Der österliche Zug im Erscheinungsbild byzantinischer Liturgie," in B. Fischer and J. Wagner (eds.), *Paschatis Sollemnia. Studien zur Osterfeier und Osterfrömmigkeit* (Freiburg, 1959), 242 and n. 7.

16. Borgia 16. Even today a red sticharion is prescribed for the bishop.

17. Borgia 16f.

18. Ibid., 17. The point of this symbolism and its connection with the symbolism of the sticharion (alb) becomes clear in the explanation of the ascent to the episcopal cathedra after the Little Entrance: "The bishop seats himself because the Son of God took fleshly human nature and lifted the sheep—that is, the mass of Adam's descendants (for that is what the omophorion [the pallium] signifies)—on his shoulders, carried them beyond all the Principalities, Virtues, and Dominations among the heavenly powers, and led them to God the Father" (Borgia 24).

19. Borgia 10.

20. Ibid., 10f.

21. Ibid., 11.

22. Ibid. This same passage of scripture is also cited in the description of the sacrificial bread on the table of preparation (Borgia 19) and carries a simultaneous allusion to the prothesis prayer (Br 309, 8ff., left-hand column).

23. See below, pp. 91–92.

24. Borgia 11.

25. Ibid., 13.

224

26. Ibid., 13f.

27. Ibid., 14.

28. This description seems to be inspired by the hymn *Sigêsatô*, which is still sung at the Great Entrance on Holy Saturday.

29. Borgia 29f.

30. Ibid., 30f. This passage in Germanus seems to presuppose the troparion, "Noble Joseph" (*Ho euschêmôn Iôsêph,* Br 379), which however is not contained in the Barberini Codex. In any case, the Letter of Isidore of Pelusium, which virtually provides a model for the hymn (see above, p. 19), is also used in explaining the liturgy. A citation from Isidore was also interpolated in the commentary of Germanus (Borgia 8 and 43).

31. Borgia 31.

32. The reference is probably to the profession of faith. The allusion was evidently felt to be insufficient, and passages from the *Mystagogy* of Maximus on the kiss of peace and the profession of faith are included among the most recent interpolations.

33. Contrary to present-day practice, the veil was removed only immediately before the anaphora, and the deacon showed it to the people from the ambo (see Hanssens n. 1179–1181). The symbolism of burial and resurrection in these rites acquired a particularly pictorial character when the aer was remodeled and became the epitaphios (see below, pp. 110f.).

34. Borgia 32f. See Br 321.

35. The *Apostolic Constitutions* (Br 14, 3ff.) had already prescribed that a deacon should stand at the right and left of the altar and keep flies away from the sacrificial gifts.

36. Borgia 33, lines 24f.

37. Ibid., 36, lines 12f.

38. Ibid., 36f.

39. Ibid., 21.

40. Ibid.

41. Ibid., 22.

42. Ibid., 24.

43. Ibid., 26.

44. See above, pp. 65ff.

CHAPTER FIVE

Section A

1. This meaningful location was chosen with good artistic sense, for the curved surface of the niches makes it possible to represent all the figures in the scene as facing the viewer (this is in keeping with the nature of images connected with worship), while not disturbing the internal coherence of the scene. See O. Demus, *Byzantine Mosaic Decoration* (London, 1947), 7–9. In addition, the area above which the dome rises is the area of the ecclesial cosmos in which heaven (the dome) and earth (the nave) meet and is therefore the proper location for the pictorial rendering present of the God-Man's saving deeds.

2. See E. Giordani, "Das mittelbyzantinische Ausschmückungssystem als Andruck eines hieratischen Bildprogramms," *JÖBG* (1951) 103–134 at 107ff. (with plan showing arrangement of pictures).

3. Ibid., 109f. See Demus, Plate 43 (plan showing arrangement of pictures).

4. Giordani 110f. See Demus, Plate 43B (plan showing arrangement of pictures).

5. The scenes are for the following feasts: Nativity of Mary (Sept. 8), Exaltation of the Cross (Sept. 14), Entry of the Mother of God into the Temple (Nov. 21), Nativity of our Lord Jesus Christ (Dec. 25), Epiphany of the Lord (Jan. 6), Meeting (= Presentation) of the Lord (Feb. 2), Annunciation (March 25), Entry into Jerusalem (Palm Sunday), Ascension of Christ, Pentecost, Transfiguration of the Lord (Aug. 6), Dormition (Assumption) of Mary (Aug. 15). Easter, as the feast of feasts, stands above the twelve major feasts.

6. G. Millet, *Recherches sur l'iconographie de l'évangile* (Paris, 1916), 15–30. Millet also gives here the literary sources most informative for the development of the calendar and the cycle of feasts.

7. Thus, e.g., A. Grabar, "Un rouleau liturgique constantinoplitain et ses peintures," *DOP* 8 (1954) 161–199 at 189f.

8. Br 328f.

9. Borgia 10.

Section B

1. A. Papadopoulos-Kerameus, *Hierosolymitikê Bibliothêkê* III (St. Petersburg, 1897), 169–175, and A. Grabar, "Un rouleau liturgique constantinoplitain et ses peintures," *DOP* 8 (1954) 161–199 (with reproductions of all the illustrations of the scroll and a facsimile).

2. Beck 645.

3. Grabar 166.

4. Ibid. In the form given, the prayer offered for the authorities during the anaphora ("for our most faithful kings, dear to Christ. . . . for the queen, dear to Christ") presupposes that several emperors are coreigning. Within the time of origin that is possible from the iconographic and paleographic standpoints, the presupposition was verified in 1067–1071 and 1092–1118; the second of these two periods is the more likely time of origin for the scroll because it is a longer period and because by this later period iconography had developed still further.

5. Grabar 165f. and 174. St. George is twice represented in privileged places: first, at the head of the scroll, along with Christ, Mary, Basil, Chrysostom, and a contemporary bishop, and in a decorative setting that is reminiscent of the architecture of a cruciform, domed church; and, second, together with John the Baptist in an illustration at the commemoration of the saints during the anaphora. This association with saints of higher rank is best explained if George was patron of the church, since the patron of a church was also presented on the iconostasis with Christ, Mary, and John the Baptist.

6. Grabar 164 and 174. Accompanied by the caption *He Kôn(stanti)noupolis*, the walls of the city serve as an illustration at the prayer offering in the anaphora for the city "in which we live."

7. Grabar describes three other scrolls of this kind, 168f., 170f., and 171f. A list of about a hundred illustrated Byzantine scrolls on various subjects is given in B. V. Farmakovskij, in *Communications of the Russian Archeological Institute of Constantinople* (in Russian) 6 (101) 25ff.

8. The scroll, done in a fine hand, gives the prayers of the priest for the Liturgy of Chrysostom, along with abridged rubrics. The quietly spoken main parts of these prayers are written in small letters; the parts to be spoken aloud (especially the con-

cluding doxology) and the rubrics are in capitals. All the incipits of the prayers have elaborate initials which are made up of one or more figures and stand to the left of the text. Figures corresponding to each initial are in the right-hand margin and, together with the initials, sometimes form depictions of scenes. In addition to the initials (and their corresponding pictures), the scroll also has the following depictions: (1) the ornamentation described above in n. 5; (2) eight individual angels (1 cherub, 1 seraph, 45 archangels, 2 angels) as an illustration of the silent prayer at the Thrice Holy; (3) before and after the words of institution a two-part representation of the communion of the apostles; and (4) a representation of the heavenly liturgy, which is spread across the entire width of the text at the silent prayer of the Great Entrance.

9. See Grabar 187f., where the evidence from the monumental painting of the eleventh and twelfth centuries is adduced for pictorial theme in the scroll.

10. Of the subjects in the cycle of festal pictures that later became obligatory for the churches, the ascension and the sending of the Spirit are missing here. The number twelve (not yet canonized) is reached by including the raising of Lazarus and the scene on the Mount of Olives.

11. Grabar gives some suggestions for the interpretation of this association, but these are deliberately fragmentary (182), and he declines to appeal to individual commentaries on the liturgy.

12. Br 312, 15.

13. *Mystagogy* 8 (PG 91:688C; H. U. von Balthasar, *Kosmische Liturgie. Das Weltbild Maximus' des Bekenners* [Einsiedeln, 1961], 386).

14. See the continuation of the passage just cited: ". . . in virtue of which he prepared himself to redeem and ransom . . . human nature. He paid the entire ransom for it as though he were the debtor instead of being in fact innocent and sinless, and thus he brought it back to the original grace of the kingdom, offering himself as price and ransom for us."

15. Correspondingly, the *Protheoria* and later interpreters of the liturgy see in the Little Entrance a symbol of the first public appearance of the Lord and of his manifestation at his baptism.

16. PG 140:429C.

17. At the same time, however, the picture of the annunciation enjoys a priority both in form and in temporal content, as can be seen from the fact that the compositional movement within the two pictures is from right to left (this is universally true in the pictures of scenes in this scroll).

18. Br 317, 9.

19. Br 318, 4.

20. For the representation of the heavenly liturgy see below, pp. 111–114.

21. Br 321, 28.

22. Br 332, 8f.

23. Br 328.

24. On the anastasis (resurrection) see H.-J. Schulz, "Die 'Höllenfahrt' als 'Anastasis,' " ZKT 81 (1959) 1–66.

25. Br 324, 14ff.

26. On the representation of the communion of the apostles see below, p. 103.

27. Grabar does not pay sufficient heed to this symbolism when he says (184) that the picture of Pentecost would be equally appropriate as an illustration here. See, however, ibid., 193.

28. Ibid., 193.

29. Br 329, 12.

30. Br 330, 13ff.

31. Br 325, 26ff.

32. Br 338.

33. G. Millet, "La vision de Pierre d'Alexandrie," in *Mélanges Charles Diehl* II (Paris, 1930), 99–115 at 107.

34. Ibid., 113. Millet provides the Latin text of Codex Vaticanus 622, fol. 114–117 (tenth century); this is closely related to the Greek text on which the redaction of the life in the Greek synaxaria depends and which in turn inspired the iconographic presentation.

35. Ibid., 106ff.

36. Br 340, 23f.

37. See *The Protoevangelium of James* 7,2 to 8,1, in E. Hennecke and W. Schnee-melcher, *New Testament Apocrypha*, translation ed. by R. McL. Wilson, I (Philadelphia, 1963), 378: "And when the child was three years old, Joachim said: 'Let us call the undefiled daughters of the Hebrews, and let each one take a lamp, and let these be burning in order that the child may not turn back and her heart be enticed away from the temple of the Lord.' And he did so until they went up to the temple of the Lord. And the priest took her and kissed her and blessed her, saying: 'The Lord has magnified your name among all generations; because of you the Lord at the end of days will manifest his redemption to the children of Israel.' . . . And her parents went down wondering, praising and glorifying the almighty God because the child did not *turn back* [to them]. And Mary was in the temple nurtured like a dove and *received food from the hand of an angel*."

38. See the *Transitus Mariae* 7 (according to the Latin version attributed to Bishop Melito of Sardis), in H. Daniel-Rops, *The Book of Mary*, tr. by A. Guinan (New York, 1960), 197: "And behold, suddenly the Lord Jesus Christ came with a great multitude of angels. . . . Then the Saviour spake, saying: Come, thou most precious pearl, enter into the treasury (receptacle) of eternal life." For the iconography of the Koimesis see L. Wratislaw-Wratislaw-Mitrovic and N. Okunev, in *Byzslav* 3 (1931) 134–174.

39. Br 341, 8.

40. Br 342.

41. Br 397f. This prayer has a different form in the Codex Barberinus from the end of the eighth century.

42. Br 344.

43. Thomist sacramental theology distinguishes in the sign not only a memorial but also a demonstrative and prophetic dimension, as well as an aspect of obligation.

44. *Protheôria kephalaiôdês peri tôn en tê theia leitourgia ginomenôn symbolôn kai mystêriôn* (PG 140:417–468).

45. Nicholas and Theodore refer to Germanus' commentary under the name of St. Basil. He intends to suppose as valid and not repeat what is already said there about the church, the pontifical vestments, and the rites of the liturgy (424B).

46. While the commentary of Germanus is written in the concise style of a catechism and avoids theological discussions, Nicholas and Theodore have a liking for detailed explanations. Their commentary is intellectually a unified whole. Its scholarly character can be seen in the already-mentioned citation of authorities and in the different value placed on generally-held views as distinct from material that is their own.

47. Ch. 1 (PG 140:417A).

48. Mansi XI, 977–980.

49. Mansi XIII, 265BC.

50. Ch. 1 (PG 140:420A).

51. Ch. 2 (420BC). On the question of unleavened bread see Hanssens nn. 206–261.

52. Ch. 3 (420CD). The classical Middle Byzantine system of decoration does not by any means show a liturgical rendering-present of individual episodes in the public ministry of Christ (choice of the apostles, miracles, etc.), as the *Protheoria* would like to claim. It is possible, however, that in the authors' Cappadocian homeland there were more preiconoclastic monuments than in the larger urban centers. Moreover, the strict Middle Byzantine system did not become fully established in Cappadocia, as its cave monasteries attest.

53. Ch. 3 (421AB).

54. Ch. 18 (441CD).

55. Ch. 9 (429B). But on this see below, p. 98.

56. Ch. 10 (429C).

57. Ch. 11 (432B).

58. Ch. 12 (433C).

59. Ch. 14 (436D).

60. Ibid.

61. Chs. 15–16 (437B–440A).

62. Ch. 17 (440C).

63. Ibid. (440D).

64. Ibid. (442A).

65. Ch. 18 (442D).

66. Ch. 19 (444B).

67. "*Stômen kalôs, stômen meta phobou, proschômen tê hagia anaphora.*" The call takes an unusual form here. Elsewhere it reads: ". . . *tên hagian anaphoran en eirênê prospherein*" (Br 383, 18f.: "to offer the holy anaphora in peace"). See Taft, "Textual Problems," in the Bibliography.

68. Ch. 19 (444CD).

69. Ch. 21 (445BC).

70. Ch. 23 (448B).

71. This prayer, spoken before the communion of the celebrants and of the faithful, reads as follows (in its second part): "In your holy supper, Son of God, allow me to share today. Never will I betray the mystery to your enemies. Never will I give you a traitor's kiss, as Judas did, but rather like the thief on the cross I confess to you: Remember me, Lord, in your kingdom" (Br 395, 25ff., and 396, 5ff). The same words are sung at the Great Entrance on Holy Thursday in place of the Cherubikon.

72. Ch. 25 (449BD).

73. Ibid. (452C).

74. Br 330, 9ff.

75. Ch. 27 (453A).

76. Br 330, 21.

77. Br 331, 12ff.: *eti prospheromen . . . hyper* ("we also offer for . . .").

78. Chs. 27–28 (453–456A). Cabasilas will sternly reject this explanation of *prospheromen hyper tôn hagiôn* ("we offer for the saints") (Ps 150:473–484). But Symeon of Thessalonica (d. 1429) will propose it in an even more extreme form; see below, p. 121.

79. Ch. 29 (457A).

80. Br 331, 22.

81. Br 318, 34f.

82. *Hyper hôn hai prosphorai:* Ch. 33 (460D).
83. See below, pp. 98f., 121f.
84. Ch. 37 (464D).
85. Ch. 36 (464B).
86. Ch. 37 (464C).
87. Ibid. (464D–465A).
88. Ch. 38 (465AB).

Section C

1. PG 140:429C.
2. Hanssens n. 334. The same document contains the earliest indications that in addition to the first prosphora, others are needed from which particles (*merides*) are to be taken for the commemoration of Mary, the angels and the saints, the living and the dead. On the form and number of the prosphoras see Hanssens, nn. 310–321, 326–351.
3. According to the commentary translated by Anastasius, it is the priest who performs the prothesis ritual. According to the order followed in tenth-eleventh-century Constantinople, a deacon may also do it. This is attested by the Order for the Proscomide (*Diataxis tês proskomidês*): "The priest or deacon—for both are suitable officiants—approaches the table of preparation, takes the divine bread in his hand and the lance as well . . ." (Hanssens n. 789). Because the symbolism refers to the angels, the Andidans regard the deacon as the more suitable officiant, but do admit that the prothesis is not everywhere entrusted to him (429C): "Although priests undertake the cutting, we should keep in mind that it was the ancient custom in the Great Church for the prosphora to be cut by deacon." See M. Mandalà, *La protesi della liturgia nel rito bizantino-greco* (Grottaferrata, 1935). 73–96 ("Il ministero della prothesi").
4. From the time of Theodore of Mopsuestia, the deacons were the privileged representatives of the angels who assisted in the work of redemption.
5. Even the custom that the deacon should himself directly (and not via the priest) lay the particles on the discos will be sternly rejected by Symeon of Thessalonica, among others (Mandalà 86–96).
6. S. Pétridès, "Astérisque," *DACL* 1, 3003.
7. Borgia 31, lines 11ff.
8. Beginning in the twelfth century with Cod. Vat. gr. 1973 fol. 2 (Mandalà 158f.).
9. Mandalà 160.

CHAPTER SIX

Introduction

1. *Diataxis tês hieras diakonias* (PG 154:745–766) and *Diataxis tês hieras leitourgias* (crit. ed. by P. N. Trempelas, *Hai treis leitourgiai* [Athens, 1935] 1–16; also in the editions of liturgical texts).

Section A

1. The exclusivity of the Middle Byzantine canon no longer prevailed at this period; consequently, in addition to new, specifically Late Byzantine, iconographic themes, Early Byzantine themes (such as the miracles or certain Old Testament events) made their way back into the pictorial decoration of churches. Alongside the

festal cycle other cycles of pictures arose and acquired their fixed place in the church building; the various cycles were not intermingled.

2. The principle of a hierarchic ordering of pictures was probably applied to the new cycles, but the further principle that selection was to be in strict accord with the degree of a picture's capacity for rendering the original present was lost from view more and more with the increasing temporal and local distance from iconoclasm and the place where it manifested itself. The custom of covering the entire interior surface of the church with paintings, which arose in the fourteenth century, further diminished the cultic significance of the major iconographic themes. O. Demus, *Byzantine Mosaic Decoration* (London, 1947), has a very clear description of this radical change (13f.).

The *Painter's Manual of the Painter-Monk Dionysius of Mount Athos* (in Greek; German tr., published by the Slavic Institute of Munich, 1960: *Das Malerhandbuch des Malermönchs Dionysios vom Berge Athos*) is especially far removed from the traditional iconographic principle that the original is to be rendered present. In the description of the individual pictorial themes (ibid., 45–177), the themes of Middle Byzantine iconography, given their position in the church building (see 178–182), must continue to be regarded as the principal themes of ecclesial iconography, and yet they are almost lost from sight in a profusion of about 350 representations (not including individual pictures of saints) that are treated as of equal value.

3. In the prothesis of the Peribleptos church in Mistra.

4. L. Ouspensky and V. Lossky, *The Meaning of Icons*, tr. by G. E. H. Palmer and E. Kadloubovsky (Boston, 1969), 204, n. 4. The Mount Athos *Malerhandbuch* considers it quite natural to represent God the Father (186, 187, etc.); it appeals to Dn 7 for justification.

5. On the early example in the Serbian monastery at Gracanica see A. M. Ammann, *Die Gottesschau im palamitischen Hesychasmus. Das östliche Christentum 3–4* (Würzburg, 1948[2]), 179f.

6. In accordance with the words: "Behold, I send my messenger (*angelon*) before your face" (Mt 11:10). See Ouspensky and Lossky 108.

7. Beck 323ff.

8. These relate primarily to the eucharist, the liturgical year, and liturgical hymns. As previously, account is taken of the liturgical year in the festal cycle of the nave and in a further special cycle in the narthex that contains representations of saints and of events from the Bible and Church history (including the Seventh Ecumenical Council) according to their sequence in the church's calendar. Especially noteworthy among the illustrations of liturgical hymns is the cycle for the Akathistos hymn; this cycle too is in the narthex.

9. From among the Old Testament prefigurations of the eucharist in Early Byzantine iconography, the sacrifice of Isaac, the hospitality of Abraham, and others now reappear.

10. The theme of the communion of the apostles does occur in Early Byzantine iconography. On the other hand, the representations of it that appear again in post-iconoclastic monumental painting only beginning in the middle of the eleventh century (Kiev and Ohrid) are typically Late Byzantine in their nuanced content and their affinity with the heavenly liturgy. For information on the occurrence of the communion of the apostles see H. Aurenhammer in *Lexikon der christlichen Ikonographie* (Vienna, 1959ff.), 222.ff.

11. See above, p. 81.

12. On the pictorial decoration of the Sophia church in Kiev see O. Wulff, *Altchrist-*

liche und Byzantinische Kunst II. *Byzantinische Kunst* (Postdam, 1924), 560f., with illustrations, and E. Giordani, "Das mittelbyzantinische Ausschmückungssystem als Ausdruck eines hieratischen Bildprogramms," *JÖBG* (1951), 103–134 at 112 (with plan showing arrangement of pictures).

13. For the pictorial decoration of the Sophia church in Ohrid, the main themes of which go back to the time of Bishop Leo (1037–1056), who is known from the dispute over unleavened bread, see R. Hamann-MacLean and H. Hallensleben, *Die Monumentalmalerei in Serbien und Makedonien vom 11. bis zum frühen 14. Jahrhundert* (Giessen, 1963), Plates 1–28; Plans 1–5.

14. Characteristically, Byzantine iconography originally showed Paul as the first of the apostles on the chalice side (although he was not present at the Supper). As a result of western influence, John is often shown as the first of the apostles on the chalice side, while Paul is missing and Judas is included in the painting (*Malerhandbuch* 114).

15. The two angels thus exercise the diaconal function on which the eighth book of the *Apostolic Constitutions* (Br 14, 3ff.) had already laid great emphasis and which Theodore of Mopsuestia had insisted made the deacon like the angels.

16. Borgia 32.

17. Ibid., 33.

18. Christ already appears in episcopal vestments in the picture of the communion of the apostles in the Serbian monastery at Dečani; the picture is remarkable in that it shows the iconostasis with its doors.

19. Ammann (101) maintains that judging by the attitude of Peter, the precise moment in the course of the liturgy that is being depicted is the summons to the reception of communion ("Come forward with faith and fear of God!"). But at that point the holy bread would have to be already broken into small pieces for distribution.

20. See above, pp. 83f.

21. The eight bishops are those regarded as the authors of liturgical formularies—Basil, Chrysostom, Gregory the Great (Liturgy of the Presanctified), and Clement of Rome (Liturgy of the *Apostolic Constitutions*)—along with Nicholas, Gregory of Nazianus, Gregory Thaumaturgus, and Epiphanius.

22. See G. Millet, *La peinture du moyen âge en Yougoslavie* I (Paris, 1954), Plate 33, 3–4; Hamann-MacLean and Hallensleben, Illust. 72.

23. The same traditional mode of representation is described in the *Malerhandbuch:* "Basil the Great, gray-haired, long-bearded, with arched eyebrows, reads from a sheet of paper: 'No one of those who bound by fleshly ties is worthy. . . .' " "St. John Chrysostom, with a shorter beard, says: 'God, our God . . .' " (135).

24. A. Grabar, *La peinture religieuse en Bulgarie* (Orient et Byzanz I, Paris, 1928), 88ff.

25. Grabar assumes that Gregory the Great and Germanus are the third and fourth bishops; the picture is not well-preserved.

26. Borgia 31.

27. G. Millet, *La peinture du moyen âge en Yougoslavie* II (Paris, 1957), Plate 1, 3–4; VI. R. Petković, *La peinture serbe du moyen âge* II (Belgrade, 1934), 15; Hamann-MacLean and Hallensleben, Plan 16–17.

28. See above, p. 66.

29. G. Millet, *La peinture du moyen âge en Yougoslavie* III (Paris, 1962), Plate 31, 1–2.

30. Ibid., Plate 55, 3.

31. Br 357, 15.

32. Br 393, 26ff.

33. The breaking takes place immediately after the elevation of the "sacred body," in which Theodore symbolized the elevation of Christ on the cross (PG 140:464D).

34. Reproduction of the Mateič fresco in G. Millet, "La vision de Pierre d'Alexandrie," in *Mélanges Charles Diehl* II (Paris, 1930), 108. Reproduction of the Ljuboten fresco in I. D. Ştefanescu, *L'Illustration des Liturgies dans l'art de Byzance et de l'Orient* (Brussels, 1936), Plate 68 = Petković, Plate 132b.

35. On the role of visions in Byzantine mysticism from Symeon the New Theologian (d. 1022) on, see Beck 362ff., espec. 365. On the influence of hesychasm in the Serbian patriarchate see M. Vasić, *L'Hesychasme dans l'Eglise et l'Art des Serbes du Moyen Age* (L'Art Byzantin chez les Slaves I; = Orient et Byzanz IV; Paris, 1930), 110–123.

36. PG 151:272C.

37. Borgia 31, 5–8. See above, pp. 72f.

38. The passage in the explanation of the prothesis (PG 140:429BC) that comes from the Andidans is in the interpolated text of Germanus (PG 98:397D) and in Pseudo-Sophronius (PG 87:3988D). See the texts in parallel columns in Br 540 (Appendix Q). N. Krasnosel'cev, in *Jahrbuch der Hist.-Phil. Gesellschaft der Univ. Odessa* 4, Byz. Abt. 2 (1894) 178–257, has shown the priority of the Andidans. Review by E. Kurtz in *ByZ* 4 (1895) 617f. Approximately half of the *Logos periechôn tên ekklêsiastikên historian hapasan* (PG 87:3981–4002) of Pseudo-Sophronius comes from the Andidans.

39. Thus, e.g., in the already-mentioned monastic church at Sopoceni (middle of the thirteen century): Millet II, Plate 42.

40. See the prothesis prayer in the Barberini Codex (Br 309), which is modeled on the epiclesis.

41. A sign of this is the often exaggerated manifestations of devotion at the Great Entrance, which usually do not reappear during the remainder of the liturgy.

42. Millet I, Plate 43, 1; Hamann-MacLean and Hallensleben, Illust. 76. While the church was built ca. 1190 and the painting of it continued until 1209, the exonarthex was not added until 1230.

43. Vl. R. Petković, *La peinture serbe du moyen âge* I (Belgrade, 1930), Plate 98a.

44. Vl. R. Petković and G. Boskovic, *Dečani* (Monumenta serbica artis mediaevalis II), II (Belgrade, 1941), 55, Plate 283.

45. I. D. Ştefanescu, *L'Evolution de la Peinture religieuse en Bucovine et en Moldavie. Nouvelles recherches* (Orient et Byzanz VI; Paris, 1929), 74. Idem, *L'Illustration* 99 and Plate 56.

46. Ibid., Plates 36 and 55. W. Felicetti-Liebenfels, *Geschichte der byzantinischen Ikonmalerei* (Olten-Lausanne, 1956), Plate 19AB.

47. Thus in a fresco at Dobrovăţ (Moldau; 1528), in Ştefanescu, *L'Evolution*, with illustrations; idem, *L'Illustration*, 190f. The epitaphios procession at the Orthros is a sixteenth-century development based on analogy.

48. Symeon of Thessalonica, *Expositio de divino templo* 76 (PG 155:728B), says in his description of the Great Entrance: ". . . also in the procession are those who carry the sacred veil on their heads, thus symbolizing Jesus naked and dead." See Taft 216–219.

49. G. Soteriou, *Guide du Musée Byzantin d'Athènes* (Athens, 1932), 134ff., with Plates 78, 80, 81. Ph. Schweinfurth, *Die byzantische Form* (Mainz, 1954), Plates 123B.

50. On the picture of the heavenly liturgy, which appears with special frequency from the fourteenth century on in Serbia, Athos, and Rumania see Ştefanescu, *L'Illustration*, 72–77, 189–191; idem, *L'Evolution*, 73–76; idem, *La Peinture religieuse en Vala-*

chie et en Transylvanie (Orient et Byzanz VIII; Paris, 1930–1932), 305–309; H. Brockhaus, *Die Kunst in den Athosklostern* (Leipzig, 1924²), 71; also G. Millet, *Monuments de l'Athos* I. *Les Peintures* (Paris, 1927), and Petković II (Indexes).

The picture is found in the dome in Serbian churches of the fourteenth–fifteenth centuries (Petković II, 19, 23, 26, 40, 46, 54, 57, 60): in the Athos monasteries of Chilandri, Vatopedi, Xenophontos, and Stavronikita (Brockhaus 273, 282; Millet, Plates 64, 1; 262, 1–2), in some Moldavian (Ştefanescu, *L'Illustration* 18) and Wallachian churches (Ştefanescu, *Valachie* 296), and in the Sophia church at Mistra (G. Millet, *Monuments byzantins de Mistra* [Paris, 1910], Plates 132, 2).

The heavenly liturgy is depicted in the sanctuary in most of the Athos monasteries (Millet, Plates 118, 2–3; 168, 2; 218, 2; 219, 3; 256, 2; 257, 2; 261, 2), as the *Malerhandbuch* also indicates (179), but less frequently in Wallachia (Ştefanescu, *Valachie* 298). The theme appears in the prothesis of the Probleptos church at Mistra (Millet, *Mistra*, Plate 113, 1).

51. Millet, *Athos*, Plate 64, 1. Despite an eighteenth-century restoration this church is accepted as being a work of the early fourteenth century.

52. Because of its depiction of Seraphim, Thrones, Angels, and Archangels, Ştefanescu (*L'Illustration* 76) regards the mosaic in the dome at Chilandri as an illustration of the Cherubikon in the Liturgy of the Presanctified ("Let us now venerate the heavenly powers who are invisibly with us"). But this interpretation does not take into account the very special function of this hymn and does not do justice to the general significance of pictures of angels in domes.

53. Ştefanescu, *L'Illustration* 74f.

54. Petković II, Plates 103, 105. The picture in the dome at Gračanica, which originated in the final years of King Miljutin (d. 1321), is very like this one. See Hamann-MacLean and Hallensleben, Illust. 325.

55. Ştefanescu, *L'Illustration* 72f, Plate 27.

56. The omophorion is mentioned along with the epitaphios in the description of the Great Entrance in Symeon of Thessalonica (PG 155:728B).

57. Millet, *Mistra*, Plate 113.

58. Ibid., Plate 132.

59. Borgia 30.

Section B

1. The book is a collection of dogmatic and liturgical treatises. A first section of thirty-two chapters on heresies is followed by the very detailed discussion of the sacraments and the prayer of the hours (see Beck 752).

2. *Peri tês hieras leitourgias* (PG 155:253–304).

3. PG 155:687–749.

4. Dionysius is already mentioned several times in the introduction (253). His *Ecclesiastical Hierarchy* serves as the model for Symeon's teaching on the sacraments.

5. The sections of this work will be called "Questions" in the following footnotes; the sections of the first-named work will be called "Chapters."

6. Qu. 2 (701A).

7. This passage is noteworthy for attesting that concelebration by priests without an episcopal principal celebrant was already customary in Symeon's time.

8. Qu. 2 (701B).

9. Gregory, known as *Ho Dialogos* because of his *Dialogues*, was regarded as the

author of the Liturgy of the Presanctified. "We do not know when this liturgy was linked to the name of Gregory Dialogus. . . . The connection probably does not antedate the tenth century" (Beck 243).

10. On Isidore of Pelusium see above, p. 19.

11. Qu. 2 (701D).

12. Qu. 4 (704AB).

13. Qu. 5 (704C).

14. Qu. 19 (705D).

15. Qu. 23 (708B).

16. This title was attached especially to the twelve gospel pericopes that deal with Easter and are proclaimed in sequence throughout the year at the Sunday orthros.

17. Qu. 28 (708D).

18. Qu. 18 (705D).

19. Qu. 12 (705B).

20. Qu. 37–38 (712CDB). In connection with the *potamoi*, Jn 7:38 is cited.

21. Qu. 35 (712AB).

22. Symeon uses the less common form of the word: *phainolion* (713D, etc.).

23. *On the Sacred Liturgy*, Ch. 79 (256B).

24. Qu. 40 (713B).

25. Qu. 41 (713BC).

26. Qu. 44 (716BC). This interpretation comes from Germanus and had meanwhile become part of the prayer for putting on the omophorion. In addition, especially "outstanding" bishops wear the sakkos instead of the phelonion (716A). The sakkos looks like a dalmatic; it was originally an imperial garment, but was granted to the patriarchs of Constantinople after 1054. After 1453 its use was allowed to all bishops. In fourteenth-century pictures of the heavenly liturgy we see Christ wearing the sakkos, while (e.g., in pictures of the liturgy of the church fathers) the saintly hierarchs wear the phelonion.

According to Symeon (ibid.), "the other bishops wear a phelonion which is covered with crosses and is known as a polystaurion" and which symbolizes the sufferings of the Redeemer. (Compare, once again, the iconographical representations.)

27. Qu. 46–48 (717BC).

28. Qu. 53–54 (720BC).

29. Qu. 55 (720D).

30. Qu. 101 (748A). Symeon does not say which of the Fathers, in his view, have explained the prothesis. He claims only that they are "the same ones" to whom he owes the rest of his explanation.

31. Qu. 64–74 (724A–725D).

32. Qu. 76 (728AB).

33. Qu. 77 (728CD).

34. Qu. 78 (729AD). Symeon here correctly repeats the teaching of the Second Council of Nicea (see above, p. 67, with note 23).

35. Qu. 86 (733A). The final words are strongly reminiscent of the iconography of the Lamb, especially of those pictures which, like the one at Čučer (see above, p. 107), also show the sign of the cross at the epiclesis.

36. Qu. 92–94 (741CD).

37. Qu. 100 (745B). Br 396, 30.

38. *On the Sacred Liturgy*, Ch. 83 (261AB).

39. Ch. 85 (264C).

40. Ch. 85 (265A).

41. Ch. 86 (265B). This passage is followed by polemical remarks against the customs of the Latins and the Armenians (265C–280B).

42. Ch. 93 (280BC).

43. Ch. 94 (280D).

44. Ch. 94 (281C).

45. Qu. 102 (748C). To the faithful who join in the celebration and to those who participate in the sacrifice through particles the liturgy also brings forgiveness of sins, provided their participation is marked by a proper spirit of repentance. But in accord with the example of the early church, serious sinners are excluded not only from communion but even from celebrating the liturgy of the faithful and participating in the sacrifice through particles (as long as they have not yet received the sacrament of penance). See above, p. 118, and what follows here, with note 46.

46. Qu. 103 (748D). Before (in the Russian rite: after) the communion of the faithful, the particles are placed in the sacred blood; at that time (in the Russian rite) the priest says: "Lord, at the intercession of your saints, wash away with your precious blood the sins of all whom we have remembered here."

47. *On the Sacred Liturgy*, Ch. 94 (284C).

48. Ch. 96 (285D).

49. Ch. 96 (285D).

50. Ch. 96 (288AB).

51. Ch. 96 (288C).

52. Ch. 96 (289A).

53. Ch. 96 (292A); Qu. 63 (721D–724A).

54. Ch. 83 (261A).

55. Ch. 96 (288D).

56. Ch. 96 (288D).

57. Qu. 48 (717C); Ch. 96 (289CD).

58. Ibid.

59. Ch. 96 (289A).

60. Qu. 65 (724AB).

61. This is actually stated in connection with the donning of the vestments 261C), the enarxis (717C, 720B), and the Little Entrance (291C, 720C). At the Great Entrance the faithful prostrate themselves before the priests carrying the gifts and ask for prayers and intercessions during the sacrificial action (729A).

62. Thus, e.g., the actual saying of the anaphora in common by the concelebrants is not always customary among the Greek Orthodox (unlike the Russian Orthodox and all Byzantine Catholics); see A. Raes, "La concélébration dans les rites orientaux," *MD*, no. 35 (1953) 24–47, espec. 30–33. It may not be concluded, however, that therefore the officiants do not concelebrate the anaphora in a specifically priestly way. On this whole question see R. Taft, "*Ex* Oriente lux? Some Reflections on Eucharistic Concelebration," *Worship* 54 (1980) 308–325.

63. Since these are superior to deacons and differ from them by ordination, the reference must be to priests, a point that also emerges from the next passage cited. The reference is probably to priests who do not concelebrate (and therefore have, here and now, a lower rank) and for this reason cannot exercise, with the other priests, the power they have by their ordination. This kind of priestly participation, in the sanctuary, in the form of a priestly reception of communion at the altar is found frequently. No other explanation is available, since distinctions of rank among

concelebrating priests could not be the basis for a different kind of participation in the sacrificial action.

64. During the anaphora concelebrants can therefore "say" something not permitted to the other priests present in the sanctuary (nor, probably, to the actively participating deacons). This can only be the anaphora itself, which seems, according to Symeon, to have been spoken softly, at least in part, by the concelebrants.

65. Ch. 99 (296D).

66. Ch. 99 (300C).

67. *Hermêneia tês theias leitourgias* (PG 150:368 = 492); critical edition by R. Bornert, J. Goullard, P. Perichon in *Sources Chrétiennes*, no. 4 bis (Paris, 1967); ET: *A Commentary on the Divine Liturgy*, tr. by J. M. Hussey and P. A. McNulty (London, 1960). (References to this translation will be identified simply by page number in the following notes.)

68. See, e.g., M. de la Taille, *Mysterium Fidei* (Paris, 1931³); J. Kramp, *Die Opferanschauungen der römischen Messliturgie* (Freiburg, 1923), 112–167; J. Rivière, *Le dogme de la rédemption* (Louvain, 1931), 281–303.

69. Kramp 114–117.

70. An initial and very stimulating orientation was given by N. Gass in connection with his edition of Cabasilas' principal work, *Life in Christ*; see Gass, *Die Mystik des Nikolaus Cabasilas. Vom Leben in Christo* (Greifswald, 1849; Leipzig, 1899²), 154ff., and the same author's *Symbolik der griechischen Kirche* (Berlin, 1872), 300ff. On Cabasilas' commentary as such see G. Gharib, "Nicolas Cabasilas et l'explication symbolique de la liturgie," *PrOrChr* 10 (1960) 114–133. S. Salaville has a general overview of the life and work of Cabasilas in his edition of the commentary in *Sources Chrétiennes* no. 4 (Paris, 1949). Literature on Cabasilas in Beck 782.

71. Ch. 1 (368D–369A, p. 25).

72. Ch. 1 (369D–372B, pp. 26–27).

73. See above, p. 91.

74. Ch. 7 (384A, p. 36).

75. Ch. 6 (380D, p. 34).

76. Ch. 24 (420CD, p. 66).

77. Ch. 1 (372C).

78. Ch. 1 (372D, p. 28). [The clarifications in square brackets are added by the author of the present book.—Tr.]

79. Chs. 3–4 (377–380).

80. Ch. 5 (380BD).

81. Chs. 6–10 (380–389).

82. Ch. 11 (389).

83. Ch. 22 (416CD, p. 62).

84. Ch. 24 (420B).

85. Ch. 24 (420C).

86. Ch. 27 (425BD, p. 70).

87. Ch. 30 (433–437).

88. Ch. 37 (452A, p. 90).

89. The connection between epiclesis and Zeon had already found expression in the formula for the commingling (or the Zeon) in the Barberini Codex (Br 341, 20): *Eis plêroma Pneumatos Hagiou* ("For the fullness of the Holy Spirit").

90. In the fourteenth century the formula for the commingling is: *Plêroma potêriou pisteôs Pneumatos Hagiou* (Br 394, 3: "The fullness of the cup of faith of the Holy

Spirit"); the formula of blessing for the Zeon: *Eulogêmenê hê zesis tôn hagiôn Sou* (Br 394, 10: "Blessed is the fervor of your saints"); and the formula for the pouring of the Zeon: *Zesis pisteôs, plêrês Pneumatos Hagiou* (Br 394, 14: "The Spirit-filled ferver of faith"). In all three formulas attention is focused not on the constitution of the consecrated gifts but on their effects in the faithful; this is fully in accord with Cabasilas' explanation.

91. Br 396, 30. See above, pp. 119–120.

PART TWO

CHAPTER ONE

1. On the place that the liturgy of Constantinople and the Byzantine rite occupy in the historical development of the overall liturgical tradition of early Christianity and Orthodoxy. The basis for the development indicated in this chapter title is described in Chapter One of Part One. There, consistent with the method used in studies of Byzantine theology, I took as my starting point the liturgical life peculiar to the Byzantine patriarchate. But current ecumenical interest in the Byzantine liturgy looks, in addition, to the expression of faith that the Byzantine liturgical order offers as a model to the *entire Church*, as well as to the continuity of this expression of faith with *early Christianity*.

2. On the primacy of Antioch from the standpoint of the history of culture and tradition, a primacy which began in apostolic times and long continued to exert an influence, see H. Grotz, *Die Hauptkirchen des Ostens* (OCA 169; Rome, 1964). On the influence of Antioch on the history of Christian art in Rome in the periods immediately before and after Constantine, see O. Wulff, *Altkirchliche und byzantinische Kunst* I (Berlin-Neubabelberg, 1914). The theology of the Antiochene school (as distinct from the Alexandrian) in the patristic period is a major theme of patristic studies.

3. See K. Gamber, "Die Eucharistiegebet in der frühen nordafrikanischen Liturgie," *Liturgica* (Scripta et Documenta 17; Montserrat, 1966), 51–65. On the correspondence between the Roman and the Alexandrian liturgies see Jungmann, vol. 1, 55f.; for a comparison between the structure of the Alexandrian anaphora and that of the Roman Canon see Schulz 56–72.

4. See J. Blank, *Meliton von Sardes: Vom Passa. Die älteste christliche Osterpredigt* (Sophia 3; Freiburg, 1963), 26–41.

5. Canon 7.

6. This is the phrase Egeria (Etheria) the pilgrim consistently uses in describing the special character of the stational liturgies; see *Egeria's Travels*, tr. and annotated by J. Wilkinson (London, 1971), passim.

7. For Rome see the Philocalian Calendar for 354 (with its older stratum from 335–336), which, in addition to Christmas (mentioned for the first time) and the memorials of local martyrs, includes only the martyrs of Carthage (Perpetua and Felicity; Cyprian) and (characteristically enough!) the Chair of Peter at Antioch (February 21: *Natale Petri de Cathedra*); the calendar is given in N. M. Denis-Boulet, *The Christian Calendar*, tr. by P. Hepburne-Scott (20th Century Encyclopedia of Catholicism 113; New York, 1960), 51f.

8. On the establishment and continuance of this tradition of the City of Rome see

J. P. Kirsch, *Die Stationskirchen des Missale Romanum* (Ecclesia Orans 19; Freiburg, 1926), 101f., 165f.

9. On the dominance of Jerusalem in this respect and on the process of exchange see A. Baumstark, "Denkmäler der Entstehungsgeschichte des byzantinischen Ritus," *OrChr* III/1 (1928) 1–32; idem, *Vom geschichtlichen Werden der Liturgie* (Ecclesia Orans 10; Freiburg, 1923), 47–50. On the Byzantine Easter Vigil: G. Bertonière, *The Historical Development of the Easter Vigil and Related Services in the Greek Church* (OCA 193; Rome, 1972). On the influence of Jerusalem on the prayer of the hours: J. Mateos, "La vigile cathédrale chez Egérie," *OCP* 27 (1961) 281–312; idem, "Quelques problèmes de l'orthros byzantin," *PrOrChr* 11 (1961) 201–220; H.-J. Schulz, "Liturgie, Tagzeiten und Kirchenjahr des byzantinischen Ritus," in *Ostkirchenkunde* 332–385.

10. See J. Mateos, *La célébration de la parole dans la liturgie byzantine* (OCA 191; Rome, 1971); henceforth cited as Mateos, *La célébration*, 27–90.

11. This is shown repeatedly by the tenth-century Typikon of the "Great Church" (ms Hl. Kreuz No. 40); see Mateos, *Typikon* I and II.

12. See Taft, espec. 179–191, 273–275.

13. Theodore Balsamon, *Ad interrogationem Marci II, patriarchae Alexandrini* (ca. 1195), Resp. I (PG 138:953); see Hanssens n. 713.

14. Ibid. (with a reference to 41 cap. 1 tit. 2 libr. Basilikon).

CHAPTER TWO

1. On the place that the Byzantine anaphora occupies in the history of tradition, from the standpoint of its basic structure and its witness to the faith. This chapter represents an expanded treatment both of the rite's special place in the history of dogma and of the authorship of Basil and Chrysostom.

2. See Hanssens n. 41. This specification of an initially more comprehensive concept (nn. 41, 59–63) was already underway in the fourth century (nn. 41, 59–63) and was introduced into all the languages in which the Byzantine rite was celebrated. For analogous names for the eucharistic celebration, e.g., *synaxis, hierourgia, mystêria,* and the equivalent terms for "celebration of the sacrifice" see ibid., nn. 65–71; on the theological concept of "liturgy" and the history of the term's meaning in the West see E. J. Lengeling, "Liturgie," in H. Fries (ed.), *Handbuch theologischer Grundbegriffe* II (2nd ed.; Munich, 1970), 77–100.

3. *Anaphora (anapherein)* refers first of all to the sacrificial action itself and, in particular (as a more specialized term than *propshora, propsherein,* which are also used for the offering of gifts by the congregation), to the priestly act of sacrifice that is accomplished by bringing the sacrificial gifts to the altar, depositing them there, and offering them. The sacrificial prayer that in the fifth century and into the sixth was still usually called *euchê tês anaphoras* (prayer of sacrifice), has since the sixth century been called simply *anaphora.* See the documentation in A. Baumstark, "Anaphora," *RAC* 1:423f.

4. Text in Botte 12–16.

5. The two most important passages (*Apologia* I, 65 and 67; *Dialogus cum Tryphone* 41, 1) are in *PE* 68–73.

6. This is shown, for example, by the fact that Greek epitaphs are found on the tombs of the Roman pontiffs in the Catacomb of Callistus until beyond the middle of this century.

7. See above, Chapter One, n. 2.

8. The "eulogies" and "eucharists" are so called after their literary form (opening

words: "Blessed be" or "I thank" or "We thank"). On the eucharistic reference of the thanksgiving in Eph 5:19f and Col 3:16 see H. Schlier, *Der Brief an die Epheser* (Düsseldorf, 1957), 249.

9. In *Dialogus cum Tryphone* 41, 1, Justine speaks of the bread of the eucharist, which the Lord "commanded us to do as a memorial (sign) of his suffering . . . so that we might at the same time give thanks." The "doing" that the Lord commanded as a memorial (account of institution!) includes, in the word "this," the actions of the Supper; when related solely to the bread (and wine) it designates a constituting or making-to-be, and this in the specific sense of "cultically consecrating" (Betz 150, n.2).

10. According to 1 Cor 11:26 the Lord's command to remember him (11:25) is fulfilled by the proclamation, through the words and actions of the concrete meal, of the "death of the Lord" (i.e., his death and resurrection).

11. In Hippolytus this reads: "Mindful therefore of his death and resurrection we offer you the bread and the cup while giving thanks to you." On the *eucharistia* of Hippolytus as a reflection of the process of sacramental actualization see Schulz 43–45 and Schulz, "Liturgischer Vollzug und sakramentale Wirklichkeit des eucharistischen Opfers," *OCP* 45 (1979) 245–266; 46 (1980) 5–19, at 45, 251ff; henceforth cited as Schulz, "Opfer."

12. The passage in *Apologia* I, 66, 2 (*PE* 70) on the "eucharistizing" of the food "through a word of prayer that comes from him" (*di'euchês logou par'autou*) is read by many scholars as meaning "through a prayer for the Logos" and interpreted as a Logos-epiclesis, similar to the one attested for the Alexandrian liturgy by Serapion (*PE* 130).

13. In Hippolytus the epiclesis (which continues the passage cited in n. 10) runs as follows: "And we ask you to send your Holy Spirit on the offering of holy Church and, having gathered it in unity, to grant to all who receive of the holy things the fullness of the Holy Spirit . . . so that they will praise you" (Botte 16; reconstructed text, 17).

14. Botte 48–50. For a more detailed comparison of baptismal confession and anaphora see Schulz 38–43.

15. Botte 50 (reconstructed text, 51).

16. In the period prior to the Apostles' Creed the words *communio sanctorum* meant "participation in the *sancta*," i.e., the consecrated gifts (*sancta = ta hagia* in the anaphora; Botte 17); see W. Elert, *Eucharist and Church Fellowship in the First Four Centuries*, tr. by N. E. Nagel (St. Louis, 1966), 209–219.

17. See the text in n. 13.

18. On the nature of the eucharist as the most representative witness to the faith see Schulz 24–43.

19. On the ecclesiology of the Byzantine anaphora see Schulz 46–55; on "eucharistic ecclesiology" from the liturgical standpoint see the Introduction, n. 8.

20. See the Introduction (with the literature indicated in nn. 4 and 5, pp. 205–206).

21. In German: Basilius von Casarea, *Über den Heiligen Geist*, with introduction and translation by M. Blum (Sophia 8; Freiburg, 1967).

22. It is addressed to the Father "with the Son and the Holy Spirit." See ibid., *passim*, and J. A. Jungmann, *The Place of Christ in Liturgical Prayer*, tr. by A. Peeler (Staten Island, N.Y., 1965), 176ff.

23. On the situation in Antioch and Caesarea and on the history of the liturgical development of the typically eastern form of the doxology see Jungmann, *Liturgical Prayer*, 172–190. It is even claimed that certain forms of the doxology are a criterion

for the authenticity of Chrysostom's sermons; see F. van de Paverd, *Zur Geschichte der Messliturgie in Antiocheia und Konstantinopel gegen Ende des 4. Jahrhunderts. Analyse der Quellen bei Johannes Chrysostomos* (OCA 187; Rome, 1970), 132–134; henceforth cited as van de Paverd.

24. See H.-J., Schulz, "Eucharistie und Einheit der Kirche nach Basileios dem Grossen," in *Die Heiligen der einen Kirche am Beispiel des hl. Basilius* (Regensberg Ecumenical Symposium 1979, sponsored by the German Episcopal Conference; Munich, 1980).

25. On the closeness of the anaphora of Basil to the *Filioque* (insofar as this last can be interpreted as an effort to restore the salvational-dynamic pneumatology of the earliest baptismal confession) see ibid. and B. Capelle, "La Procession du Saint-Esprit d'après la liturgie grecque de saint Basile," *OrSyr* 7 (1962) 69–76.

26. See Introduction with n. 8.

27. F. van de Paverd, op. cit.

28. Ibid., 287–340.

29. Thus he even speaks occasionally of the anaphora of "Pseudo-Chrysostom" (e.g., van de Paverd 485).

30. See Jacob in the list of abbreviations, pp. 200, 201. (titles: *Recherches, Formulaires,* "Tradition," "Uspenski").

31. The group of mss known as Sevastianov 474 (at least six mss) were reconstructed as a purely "Chrysostomic" text tradition by removal of the additions from other "formularies" and especially from Basil. On the other hand, by drawing on formularies in other traditions, the mss group Barberini-Leningrad 226 and especially the group Grottaferrata β VII and Burditt-Coatts became increasingly complete collections of the prayers actually used in the liturgy (Jacob, *Recherches*, Tables, 50–53).

32. Among the groups of formularies showing greater completeness (i.e., including some or all of the prayers for the prothesis, the antiphons, the entrance, the Trisagion, etc.) mss of Italo-Greek origin are overrepresented (Jacob, "Tradition," 136).

33. Ibid.

34. Thus in the Barberini Codex the following prayers (assigned to the formulary of Chrysostom) show a striking agreement with other eastern liturgies: the prothesis prayer, with a text from the Greek Liturgy of Mark; the prayer for the entrance, with the opening prayer from the Liturgy of James; the prayer at the Trisagion, with parts from an Alexandrian blessing of water (ibid., 117–119). See also H. Engberding, "Die Angleichung der byzantinischen Chyrsostomosliturgie an die byzantinische Basiliusliturgie," *OstSt* 13 (1964) 105–122.

35. Thus the prayer at the Trisagion in Leningrad Codex gr 226 (Cod. Porphyrii) has the description: "Prayer for the Trisagion in the Anaphora of Chrysostom" (Jacob, "Uspenski," 183, n. 23).

36. G. Wagner, *Der Ursprung der Chrysostomus-liturgie,* LQF 59; Münster, 1973), 11–29; henceforth cited as Wagner.

37. Ibid., 13, 25–29. See J. Mateos, "Deux problemes de traduction dans la Liturgie Byzantine de S. Jean Chrysostome. I. La prière de la proscomide," in Mateos, *La célébration,* 174–179; also Taft 360–364.

38. Mateos, *La célébration,* 177–179; Taft 358–360.

39. Wagner 29–41.

40. Ibid., 73–132. A more detailed examination of Wagner's argument is given in my review in *ThRev* 71 (1975) 145–148. Among the reviewers G. Cuming, in particular, in *ECR* 7 (1975) 95–97, carries the discussion further.

41. Chrysostom, *De incomprehensibili* 3, 1 (PG 48:720A); similarly in *Ad eos qui scandalizati sunt* 2 (PG 52:484C); see Wagner 75–78.

42. Wagner 78–84.

43. See the anaphora of Theodore of Mopsuestia (*PE* 381f.) and the parallels in Theodore's catechetical homilies (references in Wagner 78).

44. Chrysostom, *In Col. hom.* 10, 2 (PG 62:368C); see Wagner 92–97.

45. Wagner 102–106.

46. Ibid., 109–114.

47. Ibid., 112–116.

48. See Betz 308f., 315.

49. Thus especially *In Act. hom.* 21, 5 (PG 60:170C); see Wagner 116–122.

50. Wagner 133.

51. On the giving of the gifts and the act of offering as signs of a disposition of self-surrender see Jungmann, vol. 1, 17f.; vol. 2, 218f., 2ff.; in addition, Schulz 21ff., 45, 49f.; Schulz, "Opfer," 250ff.; idem, "Ökumenische Aspekte der Darbringungsaussagen in der erneuerten römischen und in der byzantinischen Liturgie," *ALW* 19 (1978) 7–28.

52. See the use of these concepts in Hippolytus (Botte 16; 17, n. 7; 54; 55, n. 2), where the concept of soteriological "reality," which is linked to the salvation-historical once-for-all of the sacrifice of the cross, is clearly discernible in the mode of expression: the bishop eucharistizes the chalice "to be a *homoiôma* of the blood that was shed for all who believed in him."

53. See Botte 16: the description of the effect of the eucharist leads directly into the doxology ("for the fullness of the Holy Spirit . . . so that we may praise you"), in which the church is seen as the "place" of unceasing praise: "so that we may praise and glorify you through your Child Jesus Christ, through whom glory and honor is given to the Father and the Son with the Holy Spirit in the holy Church, both now and through eternity."

54. This is especially clear in Serapion who (in contrast to Hippolytus) applies this last concept unequivocally to the bread and wine as the gifts offered (he even does so in one passage *before* the account of institution: *PE* 130). On various analogous concepts see Betz 217–239, where the "restriction of the concept of symbol" as a "novelty in the eucharistic terminology of the fourth century" applies to the synonyms as well.

55. Seventh Council, Session VI (Mansi XIII, 265). Even in the time of Theodore there was direct opposition to the application of this concept to the consecrated eucharistic gifts (references in Betz 231, n. 327).

56. See Schulz, "Opfer," 259f.

57. See Betz 237.

57. See E. von Ivanka, *Rhomäerreich und Gottesvolk. Das Glaubens-, Staats- und Volksbewusstsein der Byzantiner und seine Auswirkung auf die ostkirchlich-osteuropäische Geisteshaltung* (Freiburg, 1968); E. von Ivanka, J. Tyciak, and P. Wiertz (eds.), *Handbuch der Ostkirchenkunde* (Düsseldorf, 1971), 35ff; henceforth cited as *Ostkirchenkunde*.

59. On the Easter sermon of Melito see J. Blank, *Meliton und Sardes: Vom Passa. Die älteste christliche Osterpredigt* (Sophia 3; Freiburg, 1963).˙

60. See the documents of the dispute on the date of Easter in Eusebius; on the content of the feast see O. Casel, "Art und Sinn der ältesten christlichen Osterfeier," *JLW* 14 (1938) 1–78.

61. On the continuity between the Passover lamb typology in the gospel of John (and earlier in 1 Cor 5:7) and the Quartodeciman celebration of Easter see Blank, op.

cit., and P. Grelot and J. Pierron, *Osternacht und Osterfeier im Alten und Neuen Bund* (Düsseldorf, 1959).

62. Ch. 38 (J. Wilkinson, *Egeria's Travels*, 138–139).

63. See the note on this passage in H. Pétré and K. Vretska (eds.), *Die Pilgerreise der Aetheria (Peregrinatio Aetheriae)* (Klosterneuburg, 1958), 232f.

64. Ch. 24, 8–9 (Wilkinson 125). This vigil is expressly compared here with the Easter Vigil.

65. See the New Testament resurrection accounts and the echo of their liturgical imitation in Jerusalem in the *Eulogetaria* of the Byzantine Sunday orthros; the principal elements of the Jerusalem vigil survive in the characteristic middle section of this orthros (see *Ostkirchenkunde* 354): "In the very early morning the myrrh-bearing women hurried in tears to your tomb. But the angel met them and said: 'The time for mourning is over. Weep not but proclaim the resurrection to the apostles.' "

66. See *Ostkirchenkunde* 369–374; on the liturgical order for Good Friday see also H.-J. Schulz, "Die Feier des Heilstodes Christi im byzantinischen und im römischen Ritus," *Lebendiges Zeugnis* (1966) 68–85.

67. See the designation of the gifts in the anamnesis of the Liturgy of Basil and its interpretation by the Seventh Council (Mansi XIII, 265).

68. See Taft 216–219. This form of the Great Entrance corresponds exactly to the epitaphios procession on Good Friday (after the Great Doxology of the orthros), but the former comes in fact from the tradition of eucharistic interpretation itself, whereas the corresponding form of the Good Friday procession (in which the epitaphios is carried like a baldacchino over the book of the gospels) is a secondary development of the sixteenth century and a doublet of the burial rite in the Good Friday hesperinos (after the hour of Jesus' death) (*Ostkirchenkunde* 273).

69. Taft 244–249.

70. Thus, for example, the *Protheoria* of Nicholas and Theodore of Andida (above, Part One, Chapter Five).

71. See the examples on pp. 15, 16, 17.

72. van de Paverd 287–315, espec. 292. The point of departure for the comparison between the words of the Lord as used in the liturgy and as spoken historically are the references (in word and ritual) to the identity of liturgy and Supper, according to which the words of institution possess sacramental efficacy not as "formula of consecration" but in the measure of their importance within the structure of the anaphora. On the other hand, Chyrsostom's explanation of the epiclesis (van de Paverd 316–340) no longer depends on the sacramental sign but looks instead to the (sacramental) reality. On the Orthodox conception of the consecration see Schulz, "Opfer," 255ff.

73. "Mindful of the salutary command we celebrate the memorial of all that was done for our salvation: the cross, the tomb, the resurrection. . . ."

74. Following upon the epiclesis, the effects of communion in the individual are to some extent named before the ecclesial effect (fellowship of the Holy Spirit), while in the intercessions the bishops and the various classes in the church are named before the inhabited world and the church as a whole (in both cases the anaphora of Chrysostom differs from the anaphora of Basil).

CHAPTER THREE

1. Ignatius of Antioch, *Ad Magnesios* (see *Ad Trallenses* 3).

2. On the bema (which must be presupposed to be for Chrysostom an elevated place for altar and episcopal throne) see van de Paverd 33–47.

3. Chrysostom, *De s. Pentecoste* 1, 4 (PG 50:458); see van de Paverd 86–90.

4. J. Mateos, *Le Typicon de la Grande Eglise. Ms. Sainte-Croix No. 40. Introduction, texte critique et notes*, 2 vols. (OCA 191; Rome, 1971); henceforth cited as Mateos, *Le Typicon*. Since the eucharistic celebration in the Byzantine rite represents the developed form of the liturgy of the city of Constantinople and since, on the other hand, many details of it become intelligible only through knowledge of local customs, the Typicon in ms Hl. Kreuz, No. 40, which is a "stational ordo," has shed the first light on the original function of these two hymns, as well as on the history of the enarxis, which is to be explained as a gradual accumulation of elements from liturgies celebrated at intervals along the route of the procession on stational days.

5. Mateos, *La célébration* 91–126 (on the Trisagion); also 42, 50–54 (on the hymn *Only-begotten Son*).

6. Ibid., 113f.

7. Ibid., 102–106.

8. See H. Engeberding, "Zum formgeschichtlichen Verständnis des Trisagion," *JLW* 10 (1930) 168–74; Mateos, *La célébration*, 100.

9. See Mateos, *La célébration*, 110f.

10. See the sketch of the development, ibid., 126.

11. After the silent prayer at the Trisagion and the triple signing of the hymn itself, this blessing is bestowed with the dikirion and the trikirion, i.e., the two-branched and the three-branched candelabra; during the blessing the bishop turns to the congregation and recites Ps 79:15b–16a. In this we may see a remnant of the psalm at one time recited during rogation processions, especially in connection with the Trisagion (Mateos, *La célébration*, 110).

12. See Mateos, *Le Typicon*, vol. 2 (in the index, under *Ho Monogenês*).

13. On Sundays the words "who have risen from the dead" are inserted; on weekdays, the words "who are wonderful in your saints."

14. Special antiphons (with festal troparia or specially chosen psalm-verses) are to be found in the tenth-century Typicon for Christmas, Epiphany, Easter, Ascension, and Pentecost. In the twelfth century the practice was extended to all twelve major feasts and some other days (Mateos, *La célébration*, 61–68).

15. Mateos, *La célébration*, 42f. See also 89f., the sketch of the developing relation between episcopal entrance and beginning of the liturgy.

16. Mateos, *La célébration*, 49f. See also 68–71, on the history of the Typica (Ps 102 and 104, the eight Beatitudes), which the Russians sing on all Sundays and feasts of medium rank, and the Rumanians on all days that have no special antiphons of their own.

CHAPTER FOUR

1. F. R. Taft, *The Great Entrance. A History of the Transfer of Gifts and Other Preanaphoral Rites in the Liturgy of St. John Chrysostom* (OCA 200; Rome, 1975, 1978²).

2. Ibid., 99–102, 102–105.

3. Ibid., 105–108.

4. Ibid., 108–112, espec. 110, n. 201.

5. Ibid., 83–98, 112–118.

6. Cyril of Jerusalem, *Catecheses mystagogicae* V, 4; see Jungmann, vol. 2, 110, n. 5.

7. Taft 64 (with references to the numerous occurrences of *hypodechomai* with this meaning; Br 338, 339, 348).

8. See above, Part Two, Chapter Two, espec. nn. 8, 10, 50.

9. A. M. Schneider, "Liturgie und Kirchenbau in Syrien," *Nachrichten der Akademie der Wissenschaften in Göttingen. Phil.-Hist. Klasse* (1949), 45–68 at 49.

10. Ibid., 59.

11. R. F. Taft, "Toward the Origins of the Offering Procession in the Syro-Byzantine Rite," *OCP* 36 (1970) 73–107; also Taft 3–52.

12. *Didascalia* II, 57, 6, cited in Taft 18.

13. *Testamentum Domini* I, 19; see Taft 19; Schneider 52.

14. *Offerre* (with reference to the transfer of the gifts before the anaphora: Botte 10) is here specifically mentioned as a basic liturgical function: "O God . . . grant the Holy Spirit of grace and concern and zeal to this servant of yours whom you have chosen to minister to your Church and to offer" (Botte 26, with the reference to *Testamentum Domini*; ibid., 27 with n. 4).

15. See the most important liturgy-related passage in Chrysostom, which contains an allusion to Rom 12:1 and to the relevant phrase in the anaphora: *In illud: Vidi Dom.* 6, 2–3 (PG 56:137–138); van de Paverd 279ff.

16. van de Paverd 243–251, 468–471.

17. See the list of codices with this rubric in Taft 121, n. 5, as well as the evidence for the role of the deacons in the transfer of the gifts as a whole, Taft 203–213.

18. A. Jacob, "La traduction de la Liturgie de s. Jean Chrysostome par Léon Toscan. Edition critique," *OCP* 32 (1966) 111–169 at 149f. (= Taft 197). These witnesses show that deacons were the principal singers of the Cherubikon, because they had always been regarded as images of the angels (this point is made in an especially forced way by Theodore of Mopsuestia) and because they therefore actualized in a special way the symbolism of the hymn. The early departure (during the prayer for the catechumens) to the place where the oblations were shows that the gathering of these and the procession itself took some time (since the prothesis must be supposed to have been long ended). The time element is also explained by the physical layout of the Great Church, in which the skeuophylakion (the place where the faithful deposited their offerings and the prothesis was celebrated) was separated from the main part of the church. On this see Taft 178–191.

19. But in Dionysius the statement may have a different explanation.

20. *Scholia* 3, 1 (PG 4:136) on *Hierarchia ecclesiastica* 3 (PG 3: 425; J. Stiglmayr, *Des heiligen Dionysius Areopagita* . . . , 120). According to H. U. von Balthasar, "Das Scholienwerk des Johannes von Skythopolis," *Scholastik* 15 (1940) 16–38, the scholion is from John himself and not from Maximus the Confessor. The passage from John is in Taft 204.

21. Taft 205f.

22. Thus according to the *Diataxis* of Philotheus. See the iconographic representations from this period: p. 100.

23. For *Apostolic Constitutions* VIII, see Br 13f. or R. Storf, tr., *Griechische Liturgien* (Bibliothek der Kirchenväter; Kempten, 1912), 42f; henceforth cited as Storf.

24. See the survey of the development and sequence of preanaphoral rites in Taft 48.

25. This creates a difficulty especially for understanding the kiss of peace, since the profession of faith, introduced by Patriarch Timothy (511–518), is so much felt to be the object of the expression of unanimity (with unanimity in faith predominating over unanimity in sacrifice and meal) that since the thirteenth century the exhortation "Let us love one another" has sometimes been completed by a final clause: "in order that we may confess our faith" (Taft 382) and sometimes followed immediately by a reference to the Trinity (in the accusative case: "the Father and the Son and

the Holy Spirit, the essentially one and indivisible Trinity"). Together these complements make up the definitive text.

26. On the litany of offering as a parallel formation (its petitions duplicate those of the litany of intercession before the Our Father; this litany in turn already brings together petitions that originally had a variety of functions) see Taft 311–349.

27. Mateos, *La célébration*, 174–179; Taft 350–373.

28. Mateos 175f.

29. The words *thysia aineseôs* and *(prosenegkein)* . . . *thysias pneumatikas* are from Heb 13:15 and 1 Pt 2:5. These, as biblical witnesses, along with parallel passages in the Liturgy of Chrysostom were adduced by Melanchthon (*Apol. C. A.* XXIV, 26) in favor of a spiritual conception of sacrifice.

30. *Archê tês proskomidês tou hagiou Iakobou tou adelphotheou* (Beginning of the anaphora of St. James, brother of God) (Mateos 179).

31. There is a different emphasis (and one closer to the early Christian liturgy) on the Old Testament paradigms of sacrifice in the first part of the anaphora of Mark. The prayer for acceptance appeals to them but relates them to the "gifts of the offerers," whether the latter "have offered much or little . . . wanted to offer but did not have the wherewithal" (Br 129; Storf 176). The original role of the paradigms in the *Supra quae* prayer of the Roman Canon is to be interpreted in the light of the function they obviously have in the anaphora of Mark (Schulz 65–68).

CHAPTER FIVE

1. See Beck 436ff., 356ff.

2. R. Bornert, *Les commentaires byzantins de la divine liturgie du VIIe au XVe siècle* (Archives de l'Orient Chrétien 9; Paris, 1966); henceforth cited as Bornert.

3. Ibid., 86.

4. Ibid., 85f., 90ff.

5. See Beck 347f., 357.

6. H. U. von Balthasar, *Kosmische Liturgie. Das Weltbild Maximus' des Bekenners* (Einsiedeln, 1961), 377 (PG 91:673–680). The agreement in content between this fifth chapter and an appendix to the *Little Antirrheticus* of Evagrius (PG 40:1275–1278) is explained by a later interpolation of Evagrius' work (ibid., 338, n. 2).

7. Bornert 92.

8. Ibid., 115.

9. Ibid., 116.

10. Ibid., 115.

11. Ibid., 117f.

12. For an example of the tradition that interpreted the church building in accordance with the vital functions and liturgical ceremonies of the ecclesial community, see Eusebius, *Historia ecclesiastica* X, 4. With reference in particular to the symbolic correspondence between liturgy and church structure in Syria see A. M. Schneider, "Liturgie und Kirchenbau in Syrien," *Nachrichten der Akademie der Wissenschaften in Göttingen. Phil.-Hist. Klasse* (1949), 45–68.

13. Bornert 121ff. For the application to individual rites, 106–110.

14. On the diffusion of the commentary in eastern monastic circles, as well as on its influence in the West and on parallel publications there see Bornert 123f.

15. The prayer (Br 312) reads: "Benefactor and Maker of the entire creation, accept the Church that appears before you; grant what is beneficial to each; bring all things to their fulfillment and make us worthy of your kingdom. . . ." On the place

of the prayer in the history of liturgical development and on its attestation in the mss see Mateos, *La célébration*, 79 with n. 32.

16. Bornert 109; see Taft 44.

CHAPTER SIX

1. Also referred to as "proscomide," a term first applied to the preparation of the gifts at the beginning of the liturgy by Patriarch Germanus (d. 733) in his liturgical commentary and thenceforth understood in this way. In earlier usage proscomide (on *proskomidein* see below, n. 4) was a synonym for anaphora and referred in particular to the "prayer (at the beginning) of the sacrifice" (see Part Two, Chapter Four, at n. 30). Apart from the commentary of Germanus the most important witness to the development of the prothesis is the *Protheoria* of Theodore of Andida (or his predecessor, Nicholas) from the eleventh century.

2. See Part One, Chapter Four, section B, n. 18.

3. See Part One, Chapter Six, section A, n. 34.

4. In liturgical sources written in Greek "prothesis" is more common than "proscomide." The rubics use "prothesis" for: (1) the *act* of making an offering (Br 360, 28 and 30); (2) the offering as a *gift* (Br 360, 34); (3) the *place* where the offering is made (Br 356, 15); it is called the skeuophylakion in the Barberini Codex (Br 309, 5); and (4) the *table* for the offerings (Br 356, 16). In the anaphora of Basil we find *protithenai* (Br 327, 21) and *proskomizein* (Br 332, 16) used of the same eucharistic action on the gifts (in the LXX, *prothesis artôn* is used of the showbread or loaves of proposition; see Heb 9:2).

5. This view used to be almost universally held; it lost its probability due to the research of R. F. Taft (see Taft 15f., 259).

6. See above, Part Two, Chapter Four, nn. 23–24.

7. Br 309. The prayer which the Barberini Codex here makes part of the Liturgy of Basil was, then as now, the one proper to the Byzantine liturgy (whereas the seldom-used prayer that the same codex assigns to the Liturgy of Chrysostom was probably non-Byzantine in origin and could not prevail).

8. Br 41. Further references: Taft 260f.

9. Taft 262.

10. On the recent origin of and lack of unity in the pertinent rubrics for the episcopal liturgy see Taft 265ff.

11. According to Johannesberg translation (into Latin) of the tenth-century Liturgy of Basil, ed. by J. Cochlaeus in his *Speculum antiquae devotionis circa missam* (Mainz, 1549), 119. See Taft 267f.

12. A similar but far more urgent problem arose in the effort to reform the Roman Mass. Since the High Middle Ages all liturgical functions had been absorbed by the priest, but the fact that he filled all these roles at the altar (until 1955) made the original functions almost unrecognizable.

13. Taft 274, n. 73, lists the references. The passage of the eleventy-century *Protheoria* is cited in Part One, Chapter 5, section B at n. 55.

14. O. Bârlea, "La proscomidie. L'offrande dans le rite byzantin. Son écho sur la communion," *Societas Academica Dacoromana. Acta Phil. et Theol.* II (Rome, 1964), 11–66 at 26.

15. M. Mandalà, *La protesi della liturgia nel rito bizantino-greco* (Grottaferrata, 1935), 79.

16. This was Mandalà's conjecture (76).

17. Bârlea 26.

18. V. Laurent, "Le rituel de la proscomidie et le Metropolite de Crete Elie," *REB* 16 (= Melanges Sévérien Salaville) (1958) 116–142 at 130f. (139). Noteworthy also is the mention of a (first) rite of the Zeon at this point.

19. "And when he [the deacon] has completed everything, then the priest recites the prothesis prayer over the sacrificial gifts" (ibid.).

20. Ibid., 135 (141).

21. Nicholas Cabasilas, *A Commentary on the Divine Liturgy*, tr. by J. M. Hussey and P. A. McNulty (London, 1960), ch. 30 (pp. 76ff.), rightly views this passage of the Canon as equivalent to an epiclesis; see also Schulz 63ff.

22. Bârlea 15–25 emphasizes pertinently the extent to which an analogous liturgical development took place in East and West, and the ecumenical relevance of this fact.

23. Bornert 125–180.

24. See ibid., 142–144, for a list of the mss that name Basil as author.

25. For the grouping and genesis of the various forms of the text see ibid., 128–142.

26. See ibid., 140f., for Group Dp with its interpolations from the *Protheoria*.

27. On the later history of liturgical explanation and the influence of Symeon see the comprehensive study by K. Chr. Felmy, *Die Deutung der Göttlichen Liturgie in der russischen Theologie* (in preparation).

28. See Bornert 170.

29. See ibid., 171f.

30. See the list of titles, ibid., 128–142.

31. See G. Lange, *Bild und Wort. Die katechetischen Funktionen des Bildes in der griechischen Theologie des 6. bis 9. Jahrhunderts* (Würzburg, 1969), 201–216 (Nicephorus), 217–232 (Theodore); also Beck 303–305.

32. The notion of *historia* is taken as a parallel to ideas of Nicephorus in Lange 211, but in the chapter on Germanus no attention is paid to the latter's commentary (the author of which is still uncertain according to Lange).

33. See Lange, 208, 216.

34. Ibid., 220–222; see also Beck 305.

35. Lange 222f. (PG 99:432D–433A).

36. Lange 221, 223f., 226.

37. Ibid., 221.

38. On the First Sunday of Lent in 843 a Synod of Constantinople celebrated the definitive victory over iconoclasm and appointed this day for an annual "Feast of Orthodoxy" (Beck 56).

39. Bornert 181–213.

40. Ibid., 185f.

41. Ibid., 290f. (PG 140:429C; but a different view is expressed in 429B, cited in Part One, Chapter Five, Section B, n. 55).

42. Bornert 192 (PG 140:120C). Nicholas, regarding whom we have no other historical information, is named in a Jerusalem ms as the author of a special treatise on the subject of unleavened bread (ibid., 183, n. 4).

43. See P. Joannou, "Aus den unedierten Schriften des Psellos: Das Lehrgedicht zum Messopfer und der Traktat gegen die Vorbestimmung des Todesstundes," *REB* 51 (1958) 1–16 at 3–9.

44. Bornert 194.

45. They are called "Phundaitai (Phundagiagites)" (PG 140:461–464).

46. On the rite of the Zeon see Part One, Chapter 3 (Introduction), especially the passages (nn. 16–18) from Nicetas Stethatos that L. H. Grondijs cites on the corre-

spondence between the interpretation of the Zeon and contemporary iconography of the crucifixion.

47. J. Darrouzès, "Nicolas d'Andida et les azymes," *REB* 32 (1974) 199–210, esp. 200–203.

48. Bornert 191.

49. On the difficulty of establishing his biographical data see Bornert 215f. According to Bornert and to R. Loenertz, *REB* 7 (1949) 17, Cabasilas was still living in 1391, as letters addressed to him show. Direct information about him ceases as early as 1363, the year when Metropolitan Nilus Cabasilas died.

50. That is how Cabasilas, starting with the opening of the prothesis, argues from the content of the Lord's words (which in the Byzantine anaphora and some New Testament codices are given, in 1 Cor 11:24, in the form: *to sôma to hyper hymôn klômenon*, "the body broken for you"), insofar as they signify the "cross, passion and death" and, in accordance with them, the body of the Lord becomes present, "which took all this upon itself—being crucified, rising, and ascending to heaven."

50. In thus understanding the *historia* of the gospel—an understanding that has always been attached to the liturgical proclamation of the gospel, to sacramental theology, and to the celebration of the liturgical year and that is persistently reflected in the authentic theology of icons—ecclesial tradition has long since done justice to the legitimate concerns which the exegetical school of Bultmann has advanced in response to an understanding of the Bible (current in the modern age and even in church circles) that reduces the reading of the Bible to the reading of any book whatsoever and the content of the Bible to a historical report.

52. The conciliar definition (the *horos*) decrees that "as is done for the image of the revered and life-giving cross and the holy gospels and other sacred objects and monuments, let an oblation of incense and light be made to give honour to those images [i.e., icons]" (DS 601; ND 1252).

53. See Part One, Chapter 4, section B, n. 23.

54. See the whole passage cited in Part One, Chapter 6, section B, n. 71.

55. *A Commentary on the Divine Liturgy*, ch. 37 (PG 150:452A; Hussey and McNulty 90).

56. Ibid.

PROSPECT

1. See above, Part Two, Chapter 2, section 2, the final characteristic in which the anaphora of Basil is at one with the treatise *On the Holy Spirit*.

2. Ch. 29 (PG 150:429A; Hussey and McNulty 72). On Chrysostom, *De prod. Judae* 1, 6 (PG 49:380) see van de Paverd 295ff.

3. Ch. 30 (PG 433D); see Schulz 63ff.

4. Ch. 32 (PG 440AB; Hussey and McNulty p. 80).

5. Ch. 32 (PG 440CD; Hussey and McNulty pp. 81–82).

6. On Melanchthon's effort to understand the eucharistic sacrifice entirely from this vantage point see Part Two, Chapter 4, n. 29.

7. Ch. 51 (485AB; p. 116).

8. Ch. 36 (448f., p. 88).

9. Ch. 37 (449–451).

10. See above, Part Two, Chapter 2, n. 15. In addition: H.-J. Schulz, "*Sanctorum communio*. Glaubensausdruck einer eucharistischen Ekklesiologie der Ökumene," in L. Hein (ed.), *Die Einheit der Kirche. Dimensionen ihrer Heiligkeit, Katholizität und Apostolizität (Festgabe Peter Meinhold zum 70. Geburtstag)* (Wiesbaden, 1977), 16–29.

11. See the prayer for the church in the anaphora of Basil (for the wording of the passage see above, Part Two, p. 148) and the interpretation of it along the lines of a pneumatological and eucharistic ecclesiology (in the literature listed above in the Introduction, n. 11, and in Part Two, Chapter Two, n. 23.

12. See, e.g., the Declaration on the Eucharist of the Commission for Faith and Order (in the Introduction, n. 12), the Declaration of the Joint Roman Catholic and Evangelical Lutheran Commission, *Das Herrenmahl* (Paderborn and Frankfurt, 1978), espec. nos. 21–28, and *Die Anrufung des Heiligen Geistes in Abendmahl. Eine Dokumentation über das Friedewald-Gespräch* (Beiheft 31 of *Ökumenische Rundschau;* Frankfurt, 1977). On the question of sacrifice in particular see also *Das Opfer Christi und das Opfer der Christen* (Beiheft 34 of *Ökumenische Rundschau;* Frankfurt, 1979).

Bibliography

Afanassieff, N., N. Koulomzine, J. Meyendorff, and A. Schmemann. *The Primacy of Peter*, tr. by K. Farrar et al. Westminster, Md., 1963.

Aldenhoven, H. "Darbringung und Epiklese im Eucharistiesgenet," *Internationale Kirchliche Zeitschrift* 61 (1971) 79–117, 150–189; 62 (1972) 29–73.

Altaner B. and A. Stuiber. *Leben, Schriften und Lehre der Kirchenväter.* Freiburg, 1978⁸.

Ammann, A. M. *Die Gottesschau im palamitischen Hesychasmus.* Das östliche Christentum 3–4. Würzburg, 1948².

Antoniadis, S. *Place de la liturgie dans la tradition des lettres grecques.* Leiden, 1939.

Arranz, M. *Le Typicon du monastère du Saint-Sauveur à Messine.* OCA 85. Rome, 1969.

Atchley, F. *On the Epiclesis of the Eucharistic Liturgy and in the Consecration of the Font.* Alcuin Club Collection 31. London, 1935.

Balthasar, H. Urs von. *Kosmische Liturgie. Das Weltbild Maximus' des Bekenners.* Einsiedeln, 1961.

Bârlea, O. "La proscomidie. L'offrande dans le rite byzantin. Son écho sur la communion," *Societas Academica Dacoromana: Acta Philosophica et Theologica* 2 (Rome, 1964) 1–66.

Baumstark, A. *Die Messe im Morgenland.* Kempen, 1906, 1921².

———. "Der 'Cherubshymnus' und seine Parallele," *Gottesminne* 6 (1911–1912) 10–22.

———. "Zur Urgeschichte der Chrysostomosliturgie," *TG* 5 (1913), 299–313, 394–395.

———. *Vom geschichtlichen Werden der Liturgie.* Freiburg, 1923.

———. "Das Gesetz der Erhaltung des Alten in liturgisch hochwertiger Zeit," *JLW* 7 (1927) 1–23.

251

————. "Denkmäler der Entstehungsgeschichte des byzantinischen Ritus," *OrChr*, 3rd series, 2 (1927) 1–32.

————. "Anaphora," *RAC* 1 (1941) 422–425.

————. *Nocturna Laus. Typen frühchristlicher Vigilienfeier und ihr Fortleben.* Ed. by O. Heiming. LQF 32. Münster, 1957.

————. *Comparative Liturgy*, tr. by F. L. Cross. London, 1958.

Beck, H. G. *Kirche und theologische Literatur im byzantinischen Reich* (Byzantinisches Handbuch II, 1) Munich, 1959.

Benz, E. *The Eastern Orthodox Church: Its Thought and Life,* tr. by R. and C. Winston. Garden City, N.Y., 1973.

Bertonière, G. *The Historical Development of the Easter Vigil and Related Services in the Greek Church.* OCA 193. Rome, 1972.

Betz, J. *Die Eucharistie in der Zeit der griechischen Väter I/1. Die Aktualpräsenz der Person und des Heilswerkes Jesu im Abendmahl nach der vorephesinischen griechischen Patristik.* Freiburg, 1955.

————. *Die Eucharistie in der Zeit der griechischen Väter. II/1. Die Realpräsenz des Leibes und Blutes Jesu im Abendmahl nach dem Neuen Testament.* Freiburg, 1964.

————. *Eucharistie in der Schrift und Patristik* Handbuch der Dogmengeschichte IV/4a. Freiburg, 1979.

Biedermann, H. "Die Lehre von der Eucharistie bei Nikolaos Kabasilas," *OstkSt* 3 (1954) 29–41.

Bobrinskoy, B. "Liturgie et ecclésiologie trinitaire de s. Basile," in *Eucharisties* (cf. Abbreviations) 2 (1970) 197–240.

Borgia, N. *Il commentario liturgico di S. Germano patriarca constantinopolitano e la versione latina di Anastasio bibliothecario.* Grottaferrata, 1912.

————. *Origine della liturgia bizantina.* Grottaferrata, 1933.

Bornert., R. *Les commentaires byzantins de la Divine Liturgie du VIIe au XVe siècle* (Archives de l'Orient Chrétien 9). Paris, 1966.

Botte, B. "Note historique sur la concélébration dans l'église ancienne," *MD* 35 (1953) 9–23.

————. "Problèmes de l'anamnèse," *JEH* 5 (1954) 16–24.

————. "L'épiclèse dans les liturgies syriennes orientales," *SE* 6 (1954) 48–72.

Bouyer, J. *Rite and Man: Natural Sacredness and Christian Liturgy,* tr. by M. J. Costelloe. Notre Dame, 1963

————. *Eucharist: Theology and Spirituality of the Eucharistic Prayer*, tr. by C. U. Quinn. Notre Dame, 1968.

Brakmann, H. "Zum gemeinschaftliche Eucharistiegebet byzantinischer Konzelebranted," *OCP* 42 (1976) 319–367.

Braun, J. *Die liturgische Gewandung im Occident und Orient nach Urprung und Entwicklung, Verwendung und Symbolik.* Freiburg, 1907.

————. *Das christliche Altargerät in seinem Sein und seiner Entwicklung.* Munich, 1932.

Brightmann, F. E. "The Historia Mystagogica and Other Greek Commentaries on the Byzantine Liturgy," *JTS* 9 (1907–1908) 248–267, 387–397.

————. "The Anaphora of Theodore," *JTS* 31 (1930) 160–164.

Brinktrine, J. "Ein auffallender Brauch der byzantinischen Messliturgie. Zum Ritus der Zeon," *TG* 29 (1937) 637–643.

Brockhaus, H. *Die Kunst in den Athosklöstern.* Leipzig, 1924².

Bulgakov, S. V. *Nastol'naja kniga dlja svjaščenno-cerkovno služitelej* [Manual for Priestly Celebrants]. Charkow, 1900.

Camelot, P. T. *Die Lehre von der Kirche: Väterzeit bis ausschliesslich Augustinus.* Handbuch der Dogmengeschichte III/3b. Freiburg, 1970.

Capelle, B. "Les liturgies 'basiliennes' et saint Basile" = Appendix in J. Doresse and E. Lanne, *Un témoin archaïque de la liturgie copte de s. Basile.* Louvain, 1960.

————. "La procession du Saint-Esprit d'après la liturgie grecque de s. Basile," *OrSyr* 7 (1962) 69–76.

Casel, O. "Das Mysteriengedächtnis der Messliturgie im Lichte der Tradition," *JLW* 6 (1926) 112–204.

————. "Mysteriengegenwart," *JLW* 8 (1928) 145–224.

————. "Älteste Kunst und Christusmysterium," *JLW* 12 (1932) 1–86.

————. "Das ostchristliche Opferfeier als Mysteriengeschehen," in J. Tyciak, G. Wunderle, and P. Werhun (eds.), *Der Christliche Osten. Geist und Gestalt.* Regensburg, 1939, 59–74.

————. "Glaube, Gnosis und Mysterium," *JLW* 15 (1941) 155–305.

————. *Das christliche Opfermysterium*, ed. by V. Warnach. Graz, 1968.

Casper, J. *Weltverklärung im liturgischen Geiste der Ostkirche.* Ecclesia orans 22. Freiburg, 1919.

————. "Der Verkündigungs charakter der orientalischen Liturgie," in F. X. Arnold and B. Fischer (eds.), *Die Messe in der Glaubensverkündigung*. Freiburg, 1953², 165–205.

Congar, Y. *L'Eglise de saint Augustin à l'époque moderne*. Histoire des dogmes 3. Paris, 1970.

Connolly, R. H. *The Liturgical Homilies of Narsai*. With an Appendix by E. Bishop. Texts and Studies 8/1. Cambridge, 1909.

Connolly, R. H. and H. W. Codrington. *Two Commentaries on the Jacobite Liturgy by George, Bishop of the Arab Tribes, and Moses Bar Kepha*. London, 1913.

Cottas, V. "Contribution à l'étude de quelques tissus liturgiques," *Studi bizantini e neoellenici* 6 (1940) 87–102.

Craigh, R. N. S. "Nicolas Cabasilas. An Exposition of the Divine Liturgy," *Studia Patristica* II. TU 64. Berlin, 1957, 21–28.

Cullmann, O. *The Earliest Christian Confessions*, tr. by J. K. S. Reid (London, 1949).

————. *Early Christian Worship*, tr. by A. S. Todd and J. B. Torrance. Studies in Biblical Theology 10. Chicago, 1953.

————. *Christ and Time. The Primitive Christian Conception of Time and History*, tr. by F. V. Filson. London, 1962².

Dalmais, I. H. *Eastern Liturgies*, tr. by D. Attwater. Twentieth Century Encyclopedia of Catholicism 112. New York, 1960.

————. "Place de la Mystagogie de saint Maxime le Confesseuer dans la théologie liturgique byzantine," *Studia Patristica* V. TU 80. Berlin, 1962, 277–283.

Daniélou, J. *The Bible and the Liturgy*. Notre Dame, 1956.

————. *From Shadows to Reality. Studies in the Biblical Typology of the Fathers*, tr. by W. Hibberd. Westminster, Md., 1960.

Demus, O. *Byzantine Mosaic Decoration*. London, 1947.

Dix, G. *The Shape of the Liturgy*. London, 1945.

Dmitrievskij, A. *Opisanie liturgičeskich rukopisej chranjasčichsja v bibliotekach pravoslavnago Vostoka* [Description of Liturgical Manuscripts in the Libraries of the Orthodox East], 3 vols. Kiev, 1895–1901. Reprinted: Hildesheim, 1965.

Dobschütz, E. *Christusbilder. Untersuchungen zur christlichen Legende*. TU 18. Leipzig, 1899.

Dolger, F. J. *Die Sonne der Gerechtigkeit und der Schwarze. Eine religions-geschichtliche Studie zum Taufgelöbnis.* LF 2. Münster, 1919.

————. *Sol Salutis. Gebet und Gesang im christlichen Altertum, mit besonderer Rücksicht auf die Ostung in Gebet und Liturgie.* LF 4–5. Münster, 1925².

————. "Die Heiligkeit des Altares und ihre Begründung im christlichen Altertum," *Antike und Christentum* 1 (1930) 162–183.

Drower, E. S. *Water into Wine. A Study of Ritual Idiom in the Middle East.* London, 1956.

Edelby, N. "Pour une restauration de la liturgie byzantine," *PrOrSyr* 7 (1957) 97–118.

Elert, W. *Eucharist and Church Fellowship in the First Four Centuries,* tr. by N. E. Nagel. St. Louis, 1966.

Engberding, H. *Das eucharistische Hochgebet der Basileiosliturgie.* Münster, 1931.

————. "Die syrische Anaphora der Zwölf Apostel und ihre Paralleltexte," *OrChr,* 3rd series, 12 (1937) 213–247.

————. "Der Einfluss des Ostens auf die Gestalt der römischen Liturgie." in *Ut omnes unum sint.* Münster, 1939, 61–89.

————. "Das chalkedonische Christusbild und die Liturgien der monophysitischen Kirchengemeinden," *Chalkedon* [cf. Abbreviations] 2 (1951–1954) 697–733.

————. "Das anaphorische Fürbittgebet der byzantinischen Chrysostomos-liturgie," *OrChr* 47 (1963) 16–52; 49 (1965) 18–37.

————. "Die Angleichung der byzantinischen Chrysostomosliturgie an die byzantinische Basileiosliturgie," *OstkSt* 13 (1964) 105–122.

————. "Die *Euchē tēs proskomidēs* der byzantinischen Basileiosliturgie und ihre Geschichte," *Muséon* 79 (1966) 287–313.

Engdahl, R. *Beiträge zur Kenntnis der byzantinischen Liturgie. Texte und Studien.* Berlin, 1908.

Felicetti-Liebenfels, W. *Geschichte der byzantinischen Ikonenmalerei.* Olten-Lausanne, 1956.

Felmy, K.–C., et al. *Symbolik des orthodoxen Christentums und der kleineren christlichen Kirchen in Ost und West. Tafelhand.* Symbolik der Religionen, ed. by F. Herrmann, 16. Stuttgart, 1968.

————. "Der Christusknabe auf dem Diskos. Die Proskomidie der orthodoxen Liturgie als Darstellung von 'Schlachtung des Lammes' und Geburt des Herrn," *JLH* 23 (1979) 95–101.

Fittkau, G. *Der Begriff des Mysteriums bei Johannes Chrysostomus.* Theophaneia 9. Bonn, 1953.

Forte, B. *La Chiesa bell'Eucaristia.* Naples, 1975.

Gamber, K. *Ordo antiquus Gallicanus. Der gallikanische Messritus des 6. Jahrhunderts.* Textus Patristici et Liturgici 3. Regensburg, 1965.

————. *Die Autorschaft von De Sacramentis.* StPL 1. Regensburg, 1967.

————. *Sacrificium laudis. Zur Geschichte des frühchristlichen Eucharistiegebets.* StPL 5. Regensburg, 1973.

————. *Liturgie und Kirchenbau. Studien zur Geschichte der Messfeier und des Gotteshauses in der Frühzeit.* StPL 6. Regensburg, 1976.

————. *Sakramentarstudien und andere Arbeiten zur frühen Liturgiegeschichte.* StPL 7. Regensburg, 1978.

Gass, W. *Symbolik der griechischen Kirche.* Berlin, 1872.

————. *Die Mystik des Nikolaus Cabasilas vom Leben in Christo.* Leipzig, 1899[2].

Gharib, G. "Nicolas Cabasilas et l'explication symbolique de la liturgie," *PrOrChr* 10 (1960) 114–133.

Giordani, E. "Das mittelbyzantinische Ausschmückungssystem als Ausdruck eines hieratischen Bildprogramms," *JÖBG* 1 (1951) 103–134.

Gogol, N. *The Divine Liturgy of the Eastern Orthodox Church,* tr. by R. Edmonds (London, 1960).

Grabar, A. *La peinture religieuse en Bulgarie.* Orient et Byzance 1. Paris, 1928.

————. *Martyrium. Recherches sur le culte des reliques et l'art chrétien.* II. Iconographie. Paris, 1946.

————. *Byzantine Painting: Historical and Critical Study,* tr. by S. Gilbert. Great Centuries of Painting. Geneva, 1953.

————. "Un rouleau constantinopolitain et ses peintures," *DOP* 8 (1954) 161–199.

————. *Byzanz. Die byzantinische Kunst des Mittelalters vom 8. bis zum 15. Jahrhundert.* Baden-Baden, 1964.

Grillmeier, A. "Der Gottessohn im Totenreich," *ZKT* 71 (1949) 23–53, 184–203.

————. "Die theologische und sprachliche Vorbereitung der christologischen Formel von Chalkedon," *Chalkedon* [cf. Abbreviations] 1 (1951) 5–202.

————. *Der Logos am Kreuz. Zur christologischen Symbolik der älteren Kreuzesdarstellung.* Munich, 1956.

————. *Christ in Christian Tradition* 1, tr. by J. Bowden. Atlanta, 1975.

————. *Mit Ihm und in Ihm. Christologische Forschungen und Perspektiven.* Freiburg, 1977.

Grondijs, L. H. *L'iconographie byzantine du Crucifié mort sur la croix.* Leiden, 1941, 1947².

Grotz, H. *Die Hauptkirchen des Ostens. Von den Anfängen bis zum Konzil von Nikaia.* OCA 169. Rome, 1964.

Grumel, V. "L'iconologie de s. Théodore Studite," *EO* 20 (1921) 257–268.

————. "L'iconologie de saint Germain de Constantinople," *EO* 21 (1922) 165–175.

————. "L'auteur et la date de composition du tropaire *ho monogenēs*," *EO* 22 (1923) 398–418.

————. "Les 'Douze chapitres contre les iconomaques' de s. Nicéphore de Constantinople," *REB* 17 (1959) 127–135.

Hamann-MacLean, R. and H. Hallensleben. *Die Monumentalmalerei in Serbien und Makedonien vom 11. bis zum frühen 14. Jahrhundert.* Osteoropastudien der Hochschulen des Landes Hessen, Reihe II, 3–5. Giessen, 1963.

Hammerschmidt, E., P. Hauptmann, P. Krüger, L. Ouspensky, and H.-J. Schulz, *Symbolik des orthodoxen und orientalischen Christentums.* Symbolik der Religione, ed. by F. Herrmann, 10. Stuttgart, 1962.

Hanssens, J. M. *Institutiones liturgicae de ritibus orientalibus.* II–III. *De missa rituum orientalium.* Rome, 1930–1932.

Heiler, F. *Urkriche und Ostkirche.* Munich, 1937. Revised version: *Die Ostkirchen.* Munich, 1971.

Hendrix, P. "Der Mysteriencharakter der byzantinischen Liturgie," *ByZ* 30 (1929) 333–339.

Holl, K. *Gesammelte Aufsätze zur Kirchengeschichte* 2. Tübingen, 1928.

Hotz, R. *Sakramente—im Wechselspiel zwischen Ost und West.* Zürich-Cologne, 1979.

Hunger, H. *Reich der Neuen Mitte. Der christliche Geist der byzantinischen Kultur.* Graz, 1965.

Hussey, J. *The Byzantine World.* New York, 1961.

Ivánka, E. von. *Dionysios Areopagita. Von den Namen zum Unnennbaren.* Sigillum 7. Einsiedeln, n.d.

————. *Plato Christianus. Übernahme und Umgestaltung des Platonismus durch die Väter.* Einsiedeln, 1964.

————. *Rhomäerreich und Gottesvolk. Das Glaubens-, Staats-, und Volksbewusstsein der Byzantiner und seine Auswirkung auf die ostkirchlich-osteuropäische Geisteshaltung.* Freiburg-Munich, 1968.

Jacob, A. *Recherches sur la tradition manuscrite de la liturgie de saint Jean Chrysostome.* Lic.-Diss., Catholic University of Louvain, 1963.

————. "L'Euchologe de Porphyre Uspenski. Codex Leningr. gr. 226 (Xe siècle)," *Museon* 78 (1965) 173–214.

————. "La traduction de la Liturgie de s. Jean Chrysostome par Léon Toscan. Edition critique," *OCP* 32 (1966) 111–162.

————. "Zum Eisodosgebet der byzantinischen Chrysostomosliturgie des Vat. Barb. gr. 336," *OstkSt* 15 (1966) 35–38.

————. "La traduction de la Liturgie de s. Basile par Nicolas d'Otrante," *Bulletin de l'Institut Historique Belge de Rome* 38 (1967) 49–107.

————. *Histoire du formulaire grec de la liturgie de saint Jean Chrysostome.* Diss., Catholic University of Louvain, 1968.

————. "La concélébration de l'anaphore à Byzance d'après le témoignage de Léon Toscan," *OCP* 35 (1969) 249–256.

————. "La tradition manuscrite de la liturgie de S. Jean Chrysostome (VIIIe–XIIe siècles), in *Eucharisties* (Paris, 1970) 109–138.

Janeras, S. "Les byzantins et le Trisagion christologique," in *Miscellanea Liturgica in onore de S. E. il Cardinale G. Lercaro.* 2 (Rome, 1967) 469–499.

————. *Introductio in Liturgias orientales.* Rome, 1969.

————. *El viernes santo en la tradición liturgica bizantina.* Dissertation, Pontifical Institute of Oriental Studies, Rome, 1970.

Jong, J. P. de. "La connexion entre le rite de la consignation et l'épiclèse dans saint Ephrem," *Studia Patristica* II. TU 64. Berlin, 1957, 29–37.

————. "Le Rite de la Commixtion dans la Messe Romaine dans ses rapports avec les liturgies syriennes," *AL* 4 (1956) 245–278; 5 (1957) 33–79.

Jugie, M. *Theologia dogmatica Christianorum Orientalium.* 5 vols. Paris, 1926–1935.

————. *De forma Eucharistiae. De epiclesibus eucharisticis.* Rome, 1943.

Jungmann, J. A. *The Mass of the Roman Rite: Its Origins and Development (Missarum Solemnia)* tr. by F. A. Brunner. 2 vols. New York, 1951, 1955.

————. *Symbolik der katholischen Kirche.* Symbolik der Religionen, ed. by F. Herrmann, 6. Stuttgart, 1960.

————. *Die liturgische Feier.* Regensburg, 1961³.

————. *The Place of Christ in Liturgical Prayer,* tr. by A. J. Peeler. Staten Island, N.Y., 1965.

Kern, K. (Archimandrite Cyprien). *Evcharistija* (=The Eucharist. A Theological and Liturgical Exposition). Paris, 1947.

Khouri-Sarkis, G. "Les saintes mystères," *OrSyr* 4 (1959) 307–318.

————. "La liturgie de saint Jean Chrysostome et son origine syrienne," *OrSyr* 7 (1962) 3–68.

Koch, L. "Zur Theologie der Christusikone," *BM* 19 (1937) 375–387; 20 (1938) 32–47, 168–175, 281–288, 437–452.

————. "Christusbild und Kaiserbild," *BM* 21 (1939) 85–105.

Kohlhaas, R. *Jakobitische Sakramententheologie im XIII. Jahrhundert.* LQF 36. Münster, 1958.

Kolping, A. "Amalar von Metz und Florus von Lyon. Zeugen eines Wandels im liturgischen Mysterienverständnis in der Karolingerzeit," *ZKT* 73 (1951) 424–464.

Kondakov, N. P. *Ikonografičeskij Podlinnik I. Ikonografija Gospoda, Boga i Spasa našego Iisua Christa* (=Iconographical Podlinnik I. Iconography of the Lord and God, our Savior Jesus Christ). St. Petersburg, 1905.

Krasnosel'cev, N. F. *Svedenija o nekotorych liturgičeskich rukopisjach Vatikanskoj Biblioteki* (=Notes on Some Liturgical Manuscripts in the Vatican Library). Kazan, 1885.

————. *Materialy dlja istorii činoposledovanija liturgii sv. Ioanna Zlatousstago* (=Materials for the History of the Liturgical Organization of the Liturgy of John Chrysostom). Kazan, 1889.

Kretschmar, G. "Die frühe Geschichte der Jerusalemer Liturgie," *JLH* 2 (1956) 22–46.

————. "Opfer Christi und Opfer der Christen in den eucharistischen Texten der Russischen Orthodoxen Kirche," in *Das Opfer Christi und das Opfer der Christen,* ed. by the Aussenamt der EKD. Ökumenische Rundschau, Beiheft 34. Frankfurt, 1979, 56–75.

Kucharek, C. *The Byzantine-Slav Liturgy of Saint John Chrysostom.* Allendale, N.J., 1971.

Ladner, G. "Der Bilderstreit und die Kunstlehre der byzantinischen und abendländischen Theologie," *ZKG* 50 (1931) 1–23.

Lange, G. *Bild und Wort. Die katechetischen Funktionen des Bildes in der griechischen Theologie des 6.–9. Jahrhunderts.* Würzburg, 1968.

Laurent, V. "Le rituel de la proscomidie et le métropolite de Crète Elie," *REB* 16 (1958) 116–142.

Lécuyer, J. "Die Theologie der Anaphora nach der Schule von Antiochien," *Liturgisches Jahrbuch* 11 (1961) 81–92.

Leeb, H. *Die Gesänge im Gemeinegottesdienst von Jerusalem vom 5. bis 8. Jahrhundert.* Vienna, 1970.

Lengeling, E. J. "Überwundenes in der Messerklärung," in A. Kirchgässner (ed.), *Unser Gottesdienst. Ein Werkbuch.* Freiburg, 1960, 24–36.

———. "Liturgie," *Handbuch Theologischer Grundbegriffe,* ed H. Fries (2 vols.; Munich 1962–1963), 2:75–97.

———. *Die Konstitution des Zweiten Vatikanischen Konzils über die hl. Liturgie. Texte, Einleitung und Kommentar.* Reihe Lebendiger Gottesdienst 5–6. Münster, 1964.

———. *Die neue Ordnung der Eucharistiefeier. Allgemeine Einführung in das römische Messbuch. Text, Einleitung und Kommentar.* Reihe Lebendiger Gottesdienst 17–18. Münster, 1971.

Leroy, F. J. "Proclus, 'de traditione divinae Missae': un faux de C. Palaeocappa," *OCP* 28 (1962) 288–299.

Lietzmann, H. *Mass and Lord's Supper,* tr. by D. H. G. Reeve. Leiden, n.d.

———. "Die Liturgie des Theodor von Mopsuestia," *Sitzungsberichte der Preussischen Akademie der Wissenschaften, Phil.-Hist. Kl.* Berlin, 1933, 915–936.

Lubac, H. de. *Histoire et Esprit. L'intelligence de l'Ecriture d'après Origène.* Théologie 16. Paris, 1950.

Lubatschiwskyi, M. J. "Des heiligen Basilius liturgischer Kampf gegen den Arianismus. Ein Beitrag zur Textgeschichte der Basilius-liturgie," *ZKT* 66 (1942) 20–38.

Mandalà, M. *La protesi nella liturgia bel rito bizantino-greco.* Grottaferrata, 1935.

Mateos, J. "L'action du Saint-Esprit dans la liturgie dite de S. Jean Chrysostome," *PrOrChr* 9 (1959) 193–208.

———. *La célébration de la parole dans la liturgie byzantine.* OCA 191. Rome, 1971.

Mateos, J. and N. Edelby. "Autour d'un projet de restauration de la liturgie byzantine. Présentation d'une audition enregsitrée," *PrOrChr* 7 (1957) 250–260.

Mathews, T. F. *The Early Churches of Constantinople: Architecture and Liturgy.* London, 1971.

Meester, P. de. "Les origines et les développements du texte grec de la liturgie de saint Jean Chrysostome," *Chrysostomika: Studi e ricerche intorno a S. Giovanni Crisostomo.* Rome, 1908, 254–357.

———. "Grecques (Liturgies)," DACL 6:1591–1662.

———. "The Byzantine Liturgy," *ECQ* 3 (1938) 19–25, 63–71, 131–137, 189–192.

———. "De concelebratione in ecclesia orientali praesertim secundum ritum byzantinum," *EL* 37 (1923) 101–110, 145–154, 196–210.

Menges, H. *Die Bilderlehre des heiligen Johannes von Damaskus.* Münster, 1938.

Meyendorff, J. "Notes sur l'influence dionysienne en Orient," *Studia Patristica* II. TU 64. Berlin, 1957, 547–552.

Michel, A. *Humbert and Kerullarios.* 2 vols. Paderborn, 1924–1930.

Millet, G. *Monuments byzantins de Mistra.* Paris, 1910.

———. *Recherches sur l'iconographie de l'évangile aux XIVe, XVe et XVIe siècles.* Paris, 1916, 1960².

———. *Monuments de l'Athos* I. *Les peintures.* Paris, 1927.

———. "La vision de Pierre d'Alexandrie," in *Mélanges Charles Diehl* II. Paris, 1930, 99–115.

———. *La peinture du moyen âge en Yougoslavie* I–III. Paris, 1954, 1957, 1962.

Moeller, C. "Le chalcédonisme et le néo-chalcédonisme en Orient de 451 à la fin du VIe siècle," *Calkedon* [cf. Abbreviations] 1:637–720.

Moraitis, D. (Mōraitēs, D.). *Hē archaiotera gnōstē morphē tōn leitourgeiōn Basileiou kai Chrysostomou.* Thessalonika, 1957.

Neunheuser, N. (ed.). *Opfer Christi und Opfer der Kirche.* Düsseldorf, 1960.

Nikolskij, K. *Posobie k izučeniju ustava bogosluženija pravoslavnoj cerkvi* (=Textbook on the Worship of the Orthodox Church). St. Petersburg, 1907.

Nussbaum, O. *Der Standort des Liturgen am christlichen Altar vor dem Jahre 1000. Eine archäologische und liturgiegeschichtliche Untersuchung.* Theophaneia 18. 2 vols. Bonn, 1965.

———. (ed.). *Die eucharistischen Hochgebete II–IV. Ein thelogischer Kommentar.* Reihe Lebendiger Gottesdienst 16. Münster, 1970.

Nyssen, W. *Das Zeugnis des Bildes im frühen Byzanz.* Sophia 2. Freiburg, 1962.

Onasch, K. "Raub der Eschatologie. Zur Kritik ostkirchlicher Theologie und Frömmigkeit," *TLZ* 74 (1949) 267–274.

———. "Der Funktionalismus der orthodoxen Liturgie. Grundzüge einer Kritik," *JLH* 6 (1961) 1–48.

———. *Einführung in die Konfessionskunde der orthodoxen Kirchen.* Berlin, 1962.

Ostrogorski, G. *History of the Byzantine State*, tr. by J. Hussey. New Brunswick, N.J., 1957.

Ouspensky, L. "Symbolik des orthodoxen Kirchengebaudes und der Ikone," in *Symbolik des orthodoxen und orientalischen Christentums* (Symbolik der Religionen, ed. by F. Herrmann, 10). Stuttgart, 1962, 54–89.

Ouspensky, L. and V. Lossky. *The Meaning of Icons*, tr. by G. E. H. Palmer and E. Kadloubovsky. Boston, 1969.

Pallas, D. I. *Passion und Bestattung Christi in Byzanz. Der Ritus—Das Bild.* Miscellanea Byzantina Monacensia 2. Munich, 1965.

Paverd, F. van de. *Zur Geschichte der Messliturgie in Antiocheia und Konstantinopel gegen Ende des 4. Jahrhunderts. Analyse der Quellen bei Johannes Chrysostomos.* OCA 187. Rome, 1970.

Peterson, E. "MERIS, Hostien, Patrikel und Opferanteil," *ELit* 61 (1947) 3–12.

———. *The Angels and the Liturgy*, tr. by R. Walls. New York, 1964.

Petković, Vl. R. *La peinture serbe du moyen âge.* 2 vols. Belgrade, 1930–1934.

Petković, Vl. R. and G. Bosković. *Dečani.* Monumenta serbica artis mediaevalis 2. Belgrade, 1941.

Pétridès, S. "Traités liturgiques de saint Maxime et de saint Germain traduits par Anastase le Bibliothécaire," *ROC* 10 (1905) 289–313, 350–364.

Philaret (of Chernigov). *Geschichte der Kirche Russlands nebst einer Erläuterung des Gottesdienstes der morgenländischen Kirche nach seiner symbolischen Bedeutung*, tr. by Blumenthal. Frankfurt, 1872.

Piana, G. La. *Le rappresentazioni sacre nella letteratura bizantina dalle origini al secolo IX.* Grottaferrata, 1912.

Pinsk, J. *Die sakramentale Welt.* Ecclesia orans 21. Freiburg, 1941.

Raes, A. *Introductio in liturgiam orientalem.* Rome, 1947.

———. "Antimension," *PrOrChr* 1 (1951) 59–70.

———. "Le dialogue de la grande entrée dans la liturgie byzantine," *OCP* 18 (1952) 38–51.

————. "La concélébration dans les rites orientaux," *MD* 35 (1953) 24–47.

————. "L'authenticité de la liturgie byzantine de s. Jean Chrysostome," *OCP* 24 (1958) 5–16.

————. "L'authenticité de la liturgie byzantine de saint Basile," *REB* 16 (1958) 158–161.

————. "Un nouveau document de la liturgie de s. Basile," *OCP* 26 (1960) 401–411.

Rahmani, I. E. *I fasti della chiesa patriarcale antiochena.* Rome, 1920.

————. *Les liturgies orientales et occidentales étudiées séparément et comparées entre elles.* Beirut, 1929.

Rahner, H. *Greek Myths and Christian Mystery,* tr. by B. Battershaw. New York, 1963.

Rahner, K. *The Church and the Sacraments,* tr. by W. J. O'Hara. Quaestiones Disputatae 9. New York, 1963.

Reine, F. *The Eucharistic Doctrine and Liturgy of the Mystagogical Catecheses of Theodore of Mopsuestia.* Washington, 1942.

Richter, J. P. *Quellen der byzantinischen Kunstgeschichte.* Vienna, 1897.

Roques, R. *L'univers dionysien. Structure hiérarchique du monde selon le Ps.-Denys.* Paris, 1954.

Rücker, A. *Ritus baptismi et missae quem descripsit Theodorus episcopus Mopsuestenus in sermonibus catecheticis e versione syriaca ab A. Mingana nuper reperta.* Opuscula et textus, series liturgica 2. Münster, 1933.

Salaville, S. "Le catéchisme en images des églises orientales," *L'Union des Eglises* 5 (1926) 87–96.

————. *Liturgies orientales. La messe.* 2 vols. Paris, 1942.

Salaville, S. and G. Novack. *Le rôle di diacre dans la liturgie orientale. Etude d'histoire et de liturgie.* Paris, 1962.

Sauget, J. M. *Bibliographie des liturgies orientales (1900–1960).* Rome, 1962.

Sauser, E. "Symbolik des katholischen Kirchengebäudes" = Appendix in J. A. Jungmann, *Symbolik der katholischen Kirche* (supra).

Schillebeeckx, H. E. *De sacramentele heilseconomie.* Antwerp, 1952.

————. *The Eucharist,* tr. by N. D. Smith. New York, 1968.

Schneemelcher, W. "Die Epiklese bei den griechischen Vätern," in *Die Anrufung des Heiligen Geistes im Abendmahl,* ed. by the Aussenamt der EKD. ökumenische Rundschau, Beiheft 31. Frankfurt, 1977, 68–94.

Schneider, A. M. *Die Hagia Sophia zu Konstantinopel*. Berlin, 1939.

――――. "Die Kuppelmosaiken der Hagia Sophia zu Konstantinopel," *Nachrichten der Akademie der Wissenschaften in Göttingen*, Phil.-Hist. Kl., 1949. 345–355.

――――. "Liturgie und Kirchenbau in Syrien," ibid., 45–68.

Schneider, C. "Studien zum Ursprung liturgischer Einzelheiten östlicher Liturgien. 1. *Katapetasma*," *Kyrios* 1 (1936) 57–73, and "2. *Thymiamata*," *Kyrios* 3 (1938) 149–190, 293–311.

――――. "Das Fortleben der Gesamtantike in den griechischen Liturgien," *Kyrios* 4 (1939) 185–221.

――――. *Geistesgeschichte des antiken Christentums* II. Munich, 1954.

Schulz, H.-J. "Die 'Höllenfahrt' als 'Anastasis.' Eigenart und dogmengeschichtliche Voraussetzungen byzantinischer Osterfrömmigkeit," *ZKT* 81 (1959) 1–66.

――――. "Liturgie, Tagzeiten und Kirchenjahr des byzantinischen Ritus," *Handbuch der Ostkirchenkunde*. Düsseldorf, 1971, 332–385.

――――. *Ökumenische Glaubenseinheit aus eucharistischer Überlieferung*. Paderborn, 1976.

――――. "Interpretation durch liturgischen Vollzug. 'Transsubstantiation' und 'Transsignifikation' in liturgiewissenschaftlicher Sicht," in W. Beinert et al., *Sprache und Erfahrung als Problem der Theologie*. Paderborn, 1978, 61–77.

――――. "Ökumenische Aspekte der Darbringungsaussagen in der erneuerten römischen und in der byzantinischen Liturgie," *ALW* 19 (1978) 7–28.

――――. "Eucharistie und Einheit der Kirche nach Basileios dem Grossen," in *Die Heiligen der einen Kirche am Beispiel des hl. Basilius*. Regensburger Ökumenisches Symposium, 1979. Munich, 1980.

――――. "Liturgischer Vollzug und sakramentale Wirklichkeit des eucharistischen Opfers," *OCP* 45 (1979) 245–266; 46 (1980) 5–19.

――――. "Die Theologie der Ortskirche als ökumenischer Impuls," in G. Kaufman (ed.), *Tendenzen der katholischen Theologie nach dem Zweiten Vatikanischen Konzil*. Munich, 1979, 95–111.

――――. *In Deinem Lichte schauen wir das Licht. Zur Meditation frühchristlich-ostkirchlicher Tageszeitsymbolik*. Mainz, 1980.

――――. *Wiedervereinigung mit der Orthodoxie? Bedingungen und Chancen des neuen Dialogs*. Münster, 1980.

Schultze, B. "Eucharistie und Kirche in der russischen Theologie der Gegenwart," *ZKT* 77 (1955) 257–300.

———. "Ekklesiologischer Dialog mit Erzpriester Nikolaj Afanas'ev," *OCP* 33 (1967) 380–403.

———. "Die drifache Herabkunft des Heiligen Geistes in den östlichen Hochgebeten," *OstkSt* 26 (1977) 105–143.

Schwarzlose, K. *Der Bilderstreit. Ein Kampf der griechischen Kirche um ihre Eigenart und Freiheit.* Goths, 1890.

Schweinfurth, P. *Die byzantinische Form.* Mainz, 1954².

Semmelroth, O. "Die theologia symbolikē des Pseudo-Dionysius Areopagita," *Schol* 27 (1952) 1–11.

———. *Die Kirche als Ursakrament.* Frankfurt, 1953.

Sokolow, D. *Darstellung des Gottesdienstes der orthodox-katholischen Kirche des Morgenlandes,* tr. by G. Morosow. Berlin, 1893.

Solovey, M. M. *The Byzantine Divine Liturgy. History and Commentary,* tr. by D. E. Wysochansky. Washington, 1970.

Stead, J. *The Church, the Liturgy, and the Soul of Man: The Mystagogia of St. Maximus the Confessor.* Still River, Mass., 1982.

Stefănescu, I. D. *Contribution à l'étude des peintures murales valaques.* Orient et Byzance 3. Paris, 1928.

———. *L'évolution de la peinture religieuse en Bucovine et en Moldavie.* Orient et Byzance 2. Paris, 1928.

———. *L'évolution de la peinture religieuse en Bucovine et en Moldavie. Nouvelles recherches.* Orient et Byzance 6. Paris, 1929.

———. *La peinture religieuse en Valachie et en Transyvanie.* Orient et Byzance 8. Paris, 1930–1932.

———. *L'illustration des Liturgies dans l'art de Byzance et de l'Orient.* Brussels, 1936.

Strittmatter, A. " 'Missa Grecorum,' 'Missa Sancti Johannis Crisostomi.' The Oldest Latin Version Known of the Byzantine Liturgies of St. Basil and St. John Chrysostom," *Trad* 1 (1943) 79–137.

———. "The 'Barberinum S. Marci' of Jacques Goar," *ELit* 47 (1953) 329–367.

———. "Notes on the Byzantine Synapte," *Trad* 10 (1954) 51–108.

Taft, R. F. "Some Notes on the Bema in the East and West-Syrian Traditions," *OCP* 34 (1968) 326–359.

————. "Toward the Origins of the Offertory Procession in the Syro-Byzantine East," *OCP* 36 (1970) 72–107.

————. *The Great Entrance. A History of the Transfer of Gifts and Other Preanaphoral Rites of the Liturgy of St. John Chrysostom.* OCA 200. Rome, 1975; 2nd ed., 1978.

————. "How Liturgies Grow: The Evolution of the Byzantine 'Divine Liturgy,' " *OCP* 43 (1977) 355–378.

————. "The Pontifical Liturgy of the Great Church according to a Twelfth-Century Diataxis in *Codex British Museum Add. 34060*," *OCP* 45 (1979) 279–307; 46 (1980) 89–124.

————. "The Liturgy of the Great Church. An Initial Synthesis of Structure and Interpretation on the Eve of Iconoclasm," *DOP* 34–35 (1980–1981) 45–75.

————. "Byzantine Liturgical Evidence in the *Life of St. Marcian the Oeconomos:* Concelebration and the Preanaphoral Rites," *OCP* 48 (1982) 159–170.

————. "Textual Problems in the Diaconal Admonition before the Anaphora in the Byzantine Tradition," *OCP* 49 (1983) 340–365.

Tarchnišvili, M. *Die byzantinische Liturgie als Verwirklichung der Einheit und Gemeinschaft im Dogma.* Würzburg, 1939.

————. *Le Grand Lectionnaire de l'Eglise de Jérusalem.* CSCO 188–189, 204–205 = Script. Iber. 9–10, 13–14. Louvain, 1959–1960.

Theodorou, E. D. *Mathēmata Leitourgikēs.* Athens, 1979.

Treitinger, O. *Die oströmische Kaiser- and Reichsidee nach ihrer Gestaltung im höfischen Zeremoniell.* Jena, 1938; Darmstadt, 1956².

Trempelas, P. *Hai treis leitourgiai kata tous en Athēnais kōdikas.* Athens, 1935.

————. "L'audition de l'anaphore eucharistique par le peuple," in *1054–1954. L'Eglise et les Eglises* 2. Chevetogne, 1955, 207–220.

————. "Autour d'un projet de restauration de la liturgie byzantine. Point de vue orthodoxe," *PrOrChr* 7 (1957) 305–209.

Tyciak, J. *Die Liturgie als Quelle östlicher Frömmigkeit.* Ecclesia Orans 20. Freiburg, 1937.

————. "Die Feier der heiligen Messe," in P. Krüger and J. Tyciak (eds.), *Das morgenländische Christentum.* Paderborn, 1940, 130–160.

————. *Maranatha. Die Geheime Offenbarung und die kirchliche Liturgie.* Warendorf, 1947.

266

————. "Die Liturgie des Morgenlandes und die liturgische Erneuerung unserer Tage," *OstkSt* 1 (1952) 54–62.

————. *Heilige Theophanie. Kultgedanken des Morgenlandes.* Trier, 1959.

Uspenskij, N. D. "Molitvy Evcharistii sv. Vasilija Velikogo i sv. Ioanna Zlastousta (=The Eucharistic Prayers of Sts. Basil the Great and John Chrysostom)," *Studia Patristica* V. TU 80. Berlin, 1962, 152–171.

Vagaggini, C. *Theological Dimensions of the Liturgy: A General Treatise on the Theology of the Liturgy,* tr. by L. J. Doyle and W. A. Jurgens. Collegeville, 1976.

Vasič, M. "L'Eésychasme dans l'Eglise et l'art des Serbes du moyen âge," in *L'art byzantin chez les Slaves.* Orient et Byzance 6. Paris, 1930, 110–123.

Voelkl, L. "Die konstantinischen Kirchenbauten nach Eusebius," *RivAC* 29 (1953) 49–66, 187–206.

Vries, W. de. *Sakramententheologie bei den syrischen Monophysiten.* OCA 125. Rome, 1940.

————. "Der 'Nestorianismus' Theodors von Mopsuestia in seiner Sakramentenlehre," *OCP* 7 (1941) 91–148.

————. *Sakramententheologie bei den Nestorianern.* OCA 133. Rome, 1947.

Winkler, G. "Die Interzession der Chrysostomusanaphora in ihrer geschichtlichen Entwicklung," *OCP* 36 (1970) 301–336; 37 (1971) 333–383.

Wulff, O. *Altchristliche und byzantinische Kunst 2. Byzantinische Kunst.* Potsdam, 1924.

Zacharias, P. "Einführung in die orthodoxe Liturgie," in E. Benz and L. A. Zander (eds.), *Evangelisches und orthodoxes Christentum in Begegnung and Auseindandersetzung.* Hamburg, 1958, 78–100.

Zerfass, R. *Die Schriftlesung im Kathedraloffizium Jerusalems.* LQF 48.

Appendixes

I. The Byzantine Liturgy and Its Development as a Reflection of the History of Dogma

The *Anaphora* is an expression of earliest tradition of the faith and of the development of dogma in the 4th century:

1. It preserves the transmitted heritage of the early Christian Eucharistia, which is analogous in its content to the—Baptismal confessions, especially as far as their Trinitarian structure is concerned.

2. It develops this heritage by means of christological and pneumatological expansions (Christology, Pneumatology, Trinitarian expansions), and by a nuanced development of the *doxology* in accordance with Trinitarian theology:

a) In the *Thanksgiving* the address to the Father is organized in the light of *apophatic* and *kataphatic theology;* passages which speak of the Logos (and the Holy Spirit) are given a more precise homoousian expression (against the Arians and the Pneumatomachians, and in accordance with the Councils of Nicaea I and Constantinople I, while maintaining a soteriological outlook based on the economy of salvation).

b) The texts of the account of institution, anamnesis, epiclesis receive a clarification of their eucharistic and sacramental function within the anaphora as well as of their individual formulations which bear the mark of Trinitarian theology.

c) The petition for the Church in the epiclesis, the Commemoration of the saints, and the Intercessions attest (especially in the *Anaphora of Basil*), that the community of the saints (Koinonia tôn hagiôn, Eucharistic ecclesiology is a Koinonia of the Spirit.

The texts outside the anaphora and the overall form of the liturgy as a development of eucharistic symbolism and as a reflection of dogmatic development in the period of the first seven ecumenical councils:

1. The entrance of the bishop, the transfer of the gifts, and the communion rites develop (from the 5th century on) the older Syro-Antiochene symbolism in the spirit of Alexandrian Christology; (as evidenced by the Little Entrance, Great Entrance, Trisagion, Mono-genês, Cherubikon, breaking of the bread, commingling, Zeon).

2. The prothesis rite and enarxis (as developed from the 8th to the 14th centuries) give a richer expression to the Sacrificial Symbolism of the Eucharist and at the same time also represent in pictorial fashion individual phases of the Life of Jesus: (prothesis, Lamb, lance, asterisk; deposition of the gifts, aer, epitaphios; "Images" of the body of Christ, Mystery of Christ and mysteries of the Life of Jesus).

3. The many pictorial-symbolic rites (since the 8th century) reflect the significance of the Seventh Ecumenical Council (787) as a liturgy-oriented summation of the entire dogmatic tradition).

II. The Organization of the Byzantine Liturgy

The *Prothesis:*

After prayers in front of the iconostasis and after the donning of the liturgical vestments, *priest* and *deacon* go to the prothesis chamber (or table) and celebrate the prothesis rite or preparation of the gifts of bread and wine (material of the sacrifice: leavened bread, not unleavened bread, or azymes, and mixed wine). From the first *prosphora* (sacrificial bread, "sacrifice"), the sealed central portion (sacred *Lamb*, seal), is separated by means of the sacred *lance*, placed on the discos, deeply incised in the form of a cross, and pierced, and the wine and water are mixed in the chalice, melismos (Blood and water from the side of Jesus).

From the remaining four prosphoras, particles are placed beside the sacred Lamb for a memorial of the Mother of God and other saints as well as for intercession for the living and the dead. The priest then covers the gifts (asterisk, veils, aer), incenses them and recites the concluding prayer of the prothesis.

The Liturgy of the Catechumens (liturgy of the word, down to the dismissal of the catechumens):

The enarxis (opening section) consists of a *doxology*, three *antiphons* with prayers for the first, second and third antiphons, and *Li-*

tanies (before the first antiphon: litany of peace; before the second and third: a short litany).

The *Little Entrance* (with the—Book of the Gospels), to the singing of the third antiphon and an accompanying silent prayer, was originally the entrance of the celebrant into the sanctuary for the beginning of the liturgy; in the 6th century the—*Monogenes*, which today precedes it, and in the 5th-6th century the *Trisagion*, which now follows it, were sung during it.

The proclamation of the word is followed by intercessory prayer. *Insistent Litany* with a prayer (a secondary element taken from penitential liturgies—Litany and Prayer of the Catechumens (belonging, with the prayer for the faithful, to the earliest organization of the liturgy), and the dismissal of the Cathechumens.

III. The Liturgy of the Faithful (prayer for the faithful and liturgy of sacrifice):

After two litanies for the faithful (a silent prayer of the priest accompanies each) comes the *Great Entrance* in which *Deacons* and *Priest* transfer, from *prothesis* to *Altar*, the gifts which have been prepared (in the *prothesis*). During this rite the *Cherubikon* is sung (with an accompanying silent prayer of the priest: *Great Entrance*).

The gifts are then deposited on the altar on the *antimension* and covered with the *Aer*; the *priest* meanwhile recites the *troparion* of the Burial.—The litany of offering (*Litany*) and the "prayer of sacrifice" ("proscomide prayer" in the older sense of the word "proscomide"), the *kiss of peace*, and the profession of faith lead into the *anaphora*.

The communion ritual, which follows on the anaphora (understood in its narrow sense as the eucharistic prayer) includes the *Our Father*, the Prayer of inclination, the elevation of the consecrated species with the ancient *Communion* acclamation "Holy things to the holy!", the *fraction* and the Commingling of the species (union of one part of the consecrated bread with the sacred blood), at which point the *Zeon* is poured into the chalice; the communion of *priests* and *deacons* (at the altar; they receive the consecrated bread and wine as separate species); and the communion of the faithful (the bread soaked with the sacred blood). (The remaining, unconsecrated particles of prosphoras 2-5, that were used for intercession, are placed in the chalice with the remainder of the consecrated bread, carried back to the prothesis and consumed there.)

The *communion* ritual concludes with the *thanksgiving*, the *prayer behind the ambo*, and the blessing.

The blessing is followed by the distribution of the antidoron (the parts of the prosphoras that are left over at the prothesis and are blessed after the epiclesis) to the faithful as a sign of table-fellowship.

Index

274

110, 112, 113, 120, 122, 182

Cherubic hymn. *See* Cherubikon

Cherubikon, 22, 34, 35ff., 47, 72, 73, 83, 93, 94, 96, 101, 111, 114, 132, 134, 164–165, 166, 168, 171, 176, 177

Choir, 44–46, 175

Christ, depictions of, 101–102

Christology and anamnesis, 10ff.

Church building, Christological structure of, 45 ff.
 as "heaven on earth," 71
 as symbolic of cosmos, 44–45, 78ff.

Ciborium (baldachino), 33, 71, 91

Cilicia, 8, 9

Clement, pope, 5

Clementing Liturgy, 5f

Code of law, Justinian, 152

Codex Barbarini 836, 8, 66, 92, 98, 150–151, 176

A Commentary on the Divine Liturgy, of Nicholas Cabasilas, 124–133, 190ff.

Commingling of species, 8, 20, 40ff., 64, 120, 134

Communion, 15–20, 39, 47, 74, 76, 87, 94, 104, 107, 108, 119, 120, 123, 130, 135, 143, 165, 191, 195
 of the apostles, 81, 84, 85, 102, 103–105, 171, 119, 121, 122

Concelebration, 106, 115, 120, 123

Confession of faith, 24, 36, 47, 144, 149, 170

Confession of the True Faith against the three Chapters, of Justinian, 30

Consecration, 13, 19, 39, 40, 64, 84, 88, 104, 108, 127, 130, 144, 150, 194

Constantine, emperor, 86, 139, 156

Constantine II, patriarch, 52

Constantine V ("Caballinus"), emperor. *See* "Caballinus", discourse against

Constantinople, 8, 9, 10, 24, 41, 68, 80, 102, 150, 151, 154, 261, 176, 182, 183, 189
 Liturgy of, 21ff., 133, 139, 140
 Symbol of, 145, 149

Councils
 Chalcedon (451), 3, 21, 22, 45, 160, 161, 173
 Constantinople I (381), 3, 4, 7, 12, 13, 14, 150
 Constantinople II (553), 28, 30, 161
 Constantinople III (680–681), 45, 173
 Constantinople IV, 185
 Eighth Ecumenical (869–870). *See* Constantinople IV
 Ephesus (431), 3, 21, 22
 Fifth Ecumenical (553). *See* Constantinople II
 Nicea I, (325), 7
 Nicea II (787), 50, 54, 56, 61, 155, 184, 187, 190–191
 Seventh Ecumenical (787). *See* Nicea II
 Sixth Ecumenical. *See* Constantinople III
 Trent (1545–1563), 124, 193

Cucer, monastery at, 107, 110

Curtea de Arges (Rumania), church at 110

Cyril of Alexandria, patriarch, 21, 22

Cyril of Jerusalem, Saint, 13, 67, 165, 193

Daphni, monastery, 51, 78, 80

Darrouzes, J., 189

Deacon, 17, 18–19, 25, 36, 38, 66, 70, 72, 73, 74, 82, 84, 86, 92, 94, 97, 99, 104, 105, 112, 113, 114, 116, 117, 122, 124, 165, 166, 167, 168–169, 179, 181, 183, 189

278

Oblation, prayer of, 122
"Offering Prayer", 170–172
Offertory, Roman, 166, 171, 181, 184
Ohrid, church of, 102, 103, 104–105
Omophorion (pallium), 71, 75, 113, 116, 198. *See also* Pallium
On the Divine Incomprehensibility, of John Chrysostom, 152
On the Holy Spirit, of St. Basil, 148
"Only Begotten Son," hymn. *See* Ho Monogenes
Orarion, 70, 116, 198
Origen, 49, 174
Orthros, 116, 158, 163, 198
Our Father, 17, 47, 74, 97, 119

Painting, and proclamation, 72
re-presentational character of, 56, 57, 58
Palamism, 102
Palamas, Gregory, 108, 109
Pallium, 118. *See* omophorion.
Pantocrator, 57, 59, 60, 71, 100, 102, 112, 113
Parousia, 119
Particles, offering of, 97, 121–123, 178, 181
Pastophoria, 166, 167, 198
Paten of Xeropotamou, 113
Patriarchate, Byzantine, 3, 21, 141
Paul the Silentiary, 34
Paverd, F. von de, 151, 167
Péc, church at, 112
Pentecost, 85
Persian-Nestorian Church, 9
Peter of Alexandria, St., 86–87
Peter Knapheus (the Fuller), patriarch of Antioch, 23, 24, 25
Phelonion, 116, 198
Philotheus, deataxis of, 99, 114
Photius, patriarch, 50, 51, 58, 59, 60, 61, 71

Pictures
ahistorical forms, and, 101ff.
anamnetic cycle of, 55, 78–81, 88–89, 91
of anastasis (resurrection), 53, 55, 77–79, 81, 84f.
baptism and, 86
commemoration of saints and, 86
communion and, 87–88
cycle of, as description of the salvation event, 78ff.
epiclesis prayer and, 86
Eucharist and, 86–87
"festal," cycle of, 78–79
and gospel, relationship between, 54–56, 57–58, 90, 91, 186f., 190
Great Entrance and, 83–84
of heavenly liturgy, 101, 102, 111ff.
Holy Spirit and, 85–86
identified with the meaning of some part of the liturgy, 80ff.
Koimesis (dormition) of Mary, and, 88
Little Entrance and, 81–83, 84
as liturgical commentary, 80ff.
liturgical cycle of, 79f., 90
liturgical reality of Christ and, 90, 100
liturgical scrolls and, 80ff., 102, 105, 106, 111
Marian cycle of. *See* Mary, Mother of God
monumental painting and, 81, 88, 102
"mystery," 79, 80, 81, 83, 84, 88ff.
prayers of the liturgy and, 81
as proclamation, 72ff.
prothesis and, 82–83
prototype and reproduction of, 187–188

as representation, 72
scenic, and salvific meaning of
    Christ's life, 78ff.
and theology of icons of Christ,
    52–55, 57, 58ff., 63, 90f.
words of institution and, 85, 86.
    See also Icons; Images
Pneumatology and the epiclesis,
    12ff.
Pneumatomachians, 12
Pontus, 3
Prayer behind the Ambo, 8, 88, 98
Prayer over the Catechumens, 8,
    157, 169
Precious Blood, warming of, 30–
    31, 42. *See also* Zeon.
Preface, 74, 144
Presentation of our Lord, 83
Priest, 15, 17, 35, 36, 38, 44, 70,
    71, 72–73, 85, 86, 92, 93, 97,
    107, 112, 113, 114, 116, 117,
    118, 122, 123, 124, 126, 130,
    151, 160, 165, 168, 170, 171,
    179, 181, 183, 189, 194
Preparation, table of, 91–92, 93,
    109, 112, 113, 120, 131
Procession, 34, 39, 75, 113, 118,
    162, 164, 165, 166, 167, 168,
    180, 182
Proclus of Constantinople,
    patriarch, 5, 23
Procopius, 33
Prokeimenon, 93, 198
Proscomide, 65, 66, 151, 152, 179.
    See prothesis
Proscomide Prayer, 8, 64, 66, 151,
    171, 179
Proskinesis, 54
Prosphora, 66, 92, 97, 98–99, 121,
    179, 198
Protheoria, of Nicholas and
    Theodore of Andida, 39,
    89–98, 100, 131, 134, 165,
    188ff.
Prothesis, 25, 50, 64ff., 75, 76, 77,
    82, 83, 92, 97, 98, 99, 101,

102, 107, 108–110, 111, 113,
    117, 120ff., 131, 134, 135,
    140, 151, 152, 170, 171, 178,
    179, 180–184, 189, 191, 198.
    See also Gifts, preparation
    of; Proscomide
Protogospel of James, 87
Psellus, Michael, 189

Rahmani, I.E., 8
Readings, 25, 46, 91, 93, 118, 127,
    161
Resurrection of Jesus Christ, 11,
    14, 17–20, 31, 39, 42, 53, 54,
    55, 64, 65, 71, 72, 73, 75, 78,
    84, 85, 89, 90, 93, 94, 97, 98,
    104, 114, 117, 125, 127, 132,
    134, 147, 156, 166, 190. *See
    also* Anastasis
Ripidion (fan), 74, 84, 94, 95, 103,
    104, 110, 113, 198. *See also*
    fan
Ritual, as proclamation of Christ,
    63ff.
"Robber Synod", 21
Romanos Melodos, 29
Rome, 139, 140, 142

Saints, 36, 52, 55, 58, 60, 61, 62,
    77, 96–97, 105, 121–122
Sakkos, 198
Salt, 121
Sanctuary, 32, 34, 46, 56, 58, 65,
    72, 105, 111, 116, 117, 122,
    161–162, 165, 166, 180
Sanctus. *See* Thrice Holy
Satan, 27
Schneider, A.M., 166
Schneider, C., 33
Scrolls, liturgical, 80ff., 102, 105,
    106, 107, 125
Seal, 98, 120–121, 128
Semelion, as synonym for eikon,
    155
Seraphic Hymn, 96
Seraphim, 37, 61, 74, 165